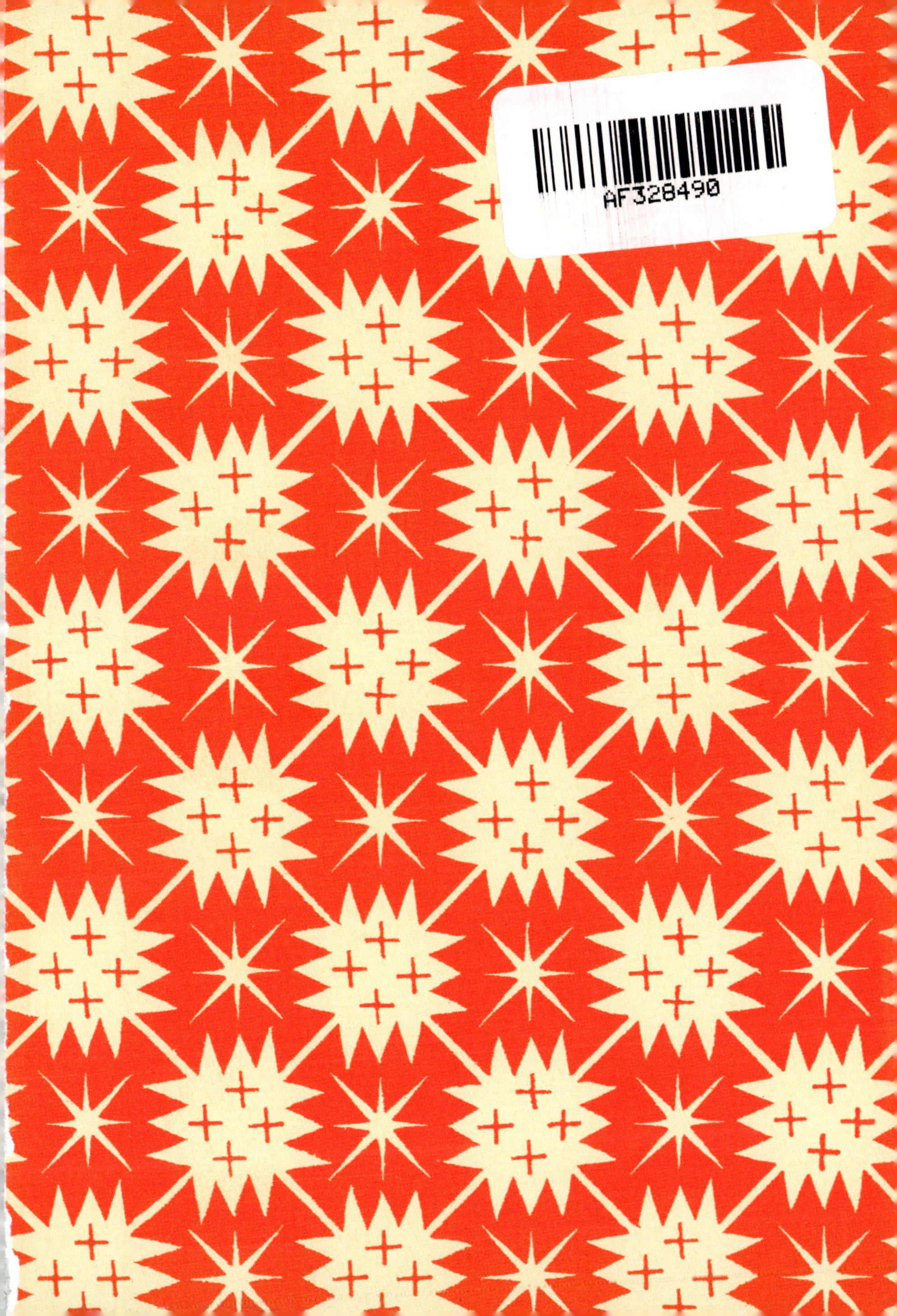
AF328490

LONG LIVE GREAT BARDFIELD:
THE AUTOBIOGRAPHY OF
TIRZAH GARWOOD

Persephone Book N° 119
Published by Persephone Books Ltd 2016
Reprinted 2018, 2021 and 2024 (twice)

First published by The Fleece Press in 2012 as Long Live
Great Bardfield & Love to You All;
this new edition has been slightly abridged

© The Estate of Tirzah Garwood

Endpapers taken from a decorative paper design,
in engravers ink red, by Tirzah Garwood

Decorative rule: border for the 1935 *Heartsease and
Honesty, being the Pastimes of the Sieur de Grammont*
(translated by Helen Simpson) illustrated by Tirzah
Garwood

Typeset in ITC Baskerville by
Keystroke, Wolverhampton

Printed and bound in Germany by
GGP Media GmbH, Poessneck

978 1910 263 099

Persephone Books Ltd
8 Edgar Buildings
Bath BA1 2EE
01225 425050

www.persephonebooks.co.uk

LONG LIVE GREAT BARDFIELD: THE AUTOBIOGRAPHY OF TIRZAH GARWOOD

edited and with a preface by

ANNE ULLMANN

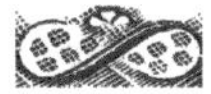

PERSEPHONE BOOKS
BATH

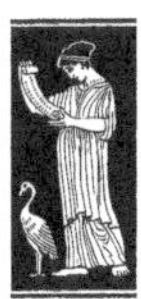

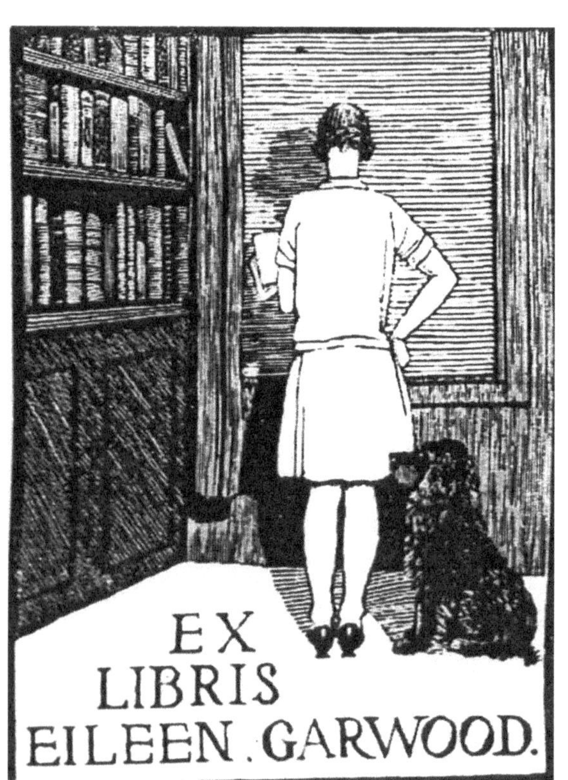

EX
LIBRIS
EILEEN . GARWOOD.

PREFACE

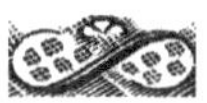

Thou art beautiful, O my love, as Tirzah: comely as Jerusalem;
terrible as an army with banners

Song of Solomon VI v 4

Tirzah was born on April 11th 1908 at Gillingham in Kent, the third child of Royal Engineer Colonel Frederick Scott Garwood and of Ella Corry, daughter of a Belfast ship builder. Though christened plain Eileen Lucy, the Colonel records that he began to call her Tertia when she was thirteen days old, and at a little over a year old she acquired her romantic Biblical name when her elder brother and sister misheard Tertia in their mother's nightly reading of the Scriptures. Her father's diary recorded on May 15th 1909 that 'she became Tirzah, which she has been ever since.'

Tirzah states clearly the reason for writing her auto-biography: 'I hope dear reader that you may be one of my descendants.' She began writing in March 1942 with a graphic description of the hospital ward where she was recovering from a mastectomy operation for primary cancer. She wrote throughout her convalescence and finished the first draft by

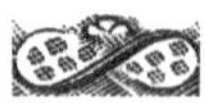

the end of May. She had added to and typed up most of the manuscript by February the following year.

Tirzah was bought up in comfort, for there was money on both sides of the family, though her mother, with a strict Presbyterian background, abhorred any showy behaviour or unnecessary extravagance. Early in her childhood Tirzah showed a gift for drawing. She went on to study at the Eastbourne School of Art from 1925 to 1928, where a new teacher, Eric Ravilious, taught drawing and wood engraving. Also from Eastbourne, he had himself attended the School of Art and then the Royal College of Art in London, where he had been one of a group of highly talented students who attended the Royal College after the First World War. Introduced by Eric, Tirzah had first shown her work at the prestigious Annual Exhibition of the Society of Wood Engravers whilst still a student, and in the autumn of 1928 moved to London in the hope of earning a living as an illustrator. In Eastbourne Tirzah had been engaged to the son of close neighbours, and both families had been delighted; but after much indecision she changed her mind, and in 1930 married Eric Ravilious. Class distinctions were rigid in the 1920s and the Garwoods felt socially embarrassed at her choice, whilst Eric's parents were equally perplexed that their son should be marrying above his station.

The couple settled in Hammersmith, London, in a flat overlooking the Thames, and Tirzah describes in detail Eric's close circle of friends from the Royal College of Art. In late 1931, tiring of too much social life, Eric and his friend Edward Bawden cycled round Essex searching for a quiet base in the

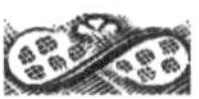

country. They discovered Brick House in Great Bardfield, which they rented together and shared until September 1934. Eric and Tirzah then moved to nearby Castle Hedingham; Essex became their home and Great Bardfield the focus of an ever-growing artistic community. With marriage Tirzah had given up wood engraving, but whilst bringing up their family of three children, John, James and Anne, she made and marketed marbled paper, a craft at which she excelled.

When war broke out in 1939, Eric became an Official War Artist. Tirzah was too preoccupied with babies, and then with illness, to be able to contribute to the war effort. She had completed much of her autobiography when the news came of Eric's sudden death. At this point in her writing there are a dozen or so heavily scribbled-out lines of type and then a gap in the manuscript. Understandably she may have found it difficult to write of this period and, possibly because her emotions were so numbed by the event, she records her lack of immediate grief with a disarming honesty. But the writing down was therapeutic, it enabled her to stand back and look at her life and helped her at a time of adversity to sort out a way forward. Her illness and the loss of her husband would have defeated many people. The autobiography, written in 1942 when life seemed vulnerable and precious, was in fact finished a full nine years before her death, during which period she found happiness in a new marriage, and a flourishing of her own artistic talents. She remarried in 1946. Her second husband, Henry Swanzy, Colonial Assistant in the BBC Overseas Service and Editor of African Affairs, produced a noted BBC programme, *Caribbean Voices*, which nurtured the

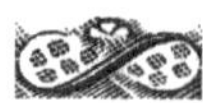

talents and broadcast the work of West Indian writers such as George Lamming, Derek Walcott and V S Naipaul.

Tirzah typed up a large part of her autobiography but she must have had doubts about exposing her personal life and it is not included in her typed pages; and Eric's affairs were only very briefly touched upon. It was not until some fifty years after her death that Henry Swanzy gave me Tirzah's original handwritten notebooks and I was able to fill in the missing story line. The two texts have now been united to make a whole. Tirzah's story stops at a crossroads in her life in 1943 when she is left widowed and penniless towards the end of the war, but a two-year period from September 1939 to March 1942 is either lost (she often gave her notebooks to friends to read) or perhaps never written. This I have filled in with extracts from letters written at the time.

I have added a biographical note covering the period from 1943, where Tirzah ends her autobiography, up to her death in 1951. Henry Swanzy's notes on Tirzah's life, given to me by his children after his death in 2004, have helped cover the later years of her life. This period, though marred by the return of cancer, produced a burst of creativity. Remarried and happily settled back in London, with her three children now at school, she could at last devote herself to her own work, making a series of enchanting oil paintings and producing her delightful collaged houses. During her final illness she was often confined to bed, and worked with a small canvas propped up on her knees, but described her last year as the happiest of her life.

Actual dates are rare in Tirzah's writing but I have been fortunate to have been bequeathed both Helen Binyon and

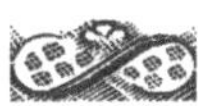

Diana Tuely's letters from my father and I have been able to use these for cross-referencing. The diaries of Tirzah's father, Colonel Garwood, which he kept meticulously for the greater part of his life from 1896 when he was a young Subaltern, until his death in 1944, have also been invaluable. He was a keen amateur photographer and the photographs of Tirzah's childhood are reproduced from those pasted into his diaries.

With regard to editing, Tirzah's notebooks had been filled in a random and haphazard manner and I have had to tackle the passages like a jigsaw puzzle, fitting the events into order. In a few instances there have been two slightly differing drafts of manuscript and I have had to choose between them. From her typed pages, I have reordered passages, so that it now reads in the correct historical sequence. I have edited out a small amount of material from over-lengthy chapters, but I have left in full all descriptions of family which may be of interest to future generations, and all descriptions of artistic work. For clarity I have added punctuation, I hope not too much.

Tirzah left a one-line gap on her typed pages indicating a change of subject matter. To facilitate my way around the manuscript, I have added to these by dividing the whole autobiography into chapters. With regard to infelicitous content, I have consulted many of the descendants of friends and relations who appear in Tirzah's text and all have agreed that the script may stand as written. My apologies to those few whom I have been unable to trace.

Time and the honesty of Tirzah's words have made this an immensely important document and it is a valuable primary record of the life of a woman who was at the centre of an

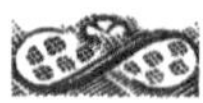

important group of artists, and who was herself a very good artist in her own right. Though written at an earlier date it is similar in its engaging style to Gwen Raverat's *Period Piece* and the enjoyment in Tirzah's writing, and indeed its strength, is in her entertainingly direct and perceptive observations of the people around her.

The work involved in editing my mother's writing and researching her art work has given me a rare and cherished insight into her life and I am very pleased to have been given this opportunity to publish her autobiography and to bring her work to a wider audience.

Anne Ullmann, Birmingham 2012 and 2016

LIST OF PICTURES

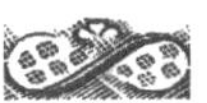

Ex Libris bookplate by Tirzah Garwood 1927 — iv

The Garwood Family 1915 (John, Betty and Margaret standing; Tirzah and Billy sitting) — xvi

The Sisters 1929 by TG — 10

Tirzah in 1919 aged 11 — 28

The Aunt or *Kensington High Street* 1929 by TG: this wood engraving was for a Curwen Press calendar called *Relations* which never appeared. It was then published (as was *The Daughter* and *The Wife*) by the *London Mercury* in March 1930. The woman crossing the street is one of Tirzah's aunts, the hunched figure following her with a briefcase saying TG is Tirzah herself. — 38

The Daughter or *The Crocodile* 1929 by TG — 56

Tirzah in 1923 aged 15 — 72

Betty with Guitar 1927 by TG — 92

The Art School 1927 by TG — 112

Eric Ravilious 1926 — 142

Eric and Tirzah's engagement photograph taken by her father May 1930 — 156

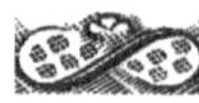

Tirzah at Alciston from *Almanack* (1929) by Eric Ravilious 170
Tirzah Garwood by Phyllis Dodd 1929 (oil painting,
    here reproduced in black and white)   192
Spring 1926 by TG   214
Eric Ravilious and TG painting the mural decoration
    for the tea room at the Midland Bay Hotel,
    Morecambe 1933   240
The Wife 1929 by TG   258
TG in 1930 aged 22   276
The Cousin 1929 by TG   294
Winter 1927 by TG   316
The Train Journey by TG   338
Eric Ravilious drawn in a sketchbook by TG 1941   356
The Grandmother 1929 by TG   380
TG with Anne, April 1941   396
Dr Davidson Nicol (1924–94), a Sierra Leonean
    academic, diplomat and friend, oil painting signed
    Tirzah Swanzy 1951   416
TG with John, Anne and James 1943 © Edwin Smith/
    RIBA Library Photographic Collection   426
TG and Henry Swanzy on their wedding day
    in 1946   448
TG 1950 © Edwin Smith/ RIBA Library Photographic
    Collection   474

To the memory of John Ravilious 1935–2014
and to the memory of James Ravilious 1939–99,
and to Tirzah's grandchildren:
John's children, Kate and Mark,
James's children, Ben and Ella,
Anne's children, Tom, Sarah and Martha

Henry reading more of my life which he says is very
readable and ought to be published when the people
who would mind are dead. I sound the most awful prig.
I did try to truthfully write in the way I had felt at the
time that the events happened.

Tirzah's diary, March 1951

LONG LIVE GREAT BARDFIELD:
THE AUTOBIOGRAPHY OF
TIRZAH GARWOOD

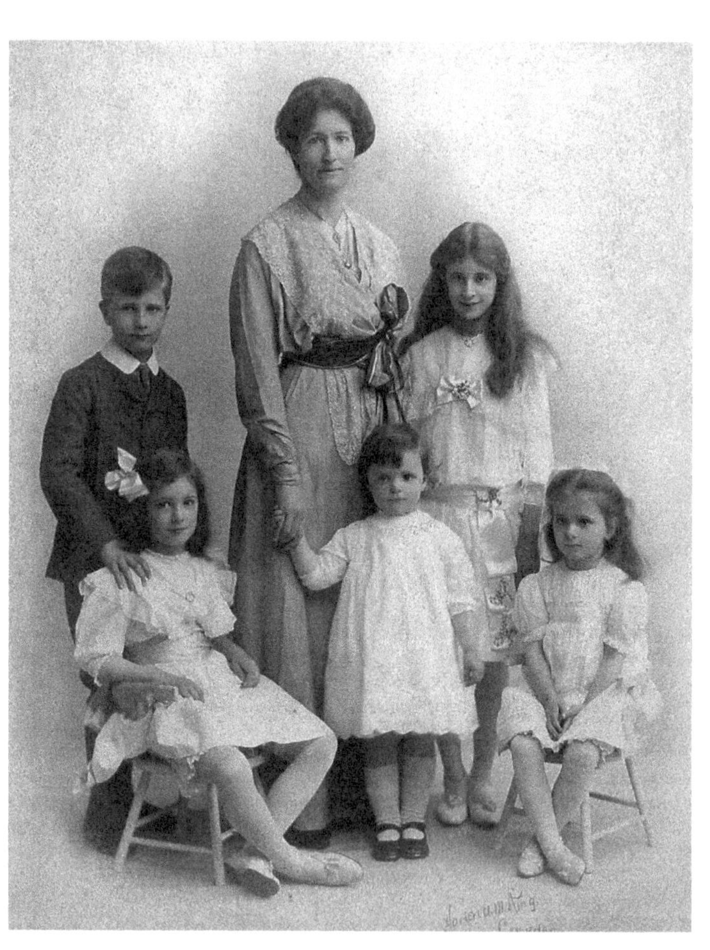

CHAPTER ONE

In 1903, on a wet afternoon in Croydon, my father was married to my mother. She was the beautiful daughter of John Corry, a ship-owner who had married a Scottish wife Margaret Galloway and come to England from the north of Ireland. They had a successful life and raised eight out of eleven children. There were three daughters, but my mother was the only one who married and she not until she was thirty years old.

My mother was lovely. She had golden hair and blue-grey eyes but she was pale and as only at fancy dress dances was it permissible in Croydon society to put any colour on your face, she only looked her very best on these occasions. She was taught singing, elocution, painting, French and German and taken for frequent holidays abroad and her mother had high hopes of her making a good match; however, the years passed and she remained unmarried. I believe one or two people proposed to her, one certainly did, a clergyman in his own churchyard: but as the custom then was that first a suitor approached the girl's mother, it was probable that if the young man was one that my grandmother considered

"

unsuitable, my mother would remain unaware that he had indeed asked for her hand.

At a dinner party in 1903, she met Captain Garwood, a young Royal Engineer who had been at Woolwich with her brother Jack. He had large brown eyes and brown hair and moustache and rather a large nose and slightly receding chin and before going out to India with her brother, he fell in love. In India, Jack invited his sisters to come and stay with him for the Delhi Durbar. There was great difficulty in getting accommodation and this plan would have fallen through had not Captain Garwood, first carefully ascertaining which sisters it was that Jack proposed inviting, asked them to come and stay in camp with him and their brother. This Lucy and Ella did and towards the end of their stay, Fred Garwood proposed to Ella and was refused with the strange statement that it would break her mother's heart.

My mother now got enteric fever and was very ill. Her golden hair started coming out as the result of her high fever and my father always maintains that it was this which finally made her change her mind and write to him, accepting his proposal of marriage.

Her mother was disappointed; my father was a mere Captain – still, things might have been worse and when they returned to Croydon, Ella's hair now an ordinary brown, the marriage took place and they went to live in Chatham.

In 1904, my sister Margaret, a very ugly baby with a large nose, was born to them, followed at two-year intervals by John Corry, Eileen Lucy [Tirzah], Mary Scott and Elizabeth Percy, called Betty. My nickname of Tirzah originated when my

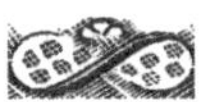

grandmother wrote enquiring after 'Little Tirtia' and Mary became known as Billy because she was said to resemble a Billikin [an American doll]. Before her birth, the family moved to Glasgow.

My father had a romantic nature and used before his marriage to fall in love very frequently, often with married women and, like a spaniel bringing a dead rabbit into the drawing room, he would lay the tribute of his unwanted adoration at their feet: this was a nuisance and embarrassing for his friends. This tactlessness in love can be traced back for many generations and came from his mother's family, called Scott. It finally extinguished one branch of the family when so far as we know, its only remaining member – my second cousin Bob Scott – having run away with his Colonel's wife while in India, was afterwards murdered in Africa by another outraged husband whose wife was taking refuge in his house.

After marriage, my father was very happy with my mother and I don't think he fell badly in love with anybody else. My mother was sentimental but not warmly affectionate. She did not like physical contact with other people and only once in my life do I remember her allowing any public demonstration of affection between herself and my father. This was in Glasgow, when he called her old henny penny and pulled her clucking and protesting onto his lap.

In 1904, when my father was sent to Glasgow we moved into a house in Aytoun Road. Our house was at the corner of the road and so had a better garden than most of the other houses. It had a small lawn at the back adjoining an orchard, a sloping grass bank on one side of the house and a sandpit

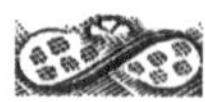

on the other. We played in the garden most of the day, making sandcastles and mud pies and finding black and white spotted stones which we called 'Simon Stones' after Uncle John's Dalmatian dog Simon. We made friends with the boys who lived opposite and I had a favourite butcher's boy and there were regular callers whom we welcomed, such as the barrel organ man with a monkey, the piper and above all the muffin man who rang a bell. I took a long time to walk as I got about more quickly on my bottom, and I can still dimly remember the pattern on the dark green linoleum over which I used to slide. I was also a good pot walker and our nurse nearly split herself with laughing when I paddled out into the hall on my pot to see the muffin man.

Almost from birth, we were interested in young men. Encouraged by our nurse who walked out with a policeman, Billy, aged two, made 'glad eyes' so successfully at a young man who lived in the same road, that he took her and the nurse for a drive in his car. This was considered a great triumph on her part, as indeed it was; in 1912 there were not many cars in Glasgow.

We had a great many changes in nurses and governesses. One nurse urged my sister Margaret so earnestly, with bribes of a penny, to 'do try hard' in her pot that she ruptured herself inside and had to have an operation. My mother had a great fear of our being constipated and would give us castor oil on very slight provocation.

My mother decided that I was quaint and used accordingly to dress me a little differently from the other children. She made me a tall thimble-shaped hat which she called the

'query hat'. Usually in the summer, we wore round flat hats made of several layers of white embroidered muslin which was gathered up to form a crown. There was no elastic and we wore a flannel under-petticoat and under-knickers and a liner petticoat and knickers which buttoned on to a top bodice. My sisters had big pansy-brown eyes but mine were small and glittering black. She asked me one day if I couldn't open them wider and sensing a criticism in her question, I ever afterwards remembered this. My hair was fair although my eyes and eyebrows were black; it was twisted up round a hairpin in ringlets at night so that I had fat sausage curls by day.

We usually went walking in Maxwell Park, where there was the excitement of seeing the waterfall: but the best walk of all was under a subway walled with dirty white bricks and up to the docks. We all loved sailors and would talk to them when we could. I wanted when I was grown up to be a schoolmistress and marry a sailor.

When one day I was given a text 'Jesus loves me' to paint, I finished it quickly and said, 'Can I have another with "I love a sailor" on it?' We drew pictures of them and I used to have trouble getting the stripes to go the right way on their collars. To tease me, Margaret sent a postcard pretending that a sailor was proposing to marry me on Wednesday. I took this quite seriously and was worried that I shouldn't be grown up enough by Wednesday. We went for long tram rides; you could go a long way for very little money and, on top of a tram, a sailor once gave Margaret a penny. I started my first collection which was foreign money that I picked up on the path; there was a lot lying about, I suppose the sailors tipped it out of their pockets.

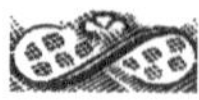

On Sunday, after church, we used to go to the house of my mother's aunt Mrs Galloway. She had four very tall sons and we loved visiting them. They initiated us into car driving. Jim had a car and took us out in it and also they took us for imaginary rides up to the ceiling, in an imaginary aeroplane from which you jumped. Then they taught us a nice irreverent grace before meals which you did by rhythmically banging your hands on the table ending with a clap of your hands, another bang, and finally your elbows on the table. I can still do it correctly, it makes all the crockery rattle and is very enjoyable. John was passing through an acquisitive stage and used to say earnestly to Mrs Galloway: 'Can I have it?' of anything he fancied in her house, and to my mother's embarrassment, she nearly always gave it to him.

The first cinema in Glasgow was the Electric Theatre and it was followed by the BBC (Bright and Beautiful Cinema). Margaret once went to the Electric Theatre but it was in the BBC that I saw my first film, *The Blue Rose*. People in film walked fast with queer jerky steps and the light flickered in a strange speckled manner but we didn't mind. I also saw my first circus, a perfectly splendid one which had an elephant that rode on a tricycle and got arrested by a policeman elephant. There was an exciting Wild West drama to finish up with. The wonderful finale to this was the bursting of the dam when water came pouring over the mountain into a specially arranged tank in the foreground of the stage, drowning the villain and splashing the delighted audience.

My father bought a gramophone with a small horn called the Kinch and we had numerous Harry Lauder records as well

as *Alexander's Ragtime Band* and a puzzle record which might play one of four tunes, you never could tell which. A great favourite was about a burglar called Jimmy Valentine who would steal a horse and cart and he would 'steal a girlie's heart for Jimmy Valentine look out!' The lovely thing in this record was that you could hear the horse and cart running away: 'Ockada, ockada, ockada' and the horrified cries from the crowd. Another record got scratched and, suitably for our family, stuck singing, 'I love you, I love you, I love you' till someone moved the needle on.

During the last year in Glasgow we had several governesses; one poor wretch was dying of diabetes, for which there was no cure in those days. Death was a terrible calamity to us. We debated the awful question, that if one of our parents were to die, which would it be worse to lose: we finally decided to sacrifice my father.

The governess we liked best was called Miss Cran. She was small and wore pince-nez spectacles. One night she was suddenly removed from the house to have an operation for appendicitis. Margaret, who shared her room, woke up and witnessed this catastrophe. Several nights later she walked in her sleep into my mother and father's room and said: 'Miss Cran is ill.' Walking in your sleep now became a new horror to me. Miss Cran, when she came back, told us that she too walked in her sleep and had once woken up and found herself on top of the chest of drawers. This wasn't quite so awful as death. At least there was always the comforting knowledge that if you kept your head and behaved calmly with the sleep walker, leading her away from the open window from which

she was just going to fall, she could be safely led back to bed where with luck, she would stay for the rest of the night.

I had a comforting belief at this age that if you shut your eyes, as you couldn't see anyone, so you yourself must be invisible. My father used to disappear behind a black piece of material when he took our photographs which he did very frequently. He had a large camera which was mounted on a tripod and into which he slid glass plates. When the photograph was being taken, he removed a round cap from the front of the camera and pulled a string which hung at the side. The photographs were either one very big one or two stereoscopic ones, and very good they were.

We heard rumours and stories of England and the outside world, the death of the King, when we pulled down the blind; the indecency of the tango and the ridiculous hobbled skirts; only a few daring Glasgow women adopted this fashion. Then there were Suffragettes and one came to tea: Miss Potter, a friend of my father's, in a skirt of narrow purple, green and white stripes. My mother did not approve of Suffragettes, she was always outraged at any display of immodesty in women. A great excitement was the visit of an aeroplane. My mother had to take us to the top of a hill where crowds of people were congregated. It was a long walk and we waited and waited; but we were not disappointed, it did arrive – one of those lovely early flying machines, a monoplane with a delicately strutted body flown by the intrepid Mr Gilmour who landed it successfully at Lanark.

Every night, my mother read some of the Bible to me. I can't believe that I could have understood much of it at the

age of five, but I was very pleased when she read from *The Song of Solomon*: 'Thou art beautiful O my love as Tirzah: comely as Jerusalem; terrible as an army with banners.' She loved reading aloud and I didn't complain because it made her stay in the room. I didn't like the dark as I was very frightened of daddy-long-legs. I had a gollywog made appropriately by the Suffragette Miss Potter and he always slept with me and was the only doll that I ever loved very dearly. I asked one night if there would ever be another war and my mother said that there was a possibility that we might go to war with Germany.

In 1914, my father was ordered to Cairo and it was decided that we should all go too. Half our furniture was sold and the rest put in store. We moved into furnished rooms for the last week, all ready packed with Miss Cran and a Nurse Macdonald engaged for the journey, but we never went because Germany marched into Belgium and we were at war.

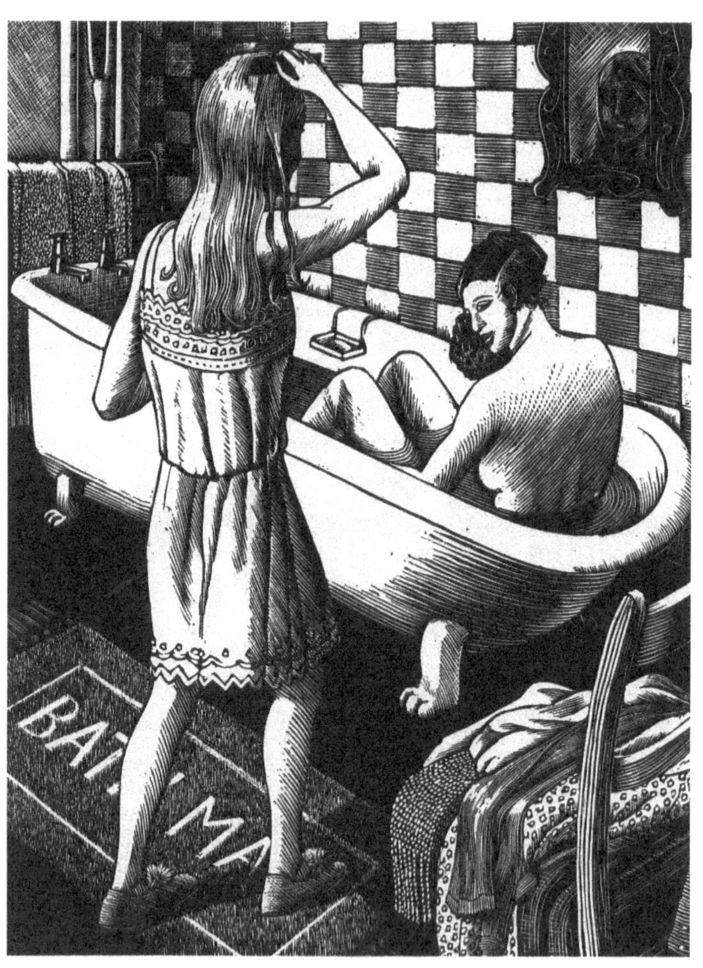

CHAPTER TWO

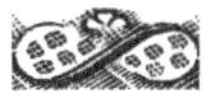

My father was ordered to join the 7th Division which was in camp at Lyndhurst so my mother took a furnished house and we all moved there to be near him. It was a huge camp by the side of a road and we used sometimes to have tea with the soldiers in a big tent. My mother did her best to provide cakes for so many people; the tea had condensed milk in it and poured into tin mugs was so scalding hot that it was almost impossible to drink. My father slept in a bell tent, we thought this lovely and examined everything he had inside very attentively and fell continuously over the guide ropes outside. Miss Cran and the army doctor fell in love with one another. There were forty ponies tethered in a line and we were allowed to go for short rides on one called Marconi. All too soon this came to an end and one evening in a lovely sunset, we watched our camp march away. They went to the Battle of Ypres and very few of them came back; the doctor and the ponies were all killed too but my father was safe and unhurt.

We were now offered a home by my mother's brother Herbert [Corry] and his wife Rose who were living in a farmhouse on the outskirts of South Croydon. We were not

allowed to have our furniture out of store as there was no way of transporting it from Glasgow, so till the end of the war we had either to stay with relations or live in furnished houses.

We arrived late one evening in Croydon. I remember nothing about the journey until the final ride along a twisting drive, and shepherded at last into Coombe Farm hall, a voice saying: 'Now kiss your little cousin'. We all hated kissing strangers and I hesitated now; but Rosemary's charms were obvious at a glance and we kissed and liked one another from the beginning.

Aunt Rose was a big, deep-chested woman, generous in every way; her husband was thin and grey-eyed with the Corry chin and penetrating look. He was the most successful of the brothers, and his ships which sailed between England and Australia gave them a more than comfortable income. Rosemary, who was the same age as I, was their eldest daughter. There was a boy two years younger called John and another called Bill, who wore white piqué suits and sat in a high chair. As there were now two Johns, my brother became Big John and John Corry, Little John.

The farm had fields on three sides and Shirley Common on the other side of the road from the lodge gate. It was about a quarter of a mile away from Coombe House where the parents of our Aunt Winifred lived, Grandma and Grandpa [Frank] Lloyd. Mrs Lloyd was delicate and only went out very occasionally in an early Rolls-Royce in which they were driven very slowly and steadily. He was a very kindly old man with a beard; his father [Edward Lloyd] had founded *Lloyd's Weekly Newspaper* [and the *Daily Chronicle*] and he had carried on his

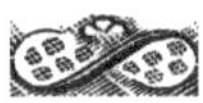

father's business but was now retired and interested himself in collecting old furniture and china.

The main charm of visiting Grandma Lloyd was the well in the rock garden. It was a very old well with a bucket and winch and we used to drop stones down and wait breathless till we heard the distant plop of their landing. There was a small tunnel in the construction of the rockery through which Big John could crawl; he was eight years old, so it must have been quite large. Coombe House garden was a very lovely one with a formal walled vegetable garden as well as the rock garden and a rhododendron walk with heavenly moss carpeting the ground. The house too was a fine one with a fernery, but I could not feel at home there because of the Blue Lady, a ghost who walked wringing her hands from a bedroom called the 'pillar room', down a secret staircase to the library below. No one seemed to have seen the Blue Lady or know very much about her except that she was unhappy. The little staircase had now been blocked up and Mr Lloyd showed us where it had ended in a cupboard in his bookcase, a very secret door indeed, its back composed of the spines of dummy books.

The thing that I chiefly associate with these early Croydon days was the change of smell. The oak trees and bracken on Shirley Common had a very strong smell, and occasionally the horse trough at the corner of the road used to smell more foully than I can remember anything else ever since. The Common land was shingle and we often found fossils there. The trees were not tall and were in consequence very good for climbing.

In the grounds of Coombe Farm there was a disused chalk-pit and this was the best place to play. It had a pond and a

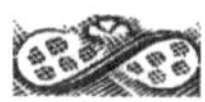

rabbit hole undermining the exposed roots of an old tree along which we could climb. There was a good-natured fox terrier called Victor, a smooth-coated black and white dog who was a very fine rabbit and rat catcher. Then my aunt brought home Punch, a brindled bulldog puppy whom we loved. Poor Punch, Victor would put up a rabbit and they both would go yapping after it, Victor disappearing finally down some rabbit hole, leaving a frantic Punch on the upper world unable to jam his enormous wedge of a head down the inviting burrow.

We were given a whirligig and this was put up for us in a clearing among some pine trees, where the ground was soft with fallen needles, their smell quite different from Shirley Common or the chalk pit which smelled of elder bushes. The whirligig was a seesaw which also went round. It had a seat at either end with a handle to hold onto so that it felt quite safe and I loved it for many years.

There was a hollow tree outside the conservatory which stood at the corner of the house; it had a convenient sized doorway and Rosemary used to call it her house. If you looked up inside it, you didn't see the sky; but it ended in rotten wood and jutting-out fungi.

Aunt Rose had two hobbies, an enormous herbaceous border and keeping chickens. She once paid us by the hour to weed and to pick up stones in the chicken runs. I was a keen competitor from infancy, my first triumph being the winning of a somersault race, and I very much enjoyed seeing how many pails I could fill with stones.

The farm was hired out to a man who bred carthorses and a field of these lovely galumphing creatures would start

moving until gradually the whole lot of them would be careering madly round and round. Aunt Rose offered a home to a horse that had been ill treated; it was thought that he would be useful to help mow the grass. However, he soon recovered from his ill treatment and escaped from his field to join the carthorses in their nursery gambols and it was a great nuisance catching him again. I think it was felt that he should somehow have been more grateful and Aunt Rose got rid of him. She also opened a home for Belgian refugees; but this too was unsuccessful because the families, boarded together in the home, fought most noisily amongst one another and as she would have put it: 'They were not satisfactory.' One of the Belgian men used to come to Coombe Farm to do carpentry and he made us two scooters which had just become popular. These first ones had small wooden wheels and so they wouldn't go very well; later we were given proper scooters and we used them until we were old enough for bicycles.

Apart from the family and servants, we didn't at first see many other people and we played very happily in the big garden and on the farm grounds. We were not supposed to go in the wood that we could see on the right of the fields that stretched away into the distance before the house. There was an old tramp with a long beard who dressed in rags and lived in the fields and ditches. We called him Rumpelstiltskin and although he was said to be quite harmless, we were naturally frightened of him. The gardener's boy told my brother that Rumpelstiltskin bathed in the sewer in the wood and we were determined to go and see this. It was a very exciting expedition. To reach the wood without being seen from the

house was quite difficult; we managed it by going out of our way to the right and scrambling in by the far side. There was no sign of Rumpelstiltskin and personally I felt quite relieved that there wasn't; but there, sure enough was the sewer, a fairly large tank roofed with an arch of corrugated iron. We stared in an awed hush at this and wondered if the gardener's boy had been telling the truth. I had no idea what a sewer was and it seemed quite reasonable to me that he should use this tank, almost as good as having a small swimming bath of your own.

Margaret and John went to school in South Croydon and a governess was engaged to teach Rosemary and me and some more children of a similar age who came and joined us for the morning. The governess was called Miss Larner, she had dark hair and blue eyes and her face was very sweet and good. We learned reading and simple crafts such as raffia work and the making of wool balls. One of the little boys died and as I was very quick at making wool balls and loved doing them, I finished off his as well as my own. One day I was dumped on his mother's doorstep and told to give her the ball; quite unembarrassed, I explained that I had finished Michael's ball and was very surprised to be so effusively thanked and kissed for something that had after all been a pleasure to me.

We did our lessons in the bow window of the billiard room and, at twelve o'clock, Billy and Little John joined us and we marched round the billiard table doing drill. Once or twice, the man who looked after the table came in and juggled for us with the balls. Every week a man with a sad face, dressed like an old-fashioned country doctor and carrying a similar black bag, came and wound up all the clocks.

I didn't understand very much about the war and there were no signs of it here till we discovered the trenches. These had been dug for practice by some recruits in a field on the left of the house. Big John discovered them and we explored them with tremendous excitement. One end terminated in a circle with a pillar of earth left standing in the middle. John said that he knew for certain that this was the lavatory; we were very impressed.

One morning I was in the garden when very suddenly, a round balloon with a large basket dangling from it nearly bumped onto the chimney of the house, I rushed in to tell everybody and they followed me out very reluctantly, not really believing my story. By this time the balloon was out of sight; however, it hadn't gone very far and we found it again descending onto a field, the basket filled with boy scouts and their scout master, very relieved to be safe on earth again.

Now the hay was cut and we had a hay party. This was one of the nicest parties I ever went to and we did everything in the way of building with hay that we could think of. We covered ourselves with it and threw it at each other and fell over in it and finished the wonderful afternoon with a lovely picnic tea. Later on in the year we went mushrooming and next best to picking raspberries, I like picking mushrooms.

At Christmas time, great preparations were made for a fancy dress party. The hall was decorated and everything prepared in Aunt Rose's lavish manner. The evening before, I went to bed rather earlier than usual and lay awake thinking about the next day. It was a wet and windy night and suddenly there was the most tremendous crash. I shouted for our nurse

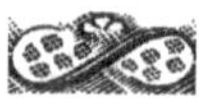

and she came in and said that a chimney pot had fallen off the house and, satisfied with this explanation, I went to sleep. The truth was that a huge branch of Rosemary's hollow elm tree house had fallen onto the roof, knocking over a large chimney which crashed through the hall ceiling and the adjoining conservatory. Poor Aunt Rose; torrents of dirt poured onto her Persian rugs of which she was very fond, and all the furniture had to be bundled out and tubs and baths put down in the dampest places. The great consolation was that at any rate, it had happened the night before and not during the party, and luckily, no one was in the hall at the time. It was a very successful party because of this accident. We squashed into the billiard room and the nursery and at the end, behind some curtains, there was a lovely Christmas tree with lighted candles and a fairy on top and Father Christmas to give us each a present from it.

This almost ideal life didn't go on very much longer because Aunt Rose was pregnant again, and in the spring we went with our cousins and their nurse Hannah to stay in Swanage.

At Swanage, we learnt to prawn and as we caught quite a lot of them, they must have been pretty plentiful. We collected shells. There were little horn-shaped white ones and fan shells and cockles but the most popular of all were tiny pink cowrie shells. With the aid of water wings, we learned to swim. Margaret and John had had lessons at the Glasgow Baths and she had been given half-a-crown because she had swum by herself. On her next visit, it was found that she couldn't swim at all but she didn't have the half-a-crown taken away from her.

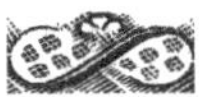

Aunt Rose was safely delivered of twins, a boy and a girl who were christened James and Susan; so we moved back to Croydon into a furnished house called Strathallan which was next door to Margaret's school, Croham Hurst.

With the help of her mother, our governess Miss Larner now opened a school. Miss Berry, who was very nice and kind, taught arithmetic and there was a weekly elocution class given by a married woman who wore a huge black hat and a neck band of black velvet ribbon supported by whalebone and net. Miss Larner had spectacles that were attached to a chain fastened onto her bosom: when she didn't want to wear them, they rolled up magically making a clockwork noise.

Miss Larner became engaged to be married. Rosemary and I were walking past some tennis courts one afternoon and came upon her sitting on her young man's knee. We were worried at the time that she might think that we had walked that way intentionally. He was, like most young men, a soldier and he went to France and very soon was reported missing: she went on with her teaching as though nothing had happened. I was walking by the school one day and saw her face when she was looking out of the window, thinking no one was by, and realised just how much she minded. I never forgot this and I hated war then just as much as I do now.

I have only a dim recollection of my first dancing lesson, given I think by Miss Wordsworth. She must have died very shortly because we didn't go very many times to her class. She had taught my mother when she went to the Croydon High School and she also taught Miss Ratcliffe, who reigned queen of dancing teachers in Eastbourne for many years.

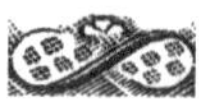

The next class that I attended was a big one in Addiscombe Gymnasium and here we learned a Welsh dance in which we bob curtsied and a Spanish dance in which we banged a tambourine, and another in which we clicked castanets; and for a scarf dance, we had various coloured chiffon scarves that we thought absolutely beautiful. On Parents' Day we dressed up in the appropriate national costumes for the dances and we also did a complicated imaginative dance in which we represented different symbols of the solar system. Our mothers had to provide all these dresses and I think that they really had to work harder than we did.

When I left Miss Larner's School and went to Croham Hurst, we stopped doing this kind of dancing and were introduced to Dalcroze methods. This was probably a better method than the other; it lacked the snobbish appeal to mothers who enjoyed seeing their daughters practising court curtsies and those aristocratic dances the minuet and the gavotte, the lancers and the polka and in descending values the waltz, the one- and two-steps, the gallop and the barn dance. For the new method, the mistress played different tunes on the piano, either slow and sad or quick and lively, and we were told to dance in the manner the music suggested to us. We did learn various turns and pirouettes and we walked or danced round the room, beating time to the music with different movements of our arms.

Later on at another school in Eastbourne, I was to learn Greek dancing. I suppose Isadora Duncan was responsible for this; she gave a display at the winter gardens in Devonshire Park. We wore Greek tunics with a cord round the waist which

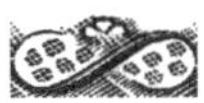

crossed at our breasts and we had no stockings or shoes. This embarrassed me because my legs were very hairy and my feet were large and flat and I was ashamed of both. I had great difficulty in throwing an orange ball about in time to music and I much preferred ballroom dancing.

Croham Hurst school was a Quaker school and it was lovely from my point of view because we were encouraged to draw as much as we liked and any homework or essay could be illustrated. I still remember the pleasure I got from painting Absalom in a royal purple cloak; the royal purple was Mummy's idea. We wore brilliant blue tunics called djibbas over tussore coloured blouses. I was worried because my hat brim was three-cornered and everyone else's was round. My mother liked it that way and refused to alter it. Margaret, when she went as a boarder to this school, found that everyone except herself wore socks, of which my mother did not approve. She thought of the clever plan of writing to an uncle, who no doubt very much enjoyed sending her a secret supply. I didn't stay very long at Croham Hurst before we had to move again. I was sorry to leave. The memorable things about my stay there were a girl called Psyche whose hair had refused to grow so that she wore a red wig; it was reported to be just sprouting when I left, and a large noisy girl called I think Jiggy, whose mother was asked to remove her daughter for saying: 'Sacré bleu'. Maybe this wasn't true.

We went now to live in Littlehampton and Margaret, Billy and I were sent to a school called Winterton House. We were rehearsing *As You Like It* which the school was going to act to wounded soldiers. I was a wood nymph, Billy a cupid and

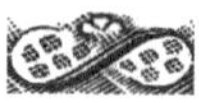

Margaret an old man. As a wood nymph I had to learn a dance and late one afternoon, carrying my slippers in a shoe bag, I left our house to go to the school to the dancing class. The way led through the churchyard where there was sometimes a deaf and dumb man wandering about. Usually he lay on the graves and took no notice of us, but this evening, to my horror, he started following me. He was smoking a pipe, and walking close behind me, he put his head over my shoulder and blew his filthy smelling smoke into my face. He kept his head in this position and I desperately walked along taking no notice of him, feeling instinctively that it would be wrong to run away from him. I can remember every step along the path, my heart thumping till at last we reached the gate at the other side and to my infinite relief, he didn't follow me through it. We had been told never to talk to strangers and we very seldom went about alone. My mother and Aunt Rose had been frightened, as well they might, by an incident which happened to Margaret at Croydon: I knew nothing about it then but she told me years later. She had been coming back from Croham Hurst along Coombe Lane; it was rather a dark overgrown lane, wide, but overshadowed with trees with a hedge on either side. Suddenly a large boy lunged towards her from the hedge and with a start of surprise, she saw that his trousers were undone displaying his penis. As if sent by providence, the car and chauffeur from Coombe House came down the lane. The boy as though on springs, leapt the hedge and ran off over the fields. The thing that impressed Margaret afterwards was not the escape from a danger of which she hardly knew the existence, but this incredible jump over the hedge.

The boy was a butcher's boy, he got into a lot of trouble, but he wasn't prosecuted because my family obviously didn't want publicity given to such an affair.

It was at Littlehampton that I became more conscious of class distinction. On our walks to and from school, we passed down a street that was often crowded with children and they would sometimes jeer at us. Some twins who wore trousers yet had long hair, I remember with particular loathing. I expect we looked little prigs but we didn't scorn them, it was they who attacked us and entirely because of our appearance. For nearly twenty years after this, I disliked and was frightened of working-class children. Sunday school children in particular I abhorred.

Littlehampton was a good seaside town for children; it didn't have such good prawning as Swanage or Bembridge where we had stayed before, but it had a big stretch of common land in front of the sea where we played and flew kites for hours on end.

My father was at home on leave before going out east and we all moved to Buxton to spend Christmas with him. I was very interested in a visit we made to some underground caves nearby. An old man led the way and we followed him into a cavernous interior dimly lit by gas light and with a subterranean river running blackly on one side, the walls made of black rock were striated with grey and white. I had never imagined there were places like this and we fingered the long stalactites that hung or joined roof and floor and with their perpetual drip, made pillars. Some parts of the ground were spotted with what looked exactly like poached eggs but were

really the products of years of dripping onto exactly the same place. My mother bought a small pot made out of the black streaky rock before we left, and later it joined the collection of china and odds and ends that she treasured in the drawing room cabinet. This sort of expedition didn't interest my father but my mother because of her past association with her brothers who had loved mountaineering and her sister Lucy, who was almost passionately interested in archaeology and Egyptology, still retained an interest in this natural phenomenon.

There was a heavy fall of snow and we spent all the time we could tobogganing down a hill with crowds of other children. To our great disappointment, my father was ordered to leave two days before Christmas although he didn't actually sail till about ten days afterwards. In command of over 4,000 officers and men, he went out to Mesopotamia and we went back to Croydon.

We were being affected more and more now by the war; my mother's brother Jack was killed while putting up barbed wire in France, he was the only casualty in our family. Aunt Rose's mother, Mrs Swaine who lived in Croydon with her son Harry, had sometimes taken Rosemary and me for drives in her carriage on Sunday afternoon but now she had sent her two horses Punch and Judy to the war: knowing that Marconi had been killed, I didn't like their going. The son Harry had become a special constable and when an air raid was expected, he would warn my mother. If it was in the night, we would go down to the cellar and be given drinks and toffees. Words like 'Zeppelin' and 'Maroons' and 'Gothas' now became part of

our vocabulary and Mummy and Martha had to stand in food queues, and sometimes bombs landed on Croydon.

Our house stood on a hill and from our top window, it was an exciting view at night. If there was a raid, we could see London with the sky above criss-crossed with searchlights searching till they held the tiny cylinder that was a Zeppelin. One night I woke up and getting out of bed, sat on my pot and the guns were banging; but there was all at once a change of noise, a throaty distant roar that grew in volume till I too on my pot and my nurse in the next room joined in that sinister cheer. 'Quick,' shouted Martha and I ran to her window while the blazing Zeppelin sank, the poor devils inside burning horribly to death.

Martha Pestridge was our new nurse and she stayed with us for many years. She had black hair and brown eyes and rather a protruding mouth and teeth and she wore spectacles. When she was disheartened, she would say: 'Well, I expect I shall die in the work house.' She was devoted to my mother and a good nurse.

I learned to ride a bicycle at this house. I never feel very confident on one to this day and am frightened of getting on and off, and like all women riding bicycles who don't happen to be wearing trousers, I am perpetually pulling down my skirts.

From her school, Margaret brought home the expression 'good egg'. Other slang we used at this time were 'keep your hair on', 'hee boo, sucks to you', 'bug wash' – for hair oil, and 'bags I'. I still got into tempers and would shout: 'I hate you I hate you, you horrid pig', at my brother when I was teased. These tempers were nearly always caused by a sense of

injustice; I expected everything to be fair in a world that seems determined to be unfair. In those days if I fought John I had some hope of winning, but later on when I grew breasts – 'stick out' as he scornfully called them – my tender body made the battles unequal and handicapped, I had to give up.

In the summer, as my grandmother and grandfather were going to Woking for their holiday we took a furnished house there, so as to be near them. John and I became entirely engrossed in collecting butterflies and moths. We had started this in Croydon where there was a taxidermist shop and John had asked an old road sweeper to collect beetles for him and these too we stuck in special boxes. They were beautifully made wooden boxes lined with cork and white paper and we had a number of different sized setting boards and special delicate pins for entomologists. We used to go far away on to the common looking for hairstreaks and hoping that miraculously we might catch a purple emperor in the woods. The bracken grew high in places so that we couldn't see very far and once or twice we got lost; I had confidence in John but it was frightening to realise that we had come back to the same place from where we had set out. I have no sense of locality and always expect the person I am with to know where we are going, and once or twice walking with friends who also have this failing, we have presently discovered that neither of us have any idea where we are heading and our laughter at discovering our foolishness does not help us to make up our minds. I loved these adventures with John and even at night I joined him in the game of dangling our butterfly nets out of the window to catch a bat. John did succeed in catching one

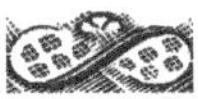

and released it on the landing, half hoping it would fly into Margaret's long hair so that he could see whether it really would be so difficult to get it out. We got into trouble for this and we were forbidden to hang out of the window any more. He also got into trouble for pouring boiling water onto a wasps' nest in the middle of the day when the wasps were all out; returning, they furiously stung every member of the house with the exception of John.

In spite of our hunting, it was our little sister Betty who found the biggest treasure; she came in one day and told us there was a beetle on the gate. 'How big?' we asked. 'Not very.' John ran out and returned with an enormous big stag beetle. He took it to Marlborough where he was at school and swapped it for a butterfly; privately I didn't approve of this, after all it had been Betty's beetle.

With my mother I collected wildflowers. She had a flower book in which each specimen was drawn in black and white, when we found the flower she coloured its picture and wrote underneath where we had found it. I also collected pieces of glass china printed with the arms of the towns where I had stayed and foreign stamps and later on I was to collect fossils, postcards and crests and indeed I still have a tendency to collect things once I have more than one or two of anything I like. I have never collected birds' eggs. I love birds' nests and feel sometimes that like the Pre-Raphaelite painter Holman Hunt, I should like to paint them very carefully in a vain endeavour to keep them for ever, the eggs still fertile yet unhatched.

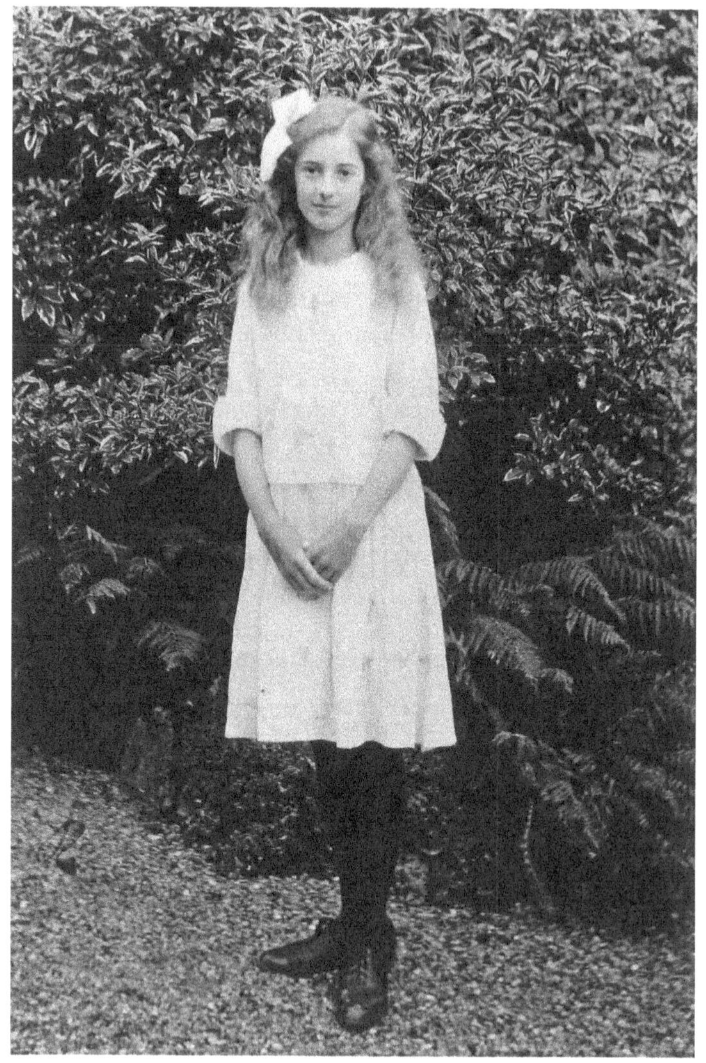

CHAPTER THREE

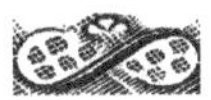

My mother was very tired of continually moving about, and finding that the ban which had prevented her getting her furniture out of store was lifted, she decided to settle into a house of her own. She chose Eastbourne because there were plenty of schools there and with four daughters to educate, she would have to be near schools for some years. We moved again, to Elmwood, 5 Arundel Rd, Eastbourne on [April 11th 1918] my tenth birthday. It was an Edwardian gabled house, semi-detached and built of red brick. It stood at the back of Eastbourne high up on a hill, so that it had a sloping front garden and pebble drive. There was a flat lawn at the back and it really justified its name of Elmwood by having a small wood at the back and two elm trees in front. It had a nice big garden and we were very pleased with it.

My mother had very decided opinions about taste and did the best she could with the furnishing of Elmwood but at the end of the war, furniture was very shoddy or very expensive, so that she was forced to buy things which she didn't really like.

She believed that furniture should be mahogany or walnut unless you lived in an old-world cottage or Tudor manor, in

which case it should be oak. She didn't consider herself rich enough to indulge in the collection of period pieces.

Most walls had cream or buff-coloured papers but the bedrooms were permitted flower-patterned wallpapers of a restrained nature. Paint downstairs was mostly dark brown but a few years later, she had the outside of the doors leading into the hall coloured a bold turquoise blue. Bathrooms and lavatories had real tiles or waterproof papers which imitated tiles.

On the floors of the lavatories and halls and nursery there was linoleum and the maids' rooms and bedrooms had rush mats before the marble-topped washstands and they were either carpeted with hair cord or linoleum. The carpets and mats in the downstairs rooms were always Persian or Indian.

Drawing room armchairs and sofas had loose-covers of chintz or cretonne with a floral design of delphiniums if possible and the room was decorated with Chinese crockery, Buddhas and a clock in a glass case. My mother was unfortunate enough to have been married when the fashion for pewter pots was at its height and she had several examples of the inevitable tulip-pattern type. A pottery dish held Christmas cards mixed up with photographs of relatives, whose pictures also ornamented the upright piano in the corner by the French windows; other iridescent bowls had rose petals or flowers, she was particularly fond of Chinese blue pottery or greeny-blue lustre ware. A brass Indian plate or a silver wedding present salver was used for visiting cards; there were quantities of small Indian brass ornaments about the house. I suspect that my parents had been bullied by the

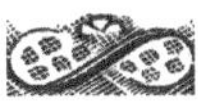

natives into buying them and afterwards they had to pretend that they really wanted them, not liking to admit that they had been weak-minded and at any rate it showed that they had travelled.

Quite a large proportion of the ornaments and pictures about the house were just there because someone had given them to us and no one had thought of throwing them away. The more valuable silver and remains of old tea sets and other treasures lived in a glass-fronted cupboard over a Sheraton desk in the drawing room.

About half the pictures had been painted by my mother herself or by my father. His were usually boating scenes while hers were flowers or autumn trees in watercolour. She thought that my father had no eye for colour and that he was better at drawing figures than she. My father liked drawing nudes and later on in life when he felt that it was improper to indulge in this sport, he took to buying books of photographs of nude models. We didn't like these books and thought them disgusting. There was rather a nice oil painting which someone had given them for a wedding present, of a windmill with a dark stormy blue sky coming up behind which hung above my great-grandfather's sounding board that had been made into a table in the dining room.

My mother at one time before her marriage had taken a great many photographs of Swiss mountains and had had them exhibited at the Alpine Club and some of these very cold photographs hung in the spare room which was a big cold room even without them. There were more photographs in the passages and some of those Egyptian pieces of appliqué

work and they hung as well in descending order down the walls of the staircase. Near the foot of the stairs was a huge brass pot which I had borrowed to take to school when we acted *The Brass Bottle*. The only other use I ever saw it put to was to hold pampas grass.

The furniture was so various that it is too difficult to describe in detail; it was solid and not elegant. In nearly every bedroom there was an excellent travelling clock in a morocco case; they kept good time, struck the hour and went on working for years.

The books were nearly all my father's; it would never have entered my mother's head to buy a book. She occasionally sat with her feet up on the sofa on Sunday afternoon and read a little Sir Philip Gibbs which one of her daughters had got out of Boots Library. My father's books were many of them inherited, his favourites were *Tristram Shandy*, Burton's *Anatomy of Melancholy*, *The Golden Ass of Apuleius* or Gibbon's *Decline and Fall* etc. He enjoyed the feeling that his old books which looked so respectable in their musty leather covers, were in reality much more salacious reading than Margaret's garish American hot sex novels.

My mother's rules of good taste were also applied to the garden. It was wrong because it was common to cut up the garden into small beds, a large herbaceous border was the right thing. Fine pink cabbage roses were out of fashion and she preferred the varieties with fewer petals and sentimental colouring like the *Daily Mail* rose. She hated any brilliant garish flowers like marigolds or magenta everlasting sweet peas, nor did she like unnatural flowers or trees such as

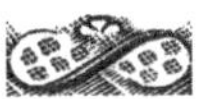

calceolarias, cactus plants or monkey puzzle trees. She loved delphiniums and anemones and scabious.

The first school we went to here was a kindergarten called Knockmaroon run by two Irish Miss Semples. It was next door to a house occupied by one of Eastbourne's eccentrics, an Austrian countess who at that time kept a number of dachshunds and one fox terrier. She dressed like a man, excepting that she wore a skirt instead of trousers, her hair was short and she wore a trilby felt hat, or was it perhaps a Homburg, and long boots. She was notorious in Eastbourne then because when she was living in another house nearer to the sea front, a burglar one night had climbed onto her porch. She had telephoned the police station and the unfortunate constable coming to investigate was shot dead by the burglar. I expect that, owing to her Austrian husband and her German dogs, in spite of the fact that she herself was an Englishwoman, she had been suspected of being a spy by some of the people in Eastbourne and this incident made her into something of a heroine. She was an amiable old person; but to children anything peculiar is suspect and we were rather frightened of her.

I was passing her house one day when her dachshunds were in the road eating an assortment of unpleasant-looking bones. They were very fat dogs, and I remarked on this to a little girl who was with me. The countess was standing at her window drinking cocktails with a friend, a young woman who, to the shame of her parents, imitated her masculine dress. She opened the door and shouted at me that we were the rudest children she had met. We were noisy, we abused dogs, and a lot more that I was too surprised and frightened to hear.

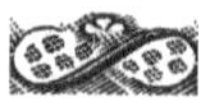

She was possibly quite right but she had no support from our parents or teachers who suspected her of being a lesbian and she eventually moved. My mother very often took me to the theatre now as Margaret was away at boarding school and I remember at one play while we were waiting for the curtain to rise, a number of women dressed like the countess came into one of the boxes at the side, and were greeted with a disgusted hiss from the more forthright elements of the audience.

Eastbourne was rich in eccentrics. The most spectacular one was Percy Hurst. He was a fairly wealthy man who owned quite a lot of land in the old part of the town. At some time in his life, he became involved in a lawsuit and emerged with a fanatical hatred of lawyers. He made for himself a white wooden top hat which he always wore; this revolved in the wind and had 'Beware of Lawyers' written round it. Very carefully in pen and ink, he drew a great number of pictures which he displayed in the window of an otherwise empty shop. The villain of the picture was of course always a lawyer, though he might be disguised as a spider or some other uncomplimentary symbol. There were captions either written underneath or coming from the mouths of the figures like distorted balloons; they had some resemblance to the drawings of Max Beerbohm. Outside the shop hung a sign, a wooden shark which he had carved. He had erected on his estates two or three enormous notice boards with 'Beware of Lawyers' written on them.

Aunt Rose and her family had come back from Australia where they had been living for two or three years, and she

came to stay with us. I think it was after the death of her little girl Sue, who had to have a couple of quite mild operations to cure a squint in her eye, and during the second operation she suddenly collapsed and died and it was found that she had that rare and odd complaint, *status lymphaticus*. Another little girl who was at school with us at Knockmaroon also died of this same thing while she was having her tonsils out.

Before she went, Aunt Rose decided to give us all a treat and she arranged that Margaret, John and I should go up in an aeroplane or sea plane and Billy and Betty, who were considered too young for this, should be compensated by a large lunch at a shop. We chose the sea plane. I went up first with Margaret while John held our hats. We had to wear helmets and the rubbery smell of them reminded me of having gas at the dentist. We taxied over the bumpy grass, the engine making a deafening roar. When we were safely up in the sky, Margaret, in front of me, wondered if eating would feel any different in the air and she passed me a sticky boiled sweet. I couldn't hear what she said and didn't notice the sweet and it must have got left in the cockpit. We hadn't expected quite such powerful wind and were more interested in the pilot's hair than the landscape underneath us with apparently motionless figures dotted about in it. Men had very long hair at this time, brushed back from their foreheads and liberally greased; our pilot's was fair and remarkably long and it blew in all directions in the most astonishing manner. When we landed, Aunt Rose asked me if I had felt frightened and although I said no, she pointed out that the red had run from my ticket which I had been clutching in my hand.

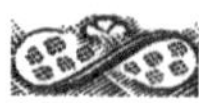

At last the armistice was signed. We were made to stay indoors after lunch because of the jubilations in the town: two men broke into our house that night looking for something to drink. As my mother never drank anything intoxicating while she was alone, they couldn't find any and they went to another house further along where they had better luck.

John and I caught more butterflies and moths, adding chalk hill blues, fritillaries and emperor moths from the downs to our collection; but we had a new interest which was collecting fossils and, with hammer and chisel, we explored the cliffs and rocks under Beachy Head and Birling Gap. Birling Gap was particularly attractive as it had a wrecked schooner that was breaking up on the beach and later a German submarine was washed ashore just beside the first wreck. The submarine was sold to the Japanese for scrap iron and a little yacht called paradoxically *The Dove* used to come and fetch pieces of it away.

Two maiden ladies who lived next door gave me two white doves, we thought they were a pair till both laid eggs and sat fruitlessly on them side by side. We got a cock for one but the other called 'Dovey' having no mate, attached herself to me and she would coo into my mouth and caress me gently with her beak putting it between my fingers and round by my ears. She usually sat on my head and I trained her to go downstairs saying 'Do do do' in that higher tone which doves use when they land from flying. Her usual call was 'Coo-coo-roo-oo-er.' The next year when she had a mate of her own she lost interest in me, but her intimacy with me had spoiled her as a dove and she was never a good mother; in all the years we

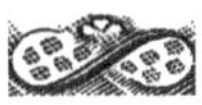

kept her, she only raised one child. There was a lot of rivalry between the two pairs and the cocks fought terrifically, banging one another with their wings and pecking viciously: why they are symbolic of peace I don't know. If the eggs of the other hen Lovey hatched first, Dovey in a passion of jealousy would leave her nest to swear at the other cage and in that way, she let her own eggs get cold. We had a lot of casualties in birds one way and another and started a cemetery for them. When my father came back, he made grave stones by pouring cement into the lid of a Lyons Dundee cake tin and while it was still wet we inserted a suitable inscription written in those alphabet letters that are made for soup. When the cement hardened, the letters either fell out or were eaten by other birds, a fact which particularly delighted my father. This was some years later, because at the close of the war he was in Mesopotamia and from there he was ordered to go to India. Knowing that he would have to stay there for about five more years to finish his foreign service, he wrote to Mummy suggesting that she should go out to stay with him and this she did, leaving us once more homeless. Margaret and John went to boarding school and Billy and I were sent with Martha to stay with Aunts Lucy and Edith in Kensington.

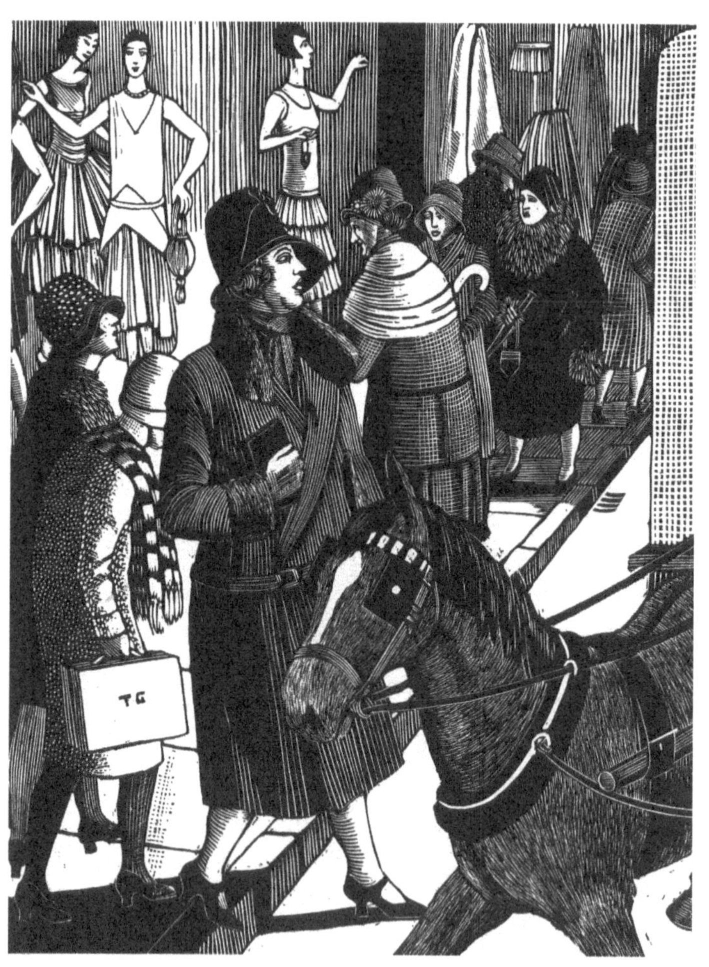
TG

CHAPTER FOUR

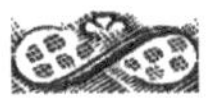

Aunt Lucy was my mother's eldest sister. She had grey eyes and regular features, her nose was slightly more Roman than my mother's and like her, she was very pale. As a girl she looked, so far as I have been able to judge from photographs, quite charming and why no one ever married her, I can only guess; perhaps she was too good, there was no suggestion of any sexual attraction about her and she loved romantic poetry and archaeology. My father's younger brother Harry said one day to me, 'I think your Auntie Lucy is the most Christian woman I know'. The only defects in her that I ever noticed were inquisitiveness and snobbishness. Neither of them mattered; if she asked you questions she forgot your answers and the snobbishness was more a theoretical attitude and did not really apply to her behaviour – she was in fact all those things which a lady should be. She loved going to lectures and was a member of the Lyceum Club.

Aunt Edith was shorter than her sisters and although not so good-looking or so good, she had a sense of fun and a rather vulgar taste which was, at that time and in contrast to her ladylike sisters, endearing. She wore coats and skirts and

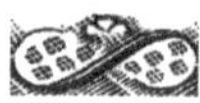

usually a green hat. John called it bice green and we could recognise her in crowds by its bright colour. As a girl, she had suffered as I did from very bad pains every month and also from a bad complexion. She did not get on at all well with her mother and she used to tell us stories about her school and home life. She was the first grown-up I knew who criticised other grown-ups.

My grandmother, as seen through Aunt Edith's eyes, was a great deal too managing. She enjoyed entertaining and although she might have no very great knowledge of any subject, she could as a hostess 'keep her end up' and appear to be well informed. She was actually interested in a large variety of different things and, having great energy, she very conscientiously looked after her children.

Aunt Edith had no particular talents. She couldn't sing or act or paint or even do housework in spite of a course of domestic science and though she might have felt sympathetically about women's suffrage and women's rights, she was too influenced by her family to break away. As a girl she had been very fond of *Vanity Fair* and had been nicknamed Becky by her family and she prided herself on her wit. This wasn't very great but it was something and she was the only one of the family to have any sense of humour at all and she wasn't good like the others; she was bad mannered, selfish and greedy and she fell embarrassingly in love. But she was in a way aware of her failings and she had many more friends than her sisters. Her faults were products of an inferiority complex and no amount of psycho-analysis or courses of Pelman could take away the misery that a girl with a spotty face must have endured.

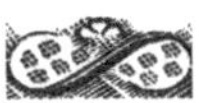

I don't think my grandmother could have avoided conflict between Edith and herself, she was used to being successful and Edith wasn't a success or a credit to her and resented her domination. Aunt Edith's stories of her mother's narrowness were not particularly damning considering the Victorian times in which she lived. On Sundays only certain books were allowed and Mrs Corry, coming into the room and finding her family reading, would snatch all their books from them and substitute others, not necessarily more pious but at any rate of her choosing. Sometimes the rebellious Becky would change the cover of her book, hoping to disguise her novel in the jacket of some missionary book. I doubt whether my grandparents were any more strict than other parents at that time and a big family is a strong defence against parental tyranny.

Everyone who knew my grandfather, John Corry, said that he was an exceptionally nice old man, both handsome and kind. As well as running his [Star Line] sailing ships to Australia, he invented things in his spare time. One of these inventions was a sewing machine but he refused to patent it on the presumption that if it succeeded it would throw many people out of work and so ultimately do harm. Being passionately attached to his lovely sailing boats, he hated the introduction of steam boats. He refused at first to have anything to do with them but his brothers who were in the business with him bought them without telling him. Aunt Edith only saw this distaste for change as a weakness which impaired the family's financial interests: 'We ought to have come out of sail quicker and gone into steam,' she said.

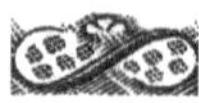

After the death of their parents, Aunt Lucy and Aunt Edith bought a house in Kensington and shared it between them. They both did voluntary work, Aunt Lucy helping the poor in Fulham and arranging country holidays for children, and Aunt Edith went to the office of the Charity Organisation Society as well as keeping the index of mental defectives for the Eugenics Society. She developed a habit of spotting mental deficiency in the people around her which was disconcerting, instead of the White Queen's 'Off with her head!', 'She ought to be certified!' was her cry.

The house was a very tall one and built with no thought for the comfort of the servants, whose kitchen was in the basement and whose bedrooms were at the top of the house. There was a small lift from the basement to the ground floor, it was only large enough to carry the meals and rumbled up into a cupboard in the hall. The only other labour-saving device was a system of speaking tubes like a telephone which ran down the landings to the basement. If you took out the cork at the mouth of the tube and blew down it, this attracted the attention of the cook because there was a whistle attached to the kitchen end of the tube and she would then take out the whistle and listen to what you had to say.

Martha, Billy and I were put into a bedroom at the top of the house; the cook, a tiny old woman resembling a parrot, who had been my grandmother's cook, was on one side and a nice parlour maid called May in the tiny room on the other side. Poor Martha had varicose veins and as well, she used to become ill and sick every month. The stairs were hell for her and occasionally when I was in bed, I used to wake up and find

her retching and groaning and utterly miserable. She always said that it was her varicose veins and in consequence I grew up with a very exaggerated horror of this complaint. My nights were also disturbed by Billy who used to cry in her sleep and once or twice she had nightmarish fights with me, although when awake we seldom fought. There was a water tank outside the bedroom and in a tobacco tin on top of this I kept two goat moth caterpillars of my brother's. I used to feel comforted in some way by these, imagining I could hear them eating away through their rotten wooden meals. They didn't survive their three years' caterpillar life, London didn't suit them and they slowly died, I expect I didn't give them enough old wood.

Billy and I were sent to school in Church Street. On the first day, Martha was instructed to tell the headmistress to take no notice if Billy wanted to go home or say she felt ill, as it was a habit of hers and was only nerves. When we arrived, some of the girls kissed one another in the cloakroom and that seemed peculiarly terrifying to Billy and me. We separated for morning lessons and met again at lunch time. 'I feel ill,' said Billy, now green with misery. Sternly we took no notice, but she was quite right and to my horror was sick on the floor in the middle of lunch.

We weren't very happy at this school. The mistresses were particularly kind and also very good teachers but the school was too small, so that there was too much intimacy and not enough exercise. Also for the first time I experienced the misfortune of having someone hate me. She was a strange girl with very deep-set eyes and I never did anything so far as I

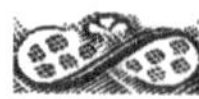

know to upset her, I suppose she just didn't like my face and she was even rude to Martha.

The day on which my mother sailed to India was a ghastly one. We were having a French lesson and with our textbooks open, answering questions about beastly verbs like 'boire'; worrying about my mother leaving us, I wasn't thinking much about the lesson and didn't hear Mademoiselle say 'Fermez vos livres'. She continued asking questions and I tried to answer them when my turn came but even with the aid of a book, I got them wrong. Suddenly I was aware of the girl at the next desk looking at me with fixed intensity and realising what had happened, I hastily shut my book. Miserably, I wondered if I should own up to this but I hadn't got a single answer right even with my book, so it seemed absurd to speak and I said nothing. Afterwards down in the basement cloakroom, the girl who had sat next to me whispered to the other girls and kept looking at me and the head girl came and sat at the other end of the form on which I was sitting and stared at me without speaking. I got more and more miserable and far too shy to say anything in case I was imagining this interest in me. It wasn't any use trying to comfort myself by thinking that when I was grown up this would seem quite unimportant and anyway, they were in the wrong. Eight or nine years later at a dance in Chatham I saw the girl who had sat next to me and I longed to ask her whether she really had believed I had been cheating; but, picturing the astonishment of the young gentlemen cadets who surrounded us, at my asking such a question, my courage failed me again. I don't know why I never told anybody about these troubles at the time. I suppose

children think that grown-ups will laugh at them or perhaps it is a form of pride, an unwillingness to admit that you aren't popular and a dislike of appealing for help outside the school.

My Garwood grandparents lived in a ground floor flat in Camden Hill Court which was on the way to school and we used to go and see them every week. My grandmother had become gradually paralysed and for thirty years she lived in a wheelchair looked after by her maid Ellen and her husband.

My grandfather, the son of a clergyman, had been a Royal Engineer. He was the only son and his three sisters never married but stayed in Kilburn, where my great-grandfather had his last living. He was a nice old man and my father and Uncle John took after him in appearance.

My father once read about a theory that women, growing old and finding that their youth and charming appearance no longer gave them power over other people, took what was termed a 'flight to illness' and by this means retained their importance in the family circle. His mother appeared to him to be an example of this type and he believed that her disease, being a nervous one, was possibly caused by her subconscious desire to be ill. Like Aunt Edith's views on her mother, my father's opinion of his mother was biased because in later life they didn't get on at all well together. She certainly had queer prejudices against certain people for rather absurd reasons. She adored Margaret and gave her expensive presents, but she disliked me because she said I had slapped her when I was a baby. Although the company of Billy, Martha and me gave her no pleasure that we could see, she would have been very

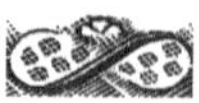

upset if we had not regularly visited her. I remember poor Martha being nearly in tears of indignation when my grandmother said that she was sure our hair was not being sufficiently brushed.

The one thing that always gave us pleasure in these visits was the cuckoo clock which hung in the passage outside the drawing room and what a relief it was to have an excuse to leave the room and wait under the clock till the hour struck and the magic door opened to release the lively cuckoo and for a few seconds the dead flat came to life, until all too soon the little door closed and for us that was the end of him for that day. We never stayed long enough to hear him strike twice.

Perhaps if my grandfather had had a firmer character and had he not been so patient with his wife, she might have been different. When she argued in front of us both one day on some point on which she was as obviously wrong as if she was affirming that black was white, he made a sign to me from behind her back to say no more, giving me to understand by his expression that he knew I was right but that it was useless to think that I could convince her that she was wrong. Poor Grandfather, the end of his life was spent in playing patience or slowly wheeling her along in a bath chair to Kensington Gardens, the monotony only relieved by occasional visits to his son John or holidays in places within a twenty-mile radius of London so that my grandmother could be driven there by car.

We were taken on Sundays to the Presbyterian church in Scarsdale Road and after the service we met some Scottish

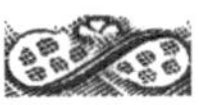

cousins called Clark and walked with them to their house which stood at the corner of Cromwell Road and Earls Court Road. This routine was occasionally broken by Aunt Edith taking us to a Wesleyan chapel where the preacher was a friend of hers. In this chapel I heard the most rousing sermon that I shall ever hear. It was preached by a converted Indian who recounted the most stirring adventures he had gone through to escape with his Christian faith from India. They included a vision seen on his bedroom wall by the English Missionary who had refused to baptise him, but convinced by this vision of his faith, he got baptised which distressed his family very much. His mother killed herself before his eyes saying that as his Christ had died to save him, so would she. He had a lot more adventures escaping from his family, who had tied him up and put him out in the midday sun but just in time he got away and went into retreat on a desolate mountain where he was nearly eaten by a tiger, but he was rescued by the Lord and in the pulpit he showed some of the scars on his person that had resulted from all these trials. From my point of view this was lovely and a change from associating Christianity with respectable dull middle-class and elderly women. I saw that in other countries it really might be an alive religion and perhaps these miracles which the Bible assured one were true really did happen, though not in Kensington where they presumed there was no need for them. I wished that a miracle would remove all the beggars who lined the kerb in Kensington High Street, ex-service men, incurable cancer sufferers, the blind with no pension, flower sellers, fruit sellers and men who produced from an

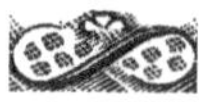

instrument with one string sounds that suggested that the cat gut still remembered the cat from which it had come. All this assortment of poor wretches Billy and I noticed and because of their appeals to our sympathy they harrowed us, and unable to relieve their suffering, we were frightened of them and hated having to pass them.

Nearly every day Martha took us to Kensington Gardens and, always self-conscious and frightened of other children, we walked to see the statues and the black swans, fed the gulls and watched the boys and men sail their boats on the round pond. If the weather wasn't good we went to the Natural History Museum at South Kensington and this I loved doing and I made drawings, always being careful that I was unobserved while doing them, I didn't like being watched. When we were visiting the National Gallery one day, Billy growing curious about male anatomy slipped away from Martha and me and went back to a statue we had passed to stand underneath it, observing with interest its sexual organs. She was discovered in this contemplation by a surprised man and she ran away to find us again, to giggle and whisper to me what had happened.

When my mother came back from India we went back to Eastbourne. I started going as a day girl to a school called West Hill and later, when she decided to go out to India again taking Margaret with her, I became a boarder at West Hill and returned to the aunts in Kensington for the holidays, this time with John as companion instead of Billy who with Betty was sent to Coombe Farm.

One of the Scottish relations called Clark whom we visited after church, took John and me to see the Turners at the Tate

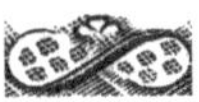

Gallery. She rather overdid it or perhaps at that time the Tate Gallery had rather overdone Turner and we saw far too many of them, even looking at drawings in obscure places under blinds and in drawers. Privately John and I thought them boring with the exception of *The Fighting Temeraire*. Another aunt, Lilian, took us to see a collection of modern French painting, an exhibition for which Roger Fry was responsible. Of course, we were as rude about them as the rest of the British public who went to see them and said that we could do better ourselves and I even did a few to prove this. At my various schools I had always been considered good at drawing but my drawings by now were pretty bad, because they were no longer innocent but influenced by the story-book illustrations of that period.

John and I were sent for the holiday to stay with another Corry uncle, Claude, who was married to Aunt Gladys and who with their three children lived at Gately Hall in Norfolk. This was a great change for us and we had a lovely time. He was the perfect uncle and disregarding his own younger children he taught us carpentry and how to shoot with an air gun or a catapult, how to ride the pony and a motor scooter that he had just bought and he took us for drives in his car to Fakenham, to Wells and to Norwich. He was a great talker and we drank in every word that he told us. It was Christmas time and snowy weather and I went out one morning and made a big snowman. All the time I was working I was harrowed by the dying screams of an enormous pig that was slaughtered that day. It quite spoilt any pleasure there was in my snowman and even when my uncle put gunpowder inside the snowman

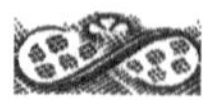

and tried to blow him up, I didn't feel very amused. The result was very disappointing as only a small proportion of the man blew up and there was no loud explosion. On the next morning, huge pieces of pig were put on the billiard-table in the gun room and I helped Aunt Gladys clean and salt the hams while John and Uncle Claude made sausages. The maid didn't like washing the gut and sent out a protest. John had a very happy time with the sausage machine and made some special double ones for himself. We had them for our last breakfast and they were quite different from shop sausages.

Years later when I was twenty-one I again went to stay; but what a sad disillusionment faced me. It was true that the house was a far nicer one than I remembered it but my uncle was a bore. He had not changed a scrap, but no longer could he hold my attention with his instructive 'how to make a canoe' talk. I had remembered from my previous visit all he had to say and there was nothing more, ungrateful pig that I am; he made me a lovely canoe. He talked incessantly and if he paused, he kept the conversation in his own hands by a succession of 'Whats', not interrogatory but simply to stop anyone else saying anything. He was obsessed with a theory he had about the method that had been employed by prehistoric men to move the big stones from Wales to Salisbury.

For our summer holiday, Aunt Lucy, who also was interested in prehistoric remains, decided to take us to Carnac in Brittany where there was a large number of stones similar to those at Stonehenge but not as big.

Travelling with either of the aunts was always a bit of an ordeal. Aunt Edith was impatient and suffered from a nervous

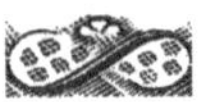

dread of being late. If arrangements went wrong as they tend to do with the over-cautious, she would curse porters because the train was late and bus conductors for the scarcity of their buses. Aunt Lucy lost her possessions in a capacious bag, and unconscious of a queue grown almost murderous behind her at the ticket office, she would mumble and fumble for her purse making futile enquiries about trains from the ticket official who naturally didn't know the answers. Her beautiful lack of business sense made this long journey doubly complicated and we arrived at Carnac without our luggage which we had been told to label to Auray and from Auray, they refused to send it any further. The hotel misleadingly called 'Hotel de la Marine' was a long way from the sea but the proprietor and his wife were so nice that we didn't mind.

We were very happy at Carnac, exploring with excitement the lines of prehistoric stones and the little chapel on the hill called Mont St Michel. There were underground passages in this mount with burial chambers of a prehistoric king and his family; Swallow Tail butterflies flew about on the hill above and John caught one in his hat. We learned the names of the different stones and could distinguish between menhirs, dolmens or cromlechs. The fields were divided by walls built of small stones and when Aunt Lucy was walking with us we would unbuild the wall for her to pass through and fill up the gap again behind her.

The girls of Carnac had a saint-like beauty, usually their hair was fair and parted in the centre. They wore white caps and black dresses and invariably they carried a long loaf of bread under one arm.

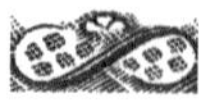

After we had been there about a week, a huge menhir made entirely of brown paper was put up in the square in front of the church and I had my photograph taken beside it with a background of the gay white town hall; a menhir is an upright stone, greyish-brown in colour, an enlarged Lot's wife. This was for a celebration called 'Le pardon des menhirs' and on the day of the pilgrimage everyone put on their best dresses. I wish that English country women had such best dresses and the men too had their Sunday suits with short jackets and large buttons and wide-brimmed black hats with long ribbons hanging down their backs instead of their usual berets. They all assembled in a field and after a competition for the prettiest dressed couple, the men wrestled and four pipers stood on tubs and played their bagpipes.

When it grew dark there was a torchlight procession. Carrying burning flares, the people processed round the base of Mont St Michel and then to the alignments of menhirs where they lit five huge beacons. Now everyone enjoyed themselves; the fires, warm and fiercely beautiful, sent up clouds of tiny sparks which changed into dense smoke floating away into the night sky. The people sang and joined hands to dance around their beacons and as they gradually burned out, coloured flares were lit and men dressed as Druids mounted on the tallest stones and waved their arms in the magnesium light. We didn't understand their play acting; it had some connection with the huge flat altar stone which stood at the head of the alignments, a sinister rock with its unknown history forever eluding us.

We went on many expeditions, stuck pins into wax saints, lit candles and kneeled to pray on each step of a magic staircase

that let you off years of purgatory. It didn't matter to us that we weren't Roman Catholic. I never appreciated the differences in Christian religions. I thought the way they gabbled through Mass in Carnac Church very silly but so was a lot of our English service.

John and I went out sketching and were horribly plagued by a number of children who used to attack visitors to the menhirs, following in a menacing band behind, chanting the history of the stones, begging for money. I grew very frightened of them and we hated their watching us. Once John was brave enough to send one of them to fetch paint water.

There was one major trouble which was the lavatory. It was a water closet, but there wasn't enough water in the summer to spare for pumping into the cistern, so the pan just filled up and, ignorant of plumbing, we didn't know how to empty it. Fascinated and horrified one day, I watched white worms with long divided tails crawl round. The smell was so bad that even Aunt Lucy had to smoke.

As it was a small hotel, we made friends with most of the people in it. The most amusing to us was a countess called by the lovely name of Comtesse de la Porte aux Loups. She was an alarming little woman with nutcracker features and an abrupt manner. She had a daughter Hélène, who in my eyes was a real princess, the possessor of beautiful golden hair, blue eyes and a lovely rose pink complexion. They went on several expeditions with us and shook with laughter at my remarks in French. They liked it particularly when the chauffeur disappeared while we were sightseeing and I said that I expected he

was in 'le débit de boisson'. We were surprised when they squatted down under a tree in very full view from the crowded street, but as they were nobly born I presumed that even countesses did without lavatories in France.

The two sons came for the day and, presented to the two young men, I noted appreciatively their blue eyes. We all went to the beach but only John and I bathed. The sea bed was carpeted with soft strands of brown seaweed called bathers' peril. Aunt Lucy, sitting on the beach with the Porte aux Loups was surprised to observe the young viscounts taking turns to watch me undressing through a pair of field glasses.

Aunt Lucy never told me about this or that the Porte aux Loups family thought I was charming because I was to them so wonderfully English. I suppose she thought that at that time I was quite unconscious of my being a possible object of attraction to young men, which was true enough but it wasn't because I didn't wish to be so but was due to humility about my appearance and shyness.

Margaret had turned from an ugly baby into a pretty little girl; her large eyes and long hair had very early in her life attracted admirers. There was one in particular who used to come to our house in Croydon and who kissed her when she was only twelve. I didn't like this fifteen-year-old boy with his foxy face, and when he and Margaret put some dead cockroaches out of the beetle trap into my bed because I wouldn't go to bed as soon as they wanted me to, my contempt for them both was increased; he made a bad mistake with the beetles, they held no terror to a budding entomologist. This

contempt for Margaret gradually grew greater and when she powdered her nose and made up her face I was very scornful, and I think it was this antipathy to her flirtations that was responsible for my reserved and 'touch-me-not' expression.

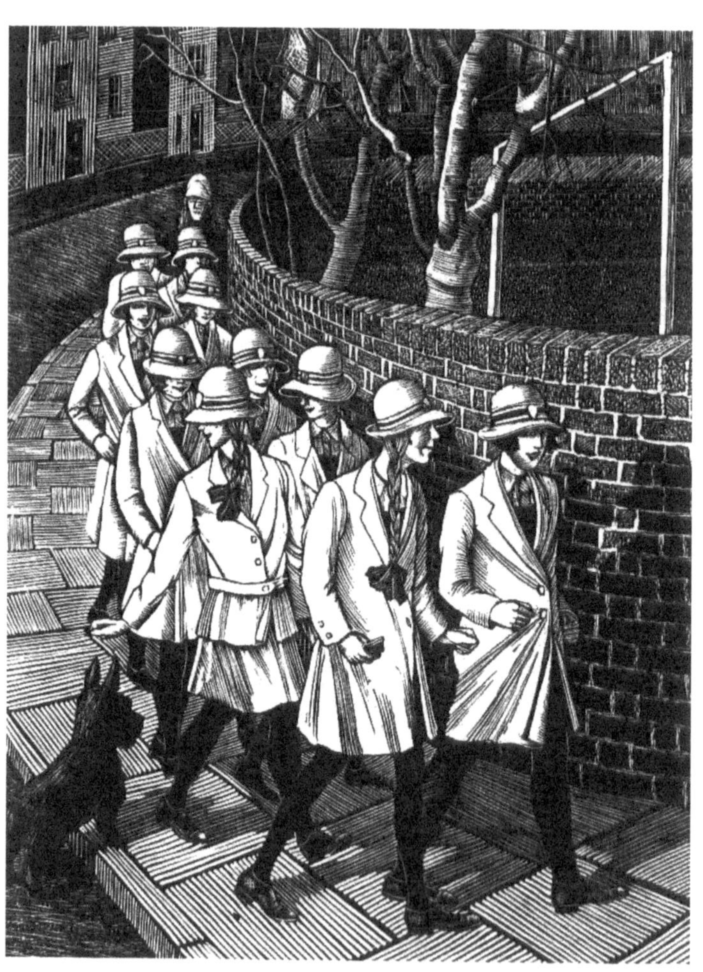

CHAPTER FIVE

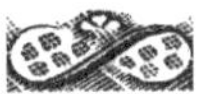

When I first went to West Hill as a day girl [in 1920], I was new at the same time as a girl of my own age called Marjorie Davidson. She was a long, pale, moon-faced girl with large limpid grey eyes and although she resembled a Raphael Madonna, she was generally thought to be very plain. At first our names were always coupled together and Eileen Garwood and Marjorie Davidson meant just two pale-faced new girls. We were persecuted by a gang of small children led by an undersized infant called Squit, our ignorance and shyness making us vulnerable targets for their practical jokes; but this didn't last very long because there were always other new girls coming along when we had grown stale to them.

The headmistress, Miss Wiles, was a tall thin woman with large sunken grey eyes and a big nose with a square end to it, which with her determined chin, gave her a witch-like appearance so that she was nicknamed the 'hag'. She was an able teacher but she kept order by being sarcastic so that I was always frightened of her. She was fairly popular both with the staff and the girls and although I didn't like her, I did respect her.

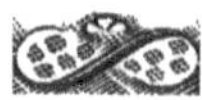

It had been expected that when the old, original head Mrs Barber died, this Miss Wiles would inherit the school; but contrary to all expectations Mrs Barber left the school to her married sister. Miss Wiles couldn't afford to buy the school and it was sold to a Miss Thomas who owned another school in Leicester but she still employed Miss Wiles as headmistress. Miss Thomas moved the senior part of her Leicester school to a nearby house in Eastbourne called South Lynn, hoping eventually to amalgamate the two schools. She didn't know she had as much hope of amalgamating West Hill to a school full of girls who talked with Midland accents as she would have if she'd tried to amalgamate it with the Tiller Girls.

The girls at West Hill were middle-class and their politics, like those of their parents, were Conservative. We looked down on the grammar school and had I known at this time that I was going to marry a 'Muny Boy', as we called them, I should have been most awfully upset.

The school uniform was a navy-blue serge gym tunic over a white blouse with a white girdle tied round our waists. In summer, the tunics were alpaca and the navy-blue round woollen caps worn in winter were changed for straw hats with the school blue and white ribbon round them. The boarders on Sundays had white coats and skirts in winter and white silk dresses in summer. Eastbourne was such a clean town that quite a number of the schools paraded spotless white crocodiles on Sundays. There were supposed to be over two hundred schools in the town but I'm sure there weren't.

The first headmistress had been a friend of Lewis Carroll's and in the school library there was a copy of *Alice in*

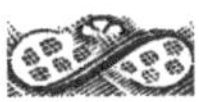

Wonderland with a dedication from Dodgson on the fly leaf, and there was a fine set of Dickens novels with the original terrifying illustrations.

For my first term I was a day girl, but when Mummy decided to go to India again I had to become a boarder which I very much dreaded. There were a number of rather petty and complicated rules and traditions that were difficult for a new girl to learn and I didn't like the way some of the girls ill-treated other children who, having come to West Hill from the grammar school, were considered inferior. I was a social snob like the majority of the school, but I didn't approve of active persecution like hair pulling; I believed that time and example would change their common accents. 'Common' was a word that haunted my upbringing, my mother far more frequently exhorted us to behave like ladies than be good. My family were unconsciously obsessed with a fear of being thought common by other people and paradoxically, the more they eradicated any peculiarity of behaviour or dress that might suggest this dreaded vulgarity, in fact the more common, used in its true sense, they became.

My mother had arranged with another Anglo-Indian acquaintance of hers called Mrs Beazley, whose children were at the school, that I should go to them on Sundays. There were four Beazley girls, three of them had brown eyes and pink cheeks with smooth features and straight brown hair but the other one was different, as she had grey eyes and she wore glasses and had a reputation for humour. The eldest one Rozelle was in the form below me and it was she who had pulled the hair of the Muny girl but apart from that, I liked

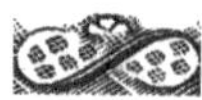

her very much. She skated beautifully but was worried by the size of her legs which were like fat bottles. She had offered to look after my white doves and from continually making their cookeroo noise, she seemed to grow very like them. The Beazleys didn't stay very long; their governess died after her bath one morning – she insisted on having cold baths – and they went to live in Jersey, but Rozelle and I still remained friends and wrote occasionally to one another.

An extraordinarily nice woman called Dorothea Moore was Guide Captain to the school and she came every Saturday morning to organise the company. She was the successful authoress of school and adventure stories, not perhaps as renowned as Angela Brazil but her books were translated into several languages. She had very large grey eyes with a queer spiritual and fanatical expression in them, Gertrude Stein would have recognised a genius. She was in delicate health and was looked after by her brother, a doctor, with whom she shared house; he had been in the army and was always referred to as Captain Moore. He was the school doctor but my mother didn't fancy him and insisted that I kept on with my own family doctor, an elderly man called Harper.

Captain Moore spent a lot of time at the school playing with the girls and giving the Guides drill. He enjoyed himself enormously over this. He also played the piano if it was needed and embarrassed me terrifically when I was new by suddenly stopping his playing and swivelling round on his stool and pointing a finger at me saying, 'Do you feel ill?' I said: 'No' and his sister persuaded him to go on. It was awkward for me having such a white face because grown-ups

invariably thought I was ill and Miss Thompson nearly stopped me taking my Fireman's Guide badge because she thought that someone with such a white face couldn't possibly be allowed to climb down a rope ladder from the top of South Lynn Tower.

Captain Moore also organised fire drill for the school and he loved this too. He did it thoroughly and made pretend fires with magnesium flares and had all of us running up and down the fire escapes in the middle of the night, everybody quite delighted, especially the girls who were allowed to jump from the porch into a blanket. I don't know if he was any good as a doctor, he had a reputation for being advanced and he gave the small girls puppy pills to make them grow.

Eastbourne, because of its richness in schools, had a remarkable number of Girl Guides and before I went to West Hill I had been with my mother to a huge Girl Guide rally in Gildridge Park. The Guides, after doing various exhibitions of putting up tents and lighting fires quickly or dealing with horrible accidents, paraded round the park. Some of them had white handkerchiefs covering the crowns of their navy blue hats and some of them had red handkerchiefs and they went on marching round until they had formed the design of a huge Union Jack. Lady Baden-Powell amid cheering then gave a speech but we couldn't hear much of what she said.

Later on, as a patrol leader, I took part in these rallies and I believe our company won a rally and we got a cup. Dorothea Moore was a very keen actress and a playwright and I know we had the highest score for acting. I always seemed to get the part of villains at school and played Mr Squeers and Colonel

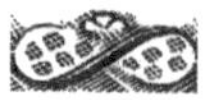

Kemp and other foul people with the greatest difficulty as I had a high voice and a feminine hesitating step. I had got into trouble with Miss Wiles for never boldly entering the staff-room door but knocking and then sticking my head in first before summoning up enough courage to follow it with the rest of my body. It wasn't till I was about fifteen that I blossomed out into a smart French dressmaker in a curtain-raiser about a lift that stuck. Dressed in my sister Margaret's black velvet toque, and my face covered with rouge, I found I looked much better and after this I decided that I should have to make my face up when I was grown up.

The Guide Company with South Lynn Guides went to camp at Chiddingly, where there was a special camping site for Guides with a large wooden hut and properly built earth latrines. A few privileged patrol leaders slept in bell tents but I was in the hut where we slept on straw palliasses which harboured earwigs, otherwise it was heavenly. In the evening we all stood round and sang that song about 'gone the sun' and on the last evening Dorothea Moore told us an extremely creepy ghost story while we sat round the camp fire, she said that she made it up as she went along. It was about two lovers who look over a country house with a view to taking it. There was a large pollarded willow outside and inside there was a marble statue half way up the stairs with its finger beckoning. The girl light-heartedly puts her wedding ring onto this finger and later, going to retrieve it, finds that the finger had closed and the ring turned to marble. After that things go from bad to worse and the pollarded willow does something awful to the young man, unfortunately I can't remember any

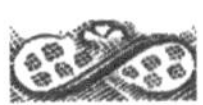

more until the end where the whole house, by now completely overgrown with ivy and creepers, collapses: it was worse than Borley Rectory.

Except for being better than the other girls at drawing I was of average intelligence. Being tolerably good at mathematics, I kept quite high up in my form and was occasionally top. Once I got a 100 out of a 100 for a geometry exam which was very astonishing because I made a fuss abut learning geometry as I thought it a waste of time to go proving something that you could obviously see was right. I was very bad at languages and hated French and Latin lessons. I would have liked science but we had so many different teachers that we never got really interested.

I also had far too many music teachers and each successive one had a personal theory of how you should hold your hands, so that I had to keep on beginning all over again. I was pretty miserable in music lessons and, staring so closely at the black and white sheets of music in front of me, my eyes used to fill with tears of fright because I had usually skimped practising my scales. I did begin to improve when I was taught by an old man called Mr Meade. He started every pupil off with Grieg's *Albumblatt*. I suppose the whole business of teaching being painful, it was less painful to hear one piece continually murdered than a larger number. Once he kissed one of his pupils and after this we had to have a chaperone in the room during our lessons. In spite of this, he managed to marry one of the girls after she had left and then quite suddenly he died. A tall pale girl who used to come in for private tuition from

him waited very patiently for him in the hall. At last she enquired from a girl who was passing when she could have her lesson, she baldly replied: 'You can't, he's dead', which gave the poor girl such a shock she fell down in a faint.

My last teacher was called Miss Thorne. She used to make me cry more than the others, but she did allow me to learn 'To the Spring' which I thought quite perfect. I had difficulty in striking so many notes together all at the same time I remember. I heard later that she had gone mad, she had been behaving very oddly my last term.

There was a very pathetic girl called Joan Lyle whose parents were Christian Scientists so she had no doctoring. She had been born with her spine slightly crooked and her people had done nothing about this, so that half of her brain had been affected; her shoulder and neck were crooked and her face with its undeveloped nose and round monkey eyes showed traces of Mongolism. When she was talking her eyes sometimes disappeared upwards like new-born babies' eyes. We felt indignant with her parents because although she did have massage and special treatment from the gym mistress, she could obviously have been put right as a baby and it seemed such a waste of what would have been a good-looking and nice girl. She was not defective enough to be unaware of her deformities and it made her pathetically eager to please and embarrassingly devoted if she was encouraged. As she talked incessantly, it was hard for us to be patient with her. We used to tease her if she yelled when she banged herself because she was supposed not to allow herself to give way to expressions of pain, but she seemed to hurt herself even more

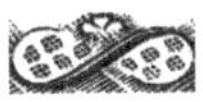

than we did. I sat next to her at meals for two terms in succession and for years afterwards I talked at terrific speed because I had had to talk so quickly to be heard through Joan's continual gabble.

Her mother didn't take much trouble with her clothes and never came to the school to take her out. She did have a bedroom to herself but that was the only admission that she wasn't quite normal. She had a pretty elder sister who when out in India became engaged. When she came back to England with her young man, she wrote to Joan that they were coming for the weekend to see her. Joan was bursting with excitement about this visit and we wondered whether the sister had prepared the young man in any way for the shock he might get in meeting her or did she too pretend that Joan was perfectly normal? At last for her, the great day came and she waited breathlessly after lunch for their arrival but no one came and when at last the message arrived that they were unable to come, poor Joan burst into tears. I don't know if Aunt Edith's work for the Eugenics Society made me particularly interested in this kind of problem but I know that if I ever had the opportunity of meeting Mrs Lyle, I should have felt it my duty as a Girl Guide to tell her just what I thought of her.

I had learned from Margaret about girls falling in love with other girls, it wasn't called falling in love but the term varied with the school. You had a 'pash' or a 'crush' on a girl or you were 'cracked'. I think only the Germans admit the existence of this adolescent love in their language and have given it the

name *schwärmerei*. Not having suffered, I had been quite scornful about it, but now I found myself becoming daily more interested in a girl called Betty Rennison. I resented at first this fascination for me that she held and pointed out to myself how ridiculous I was being; but the fact that I was having to fight against this attraction only stimulated my interest and I grew more in love and so more frightened of Betty, who was quite ignorant of this passion that she had aroused in me. I had hated being a boarder but now because of Betty, I started to love the school as well.

She wasn't a particularly beautiful girl, her eyes were grey and protruding, her jaw was square and her mouth was large and she had a big dent in the middle of her chin. She was very good at games but was not particularly remarkable in any other way. When I first loved her she had never spoken to me and I knew very little about her character, my affection was entirely for her appearance. Actually she was an extremely nice girl and she behaved very kindly and tactfully with me when she became aware of my embarrassing devotion.

So that she should approve of me, I worked very hard at my lessons and tried my best to be good at netball and cricket. It became fashionable in the middle forms of the school for girls to be cracked and most of my form had their various heroines. I became ecstatically happy if Betty so much as smiled at me and when once or twice she walked to evening church with me and sat next to me, I was filled with such joy that I wrote to Margaret who was now in India, a letter seventeen pages long describing my exaltations.

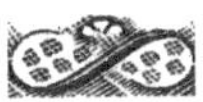

Miss Wiles didn't approve of this wave of sentimentality that was spreading over the school and she spoke to some of the older girls about it. Not fully understanding her point of view that this love might be misconstrued by parents and so give the school a bad reputation, I couldn't understand why she should wish to discourage this quite disinterested affection, which resulted only in good because it made us work harder and kept us more ordinarily happy. Before the end of the next term, Betty went to India leaving me desolate and unable to taste my food, though I managed not to cry. She wrote to me for a year or two but after she married we stopped. I practised shooting at netball until I was good enough to fill her place as Attack in the netball team and became the proud owner of a green first team girdle.

Netball can look very pretty when it is played well, but it is a delicate game of passing and dodging. Being Attack meant that I could go into the half circle at the end of the field and I and the shooter could either of us throw the ball into the net. If I got upset I couldn't shoot the far away ones and would feel very guilty and worried; the penalty for a foul was a free shot which meant the chance of shooting from the outer edge of the half circle. I usually got these in and had once when practising got six of them into the net, one after the other. This really has been useful to me because when I am cooking and want to throw egg shells or any other rubbish into the wastepaper bin, if I don't think about it overmuch and just casually throw, I can nearly always get things in from right across the kitchen.

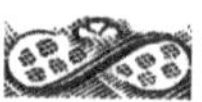

At first I had shared a bedroom with a clergyman's daughter called Norah, but she left the school and I now shared my room with Joy Holyoak whose eyelashes were so long and curly that they touched the upper part of her eyelids and whose nose turned up as well. We both went riding with a Mrs Webb instead of the usual school riding master and as we had better and faster ponies and went much further, we felt very superior. We both loved riding lessons better than anything else, it was such a wonderful escape from school and all its petty troubles. The air on the Downs was strong and wonderful and we went back to school with our cheeks glowing and our noses pink. Mrs Webb became very proud of us and when I managed not to fall off when my pony did a sequence of bucks, she said, 'I wish your father could have seen you'. My father was in India, but he wouldn't have been at all edified by this performance as he loathed riding and never got on to a horse unless he simply had to. The downland turf was marvellously springy under our horses' feet and the gorse and cowslips and later the milkworts and other minute flowers smelled gloriously of honey and waiting for the others at the end of a canter I would sniff and look around thinking how happy I was.

Miss Wiles didn't like this tremendous enthusiasm for riding any better than she liked my passion for Betty Rennison and if she could find a reason for stopping our rides, stop them she did. The weather was too bad or we must stay in on Saturday afternoon to write out lines for punishment for disorder marks or 'rules' as they were called. Soon the disagreement between Miss Wiles and Miss Thomas and South Lynn became almost open. We were asked round to

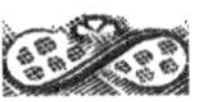

South Lynn one evening to attend a lecture. Thinking that it would be an ordinary kind of lecture on a subject like the Waifs and Strays or Wireless, we were quite unprepared for the spirited account of the end of the world which was given to us by a fervid believer in the Pyramid Inch. He worked out on the blackboard that the world would end in 1933, or failing that and leaving some small margin of error, 1935. On this momentous day, the good would all be gathered upwards while the bad and indifferent would be left to work out their salvation on the earth until the millennium. Miss Wiles walked the crocodile home in silence but after evening prayers she took up her Bible and read from the gospel of St Matthew: 'Heaven and earth shall pass away but my words shall not pass away, But of that day and hour knoweth no man, no, not the angels of heaven, but the Father only.' She left at the end of the term and most of the staff went with her and she started a school of her own at Seaford, where a few of the girls also followed her.

Miss Moore was getting too ill to continue as our Guide Captain. She was very kind to me and, knowing that I loved drawing, she offered to help with introductions to publishers if I wanted to become an illustrator. I went to tea with her and saw her spaniel dog sit up with a lump of sugar on his nose; she then repeated the names of Prime Ministers and when she reached the current Minister the dog snapped the sugar off his nose and caught it in his teeth. The last time that I can remember seeing her was leading the Guides along the road, her head held on one side, her infirmity made her lopsided, and in her eyes that look of intense patriotism

and pride in her Guides. It was good that we had done so well at the rally because she died shortly afterwards and Cecily Shackleton, the daughter of the explorer, became our new Captain.

We had often seen Miss Shackleton before because she usually won the Guides' diving competitions for St Winifred's School; she was a big, solid, masculine-looking girl like her father, and her body just went swiftly and rigidly down into the water like a stone. However, an American girl called Mary Lorraine Wilberforce Bird, who had recently come to West Hill, could do a beautiful swallow dive and so in her final competition Cecily Shackleton was defeated. She lived with an aunt in Eastbourne at that time and kept mice in her dirty clothes-basket so that the aunt who didn't like mice shouldn't know of their existence. My sister Billy who was now at West Hill too, got cracked on her but deserted her later for the new headmistress, Miss Ira Powell who was a niece of Miss Thomas's. She was a nice intelligent woman, as ugly as a bull terrier, but she worked very hard and managed to scrape most of my form through the School Certificate examination; the credit was due far more to her untiring efforts than to ours. She worked out a list of probable questions that we should get asked in her subjects of English and History and she guessed them practically all right, so we did well. I failed in Geography but was the only one to pass in Botany.

I rose to be head girl and when the family returned to Eastbourne, I became a day girl again. I fell in love with a film star called Richard Barthelmas and with another girl wrote him a fan letter, to which he replied with a photograph of himself. He was wearing an overcoat with a fur collar which, had he been an Englishman, I should have condemned as being very common and even in an American I didn't like it.

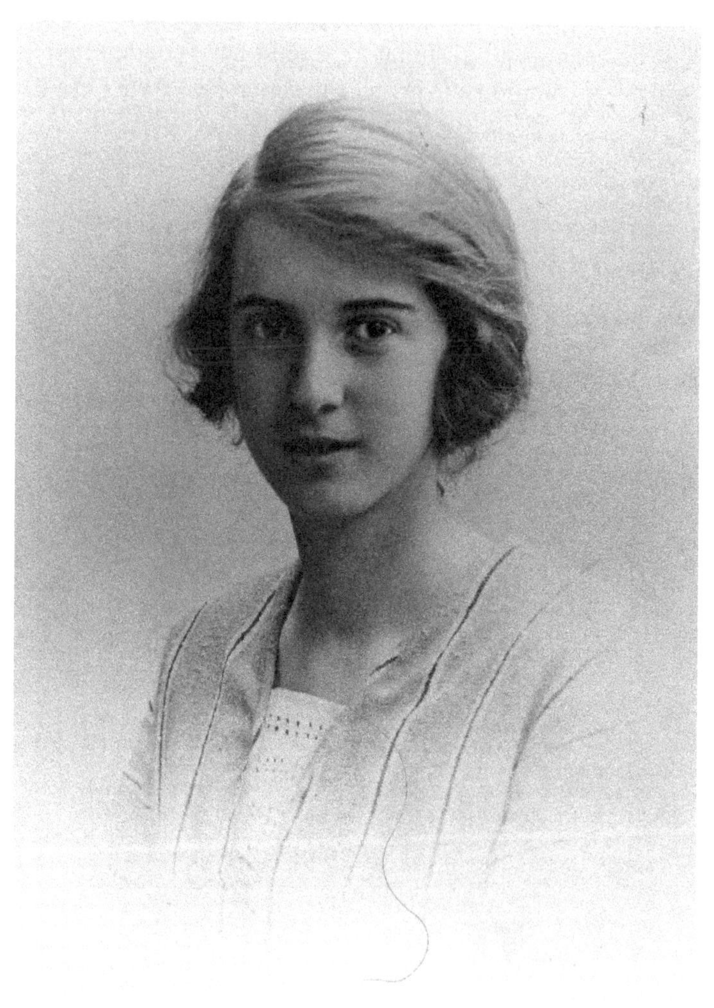

CHAPTER SIX

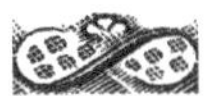

When Daddy came back from India with Mummy and Margaret, he was sent to be Commanding Royal Engineer at Oxford, so our Eastbourne house was let and we stayed in furnished houses in Oxford for about a year, during which time I still boarded at West Hill and joined the family for holidays.

Margaret had gone out to India when she was seventeen. She was an attractive girl with long, thick brown hair and a confidential manner; speaking to a young man she managed to convey the impression that she appreciated the fact that only he could have done or said this or that amusing or interesting thing. I used to listen to her fascinated and speculating whether there could be any limits to the flattery which men would swallow, provided the 'butter' was given to them by a pretty girl who danced well and who could syncopate on the piano. She and Billy, although conscious of their prettiness, were quite humble about their characters, believing them to be unimportant compared with the value of being amusing or dancing well and making the best of your appearance. As she was not an undergraduate, Margaret in

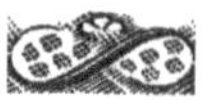

Oxford enjoyed a number of privileges that would have been barred to her had she been a member of a college. It was a matter of great satisfaction to her that proctors had no power over her, and asked 'Your name and college?' she could, if she chose, merely stick her tongue out at them. Not that Margaret would ever have done such a thing. She thoroughly enjoyed herself, her final triumph was to act with OUDS in *Hamlet*. Her most constant admirer was called Dickie [Armitage], an athletic young man from Brasenose, a scorner of aesthetes and intellectuals and above all undergraduates; they were blamed for showing their bloomers when riding their bicycles, they were hearty and had on the whole faces like the backs of cabs. At this time the word marvellous was just coming into fashion and also the verb throw, in the sense that you threw a party. Very wide trousers were replacing the narrow variety and Dickie was one of the first people to wear Oxford bags. In spite of all his attractions, Margaret couldn't agree to marry him because he had no money or prospects. He failed to get his degree and sailed to Africa as a purser with Tosti's 'Farewell' on a gramophone record which he played incessantly, till one morning it was missing from his cabin.

In the meantime, Dickie's best friend Joe Calverley had also fallen in love with Margaret and she with him. Joe didn't want to get married straight from college and I don't suppose he liked the thought that Margaret was originally his friend's girl, even though his friend wasn't in a position to do any-thing about it. There was one rather awful weekend which he spent with us in Eastbourne after Margaret had rashly said, 'I love you' to him. It was a very hot day and my mother went

bathing, which she occasionally did, wearing a voluminous alpaca bathing dress with a longish skirt. She was always very careful to wet the top of her forehead first when she went in, I think her mother had told her always to do this. It seemed a poor sort of reward for years of such caution that she should in spite of this get sunstroke, but there it was, she came home with her memory completely gone and kept offering Joe more helpings of rice pudding for lunch. My father was in a dreadful state of apprehension; but happily after an hour's sleep in the afternoon she came down quite restored for tea. Margaret afterwards thought that this might have had some bearing on the fact that Joe wouldn't see her any more, they had a quarrel of some kind and I remember Joe watching a pretty school friend of mine turn cartwheels in the garden, while in the distance we could hear the tinkle of Margaret playing nonchalantly on the piano, and that night Joe kept spinning a lot of different sized wooden tops that we had in a box, instead of kissing Margaret goodnight. She was pretty upset by losing Joe and when Dickie returned, she refused him again and he sailed for America and didn't come back.

I was very interested in Margaret and her lovers. I don't think I was jealous because I didn't want for myself any of her young men. This all happened later on at Eastbourne but I will tell you some more about Oxford first. One of the houses we lived in was just beside Tim's boathouse and we hired a punt for the summer and even Billy who was fourteen learned to punt without falling in. She did fall in from a canoe and came home on a bicycle cleverly draped in a towel and dress.

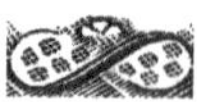

John and I were still friends and in holiday times we were nearly always together. He had started to have very bad spots on his face while he was at Marlborough and these still afflicted him when he went to Woolwich; he had passed out first from the army class at school and it was presupposed that like his father and his grandfather, he should be a Royal Engineer. We used to ride about on his new motor bike, a Rudge Multi which had a rubber belt instead of a metal gear, this belt gradually stretched and used constantly to fall off and seeing it behind on the road like some shameful article of clothing that we had dropped, we grew to hate it. When a motor bicycle is new its clutch is very stiff and in the struggle to move the clutch the engine is apt to stall. We dreaded Carfax because wherever we wanted to go, we always had to go through this crossroad and always the policeman on point duty held us up and always the engine stopped, and very embarrassed, John had great difficulty in starting it again.

We drew pictures of old cottages and suitably picturesque subjects in the neighbourhood and we explored the colleges but I only remember Great Tom at all clearly. We got the key of the tower from the man in the lodge and climbed up through two or three floors to the bell. John examined it very carefully and explained that now it was worked by machinery and the bell rope that still hung from the belfry was disconnected. We left the great bell and clambered down to the floor below, where the bell rope ended with a prettily striped sally: John, unable to resist its loveliness, put out a hand and pulled. The rope descended and with a whirring of machinery most awful to hear, the whole tower shook as the enormous bell gave one

deafening chime. I was so terrified that I ran round and round the room while John, equally frightened, stood petri-fied with the rope dangling beside him. At last we collected enough courage to leave and under the passage of the gateway John returned the key, expecting the porter, like Bluebeard when the bloodstained key was handed to him by Fatima, to break into a torrent of accusations; but he didn't say anything. Surprised, we walked out into freedom and it was only then that John looked up at the face of the clock and understood; the time was four minutes past one.

St Giles' Fair came on its annual visit to Oxford and its mushroom growth so changed the appearance of the High that it was difficult to realise that it was the same place. At night, the streets became packed and girls dodged in and out of the crowd tickling the faces and necks of young men with feather switches, giving the men licence to kiss them in return if they allowed themselves to be caught.

I hadn't any young man and felt that sixteen was a very difficult age to be. I was unwilling to give up the pleasures of being able to run when I pleased, to roll down banks and climb trees and be ridiculous and yet I found myself observing the undergraduates who passed me in the streets, though they would scorn to take any notice of a flapper like me. I knew that scornful as they might be now, it was my generation whom the majority of them would eventually marry and knowing this I shyly looked at them, wondering if I should see among them that particular one who was destined to be my husband.

When my father was finally retired with the rank of Lt Colonel, we moved back to Eastbourne and my parents,

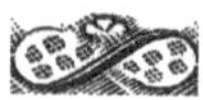

having bought the house in Arundel Rd, at last settled down. My father when he first came back from India was a stranger to us. Billy and I accompanied by Martha met him at the station. He was tanned brown from Indian sun and offended me in the first ten minutes of our reunion by walking up the road with Billy and me, absolutely ignoring Martha who was left to follow behind by herself. I insisted on walking with her in spite of her urging me to go with my father if he wished it. He wanted quite naturally to resume the relationship between himself and his family as it had been when he left; but Margaret and I hated his kissing us and sitting on his lap. He had a big moustache and I loathed the broom-like feeling of it when he kissed the back of my neck at breakfast time. He used to come into my bedroom and kiss me when I was in bed in the morning and I used to shudder with horror at this. As a family we were very averse to kissing one another and Billy invented kissing Betty as a punishment to tease her, and they would run laughing and screaming through the house. Margaret very soon quarrelled with Daddy and he refused to speak to her for a long time, addressing any remark that he wished to make to her through the medium of my mother: 'Mummy will you tell your eldest daughter to sit up and stop playing with her hair.' She had a habit of playing with her hair at this time because it had frizzed pieces each side like a matted bird's nest and with her arm up she would sit in a round-shouldered slump, either fingering her hair or letting the hand hang down limply from her wrist. In spring, she and my father got hay fever and they would sneeze thirteen or fourteen times in succession and Margaret rubbed and rubbed her large eyes so that I couldn't

bear sitting opposite her. It never seemed peculiar to us that Daddy shouldn't speak to Margaret and I thought it wrong of her to lock her bedroom door against my parents, though I longed to have a key for my door too. I grimly suffered my father, fearing to hurt his feelings and thinking it in some way my duty to allow him to kiss me. My mother too made a nuisance of herself before breakfast, shouting at us to get up and turning out our chests of drawers and making general hay; but Mummy never behaved shamefully and we felt grateful for her dignity and good manners. Her peculiarities were both endearing gifts, of being able to wiggle the bottom of her ears and to move her hair backwards and forwards, her whole scalp moving a good half inch. She did these two things when she was at all nervous, on occasions such as interviewing a new house parlour-maid or telephoning.

My brother was still my favourite of the family. He taught me to ride his motor bicycle and later on, when I was old enough to have a licence, to drive a car. I remember how proud I felt when he said: 'For a girl you're really very efficient.' I preferred the *Boy's Own* annual to the *Girl's* and hadn't much interest in pretty clothes or jewellery.

For a long time I had wanted a dog and seeing an advertisement for a terrier who was for sale, I persuaded my father to come with me and John to buy the dog. His owner was a canon, happily perhaps for his conscience he was out when we called and his wife praised the dog, Billy, a nice looking wire-haired terrier and we took him back with us.

The dog was almost mad, a borderline case Aunt Edith would have called him. He attached himself to me so far as he

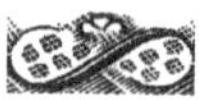

was able to attach himself to anyone; though he would growl fiercely and snap at me if I tried to turn him off the best chairs.

We kept him for quite a long time, it would have been easier to have kept a tiger; at least the public would have known what to expect when they saw his stripes. He always had to be on a lead and straining and panting against his harness he struggled along, letting off the most ghastly high pitched barks and whines if he saw another dog. If he escaped from his lead or slipped his collar he would pounce on any other dog regardless of sex or age and, getting a grip on some tender part under the belly or by the throat, he would hang grimly on. He had the most powerful grip and would practise in the garden by pulling at a rope that was attached to a tree. Even if you held him up by the tail with another dog which he was biting hanging below he would never let it go. I used to go out with pepper in my pockets but it never was much use. A workman passing one day saw him fighting and got off his bicycle and hit him hard over the head with a brick which shocked him a little.

We bought him a muzzle but he escaped from the garden and bit an old lady who was trying to protect her dog. When I got back from school, Margaret ghoulishly handed me his collar smelling of gas.

Our next dog was a black cocker spaniel called Charles and he was my chief love for two or three years. I've caught as many as seventy-five fleas in a few days on him but they didn't seem to leave him naturally and we didn't get bitten. He was very sentimental and had a tender conscience. He knew that he

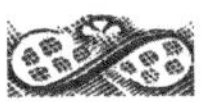

mustn't lie on beds and one day I went into my room and found him on my bed; before I had even said anything he felt so guilty that he rolled onto his back and peed into the air with fright. He was a great solace to me because he never talked or asked when I came back from a dance if I'd had a nice time and, if I was sad, with his mournful expression he was the personification of sympathy.

We all went with Aunt Edith for a summer holiday to a place in Brittany called Trébeurden and this was followed by a number of trips abroad: Switzerland for winter sports with John and Aunt Edith, a Christmas visit the following winter to Saint Jean de Luz with Aunt Edith and a friend of hers [a stockbroker] called Max Irving who showed us a little of Paris at night. We saw Maurice Chevalier performing when he was quite young and thought he had a very attractive backside. In the Moulin Rouge dance hall the Black Bottom had just come into fashion and the whole room was jigging with couples doing this remarkable dance, some of them jumping quite high into the air with both feet together.

In Eastbourne, Margaret still continued to collect young men; but it was a more difficult town for this sport as there were a great number of pretty girls to compete with. She and other 'beauts', as Daddy called them, got up rather late for breakfast and went down town, their hands clutching a handbag over their stomachs so that they became known as the tummy huggers. They assembled at Cave's Oriental Café and drank coffee and ate chocolate biscuits. While they sat and gossiped, they carefully observed each other's clothes and appearance and the young men that perhaps escorted them.

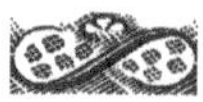

Margaret had a number of unwritten laws about flirtations and she was very down on girls who broke them. When she was sixteen she and her friends had walked about in Eastbourne, content merely to click. This translated means that you pass a young man who eyes you appreciatively, it was something between the glad eye and getting off, which went a little further. After India and Oxford she was of course ashamed of this youthful sport, dismissing it as common. The important thing at this time was that every Saturday evening she must be dancing at the Grand Hotel with an attractive man and, if possible, always in a different dress; a change of dress was I think more important than a change of partner. For a man to pass the test of being attractive was a tricky thing. They must have been to a public school and be able to dress well, a soft hat turned up all round was the sign of a boob and a bowler hat was seldom tolerated except in London. They must not be too handsome, hair set in waves was very wrong and of course it was better to be athletic rather than clever. Height was almost essential, if men were small they must be very rich, very amusing or a double blue.

Although Margaret ultimately intended to get married, she was at this time mainly preoccupied with having a good time or at any rate appearing to have a good time. She paid her young men with kisses; but was very scornful of girls who went off the deep end. She felt that they had taken an unfair advantage, a short cut and that theirs was a misplaced generosity, it was for some reason unwise to admit to any young man that you loved him. She felt that it was through saying 'I love you' to Joe Calverley that she had lost him. She

mourned very much for Joe and was eager to find out anything she could about his life after he had left her and through various channels of gossip she had come to hear, whether true or not she couldn't tell, that referring to her he had said that he didn't want to get married yet. Poor Margaret, these years were so wasted and if only she had been sure that he really would marry her, how differently she might have spent them. In the house, Margaret was rather a nuisance because she would frequently be kissing young men and one was never certain on entering a room that she wouldn't be there and as no one likes to butt in under such circumstances, the rest of the family took to knocking on the nursery door, that being the room she most frequently used.

At night too, from my bedroom above the hall porch, I could hear her slow progress up the drive by the crunching feet on the gravel until that final embrace in the shelter of the porch preceded by a stumbling up the steps and a clanging noise on the iron shoe scraping mat. Occasionally, she was accidentally locked out, so my father made a tiny secret drawer in the porch into which he put the door key. I used to resent these muffled noises, but in turn we all made love up the shingle drive and if I walk up it now, it still seems a romantic place at night time with its shadowy fir trees and the line of neat euonymus bushes. My father knew that we were making love and used to complain in a childish voice, 'Nobody ever tells me anything'.

I hated going down town and I hated shopping with Mummy and Cave's Oriental Café seemed to me to be the bottomless pit, its horrors only equalled by the lawns on

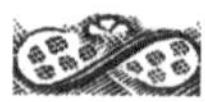

Sunday. This was an after-church parade on the front at Eastbourne which my mother and Margaret, dressed in their best clothes, very much enjoyed. Mummy insisted that I too accompanied them. I knew that it was really a form of exhibition of her daughters to other mothers with families, and because it entailed making polite conversation and introductions and was an endless waste of time, I utterly detested it. It was imposition enough that one should be forced on a lovely day to sit in an ugly red Presbyterian church and that this other indignity should also be imposed on one seemed to me quite monstrous. The alternative to the Scottish church was the nearby Protestant church, whose vicar annoyed my mother by calling the congregation 'My dearly beloved' and by his excessively intoning delivery. He was old and absent-minded and his sermons were certainly not as good as the Scottish minister's; he had on the other hand a remarkable daughter.

Dorothy when we first knew her was nearly forty. She was short and thin with brown bobbed hair and a weather-beaten complexion. Her eyes were a bright blue and they shifted and darted backwards and forwards with lightning rapidity so that she never looked at one steadily; these remarkable eyes and her nutcracker features gave her a witch-like appearance and in many ways she really was a witch.

She usually rode about on a bicycle and frequently when I have been walking along a road she has twice passed me, not as you would expect in different directions but going the same way, as though she had rapidly made a circle and was aimlessly spinning round. She was when we first met her, a Guardian, and taking a fancy to my father she helped to get

him also elected as a Guardian. She became very fond of our black spaniel Charles and looked after him when we all went to Brittany. She took him for walks on the Downs which, when I had started going to the Art School, I couldn't do, and he grew very attached to her. She then started paying a similar attention to my father who was not so easily charmed and she became a great embarrassment to him. She loved intrigue and would manufacture elaborate plans so that he should accompany her on some errand of mercy or to some public duty that it was essential that he should perform and little notes brought by various messengers were delivered at the house. She had many friends among the casuals and also among her father's parishioners whom she visited. Her mother, an eccentric person, stayed upstairs in their house, seldom going outside and doing no parish work, so that Dorothy as vicar's daughter had access to any number of houses. The old father, who was almost a caricature of a vicar, went about oblivious of his strange family and lived apparently in a world of his own.

As my father was particularly proud and fond of me at this time, Dorothy naturally didn't like me very much, but hearing that I was interested in engraving she gave me some very nice old books, among them *Gay's Fables* and a huge volume of *Aesop's Fables* illustrated by a wealth of very fine line-engravings. There were also some lovely books on insects with hand coloured illustrations, a charming little hieroglyphic Bible and a number of rare postage stamps and Mulready envelopes. These gifts were, in some way not exactly specified, bribes to help in her pursuit of my father. I thought this very amusing and cheerfully accepted the things because I

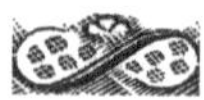

truly appreciated them. What puzzled me was how Dorothy, who took no interest in such things for their own sake, knew the difference between good, bad and indifferent books; most people in Eastbourne were incapable of distinguishing between a wood engraving and a pen and ink drawing. She said that friends had given them to her or that she had bought them in the Lanes at Brighton.

For some years Dorothy continued to entertain the family and though they complained of her irregular behaviour, she certainly livened up a rather dull parish. I've never met anybody else to whom the adjective 'bewitched' applied so accurately. She was in her small way a follower of Robin Hood, because she never took things for herself but always to please someone else. On the other hand, she was quite heartless about the blame which fell on other people for her pilfering. One of the nurses at the infirmary was sacked for stealing and the relieving officer was so worried by thefts when he was giving out money to the unemployed, that he had a nervous breakdown and subsequently died. Apparently it never entered his head that the vicar's daughter who was kindly assisting him was helping herself as well whenever his back was turned. Perhaps he did realise it and couldn't face the embarrassment of accusing her.

Soon afterwards she went to live in the asylum; her mother died a natural death and the old father married again. Pathetic now to remember her pride that when visiting Haywards Heath Asylum as a Guardian, the lunatics had always loved her and wanted to kiss her and one old man had said that her blue eyes made her look like an angel.

I was still head girl at West Hill and in the morning wore a gym dress four inches above my knees and a plait down my back. In the afternoon I divided my hair into two plaits which I crossed at the back and bringing them round to the front of my face, folded them under and pinned them up, so that my hair looked more or less as though it was bobbed like everyone else's. I usually wore a pink linen dress and with my nose powdered and my cheeks reddened, off to the Art School I trotted on high-heeled shoes.

After I had been there a term or so, Rozelle Beazley suddenly reappeared and joined me and I was very pleased to see her again, her cheeks were still as pink as ever and she hid her bottle-shaped legs under rather long skirts.

Miss Shackleton became tired of being the Guide Captain and tried to persuade me to try and take on the job. I refused, although she said that she particularly wanted me to do it because I was a nice girl. This direct piece of flattery surprised me as I never considered myself as being nice. I don't think it a very flattering adjective now but I suppose it did apply to me then.

The older I grew, the more resentful of my mother's domination I became. At first I merely noticed the things that I didn't like in her treatment of her children. I kept a notebook of items in my mind, small rules to observe when I should one day have children of my own. I always intended to write them down but I never did; she would almost certainly have found and read them had I done such a thing; we were allowed no privacy.

My father was the only person privileged to criticise Mummy, he said that he gave her full marks for everything

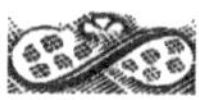

except love. He constantly complained that Corry women were frigid and disliking any reference to sex from my parents, I wished he wouldn't. I suppose his fondness for me at this time didn't make things any easier between my mother and myself, not that we were a jealous family and I didn't want him to praise me as he did.

My mother's idea of bringing up children was to order them about and shout at them from well before breakfast till bedtime. There was a wonderful peace and calm in the house when she was out shopping, which she did regularly every morning after she had written one or two letters. Usually the noise indoors was tremendous. Margaret either vamped on the piano or did chorus girl gestures, making the shape of a wheel with each hand in turn to the music of Black Bottoms or Charlestons on the gramophone while Daddy, if he was in, continually played with his wireless: he was a complete fiend. Conversation, mainly about clothes, was carried on at great speed and in high clipped voices so that the general effect was the noise of a typewriting school. When I was working for the School Certificate Examination, I had in desperation to climb to the top of the chestnut tree to get any peace and quiet.

Mummy was very energetic and practical and though she couldn't herself cook and scrub floors, she was untiring in her management of the servants who did. In fact, she very successfully ran a house and family which is all very well, so long as you don't mind being run. She never praised or flattered us and we appreciated this, because we used to laugh at those Eastbourne mothers who raved about their own daughters' charm and beauty; but this constant supervision was very

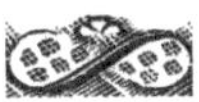

galling and had different effects on each of us. Margaret rebelled and snapped at it but she was too lazy to leave home. Billy read novels from Boots Circulating Library and, immersed in romantic literature, she just didn't hear, and she allowed Margaret and Mummy between them to completely take charge of her clothes and appearance. Betty didn't really mind, she was very like my mother, practical and interested in needlework and dressmaking. She did leave home much later on; but she didn't quarrel with my mother. John escaped altogether, Mummy loved him so much better than all of us that her attitude towards him was different; he was able to tease her which would never have been tolerated in a daughter and he surprised all his sisters by writing her the most intimate letters with details of his love affairs and his feelings, which we could never have done to my mother.

During the war, my father had written a slim volume of rather bloodthirsty poems of hate against the Germans and being an admirer of Kipling's, he called it *Lest We Forget*. This book didn't sell very well and for a long time his love of writing lay dormant and he amused himself bathing and photographing his family in Eastbourne, where his work as a Guardian took up quite a lot of his time. On his way out to Mesopotamia he had written a musical comedy called *Carissima* which was something like a Gilbert and Sullivan opera and the boat, which held about five hundred troops, had acted it with enormous success a day or two before they landed. I think the theme was the adventures of a girl who had come aboard ship disguised as a sailor. He happened to show this play and his poetry to an old man who lived in

Eastbourne and who also had literary ambitions and was flattered to find himself acclaimed as an undiscovered genius. He naturally started to write again.

The trouble with Daddy was that he couldn't do things quietly, but he lived through a succession of overwhelming obsessions in which he tried to make other people share. He was an excellent letter writer but suffered from an inability to write impersonally when he was composing fiction, so that when reading his work one was constantly irritated by small comments of his own opinions, when the subject was one which was nothing to do with him personally.

His first obsession at Eastbourne was a magazine which he produced called *The Blue Tit*. He was fond of birds and made rustic nesting boxes for them about the garden and an ingenious arrangement with hooks on a coat hanger for suspending monkey nuts and lumps of fat for tits and blackbirds. He was jealous of my mother's love of the Scottish Church and the pacifist preaching of the Reverend Jamie Reade, so that his writings in *The Blue Tit* were thinly-veiled allusions to this sort of topic and his outspoken views on puritanical behaviour in general. He loved pretty girls and if, when you were walking with him, he saw one that he knew on the other side of the road, without comment he would at once cross the road and accost her, leaving one stranded and embarrassed on the other side.

His other contributors to *The Blue Tit* pretty soon tailed off, so that latterly the magazine was almost entirely his own composition. I drew him a cover and illustrated it when I was asked with pen and ink drawings and it was for sale on the

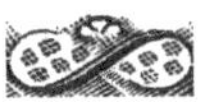

local book stalls. All the family were ashamed of this venture and troubled by the way he used to buttonhole visitors and read or make them read his poems and we were very relieved when he gave it up.

The next obsession was for archaeology. He stayed at Aunt Rose's Tudor manor and with passionate thoroughness tried to unearth a plan of what it had previously looked like, as though no one else had ever thought of doing such a thing. Later on in life Eric and I, who didn't have to suffer from his enthusiasms for very long at any one time, were very entertained by these phases, and finding that Eric was really quite well-informed and might be useful to him in his literary efforts, my father altered his opinion of this son-in-law who allowed him to read his poetry to him and he forgot all his previous antagonism and became quite fond of him.

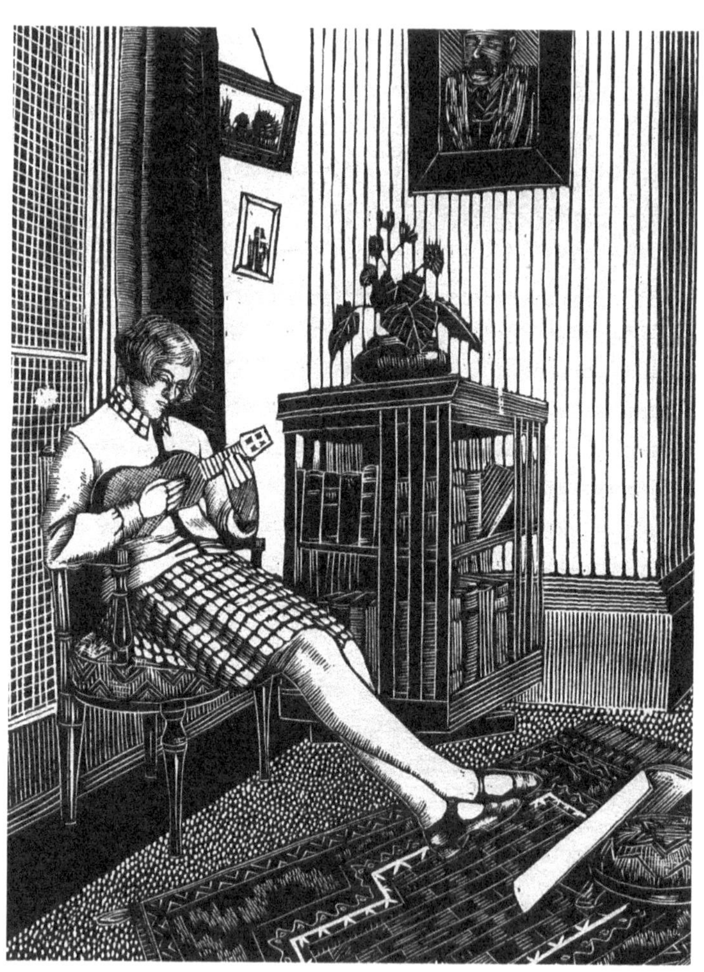

CHAPTER SEVEN

When I left school and became a full-time student at the Art School, I was most awfully happy. I quickly made friends with the other girl students and it was lovely to be able to draw and paint all day and to be actually encouraged to do this.

I first met Eric Ravilious [in the autumn of 1925] when he came as a teacher of design to the Art School at Eastbourne. He had just left the Royal College of Art at South Kensington and was still living in London. He travelled backwards and forwards, staying with his parents when he was in Eastbourne.

He had a smart double-breasted suit and shy, diffident manners not unlike those of a curate and, with my family's training behind me, I quickly spotted that he wasn't quite a gentleman and as he took no particular notice of me, conceited as well. He used to talk animatedly to the beautiful gypsy-brown Brenda Capron whom he had admired since he was a child and who had been a student at the Eastbourne Art School with him. He was tall and thin with a small head which jutted out at the back, his eyes were large, light-brown or hazel coloured with long girlish lashes which gave him an appealing look, so that motherly women often offered him cups of

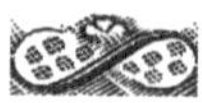

tea. This look was only superficial, he wasn't really at all effeminate nor did he need sympathy, though it was true that he was inordinately fond of tea.

The headmaster, Mr Reeve-Fowkes, was an enthusiastic teacher but an ill-balanced man. He had served in the war and sometimes wore remnants of his officer's uniform. His own work was sentimental and usually done in pastel; he liked wet water-colour painting with little villages nestling in the blue distance. His most successful class was his evening composition class; he was proud of this as it was something that other Art Schools didn't have; he had learned the method at the Royal College of Art from old Gerald Moira [Professor of Mural and Decorative Painting], a man he very much revered. These composition classes were romantic affairs which took place in the gas light and we drew with charcoal on 'Michallet' paper. The model vaguely suggested some subject, such as a man in a little hut watching a road-up excavation at night or figures in a towering landscape. Brangwyn was another god to Reeve-Fowkes. He felt uncomfortable about the modern French painters and once confided to Eric Ravilious as he was toiling up the innumerable stone stairs which led to the Art School at the top of the Technical Institute, that he thought Cézanne was all arse-wipe.

There was a certain amount of competition for his favours around Eric Ravilious and he flirted with most of the girls in turn; but he never went so far as to kiss any of them. He used to take sketching parties, mostly of female students, to country villages or places on the coast like Birling Gap or Cuckmere valley and we all enjoyed ourselves enormously but

did very little work. I made friends with him on one of these occasions and we lay back to back with one another on the downs in our bathing suits and were photographed in this position by another student when we were dozing. My dog Charles used to come too and he liked Mr Ravilious because he associated him with walks, though he got no encouragement in return because Ravilious didn't like dogs.

He also arranged a sketching holiday and I went on this with a number of students to a house near Barcombe Mills which was owned by an Eastbourne school called Clovelly-Kepplestone.

I got rather irritated by Ravilious's half-hearted flirtations, not understanding the reason for his caution. None of the girls openly encouraged him though one or two of them were badly in love; each feared the censorship of the others if they appeared too familiar. One evening, feeling particularly irritated by this cat and mouse playing, I boldly taught him to Charleston. This same evening we played sardines and after the game had been going on for some time we all found ourselves looking for a rather unattractive girl, not that she had a particularly ugly face but she was a bitter complaining girl. Her hiding place was a good one and no one could find her. As they lost interest the seekers gradually stopped looking for her, at first rather shamefacedly and then, following Ravilious's example, quite brazenly until I and another girl with an equally strict sense of fair play were the only ones left searching for her. Even we failed to find her and some time later, she reappeared with an 'I might have known it' expression on her face.

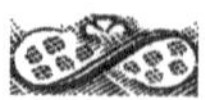

Ravilious asked me to come for a walk the next evening and I set off feeling a bit apprehensive, not knowing how someone who wasn't quite a gentleman might behave under such intimate circumstances. As nothing happened, I became more confidential and friendly and commiserated with him on the trials and embarrassments of having to teach. He liked the drawings and engravings of people that I made, though I hadn't very much interest in landscape which he loved. He liked my work because it was personal and didn't imitate his own. He was doing some drawings of Barcombe Mill, a lovely big weather-boarded place which was now disused, he painted it very dryly in pale watercolour. He also made a drawing of me for an almanac that he was engraving.

At first I resented his dislike of fairies and other conventional story book characters such as cute little rabbits or quaint little gnomes, which I associated with book illustration. I had never come across the decorative deer that showed up so frequently in drawings at the Royal College of Art; it was taken from Indian paintings of which I had never even heard but I'm sure I should have adopted it if I had known. When I complained about Ravilious's taste in subjects at home, my family approved of my dislike, but an artist friend of my father's [Clifford Webb] who was staying, warmly argued that Ravilious was right and said I was jolly lucky to have someone like that to teach me. I nearly burst into tears but saw that he was probably right.

The house where we lodged was called Camois Court and there were still a few of the mistresses and girls from Clovelly-Kepplestone in residence as it was used as a holiday house.

The headmistress Mrs Brown was mother to the theatrical producer Maurice Brown who had produced *Journey's End*, the war play by R C Sherriff which had had a spectacular run. There was another son who later committed suicide and her one daughter, Frankie.

Frankie Brown was a masculine-looking woman with short hair and she had great influence in the school, where she was very popular. She played the piano well and with her brother's connection with the stage, the girls were naturally encouraged to like acting and most of them wanted to go on the stage when they left school.

We met quite a number of these stage-struck girls who were spending their holidays at Camois Court and Ravilious nicknamed them 'Booglie' because of their romantic outlook; they were very friendly and charming. Another equally charming person was Miss Greta Douglas who taught art at the school and she and an Irish woman called Miss Widdershins were particularly interested in the spiritual value of things and in superstition and the supernatural. One morning, Miss Douglas read our hands. She very accurately foretold most of the main events of my life. She didn't know whether my husband was going to die or not but she said he wouldn't at any rate be living with me for the latter part of my life. She showed me her own hand which like mine had a number of lines round the lump at the base of the middle finger which indicated that our love affairs would be unfortunate.

I had previously been to a Madam Viola in Eastbourne to have my hand read, she was more wordy but less accurate than

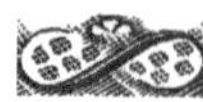

Miss Douglas. She said that I was going to marry an extra-ordinary man, 'a superman' she called him, for want of a more explicit adjective. I naturally wanted to know in what way he would be extraordinary. My aura lacked blue spirituality.

Miss Douglas was less flattering about my character than the professional Madam Viola but she said that I was very well balanced and that although my judgements and opinions would probably be sound, people would not believe me; not like Cassandra, because I was cursed, but because I could not express myself with the necessary assurance which would carry conviction. It is true that I'm very rarely respected and then never for very long. Perhaps it is because I don't wish to be.

She took a print of the hand of Eric Ravilious but he told me later that she never revealed her interpretation of it but she and Miss Brown just laughed heartily and wouldn't say anything.

Back in Eastbourne, I still continued to be friends with Mr Ravilious though I never went to his house nor did he come very often to ours; but I and another girl called Molly Stuart, a beautiful person like a pre-Raphaelite painter's model, used to walk half of the way home with him from the Art School.

The headmaster Mr Reeve-Fowkes at this time was far more interested in badminton than in art. He was an unbal-anced man who did everything with excessive enthusiasm and he felt quite unreasonably annoyed with those students who refused to join the badminton club.

He spent quite a lot of time in The Lamb, an old pub near his house, and when he came late in the evening to give his

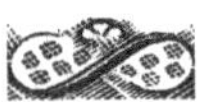

weekly talk on our charcoal composition class, he smelt very beery and gave an unnecessarily inspired talk, wonderfully high flown phrases flowing from his well-oiled throat, so that the evening classes were very popular.

The art and craft mistress from the elementary school which occupied the middle floors of the Technical Institute occasionally came up to the Art School above, and was a Miss Stanley, a bony woman with an unattractive lisp though her face was fairly prepossessing with large blue eyes. She also taught weaving to the art students and although she must at that time have been nearly thirty, she walked out with a young student of sixteen or seventeen called Edward Scroggy. He was a monstrous, overgrown child with a hideous voice, but there was something endearing about his earnestness and his rather pathetic ambition. As he was underdeveloped in some respects, it was unlikely that he could ever attain these ambitions because of his lack of intelligence. Strangely, Mr Fowkes seemed to take a fancy to Edward Scroggy and he helped and encouraged him with his work with more seriousness than he did the other students. Scroggy, with a reverence for modern art as he understood it, painted simple pictures of unorthodox subjects like cement works so that his work really was preferable to the nestling villages and windmills that were painted by the more traditionally minded students.

The painting and drawing master was a short man with merry blue eyes called Oliver Senior, a pleasant and reasonable person but wholly lacking in Mr Fowkes's more inspiring enthusiasm. He lived apart from his wife in a studio of his own, above one of the shops in the town, where he made

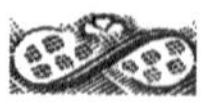

complicated wireless sets with fretwork façades. Both he and Mr Fowkes smoked excessively, so that they exuded tobacco wherever they went and one could tell that Mr Senior had gone up the stairs by the lingering smell; however he didn't have a smoker's cough like Mr Fowkes.

I complained one day to Mr Fowkes about the bad heating arrangements in the life class, it was a terrible gas affair which gave us all a headache. He said that he knew that it was bad and indeed put down his chronic cough to the bad air in the Art School; but he dared not ask the town council to alter it because they might stop the life classes altogether.

At the end of the war when buildings were blacked out because of Zeppelin raids, a warden had seen a light from one of the big Art School studio windows and he had run panting up the stairs and seeing no one about, had charged straight into a mixed life class where he stood transfixed. As later he was dramatically to describe the scene: 'There before me was a naked woman!' and he caused a great outcry in the heart of respectable Eastbourne and after innumerable meetings the Town Council decided to allow life classes only if the model was thoroughly draped and the classes were divided into male and female, so that it was small wonder that Mr Fowkes did not wish to mention this subject to them again. There was yet another reason for his wishing to avoid a council meeting which we were to discover later.

The fire station stood next door to the Art School and the head fireman, a Mr Quincy, lived in a flat adjoining the Art School on the top floor of which he had the run. He was a typical fireman in appearance with a large black moustache

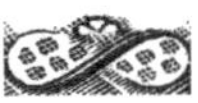

and he had a very unpleasant wife and one stodgy little girl, who was usually dressed in white right down to her boots. He had one day after Art School hours gone into Mr Reeve-Fowkes' private office and found him on a sofa with Miss Stanley and he had thought it his duty to inform the council of what he had seen.

'Fowky boy', as Miss Stanley used to call him, was naturally very upset about this as he had a wife and four children to support and they were at present living very comfortably in the nicest house in Eastbourne; the old manor house in its recently opened gardens which had been bequeathed to the town by a Mr Towner who had previously owned it.

To his alarm he heard that a council meeting was to take place in the Art School to which he was not invited. Unable to contain his curiosity as to how much they knew, he fixed up a microphone under one of the meeting tables, which he connected to a wireless set in the little staff room upstairs which was shared by Mr Senior and Mr Ravilious.

We discovered this device and were naturally curious as to why it was there and it wasn't till years later that Mr Ravilious told me the true story. The microphone broke down at the appointed hour, but it would have availed him nothing if he had overheard, because the committee decided that he must go. They were decent enough to see that this decision was bad luck on his innocent wife and family, so they allowed him to remain at the manor house and they gave him, after months of negotiating, the job of Curator to the Towner Art Gallery which occupied half of his house. His wife, a careworn looking woman who used to recite at the Art School theatrical shows,

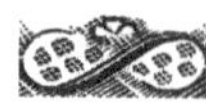

putting in all the expression, now blossomed out into a successful flower painter and was finally honoured by having a picture bought by the Queen.

These minor scandals were constantly recurring under the apparently extreme respectability of the residents of Eastbourne. Suddenly it would be found that a town councillor had for years been taking bribes and a charming old councillor called Gilbert, who owned a tea shop and incidentally gave Ravilious his first commission, was found to have been living on credit and loans for I don't know how many years; he had just felt unable to cope with the accounts of his tea shop and who shall blame him.

None of the mayors or mayoresses were I think ever accused of any of these dishonest acts, but it was certainly an advantage for your business as an electrician or a contractor to be on the council. A large stout woman called Miss Hudson, an amiable hippo, was frequently mayoress which she appeared to heartily enjoy. I remember reading in *The Eastbourne Gazette* that she had sent a casual to prison for a week, for begging for a penny from an old lady in Terminus Rd.

Apart from these underhand methods of some of the wealthier tradespeople, the life of Eastbourne was undoubtedly very respectable, until every now and then some spectacular crime like the Crumbles murder of Irene Munroe by Mr Field and Mr Gray or the Pevensey bungalow murder, shattered this illusion of nice behaviour and aroused an extraordinary amount of interest for several months. The bungalow was even bought as a speculation and people were able to visit the scene of the crime for 6d a look. On the other

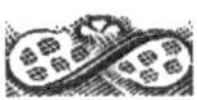

side of the town, of course, there were always the periodical suicides from Beachy Head. People even came from places as far away as Scotland just to jump off Beachy Head.

There were two Eastbourne papers: *The Gazette* and *The Herald* and my father was very pleased when his photograph appeared in either, which it did quite frequently as he was an Old Contemptible as well as a Guardian, and the female members of the family enjoyed Miss Gossip's page, in which she painstakingly described nearly all the dresses of the women at any local dance. She was in reality a Miss Pulsford, who attended the Art School and seemed to us to be very slightly dotty.

My father met in Eastbourne some old friends of his, a retired Colonel, his dark attractive wife and their two children. They had known one another in Aden when my father was unmarried and before they had had any children, and there are some photographs of them bathing together, wearing long black and white striped bathing costumes.

The children were called Bob and Barbara; Bob was at Cambridge and Barbara just about to leave the School for Officers' Daughters at Bath and go to Oxford. They were both dark with wide-apart eyes that sloped slightly downwards at each side, the opposite way to the Chinese. They had charming low voices, Bob's particularly so, a warm affectionate bumble-bee noise. Their familiar terms of endearment were Welsh expressions such as, 'There is lovely', or 'There is beautiful', but they didn't speak with a Welsh accent. I became friendly with them and went occasionally to tea or tennis. Margaret dismissed Bob as a possible young man as he was known to be

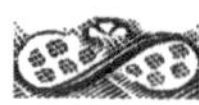

a misogynist and anyway he was dark and intellectual; my sisters, all being brown-eyed, concentrated on fair young men.

Bob had almost finished training to be a civil servant and he and his friend Alec had planned to go to Africa: Alec to Nigeria and Bob to Nyasaland [Malawi]. Bob and Barbara had been brought up with a cousin of theirs who was interested in art and he used occasionally to take Bob to see picture exhibitions, and for a short time he went to the Art School at Eastbourne. I never saw any of his drawings but when he had occasion to sit down, I did notice that he very often arranged himself like a model in some elegant pose; he was quite unconscious that he did this. He was a very good swimmer but otherwise was not particularly good or interested in sports; he and Barbara were both very honest and no peculiarities of behaviour seemed to surprise them. Bob sometimes said very nice funny things and his stories against himself were endearing. When they were at school together, he and Alec had been chased by a bull in a field and they had each tried to get behind the other.

One afternoon, I had arranged to go for a walk with Ravilious and, finding all my cotton frocks were dirty, I had to put on a rather bright Sunday go-to-meeting dress. Walking down the hill to meet him I passed Bob, who asked me where I was going. I wonder now what difference it would have made to my life if I had never gone for this walk.

On New Year's Eve, there was a big dance at the Grand Hotel to which we all went except for my sister Betty, who was still a schoolgirl: towards the end of the dance, I was sitting out with Bob in a secluded place when he said: 'May I kiss

you?' I was very surprised as I had no idea that he felt like that, but could see no reason why he shouldn't kiss me, especially as he was going away. I had never let anybody kiss me before so I shut my eyes and thought well, this is what it feels like to be kissed. We were interrupted by the band playing God save the King and I got up and inanely did a Girl Guide salute while he said that he was in love with me. He had realised this on that occasion when he passed me going to meet Ravilious, because he had felt so extremely angry that I should be meeting him in such a pretty dress.

Back in the cloakroom with its overpowering smell of powder, I whispered to Billy that Bob was in love with me, to which she warmly replied: 'Rot! He isn't.'

The family, becoming convinced of the truth of my remark, were very pleased and everyone said what a nice couple we made. When we went for a walk on the Downs and Bob in making love rolled over on top of me, I began to realise just how lovely making love really was, but he quickly sat up again and we found a clergyman smiling very benignly at us from the hill above. We went for a walk in the park and I got kissed in an ornamental rock garden; looking up I saw Eric Ravilious watching us from a tennis court. I apologised next time I saw him, but he said: 'Why? You looked charming, like Krishna and Radha in an Indian painting.'

I enjoyed being made love to very much and went about with a silly smile on my face when nobody was there to see, because I was so happy. We went to cinemas and held hands and with Barbara and Alec, who were also in love, we stayed in London and went to the circus at Olympia. After the circus,

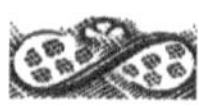

we went riding on infernal switchbacks and dodgems in the Fun Fair. In a very hot and noisy tent, where some doubtful-looking Africans beat drums and proclaimed that they were doing tribal dances, Bob asked me to marry him and I promptly replied: 'Of course not'. (I wasn't thinking of marrying anyone then, I was only eighteen and wanted to go on with my drawing and engraving.) Wondering later why it was that I had so definitely refused to marry him, I came to the conclusion that it was because he was dark and that if we had children, they would inevitably be dark-haired with black eyes and rather large noses. Not that Bob wasn't handsome enough; but he just didn't look like the kind of young man I'd been imagining I might marry. My father said I was incurably romantic and I'm afraid he was right.

Before Bob sailed for Nyasaland I promised to write to him and not to marry anybody else while he was away for his three-year tour. Watching him go down our shingle drive for the last time I felt cold and forlorn because I loved him dearly, but I had a sudden feeling of certainty that I could never marry him. I didn't tell him this, I couldn't make him more unhappy than he already was at having to go away. I think it would have made no difference to the subsequent tangles in which I found myself and I was beginning to see that love affairs were not the jolly romances of magazine stories for people like Bob and me who were proud and morbidly sensitive.

One evening, Betty stayed up later than her ordinary bed time and Mummy, having at last got her to go up, then turned on Billy and ordered her up too. Billy demurred, feeling that

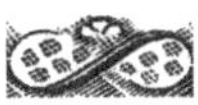

as Betty had been indulgently treated it was unfair that she should be sent to bed immediately after; they normally went up with a quarter of an hour interval between them. I was sitting at the table doing a wood engraving and was in that rather tense and irritable mood that one is in if you are trying to concentrate in a room full of conflicting noise. Margaret said that Mummy was being unfair, adding that she was silly. My father, hearing criticism of his wife, pricked up his ears and went for Margaret. Drawn against my wishes into this, I felt compelled to stick up for Margaret and Billy and added: 'Well, she is silly.' He ordered me to leave the room: but fearing for the safety of my wood block which at that state of gestation was as precious to me as a foetus in my womb, its birth that magic moment when I should lift the Japanese paper on which it would be printed, I stayed where I was. He got up, his face ashen white with rage and started to try and turn me out. He had always been very successful in running Margaret out and hadn't tried with me before. I laughed rather nervously, scrapped a bit and nearly tripped him up, I'd had quite a lot of practice wrestling at school which the family didn't know. My brother was called in to deal with this undignified scene and I went upstairs with my precious wood block, secretly rather pleased that I had defeated my father. John gave me a talking to and said that we had been badly brought up, this surprised me and I still wonder in what way he meant this. Margaret, who hated any display of emotion unless it was one of love for her, was very angry with me, although it was really her quarrel. I apologised, not feeling very sorry, nor do I now. This made me more than ever

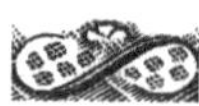

determined to go to London and earn my own living if I could. At first my parents didn't answer if I asked if I might go, but I persevered till they got used to the idea and with the help of my aunts, I eventually had my way. My father was particularly against my going and bluntly said: 'Before we know where you are, you'll start living with that fella Ramvillas.' He didn't like Eric Ravilious at all, he hoped I should marry Bob and I was indignant that our nice friendship should be doubted, and scornfully denied that there was any possibility of such a thing.

I had sent some of my wood engravings to the exhibition of the Society of Wood Engravers and they had been liked by the committee of which Eric was a member and *The Times* had given them a kind mention; this more than anything convinced my parents that they ought to let me go, though they thought my subjects hideous and that Mr Ravilious was perverting a nice girl who used to draw fairies and flowers into a stranger who rounded on them and did drawings that were only too clearly caricatures of themselves.

I was installed in an attic room at the top of a very tall house in Hornton Street, Kensington. It was a Ladies' National Club, I was surrounded on three sides by relations and there were eighty-five stairs to climb to reach my room.

I was very happy here, it was lovely to be able to go out with my latch key in my bag and have no one asking where I was going and when should I be back. In the morning I used to go to the Central School of Art and did life drawing which I didn't much like. I couldn't see why this particular subject should be so vitally important above all others. It seemed

stupid too that we were never given a model wearing ordinary clothes. A costume class usually was all it sounds. The models were dressed as Red Indians, Queens of the ball, Spanish gypsies or just fancy dress, but there were never any quite normal clothes in the Art School fancy-dress box.

Through being introduced to the Curwen Press by Eric, the BBC started giving me work: wonderful, wonderful evening when I was asked to do my first job, I danced round the room with joy. I managed to earn enough money not to feel that I was costing my parents any more than if I had been at home. They didn't think it particularly surprising that I earned any money so quickly, the inference being that in similar circumstances they could have done the same or more probably that it was the influence of Mr Ravilious which was responsible. My parents and the aunts were firm believers in influence and imagined that very few things could be accomplished without it. I had also been led to expect that editors were either ready to seduce attractive girls or else it was quite impossible to get an interview with them. Neither proved to be true. The BBC was at Savoy Hill then, the two editors that I met were very kind and they had such pretty secretaries that they were obviously contented.

I went out somewhere nearly every evening, quite often nothing more exciting than a visit to my aunts in Argyll Road which was parallel to Hornton Street; an old lady who had a room halfway down my eighty-five stairs used to pop her head out as I passed and say: 'Off on the razzle dazzle again!' The old ladies were mostly spinsters, either with private means or retired from some profession like nursing. My room

had been occupied by a sweet person called Miss Douce who had been decorated for her nursing through the Siege of Ladysmith, but the stairs were now too many for her and she moved to a lower room. I had a gas ring in my room and Miss Douce taught me how to make tea. One middle-aged woman had apparently no occupation, she just lived and read novels from the library in an unending stream.

Eric became a frequent visitor, as did my Uncle Harry [Garwood] who used to come round in the morning with his car and chauffeur and drive me to places like Richmond or Hampstead Heath. This was fun and good for me but apt to interfere with my work. One day he came particularly early in the morning and I said all right that I would come, but I would have to change my skirt, which I did in front of him. He told my grandmother with whom he lived about this and she made a great fuss and to-do, accusing him I believe of having feelings improper in an uncle towards his niece; anyway he didn't come and see me after that. My grandfather had died and he had taken his place in looking after granny. He never married and my father, although very curious to know, never discovered whether he had ever been in love with any woman. He was very impressed by *Madame Bovary* and I don't think he thought very highly of women.

He had an exceptionally big head and had gone bald at the age of twenty-eight, but he was quite an attractive-looking man and there seemed no obvious reason for his remaining unmarried. Daddy labelled him an 'eccentric fella' and a 'literary bloke'. He was in the Royal Artillery and won a DSO in the war of 1914–18. He had a reputation for being clever, he certainly

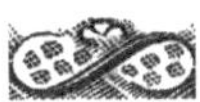

was a kind of human magpie of information and he read an enormous number of books. He quite frequently wrote letters to *The Times* and the *New Statesman* on subjects as varied as bulldogs and the drawbacks of low horse-powered cars.

I don't think Uncle Harry minded looking after his mother, she was getting very childish and feeble but he managed her quite tactfully and treated her as though she was a child. He was fond of children and would stop nursemaids so that he could talk to their babies. The nurses would probably suspect his intentions but their suspicions I am sure were quite without foundation, but it made going out with him a little difficult as he was continually talking to strangers and saying rum things to them. I'm afraid it's a family failing as my father does too and I remember my great-uncle being even worse because he talked baby language as well.

The old ladies in the National Club missed Uncle Harry and used to ask what had become of my nice uncle. I didn't know the reason for his not coming till ten years later when my father told me. I was sorry not to see him because he was a nice uncle although he had been disturbing. Eric was equally disturbing, but he made up for this in showing me pictures and books and museums and all those treasures of which London had so rich a store. As I came to know him better and learned about all his various family troubles, I admired him very much. Events that were deeply embarrassing or shameful to him were so far removed from my smug middle-class life that they seemed to me rather romantic or just funny and I was very interested to have insight to the unfamiliar and rather frightening working-class world in which he had lived.

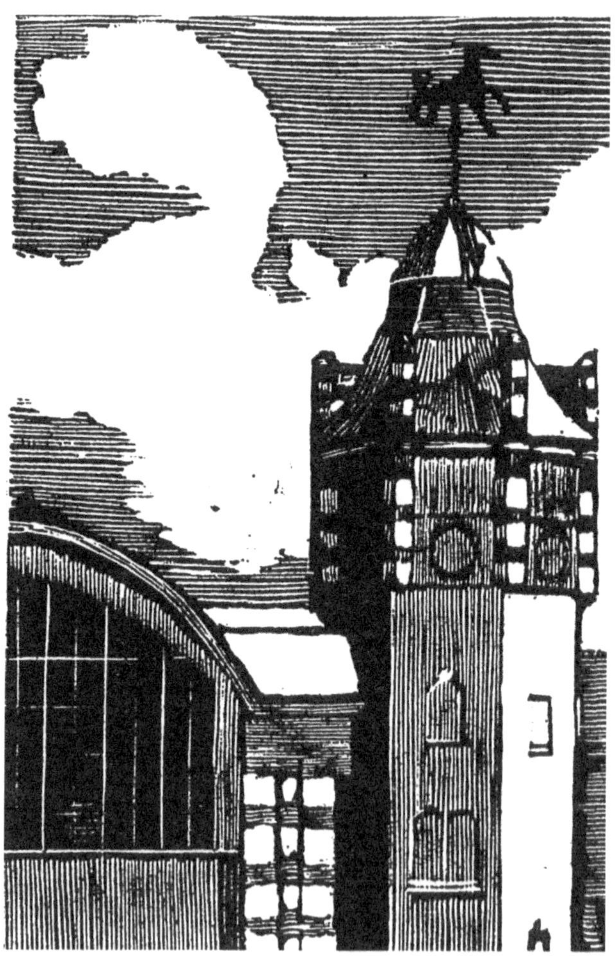

CHAPTER EIGHT

Eric's father's uncle had been deported to Van Diemen's Land for breaking open his daughter's money box. The neighbours had prevailed upon her to report this crime of his to the police and for the rest of her life the poor woman was worried by this awful thing that had happened. For of course she had no idea that such a fate would be meted out to her father, not that he probably minded very much because he did quite well out there and never came back.

Eric's grandfather was a marine, and when he retired he became coachman to a family called Carnal who lived in Tonbridge. He was a tall and fine-looking man with blue eyes. He married and, as his first son was illegitimate, possibly his wife was in trouble when he married. They lived in a tiny little white weather-board cottage [at Cage Green] where she had thirteen children, Eric's father Frank being the youngest. Frank first worked as a pageboy at the Rose and Crown and then at a school for young gentlemen before becoming apprenticed to his eldest brother who was a coach builder. He liked this work and did it very well until, unfortunately for everybody connected with him, he became ill and had to go to

hospital, where he became converted. He left the employment of his brother because he did not pay him enough and because he gave the men their wages in a public house which seemed to Frank a dreadful thing. He and another brother Albert now became preachers of Evangelism and would address the people in Tonbridge market. One day they were told about a woman who was suffering from a growth and in great pain, she was not expected to live. They prayed and hurried through a wood to her cottage where they were met at the door by the pleased and excited friends of the woman who showed them the growth in a basin and the woman recovering. This more than ever convinced them that they were chosen people and, all through his life, Dad [Eric's father] had this feeling that he was one of God's saved and this subconsciously gave him licence to behave in a rather unorthodox and sometimes quite dubious manner.

He was a very nice-looking young man with lovely blue eyes and he married a sweet and beautiful Devonshire girl called Emily Ford who was in service in Tonbridge. She was small with a neat, well-shaped head and fine dark eyes. They had a baby called Catherine, a fair blue-eyed little girl; but she died when she was two.

One of the brothers, called Lewis, had gone into the marines, as his father had done; but he didn't like it at all. To leave the service, he stole a pair of braces which caused him to be discharged. He then went to America and started an apple orchard which was very successful. Frank, fired by Lewis's accounts of America, decided to go out to join him. This trip to America was a complete failure. They didn't like Lewis' wife

and they didn't like the country, and Emily again being pregnant, they came back to England in very rough weather which as she was very sea sick did her no good. They went back to Devonshire to stay with old Mrs Ford where their baby Frank was born. Dad became very restless and unhappy in rural surroundings where he could do no work and he decided to try America again. He left for Liverpool, leaving his wife with her mother. It was bitterly cold weather and when he had bought his ticket and boarded ship, he suddenly changed his mind and took a return ticket to Devonshire. He gave poor Emily the shock of her life when without any warning, he appeared in a great snow storm in the middle of the night. They now started a furniture and upholstery business in Acton, where another brother Herbert had a tailor's shop and this business did very well. Dad joined the Salvation Army and I believe played the drum for them. They lived in Acton for many years and had three children, Frank, Evelyn and many years later in 1903, when they were both over forty, Eric William.

Dad bought too large a stock of something, mattresses I think, and instead of living on credit as he could have done till he had recovered enough money to put the business right, he got into a panic, declared himself bankrupt and sold up. He was always an apprehensive man and when in trouble would flap his very large hands and pray to God most earnestly and loudly, his gasps of: 'Oh Lord, Oh Lord' sounding like waves breaking and receding on a shingle beach.

The next move was to Eastbourne where he started a shop for the fitting and selling of blinds. He was a good craftsman

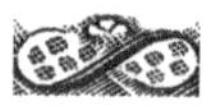

and appreciated good furniture and he drew and painted quite well, though he was very humble about this gift, preferring to have some beautiful picture to copy than having a subject of his own. One of his ancestors had been a hatchment painter, and the hatchments at Hadlow Castle were painted by him. Possibly he was a Huguenot refugee, the family thought that their name of Ravilious was of French origin but they had no definite proof of this, they knew that it had been differently spelt. His new business did well and he took a house in Hampden Park, a village about a mile away, inland from Eastbourne.

Eric's earliest recollections are mostly of Hampden Park and the dame school he went to nearby at Willingdon. Like me, the things he remembers seem chiefly connected with love and excrement, perhaps everyone's early recollections are. He started falling in love when he was very young; but was very much ashamed of doing so and if his admiration for some little girl was noticed and commented on by grown ups, he was deeply upset. Playing postman's knock he did once kiss one girl, but otherwise until he was seventeen he hid his admiration so that no one guessed. A pretty little girl called Dora Clark at his school loved him, and less secretive than he, she gave him in front of the other children in the playground, a lovely daffodil. He felt hotly embarrassed and that this was in some way shameful, so he folded up the flower and broke it into little pieces.

After living in Acton, Eric loved the fields which stretched away to the Downs behind, he had possibly always associated the Downs with these joyful evenings when he kicked cans

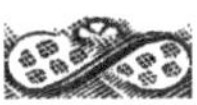

about and laughed and shouted with the other children and he had a great affection for them. Once, when angered by a boy, the son of the Wesleyan Chapel organist, he picked up a drying cow cake and smashed it over his head. He remembered very easily the names of these children and recognised them if he saw them when they were grown up.

Dad fortunately didn't take so much notice of Eric as he had done of Frank, who suffered very much from a too religious upbringing, but for Eric he was bad enough and he grew to dread Sundays when they attended both morning and evening chapel. Sometimes they would go to a Revivalist meeting and on these occasions three or four different preachers would each give a separate address and separate prayers, competing with one another in the depths of emotion and earnest feeling they could put into them. Their eyes screwed up and in hoarse voices: 'Oh Gard, O Lord', they would pray for a very long time. The sermons addressed the unsaved who weren't there to hear them, and went on for hours and hours and hours and Eric suffered agonies of boredom. Walking home after such a meeting, Dad would be in exalted high spirits: 'Ah, my boy, that is what the people need'. Eric would be madly furious and sullenly mutter: 'It was boring'. 'My boy you don't know you're born.' Dad could never put himself in anyone else's place and imagine what they might be feeling and he simply could not understand that Eric had got no pleasure from something that seemed so obviously moving and good to him. To help him, he would perhaps repeat some of the preachers' words, stressing their points so that their meaning should be quite clear to him.

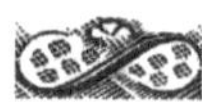

Mum, puzzled, but more tolerant, would scold Eric for fidgeting, a neighbour complained of him. Their friends all loved these occasions and sister Evelyn sang in the choir: how fine it had been and how well the preachers had brought it out, warm and slow, then they went back to the house and cold supper with pineapple chunks.

To Dad at that time, a Roman Catholic was almost as bad as the devil himself and he was very down on any signs of Popery. He smelt sulphur even in Protestant churches if the clergyman wore elaborate vestments and burned incense. He brought up his children as strictly as he could; Frank was not allowed to smoke and they all signed the pledge. Eric when he was very tiny, overheard someone say 'bugger' and he proudly repeated it at home. Dad, horrified, made him go down on his knees there and then and kneeling beside him on the hearth mat, he begged the Lord to forgive this dreadful sin, pleading the child's ignorance. Eric, very scared, burst into tears. Every morning Dad assembled the family and said prayers. He loved composing these extempore prayers and would embarrass the friends whom they had occasionally to stay by praying for them too, referring to them as 'the strangers who are within our gate'. He knew so well all the phrases and ways of expressing prayers that they sounded quite convincing; but his tangle of Bible extracts and high-sounding phrases quite often had very little relation to reality or sense. He loved expounding the Bible, the only book which he read with any concentration. He was particularly fond of St Paul, he dipped into books on prophecy and the lives of various Victorian Revivalist preachers: but he never read right through them.

This evangelical zeal was a constant bogey to Eric who dared not ask friends to the house because his father might ask them if they were saved and perhaps say a prayer for them, and he would certainly give them one or two religious tracts. He always carried tracts and in every hat that he owned, he wrote: 'God is love' in indelible pencil on the hat band. One year he carved it with a pen knife on his crop of baby marrows and, with great satisfaction, watched the message grow bigger.

The most embarrassing thing he ever did was to stand up in the Wesleyan Chapel and answer in some length one of those questions which preachers, in the heat of their sermons, sometimes fling to their congregation, not intending them to speak but to ponder silently. The preacher was very annoyed and put out by Dad and the family nearly died of shame. Mrs Ravilious wouldn't go near the chapel for months afterwards and indeed it so shook poor Evelyn that she subsequently had a nervous breakdown and suffered from nerves for the rest of her life. At her wedding reception he publicly reprimanded the clergyman who had married her to Vernon Ledger, for smoking a cigarette, a farewell exhibition of his wonderful tactlessness.

He liked picnics and jolly times. When they went on a picnic they always set a fire and boiled the kettle on it, and he had a habit of putting a hot teaspoon on the backs of girls' hands to make them jump. At getting anything he wanted of a not too ambitious nature he was unrivalled; he accomplished this by tenacity, worrying and importuning his victim until he had his way.

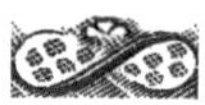

They were always rather poor, till at the end of the war, Eric's father who had been invalided out of the army with something wrong with his back which he had strained while carrying heavy stretchers in the RAMC, started an antique furniture business. This shop prospered like magic in the post-war boom and soon they had a chain of antique shops along the south coast. They had no idea how to spend this money. Dad put £10 on top of the lavatory cistern and forgot about it, Frank pulling the chain some time later was astonished by a shower of one pound notes from above. They bought a huge gramophone and a car. Frank married a nice but high-stepping brewer's daughter and they lived expensively in hotels. Frank at this time was very handsome and looked and behaved like the hero of a musical comedy, he was very generous with his money and liberally tipped the hotel servants. Evelyn married Vernon Ledger, a north-country man who had been at the South Downs convalescent camp near their house. He was appointed manager of the YMCA at Burton-on-Trent and after the war they went to live there.

Eric had been going for two years to a church higher grade school called St Saviour's and from there he won a scholarship to Eastbourne Grammar School. In comparison with the other children at St Saviour's, he had been considered clever; but at the grammar school, he didn't do so well. He worked hard enough at those subjects that interested him: but if he didn't like the master or the subject he didn't concentrate and so was a constant thorn in the side of people like the sarcastic mathematics master, who knew that Eric could have learned

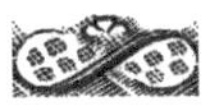

mathematics but the whole subject boring him, he never would try.

The art master at the grammar school, Mr Millington, was a very kind and nice person. He was tall and dark with a beard and black hat and he wore a loose stock tie fastened through a ring. His voice was deep and over-cultured but he drew well in the ordinary academic tradition of his time. He was very encouraging to Eric who liked and admired him very much, never having met anyone like him before; the other masters wore neat conventional suits and had voices of the self-made men they were. Unfortunately Mr Millington was a conscientious objector and because of this he was arrested and sent to prison where he died.

Eric was very much in awe of the headmaster Mr Blackburn, who also taught geography at my school West Hill. He taught English in his own school and so paralysed Eric with fright by watching him write one day, that he crossed a capital L making it into a £. This fear of Blackburn haunted him until he was about thirty and he constantly had nightmares about him. This seemed very strange to me because I never felt very frightened of Mr Blackburn. Indeed, West Hill treated him with little respect and we would tactfully lure him on to talk about his socialist politics or beer, rice pudding and margarine, pronounced with a hard 'G', which were all subjects that were guaranteed to keep him going for most of the lesson. I suppose being a headmaster made him seem different or perhaps he was different among boys.

Eric was not a nervous child but he was very sensitive to insults or imagined insults and would remember them against

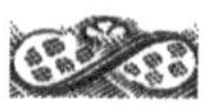

people almost indefinitely. The family went for holidays to Devonshire where they stayed at Kingsbridge with Mrs Ravilious's sister Polly Dufty, who had married a farmer. The farm was called North Upton and was on a hill overlooking a creek from the sea beyond. Eric loved these holidays and the Dufty family. The father was a very handsome man with a wide fair moustache and blue eyes like a Viking. He was tremendously hard working and outlived three wives. Aunt Polly used to be so exhausted by bedtime that she would just sit resting her head in her arms on the table. In the daytime, she fortified herself with cups of very black tea. She was very like Eric's mother in appearance and also in her love of strong tea. It probably hastened both their ends. The eldest girl Winifred went to a good school and acquired a ladylike accent which infuriated her brother, who was continually mocking the poor girl when she came home. She worked away from home and when she came back, didn't do any housework which was one of the causes of her unpopularity. She sang and played the piano and Eric's elder brother Frank had been very smitten with her which worried Dad; Eric preferred the second girl Mabel and was kissed by her in a hay field. Another cousin came to stay and commented on the fact that he was lazy, for which he never forgave her; he had hoped that his laziness would not be noticed.

Eric was popular at school and was very good at football and quite good at bowling for cricket. His father had little power to interfere with his school life but he objected to Eric joining the OTC and Mum had to go to the school and explain Dad's views to Mr Blackburn. As he was the only boy

not in the OTC he felt very resentful with his father at the time. He was very ashamed too of his family for attending chapel instead of church and he hoped that the other boys would never find out this shameful secret.

Mrs Ravilious was a very good and sweet person and kept her head through all the family's ups and downs, continuing to produce meals, do the housework and mend their clothes. I don't know if a person can be blamed for being too kind, she did spoil her family although she tried to keep Dad in order, which was no easy matter because he was a most self-centred man and his devotion to his son Frank was only in some ways a devotion to the image of himself which he saw uncon-sciously in him. Mum and Dad disapproved of both Frank and Evelyn's marriages. Frank's wife, Lilian, was frivolous and what was worse, a publican's daughter; Vern was steady enough they had to admit but his muscular Christianity was unfamiliar to them and they didn't like it. Muscular he was, short and dark and powerful, he played games very well and was kind and nice and serious as north-country people are.

His mother hoped Eric would go into something steady like the Post Office, she had at first put Frank to work as a clerk in the Gas Office but he hadn't stayed there long. She always wished that Dad would work under someone instead of these erratic changes of business in which you never knew where you were. No one thought of Eric becoming an artist and it was quite accidental that he did.

Every year the Eastbourne Art School had two scholar-ships to award. The boy who drew best in the grammar school was called Reed and he took one of the scholarships and Eric,

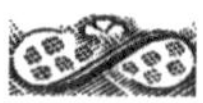

who enjoyed drawing more than anything and realising that it offered a better chance of freedom from the things that bored him – he was trying to learn shorthand – accepted the other.

He was awfully happy at the Art School and for the first time was able to speak freely with girls. The headmaster Reeve-Fowkes was very pleased with him and taught him to do art school drawings that were full of clever tricks. He became the humble adorer of Brenda Capron, a pretty and precocious little girl who also did remarkably dashing work and was a particular favourite of Mr Fowkes. He worked hard and tried to pass a teacher's examination consisting of various different subjects in each of which you had a separate examination; always he failed in plant drawing. Every three years there was a scholarship to the Royal College of Art at Kensington and after two years' work he entered for this. It was won by Miss Owen and Eric was second. This girl quite suddenly decided to be a missionary and giving up her scholarship to Eric, she sailed to Africa. Dressed in a stiff collar and a bow tie and looking even younger than he was, Eric was sent by the enthusiastic Mr Reeve-Fowkes to be interviewed by Professor William Rothenstein, the principal of the Royal College. When Eric was shown into his room, he found that he was at work on a self-portrait, peering into a mirror that was fixed into position beside his easel. He continued working for a few minutes before he attended to the apprehensive student. He then looked rapidly through Eric's folio of drawings; they showed no flicker of originality anywhere and he must have thought them appalling: 'Your quick sketches are better than your other work,' he said in his soft fruity voice. He then

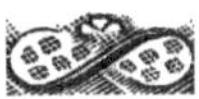

advised him to wait six months and then go into the design school, adding: 'Here you will have better opportunities than at Eastbourne'.

Fortunately for Eric, the war had made it necessary to introduce female teachers and a Miss [Lilian] Lancaster, who had been a student at the Slade School, came to the Eastbourne Art School. She drew very well and showing Eric good drawing, she encouraged him and helped to remove those clever tricks which are always so attractive to a young student.

During this time he also started his first serious love affair. The girl was older than him but she was very nice and she played tennis very well which attracted him as much as the love making part of it. He did not dare mention to his family that he now had a girl and could only have clandestine meetings round the corner, which for some reason he didn't much like.

When he eventually went to the College the affair became even more of a bore because it meant that he had to write letters as well and he hated writing letters. I don't know if it was the effect of Mr Blackburn or just natural slowness but he took hours to write letters. Meeting so many new people and becoming absorbed in work, his letters got fewer and fewer until they stopped altogether. He felt very guilty and ashamed of himself and determined not to kiss any more girls.

[Eric's brother] Frank, leading his musical comedy life, made friends with a great variety of people. He was naturally attracted to the stage and his wife and he both did a little acting. One of his shops which was conveniently behind the

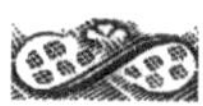

Grand Hotel, would often be visited by actors and actresses who were staying there while they performed at Devonshire Park Theatre. He entrusted the management of his other shops to doubtful young men who probably didn't know very much about antiques. Frank himself didn't know much, only Dad because he was old and therefore familiar with old things really knew and his knowledge was instinctive and couldn't be imparted. He would affectionately stroke old furniture, he had no sense of possession and didn't mind parting with anything. I imagine customers must have preferred him to Frank hoping that he might sell them a bargain. Inevitably business started to fail and one by one the shops were lost until they went bankrupt.

Frank's wife Lilian had a rich aunt who came to her assistance and she with her family started running a boarding house. This family called Boniface loved horse racing and gambling and also they were keen card players. Frank had no interest in these things and he and his wife, who had a temperamental nature, quarrelled more and more as they lost their fortune. Frank started borrowing and living on credit. Eric was at home when the doorbell rang and a man asked to see Mr Frank Ravilious. When told that he was out he handed Eric a warrant, an awe-inspiring document with *Rex v Ravilious* on it. This shock was followed by the even more painful visit of a tearful and hysterical Lilian and the gloom in Charleston Road was pretty black. Dad did an extra lot of praying and his exhortations to the Lord added to the general sense of calamity. For Lilian this was the end and she made up her mind to leave Frank.

Eric attended Frank when he had to go to Court, he gave him one or two stiff brandies and waited to hear the verdict which was six months. He went to Eastbourne and tried to get the local paper to omit an account of the trial to spare his mother's feelings but of course they wouldn't.

Poor Mum had no peace because Evelyn, after having a baby, had collapsed. The nervous strain of all these dreadful things and the shock of having a baby were too much for her. She and the baby came to stay in Charleston Road and as Evelyn couldn't feed it herself, they tried to feed it on milk and soaked bread which it could not digest. Eric was now harassed by the almost perpetual crying of the baby and the moanings and complaints of his sleepless sister; he hated noise as much as he did boredom and it was a good thing that he was earning enough money to enable him to live in London.

In London, at the Royal College of Art, Eric had been living on his scholarship money of £60 a year and some which his mother allowed him. He won the travelling scholarship and went to Italy because it was the traditional thing to do. Afterwards he regretted that he had gone there because he didn't like it. It was either intolerably hot or intolerably cold or he was constipated and lonely and he saw far too many pictures and so had no desire to paint any himself. He had become interested in wood engraving which was having a revival, and back in London he illustrated a book called *Desert* by Martin Armstrong; this and an engraving he had done of the little Sussex church at Lullington were liked by quite a lot of people and he met Eric Gill, and Robert Gibbings who ran the Golden Cockerel Press, and was given work by him. With

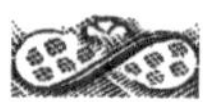

his teaching job at Eastbourne, he was now earning enough to be able to help his mother and later on, when he started working at Morley College, he was able to help her to buy the house which they had had built for them. She was wonderfully good at saving and would hide money up the chimney of her bedroom behind some newspaper, where Frank and Dad never discovered it. It was a great relief to her to feel that anyway the house was hers and when Evelyn and the baby left, she let the top floor of the house and became independent. For the rest of her life, she gradually saved up the £50 which Eric had lent her and although he said that he didn't want it back, she insisted that he took it.

Eric kept all his family troubles very much to himself. He never invited anyone to his home at Eastbourne; the fact that his father ate with a knife was enough in his view to make him impossible. I naturally felt very sympathetic when I heard a little of what had been happening.

During the summer holidays, I had been with John and Aunt Edith in Switzerland and Eric had been for another holiday to Barcombe Mills. We had both had mild flirtations and he had made love to a half-Austrian and half-Scottish girl, she had fine big breasts and could play the piano and dance on the lawn; the other more prim English Art students hadn't approved of her free behaviour but Eric was very grateful. I felt grateful to her as well because it gave him enough confidence to kiss me too. Every time that he came to see me we made love for a little longer than the last time, but I was faithful to my promise to Bob and my father's fears were not fulfilled in fact,

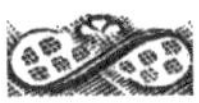

if they were in mind. We went about hand in hand. Eric didn't like arm in arm because it reminded him of going to chapel and if he tripped up or bumped into anything while I was with him, I felt the shock more deeply than he did himself. I don't know where he lived then as I never went home with him.

Bob and I wrote regularly to one another, he was seasick almost the whole way out to Africa. When he arrived in Nyasaland he had to live all by himself in a bungalow with only two or three other white people at all near. The place was called Cholo and he worked as Postmaster, settled disputes and collected hut tax from the native population. He was naturally very lonely and my letters filled with girl's chat about my new busy life didn't make him feel any less so. Aware of how miserable he was, my natural instinct was to try and cheer him up as much as possible: but I could only accomplish this by writing love letters. He was a more than ordinarily jealous man and any allusions to other men gave him awful pangs. He wrote very good letters and I looked forward to them eagerly. I was as frank as I could be in mine so far as I can remember and told him I had kissed Eric.

I went at New Year's Eve with Eric and a party of Art School friends to the Chelsea Arts Ball at the Albert Hall. If you consented to take part in one of the Art School processions, students could go to this dance with a very much cheaper ticket, so I joined the Central Art School's show. I believe that the schools were told to represent in some form or other the Arabian Nights. We had a huge model elephant; we weren't allowed a real one in case it went through the floor. The model one was only just finished in time because the boys who

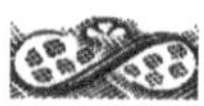

made it quarrelled. I was one of a band of slave girls who were dressed in bust bodices connected with our very small trousers by a band of purple sateen material; we had also black raffia wigs and we carried trays of flowers on our heads. By the time we had processed very slowly twice round the huge floor holding our arms above our heads to support the trays and eluded the pawings of the more drunken businessmen in the audience, we felt pretty exhausted. I managed to kick one of them rather neatly as I passed and felt the same satisfaction that I had at overwhelming my father. With a friend, I tried to go up the stairs to rejoin Eric and the others and to change my dress. I had brought a yellow Elizabethan dress with me that Eric had designed when we acted a play at Eastbourne. The Albert Hall struck me forcibly as being as badly planned inside as it could be. There seemed to be only two staircases in the whole place and as the main cloakrooms and bathrooms were below the floor and the refreshments right at the top, the staircases were a solid mass of people. I felt like bursting into tears and when a middle-aged man dressed as the devil tried to put his arm round me, I turned on him with such fury that his startled friends hastily withdrew him.

It took us about half an hour to change and find the others. After supper, I felt so fed up with the place that I would gladly have gone home but Eric found that it was nice and quiet under the floor, so we went there and sat beside an enormous organ till a kindly policeman turned us out; there were reported to be sixty policemen present because there had been a row the year before. It became intolerably hot, one poor man dressed entirely in a thick fur as a monkey became

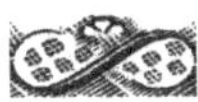

so hot that his face ran with perspiration like one in dreadful pain.

It was Sunday the next day and I went with the aunts to the Scottish church, where the minister during his sermon mentioned how sad he had felt at seeing early on this Sunday morning the revellers from the Chelsea Arts Ball going tired and haggard to their homes. I was the only member of the congregation who could possibly have gone to the Ball and I felt indignant. He was a well-fed looking man with thick white hair set in waves which shone under the lampshade recently re-covered in blue silk by Liberty's. Nearly all the artists and art students that I had met were very respectable people and I resented the inference that they were more immoral than other people or less religious. It is rum how a certain trade can acquire a reputation and how silly people class together all those belonging to that trade and judge them according to their traditional repute. Sailors, for instance, are rarely blamed for their attitude to women which generally speaking is a rather disgraceful one. Stockbrokers seemed to me to be far more immoral than artists if you wanted someone to blame for immorality, both for their activity and their dirty stories. The ones I met were sentimental overgrown schoolboys.

One of the Eastbourne art students called Valetta had recently married a stockbroker called Edric Swann. He had I think been in the navy or tea planting in Ceylon but he had given it up as being too unprofitable. Eric admired Valetta because she very much resembled a portrait of a lady by Baldovinetti in the National Gallery, though he didn't like her very much as

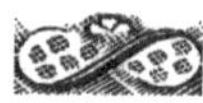

a person. He often liked people quite unreasonably because they reminded him of pictures or of other people he had known and admired.

Now that she was married and living in Elgin Crescent, she still continued to be an art student and went as I did to the Central School. Occasionally I went out in the evening with her and her husband, a nice, friendly, little man who was obviously very proud of her. He took a great deal of interest in her clothes so that she blossomed from a narrow, Eastbourne girl into a voluptuous-looking Junoesque beauty. All the same, Valetta complained to me that he still flirted with other women and they weren't altogether happy.

We met at their flat one evening when they had invited me to go to Skindles with them. I was wearing a new dress which Aunt Edith had just bought for me in the sales, it was a cheap dress made of red silk stockinette, but Aunt Edith had wanted me to wear it and I suppose it was a suitable type of dress for Skindles.

Edric, having been in the navy, didn't seem to be happy unless he had just had a drink or there was a prospect very shortly of having another drink. He didn't get tight but was just cheerful. They had invited two other men, one had been in the navy as well and who Valetta warned me was so miserable and demoralised that he would probably get drunk, she didn't say why, and another stockbroker friend of Edric's, a tough lascivious-looking man who obviously admired Valetta.

We drove very quickly along the Great West Road in Edric's fast, red car and reached Maidenhead before it was quite dark. Skindles wasn't anything spectacular, just an

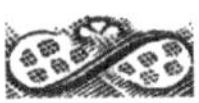

ordinary roadhouse. There was a pretty blonde in the bar and Edric chatted with her with that easy familiarity acquired by commercial travellers and sailors. We sat at a table in the dance hall and it got very crowded and hot and the naval man drank more and more and the stockbroker became more and more openly desiring of Valetta. I felt very young and unsophisticated in my hateful red dress and, not being able to drink, rather uncomfortable and proper. The stockbroker's conversation seemed to be mainly an exchange of dirty stories.

When it was time to go, the sailor, who was a tall, handsome young man, was hardly able to speak but I got into the back of the car with Valetta and the stockbroker and perched on the sailor's knee in a 'when in Rome do as the Romans do' desperation.

Valetta and the stockbroker soon became wrapt in a passionate embrace and I felt even more miserable and awkward and wondered if Edric driving alone in front was aware of what was happening behind. As though Edric sensed my distress, he stopped the car with some excuse and asked if I wouldn't prefer to come in the front and so gratefully I went and sat in security beside him.

The marriage between Edric and Valetta didn't last very long and they separated from one another. Some time later my mother came back one day to lunch and recounted to me how she had just met Valetta's mother. 'Such an unpleasant man', she said. 'He was always drinking and led Valetta an awful dance and had even taken to beating her!' she concluded with a shocked yet rather pleased voice. My mother

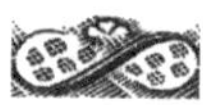

hadn't really liked Valetta but she admired her ladylike appearance and clothes. I was so surprised that, 'What rot, she's much bigger than he is', was all I said in poor Edric's defence.

In the spring [of 1929] I went back to Eastbourne and had my appendix removed in a nursing home. I had the same doctor who had taken out Bob's, he had been a rowing blue and he didn't take them out very well. Afterwards, I had far more pain from my scar than I ever had from my appendix. It took six years to get right. Later I stayed with Bob's family; I was very fond of them and preferred his parents to my own at that time. His sister Barbara was taking her final examination in French at Oxford. She felt very annoyed with her mother who in the early part of the summer holidays had invited a French girl to stay 'au pair'. Barbara had had to make conversation with her instead of getting on with French for examination which was a very different thing from ordinary French conversation, as I soon discovered when I used to hear her parts that she had learned by heart. She deplored that at Oxford you had to mug up all your work for one final examination at the end of two years while at Cambridge, you could pass half of your examination at the end of your first year and then your final at the end of two, which seemed to her a far more sensible arrangement. She knew that she hadn't enough time to stuff herself with sufficient early French to get a first. We decided to go away together to do some work.

We went to a little village called Lanvallay in Brittany; it was over the other side of the viaduct from Dinan. Our

bedroom was large and square with yellow wallpaper, green shutters and maple wood furniture. I did a picture of myself sitting up on one side of the big double bed and called it *The Wife*. It was one of a series of engravings I was doing called *Relations* for a calendar for the Curwen Press.

The dirty work of the house was done by a poor wretch of a child called Gilberte. The only place of refuge from the cries of 'Gilberte' was in the garden lavatory and she used to spend as much time in there as possible. This lavatory was inhabited by the most alarming bees. We could hear them droning and buzzing below and going to the lavatory became a nightmarish excursion till Barbara invented the happy idea of folding a Sunday newspaper into a kind of safety bucket between one's bottom and the bees.

The weather grew intolerably hot and sultry and Barbara, always sensitive to thunderstorms, became ill. After three or four days we called in a doctor, who advised an enema. I was appalled at the thought of having to buy such a thing in my halting French and enquired what I should call it; 'Oh quelque chose pour lavement,' he said. I could hardly believe that this simple phrase was really all that was necessary and full of apprehension, I set off for Dinan with a little Jewish girl from Manchester who was also staying in the house. We came back with a beautiful syringe and I was filled with admiration for Barbara who was capable of giving herself an enema.

Finally, one night the weather broke with the most terrific storm. The sea water flooded into the river and killed the river fish who rose to the top in hundreds and covered

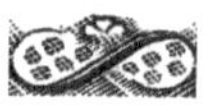

the surface with their pathetic silver bellies; soon they smelt very bad but no one thought of removing them. In spite of the phenomenal storm, our hostess set off the next morning at her accustomed hour of ten to six to play the harmonium at mass; but she came back shortly as, except for the priest, the church was empty.

Barbara's love affairs were more tangled than mine, even her girlfriends suffered from pangs of jealousy. I learned with surprise that her friend at Oxford nicknamed Brab was even jealous of me because I was staying with her on this holiday; whether from excessive humility or superiority, I have never been certain which, I never suffered very much from this gnawing monster. Living with Bob's family I began to believe that I shared with them the natural love for him that they felt. It never I think entered his mother's head that I might not want to marry her darling, his father did know of my doubts. Sitting on Barbara's bed one day after lunch, we both burst into tears. I made up my mind that I would marry Bob and I wrote to Eric and said that I thought that I'd better not see him any more when I got back to London. It was a very insulting letter, though not intentionally so; he was, quite naturally, furious.

Huge black spiders began haunting our bedroom. The wallpaper was loose in many places and they lived underneath; coming out at night, we could hear them pattering horribly on the uneven paper: there were also swarms of flies. Barbara courageously tackled both one day, the spiders with a tennis racquet and the flies with a newspaper. Our landlady didn't like the mess of squashed flies on the wall. When we

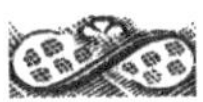

were out walking, we found strange spiders with yellow and black striped bodies like big bloated wasps. The blackberries, superbly large and left unpicked by the villagers, hung in great clusters wherever we went so that we saw them in our dreams. On our last day, Barbara who was a realist, took me for a final last look at everything: 'We shall never come back', she said.

The letters that I was having from Bob were the replies to the ones I had sent in the winter when I had been going about so much with Eric. He was miserable and jealous and I felt a pig for causing him so much anguish; I was also alarmed because he threatened to chuck up his job and come back. I suggested to his mother that she and I went out to Africa to see him. My family agreed to pay my fare and we sent him a cable. He cabled back that he couldn't have us because he was being moved to a place where it was impossible for us to stay. He half guessed that he would lose me by wiring this, but there seemed nothing else he could say.

Back again in London, I very soon began to feel the loss of Eric's friendship. He had been decorating the walls of a refreshment room at Morley College with Edward Bawden. I rang him up on some futile pretext and went to see him. Edward was a difficult person to work with and the summer had been pretty awful for Eric, but the painting was gay and charming and showed none of this distress. After seeing one another again the summer was forgotten and we resumed our friendship and love making almost as though nothing had happened, the only visible change being the moustache that he had grown.

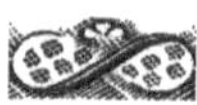

London is a difficult place for making love if you haven't very much money and don't like joining the couples in Hyde Park. We could only snatch kisses behind cases in the museums, dodging the attendants who were far too numerous or sit in cinemas and afterwards stroll about the more secluded places like Holland Walk and the passages between Kensington and Notting Hill Gate but they were pretty thickly populated by other couples. We didn't like to make love in my room as much as we had before as Miss Phillimore, a niece of the Lord, who had a room beside mine and shared the top landing, had given me a talking to because she had observed that my light was out when Eric was there. She warned me that the club had turned out a previous member for being indiscreet with her men friends and allowing them to stay later than eleven which was closing time for male visitors.

Eric was now living with Douglas and Phyllis Bliss who had a flat near Morley College, it was over a factory for making synthetic sausage skins and they were almost incessantly plagued by the local children who rang their bell and ran away. The Blisses were very kind to me and I used to go there a lot. Douglas was dark-haired and blue-eyed, quick and lively, he pounced on ideas and conversation like an exuberant Scottish terrier. Phyllis was fair with large blue eyes and a sweet face. Except when portrait painting at which she was very good, she did everything very slowly which exasperated her friends because she was invariably late. Edward Bawden mortally offended the newly wedded Bliss by saying one day after they had been waiting some time, 'If I were you, I'd put a bomb under Phyllis'.

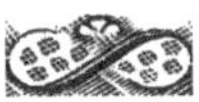

In Africa, Bob knowing that I was in London and probably falling in love with Eric, was growing more and more desperate and he finally asked the Nyasaland authorities if he could go home. He explained what it was that was worrying him so they gave him leave, though it meant that it would slightly delay his future promotion.

Eric's friends learning of my dilemma were very interested and Bliss, hearing that Bob could swim round the pier, thought that Eric's case was hopeless.

I went to stay for a fortnight in Eastbourne and Bob arrived. He said that he wouldn't make love to me because he couldn't bear it if he started to and then if after all I didn't want to marry him, he had to stop. I wished he wouldn't be so humble and when we put on the gramophone and it played a soupy waltz and I saw him looking so miserable, I naturally wanted to kiss him. I've got into a lot of trouble by naturally doing things and so it was now. The resulting confusion was dreadful. I think if I'd been left alone I shouldn't have married either of them. My father's light-hearted suggestion that I would 'live with Ramvillas' was impractical and much as I liked the idea of Bob as a comfortable pipe-smoking husband, I knew that if I did marry him I should always regret giving up my friendship with Eric and that I hadn't gone on with my drawing. It was as though Bob stood for my family's idea of life and Eric for my freedom and independence. Bob realised this and wanted to leave the civil service and try to earn his living in London as a writer. His family hadn't very much money and I knew this would be hopeless for him. I was by now in such a state of uncertainty that if either of them had

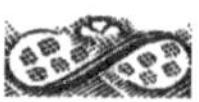

produced a marriage licence and firmly marched me off to a registry office, I might have married them for peace of mind. Eric felt that he wouldn't be a good husband and advised me to marry Bob. Tactlessly I sent them for a walk together and it was a wonder that Eric returned undamaged. Bob afterwards confessed that he had felt like murdering him.

At the end of the fortnight we went back to London and feeling absolutely miserable, I told Bob that I had definitely made up my mind not to marry him. We spent the morning weeping on my bed till we were utterly exhausted. In the afternoon Bob thought that he would shoot himself and sat down with his revolver intending to do so; the realisation of how upset his mother would be if he did, mercifully stopped him. Hearing about this, I wrote to his father for help.

Aunt Lilian, knowing nothing about these troubles, had invited me that evening to go to the Gate Theatre and meet a second cousin of hers, Jim Richards, who had just finished his training as an architect. We were both surprised to find that we liked one another, as somehow one never expected anyone introduced by an aunt to be anything more than a member of such a nice family. He was a shy-looking young man with intelligent grey eyes and rather long hair; but I detected that the shyness was more a barrier against those people who did not interest him than a real fear of them. The play was one of those Victorian revivals and was the first play of its kind that I ever saw. I didn't like the McKnight Kauffer scenery because it seemed to me to be too brightly coloured and was confusing with the figures acting in front of it. I wished Edward Bawden had done it because he really appreciated Victorian furniture.

Standing afterwards with Aunt Lilian and Jim Richards in the entrance to Earls Court Underground station, I was suddenly and vividly reminded of my own troubles by seeing Bob go by in a bus. We were making polite conversation, Jim was just going to Canada and America and I thought how startled they would look if they knew how I had been spending the day.

Bob's mother took a long time to forgive me for being the cause of so much misery to her son. She was a simple person and couldn't understand that because I loved Bob, it didn't necessarily mean that I wanted to marry him and she thought that I had 'led him on'. Barbara, who had by now about six people wanting to marry her, knew that these affairs were not so straightforward and easy to manage and she was as nice and sympathetic to me as she had always been. She and Alec and her friend Brab [Bowers], who finally married Bob, looked after him and Barbara went back with him to Africa.

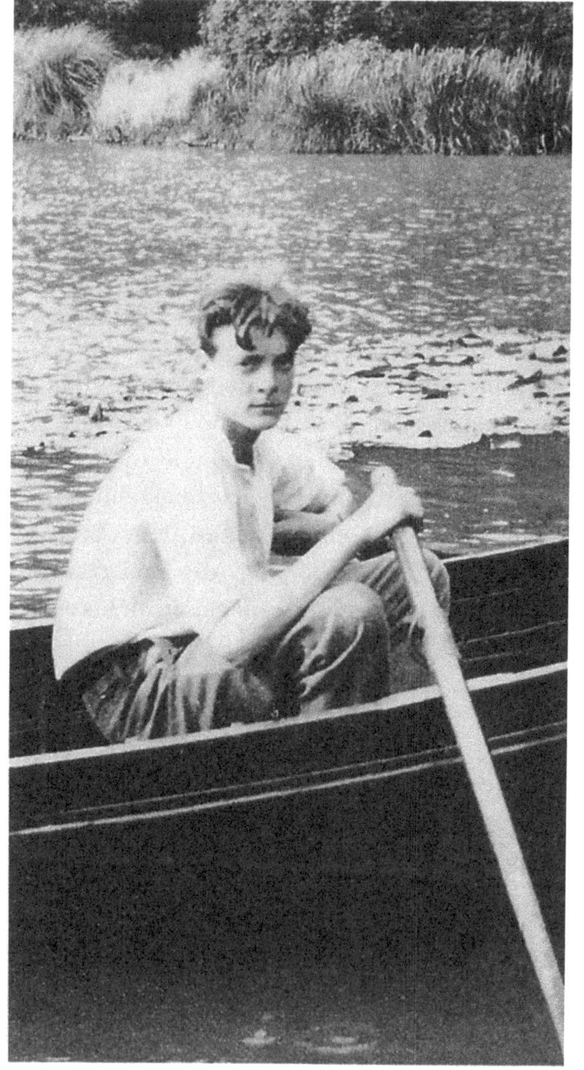

CHAPTER NINE

I was still rather run down from having my appendix out and had got adhesions under the scar on my stomach. I had hoped that the operation would lessen the pain which I had to endure every three and a half weeks when I was unwell; but it didn't seem to make much difference and in addition I had this chronic trouble from my scar as well. My family were very unsympathetic people about illness. Their own fear of pain made them unwilling to admit its existence and they disliked you for forcing their attention onto such an unpleasant subject. This is obviously an ordinary healthy person's reaction to a state of which they have no experience, but very few people admit it. I could have kissed my sweet Aunt Lucy for saying: 'I hate sick people'. I think my sister Billy is naturally sympathetic and exclude her from this attitude of the rest of the family's.

It was popular among doctors at that time to dismiss menstrual pains as being imaginary, and so many people, among them the school matron, adopted this theory that it was just nerves when I complained of having a pain, and a little exercise would soon put me right. The fact that I was

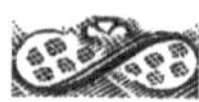

a pale green colour and suffering from diarrhoea and sickness didn't seem to convince her and when I asked to be excused from a walk or dancing, she would say: 'Well, what are you going to do when you are grown up if you give in like this now?' The awful thing about these pains was that as well as being accompanied by an unmanageable amount of blood, they were preceded by a feeling of dreadful depression. On the second morning I usually wished I was dead and would sit in the lavatory saying: 'Oh God, Oh God' and following this nonsensically with: 'God of our fathers, known of old, Lord of our far flung battle line', a hymn of Kipling's that I particularly detest. I suffered like this for fifteen years, and society not admitting such an indecent affliction to be talked about, I was constantly offending people by being unable to keep appointments and unreasonably refusing invitations and it also interfered with my work which, in spite of all these interruptions, I still enjoyed.

I was very easily influenced by people that I admired and Eric and Bob and Barbara between them had very much altered me and enlarged the number of things that interested me. It is difficult to assess one's own faults and attractions; but I think they liked me, apart from Bob and Eric's desire for 'almost a pretty girl' (Eric had been amused by hearing me described this way by a young man he was talking to in a bar), because I tried to be honest. This candour of mine was very good for Eric who, suffering from his difficult family and from being 'not quite a gentleman' was constantly trying to hide insults and mistakes that were far less grievous if they were openly talked about.

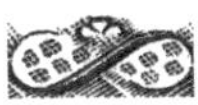

I tried to convert Eric to Christianity and was introduced by him to various books by scientists and philosophers which persuaded me that it was I who was wrong in my previous beliefs and not he. It wasn't that Eric didn't believe in God or Christ or a future life, but he didn't like the Christian churches and chapels. Edward Bawden too, had a chapel upbringing and detested them, but with not quite the same violence as Eric. He had at one time tried to work out how many pounds of stuffed cherries there were in the hats of the congregation. He replied majestically to some derogatory remark of Eric's about people in churches: 'Well anyway it keeps them off the roads'.

Edward was the son of a very successful ironmonger in Braintree. The shop was called Crittall and Winterton but really was entirely owned by Mr Bawden, Winterton having committed suicide and Crittall having sold his shares in the business a long time back. He was a delicate and difficult child and his mother never had another, saying that the difficulty of rearing him had determined her never to have more children. He was, he told me, so exasperating that she once threw a frying pan at him. She was a very ordinary middle-class woman and it was hard for her that providence had sent her this constipated and abnormal child, hard too for his father who had hoped for a son who would carry on his work as an ironmonger.

He went to the Braintree High School and later to a Quaker school at Saffron Walden where, realising that drawing was the only subject that really interested him, they let him alone to continue drawing and afterwards advised his parents to send him to an Art School.

I don't know how early it was that Edward developed an antipathy to his father; he was very much a mother's boy and his father in the hardware trade can hardly have felt much sympathy for a child who was so obviously 'soft'. Mr Bawden was a self-made man and every spare sum of money that was available he reinvested in the business. He was determined that Edward too, should make his own way. When he left school he sent him to an art school at Cambridge, lodging him with a suitable chapel-going family and allowing him 9d a week pocket money, so that poor Edward, who didn't like the family, walked about Cambridge in his spare time and bought oranges with his nine pennies.

He drew with great precision and accuracy and was quick to assimilate new ideas. His early pen drawings were remarkably mature and it was in this medium that he first impressed those people who saw his work. He was meticulous and painstaking, wiping the ink off his nib before every dip in the ink pot to avoid any clogging lumps on his pen. With a perfectly steady hand, he could place a ruler on a still wet drawing and rule confidently on it with ink. Although nervous, the things that affected him were not of the usual kind and he could draw his fingernail over linen or satin material producing that noise which sets most people's teeth on edge without it having any effect on him at all; he, on the other hand, hated tweed and woollen materials and chose for his suits a smooth grey material that to most people was quite repellent. He first appeared at the Royal College of Art in rimless pince-nez spectacles and wearing a handkerchief tie and brightly coloured socks. He walked with a springing step and held himself so upright that

he appeared to be almost leaning backwards. If a stranger asked to be directed anywhere he would stiffly put up his hand and direct it as though it was a sign post. He was extremely good at knowing his way about London because when he first came to live there he always walked everywhere, being too shy to take a bus.

In appearance he was dark, his eyes small and bright like an intelligent Essex pig's, his hair was long and brushed back off his high and slightly receding forehead, it stood up from his long narrow head as though it was very fine wire. He had black eyebrows and thick almost negroid lips, and his complexion was a pale greenish yellow colour. He was of medium height, his shoulders sloping and he had small hands and feet of which he was very proud. These individual details must suggest a monster of ugliness; but he wasn't, the whole effect was to some people quite a handsome and distinguished looking man. Eric and I thought him very ugly; but there was something attractive in the way his ears were rather pointed and sloped upwards, giving him at times when he laughed a Puckish look and one could not dismiss as wholly ugly a face that was so obviously alert and intelligent.

To strangers he appeared to be very shy and self-effacing, but once he looked on you as more than a mere acquaintance, there was a great change and no personal remark was too personal for Edward. For all that, he hated contact with people and if anyone talked to him at all animatedly he would gradually back away from them and if they in their enthusiasm advanced, he would finally be standing with his back to the wall with his arms outstretched like a film heroine whose

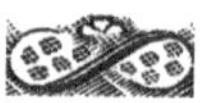

honour is threatened. It gave people, unaware of this peculiarity, an uncomfortable feeling that they were personally distasteful to him, until they learned with relief that it was his usual habit. He talked well and was very good company to his friends if he was feeling warmly towards them.

He used at this time to be very constipated and I was worried when he said that he hadn't been for a fortnight. One cure for this was a visit to see businessmen in connection with his work, the nervous apprehension before the appointment frequently causing him to have diarrhoea. He was reading Havelock Ellis and other books on homosexuality and rather proudly came to the conclusion that was probably what he was.

I felt sorry for Edward because I thought that no one, male or female, could love him; but Eric told me that he had a very devoted aunt whom he was rather ashamed of because she mothered him and, having been a nurse, she constantly enquired about his bowels. Then there was also a bald woman who loved him. He had been to stay with some relations of his father's in Cornwall; Mr Bawden was a Cornish man and the maid at this house who had no hair had fallen in love with Edward. Her affections were not returned by Edward and he showed us a letter that she had written to him which was the most pathetic letter that I have ever read. She described her feelings for him and how sitting on a seat longing for him, she had seen him coming along the road towards her. She was unaware that Edward had by then left the place and she must have been so longing for him that she had imagined another young man was him.

When he was at the College, Edward became a vegetarian. He had, he realised, been revolted by his father's prodigious appetite; Mr Bawden he said was capable of eating a whole pie all by himself. Those more intimate pieces of meat such as kidneys, livers, hearts and brains were now quite abhorrent to Edward. I think this lack of meat may have been responsible for his pale complexion and the fact that he was not eating enough for his constipation. He was also not sleeping very well and his hair was being affected.

Eric had stopped living with the Blisses and now had a couple of rooms in the same house as Edward. His room was on the third floor while Edward had the ground floor which consisted of two rooms and a kitchen. The communal bathroom and lavatory was in a terribly dilapidated state; one feared to pull the plug with any spirit in case the cistern above might fall. Eric did blow part of the geyser into the garden, by lighting his match too late. The combination of geysers and lavatories reminds me of two things which Edward used to do as a child, one was to set fire to lavatory paper and then pull the plug and the other was to sit on the seat and pull the plug in hot weather so that he had his bottom flushed with cold water: he always washed his hands after he had been to the lavatory and was personally as clean and fastidious as a cat.

Redcliffe Road was quiet in rather a sinister way, a perpetual Sunday afternoon atmosphere pervaded it; but inside the houses, one could imagine that anything might be happening. After respectable Eastbourne, I used to love sitting in Edward's front room watching the occasional passers-by. I was once lucky enough to see an elderly prostitute luring a

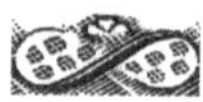

respectable-looking citizen. He didn't fancy the idea of walking along beside her, so he followed behind, every now and then looking furtively round to see if he was unobserved, while she also looked round from time to time to make sure that he was following her.

Edward's front room was distempered a greenish mustard colour and the paint was burnt umber stippled with green. On the mantelpiece there were busts of Queen Alexandra and King Edward VII. When he bought them they were marble white, but he painted them with red and blue and they didn't look so dead: between them there hung a Victorian wall mirror edged with a large gilt-leafed decoration. The chairs were elegant golden ones with thin spindle legs but they didn't last long as he had a nervous habit of spinning them on one leg or else they were broken when, sitting at meals, he became enthusiastic and tipped backwards. Occasionally he fell right over like Fidgety Philip.

He collected military uniforms and hats of various kinds, top hats and a guardsman's bearskin. There was a hat stand for the hats and a black Jemima tailor's bust for the uniforms. He had a fine Victorian ornamental piece, a dish of flowers and fruit made out of wax and beads which was covered by a large glass dome – he was one of the first people to fully appreciate such pieces at that period.

A Lambeth carpenter made him a full-sized ping-pong table, more for the amusement of his friends than for himself as he didn't play on it very often, and some expanding book shelves and a large wooden screen which he papered on one side with a lino-cut design of a pigeon and on the other

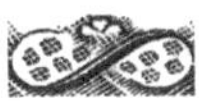

a patchwork of scraps, drawings and letters which were carefully cut in a mischievous way most calculated to annoy their authors; watching an indignant victim, he would silently laugh, shaking like a kettle that is just going to blow its lid off.

He had a gas stove in the kitchen and did quite a lot of fancy cooking. Occasionally he discovered that there were things that he had never eaten before and he would eat a lot of them, to compensate for all the years he had lived without them. When Eric first introduced him to kippers he had them daily for a week. At the time, if he poured out the tea he always held the teapot high up in the air so that it was doubtful whether the tea would land in the cups, but it always did; that was one of the remarkable things about Edward, he had the steadiest hands of anybody that I have met.

As he was on the ground floor, there were a lot of mice. He couldn't bear to set traps, so he put down crumbs in certain places so that they wouldn't go exploring into the wastepaper basket or the rubbish pail and keep him awake with their squeaks and rattling noises.

He had at this time very high moral principles and he sent any money that he earned which could be spared home to his mother, who put it in the Post Office Savings Bank. This was typical of him, he never had the courage to do this sort of thing for himself and his mother still bought his clothes for him at Pluck and Collins in Braintree. He loved his pearl-grey suits and looked after them carefully but he was very bad on handkerchiefs which he nervously fiddled with in his pockets, tying them in knots and biting them, he used a clean one

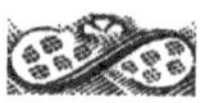

every morning. I came to the conclusion that he kept the commandments but broke most of the other laws. He got annoyed with Bowker [Beryl Sinclair] at one time and knowing that she disliked mice, he sent her a dead mouse in a matchbox by post. I think she was away when it arrived so it was pretty high by the time she opened it and she was very angry about this; he also gave her a nice little oil painting of a milkman and his van. He sent another friend, who had just had a baby, a French letter which so offended him that he didn't see Edward any more after it.

Eric found him a very difficult person to work with and painting at Morley College with him was unnecessarily complicated by a variety of troubles. He had more strongly than anyone else that I have met that habit of sensing that you were going to criticise or blame him for something, and to stop this, he forestalled you by accusing you of this very fault, however inconsistent it might be. He was also stimulated in his work by a competitive feeling which was annoying if you didn't wish to compete, and Eric didn't. He was very painstaking and would constantly repaint parts of his side of the wall so that there began to be some doubt as to whether it would be finished in time for the opening day.

These decorations at Morley College were being paid for by Sir Joseph Duveen, but he was in America and Professor Rothenstein was really the instigator of the scheme. He was keen that work of this kind should be given to young artists who would be willing for little money to have the chance of displaying their talents.

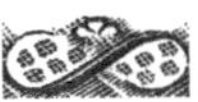

I met him for the first time at Morley College. His students were very much in awe of the little man; his correct diction, self-assurance and above all his knowledge and reputation made him very respected. As I was not one of his students and because he reminded me in appearance a little of our nurse Martha, I wasn't as terrified of him as I might have been. He was very pleased with the refreshment room. Bawden and Ravilious had, in doing so well, incidentally justified his beliefs in the merits of his pet scheme, and he hoped that further mural decorating jobs would be given to young artists now that the Tate Gallery tea room and Morley College had given a start to his plan.

On this occasion Rothenstein looked intently at the painting and having talked enthusiastically with Eric, he turned to look at Edward's wall and praised his illustrations to *As You Like It* and he went on from this to be equally enthusiastic about Shakespeare, ending with some query, I think, as to whether Edward enjoyed the comedies as much as he did. 'I don't know, I never read Shakespeare,' Edward replied in a flat cold voice. Deflated, Rothenstein without another word, turned round and walked out. I felt sorry for both of them. Poor Edward: it wasn't affected, it was perfectly true, his queer education had left the most extraordinary gaps in his general knowledge.

Edward and Eric's designs for Morley College were of different subjects but the period, except for Eric's boarding house, was all Elizabethan. To relate the different plays, they adopted a design of posts and scaffolding, so that the room looked at from a distance appeared to be the work of

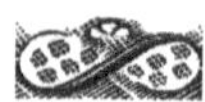

one man. Indeed very few people were able to differentiate between their painting.

On the left wall as you came in, Eric illustrated Ben Jonson's *Cynthia's Revels* and Marlowe's *Doctor Faustus*. On the wall facing the entrance, Edward did *The Tempest* and *As You Like It*. Eric did a boarding house, displayed like a doll's house with the front open. The Morley College decorations were to be opened by Mr Baldwin the Prime Minister, and a day or two before this, his private secretary Sir Geoffrey Fry came to look at the painting so that Mr Baldwin's speech should be appropriate. He was a short bald man of about forty, dark but with grey eyes. He was dressed in those discreet clothes that men with any connections with the Conservative Party usually wore, and carried the usual beautifully rolled umbrella and a dispatch case containing those most secret documents, the whole surmounted by the black hat which to me, with its past association with Augustus John, suggested that the wearer wished to counteract with this bogeyman emblem the effect of such extreme respectability as was implied by the rest of his clothes. He was familiar with the Elizabethan plays that Eric had illustrated, he talked well and afterwards invited Eric to his house.

On the opening day [February 6th 1930], Mr Baldwin said that after seeing the pictures the one thing that leapt to his mind was the feeling that the works were conceived in happiness and joy. The execution had evidently given real pleasure to the artists, and it was only in that spirit that any creative work could be done that was going to give pleasure to other people.

There were of course criticisms of the paintings in the usual papers and magazines. Only Mr Howard Hannay from the *London Mercury* bothered to look at the paintings closely and discovered which belonged to Ravilious and which to Bawden. Hardly any other critic got this right. I don't think Bawden intended to be half as comic as was supposed, he just did see people like that and he didn't like the conventional ideas of feminine beauty, like breasts or large eyes. And though Eric intended the doll's house to be satiric – it was founded on the bourgeois doll's house that I had made at Eastbourne and I was climbing up the stairs in the painting – he did not intend the other designs to be funny, and the muses floating in the sky were drawn from the Morley College mistresses.

After the official opening day, Queen Mary, learning that there was a painting of a doll's house, expressed a desire to see it. Eric and Edward were hastily sent for and, dressed in their best, they waited for her at Morley College. When she arrived she was surrounded by black-coated gentlemen like under-takers who smoothed her path in every way that they could. It was wrong to address her unless she first spoke and with the intermediary gentlemen as well, conversation with her was as difficult as though she could not speak English and was forced to have an interpreter.

Eric thought that she was fine and admired the royal bust and especially her toque. There was one rather awful moment when she lorgnetted the two pictures of King Edward and Queen Alexandra which hung in the morning room of the doll's house but she didn't say anything. She didn't really like the decorations and went away to see over the rest of the College.

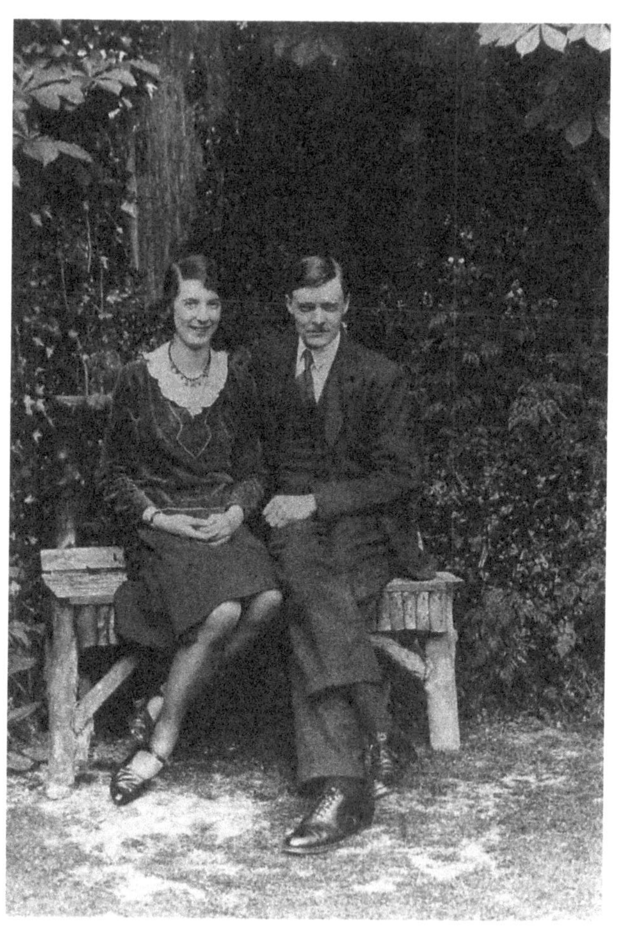

CHAPTER TEN

The problem now that Bob was gone was: what was I going to do? I wasn't absolutely sure that I was properly in love with Eric and felt that I didn't love either him or Bob as much as I had loved Betty at West Hill, although the circumstances of course were very different, but she was the only other love that I had for comparison. I realised that falling in love was largely a matter of not being able to obtain the person you wanted and because I didn't have to suffer doubts on Eric's account, I hadn't got into the desperate state that Bob had over me: on the other hand, I couldn't bear the thought of his belonging to anyone else and it obviously wasn't fair to go on making love and never getting any further. It did worry me that he wasn't quite a gentleman and that he had none of those attributes of solidity and respectability that were necessary for a family man, and I wanted a family if for no other reason than getting rid of my unfortunate menstruation.

I had now left my room in Hornton Street and a very nice woman called Miss Hughes had moved into it. I made friends with her and told her about my troubles; she was one of those people who, although they are old enough to be your mother,

treat you as a contemporary. She had already met Bob and now she asked Eric and me to tea. When he had gone she said that she thought he was charming and perfectly suitable for me to marry, she had imagined from my description that he would drop his 'aitches'. I was staying with the aunts and Aunt Edith also approved of him, though Aunt Lucy I felt was a little worried at the lack of nice people behind him. I couldn't stay with the aunts indefinitely and on the day I was due back in Eastbourne, I went round very early in the morning to see Eric in his rooms in Redcliffe Road. He was rather surprised to see me and we were constantly interrupted by his char lady who was bustling about, in fact it was a very inappropriate moment for saying: 'You are mine'. It was a large room with a pale green carpet and it was furnished with a yellow maple wood chest of drawers, two or three chairs and a child's cot with bars. This was not because he wanted or expected any children but because he liked the bars. He had a nice big wall clock which struck eighty-seven times when I was waiting for him one day. When at last the char lady had bustled into his tiny bedroom and kitchen combined, we sat on the cot and discussed whether we should have any children or not. Eric with his recent memories of the screams of his baby niece Gwen was very against them; but he said that we might have some in about five years – five years seeming such an infinite distance away that anything might have happened by then.

He wrote a letter to my father to tell him that we wanted to get married. My father wrote back saying couldn't we wait until like his friend Clifford Webb he had won his artistic spurs and he didn't like to think of his daughter developing

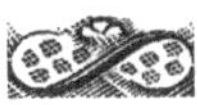

into a domestic drudge, etc. Clifford Webb was a friend of his who had been with him in Mesopotamia, he wasn't a particularly good artist and Eric wasn't flattered by the comparison and wrote back stating his income, which because of Morley College was about £400. It never got any higher than this, nor do I think it ever will. Eric was very pleased with his own work at that time because his wood engravings and Morley College were being very much praised by people whose praise was valuable. We agreed to wait till the summer and became officially engaged. Privately we didn't wait, because in the past it had been my promise to Bob and not the lack of a church service that had kept Eric from being my lover. Now that Bob was gone and we intended to get married, there wasn't any reason for my refusing any more.

Eric, having become engaged, had the unpleasant duty of visiting my family and introducing his own. The first public occasion on which our parents met was at the opening of the Morley College decorations.

He was very frightened of my family and, knowing that my parents did not approve of him, he very naturally didn't like them. I felt very emancipated by now and didn't care very much what my parents thought or said and I used to tell Eric the more ridiculous things they said about him because they amused me and, as they were my parents, they didn't seem to me to be at all important or to be taken seriously. My mother wanted to choose my trousseau and the decorating of our flat, it never struck her that it really wasn't her business. I tried to stop her but it resulted in such bitter quarrels that I gave in. She finished one of these battles, in which I had been arguing

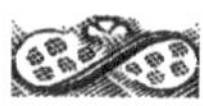

that as decorating was Eric's job, surely he ought to be able to decorate his own home, with: 'Well, artists have notoriously bad taste'.

Visiting Elmwood, Eric seemed to recede into his clothes and sat in our chairs with that apprehensive expression of a shitting dog. John and my sisters all liked him and as he appeared to be very mild, my mother did not mind him as much as she thought she was going to; but my father was still bitterly disappointed that I hadn't married Bob and being more of a snob than the others, he minded more about Eric's family.

Introduced to Eric's mother and father, I instantly liked his mother who was very sweet with that comfortable Devonshire way of calling you 'dear'. She was still very good-looking and her hair was quite black. Dad seemed quite harmless, his eyes were the most innocent blue and his hair a shining white. Looking on me as a young lady he behaved quite rationally, only putting a hot teaspoon on the back of my hand to see how I reacted. I had never seen anyone eat with a knife before and thought it was very remarkable, almost as clever as Chinese chopsticks. Dad so loved his food that he would become quite unconscious of the external world; bending low over his plate he gobbled up enormous helpings of pie. If you addressed a remark to him he would lift up his head un-seeingly and blink his eyes once or twice and enquire: 'Eh, what's that you say?'

One of the nicest things in Eric's home was the canary, which was very fond of him and would sit on his head or flut-ter on his fingers and peck at the chips from his wood-block

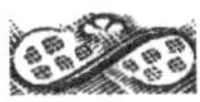

while he engraved. Eric was very good at whistling and by curling up the tip of his tongue and then straightening it in his mouth, he could produce a double note. The bird loved his whistling and would sing so loudly that we were unable to hear ourselves speak and he would have to be removed to another room.

Dad at this time was making a precarious living selling electric lightbulbs and when Frank came back to Eastbourne and was unable to get work, he joined Dad in his commercial travelling.

When I had gone, Mrs Ravilious said that she liked me and anxiously asked Eric if I realised how queer he was. He had grown so different from them that they thought there was something wrong with him (he did have sulking fits at times if he was offended and wouldn't speak very much for a day or two). She would I think rather he had married some nice chapel-going girl of his own class. She was a very humble person and knew her place and it was as embarrassing to her and Dad as it was to my parents that Eric and I should force them to meet one another. Dad was a little different; being one of the Lord's chosen he had no social stratum and was quite at ease with his bowler hat clapped well down over his ears wherever he went, that 'God is love' inside, giving him protection from the cold Philistine world. But he too was frightened of my family and Eric's presumption in becoming engaged to the Colonel's daughter.

When I stayed in London I met most of Eric's friends. When you are engaged, it is difficult to know how to introduce each other because fiancée is such an odious word, and

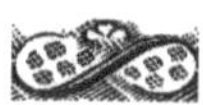

betrothed and affianced are equally ridiculous. In consequence of this, Eric would never introduce me to anyone.

At a party given by Douglas and Phyllis Bliss, I met most of his Royal College of Art friends and as most of them stayed friends I will describe them as best I can. Beginning alphabetically with B, there was [George] Branson and his wife [Mary] Brown: Branson was very tall and thin and had something wrong when young, probably an operation for glands which had affected one side of his face, giving his mouth a twisted look. He liked smart new things, Bliss nicknamed him the Bombinator. Brown was loud, cheerful and self-confident and once referred to Edward as 'that evil Bawden' which I thought very aptly described him. Then there was Bowk or Bowker who was really Mrs Beryl Sinclair; but she was so much larger than her husband whom she called 'poor little Sink' that he never succeeded in properly annexing her from her maiden name of Bowker which so suitably suggested her enormous size. At this party her hair was in ringlets and I noticed that she ate a large number of cakes. She had, as I have noticed in a great many fat women, social ambitions; it is as though their generous size encouraged them to spread themselves still further into huge country manors where they could further expand in house parties, point to points, dances and garden fêtes. Bowker's ambitions were not so much for a life in which she would be on intimate terms with the upper classes but to be herself a successful painter, surrounded by her equally distinguished friends. At this time she was backing Coxon, Moore, Ravilious and Bawden in this sweepstake.

She had a great many qualities as I learned later on and as to her great disappointment she had no children, her maternal instincts were diverted to her friends, and as my aunts had been a central bureau to our family, so in some ways was Bowker in her flat in Gloucester Terrace a centre for her friends. She was influenced at the College by Raymond Coxon's painting, an Impressionist method of putting on paint with delicate dabs and so thinly that the white canvas often showed through in places. This suited her feminine sensibilities and her pictures were fresh and sensitive. Her husband Robert Sinclair was a very successful newspaper editor; he was usually so exhausted by his day's work in Fleet Street that it was difficult to make friends with him. He grew a goatee beard and adopted an adult attitude to his wife's friends, as though they were all children and it was amusing to him to watch their nocturnal playing. He once painted two pictures and one of them was accepted by the London Group, while his wife's more mature work was thrown out by the selection committee. I think this may have given him the feeling that he too could have painted successfully if he had seriously chosen to do anything so puerile. He did not, in spite of this tolerant attitude, appear an unduly conceited man, but merely a very tired man. After years of research work, he produced a book about London called *Metropolitan Man*.

Raymond Coxon came from the Midlands and was at that time a friend of Harry Moore's. They were both short and fair and affectionate. Coxon was the more immediately likeable of the two, there was something about Moore even then that

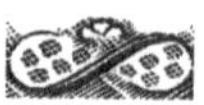

suggested he was confident of his own merits and a promising student rather than the friend of a contemporary. Coxon's wife was a very attractive Yorkshire girl called Edna Ginesi, she was as good a painter as he. They were a very popular couple and I always enjoyed going to their riverside house in Hammersmith. Every year they had a boat race party.

Barnett Freedman was from Stepney and was Jewish; he had been a particularly brilliant student and was a very amusing person and with his cockney accent, an excellent story teller. He was friendly at this time with the tall and cadaverously thin Cyril Mahoney, called 'Charlie', who was also doing a decoration at Morley College in the lecture hall. They both painted heavy and very unattractive women and were interested in tone and the effects of light and were great admirers of Sickert's painting. Barnett was short and going to be fat, his head was very big with light brown slightly curly hair growing rather far back from his dome-shaped forehead. His light grey eyes were rather enlarged by his horn-rimmed spectacles and his lips were thick like Edward's. He made his own cigarettes, carefully wrapping up the evil tobacco with his square short fingers and finishing the cigarette off with a prodigious lick from his large tongue. Once alight it would be almost engulfed in the fleshy embrace of his big lips and when it had burned almost to the root, so that watching him one wanted to warn him: 'Look out, you'll swallow it', he would in the nick of time bunch all his fingers and thumb into a tiny circle and pluck out the brown and wet remains which miraculously still burned, the smoke exuding from between his encircling fingers. Charlie too made cigarettes but not

having a mouth like Barnett's, the process was not so remarkable. Charlie had a glass eye but I thought that on the whole it improved his appearance, giving an interesting and piratical look to a face that, as nature intended it, might have belonged to a Sunday School superintendent or a postman. Barnett had recently married a design school student, a half-Sicilian girl called Claudia. Her father was a Sicilian ship's captain and her mother was a Devonshire woman. She was dark and a little resembled those ample women that Renoir used to paint. She dressed sometimes in tight-bodiced dresses with full skirts.

She was, I found, not very much liked, though no one had any definite reprehensible action against her that she had committed. When I met her, I understood this feeling of antipathy that she aroused. She spoke very carefully and sweetly to you, so carefully and sweetly that you felt convinced that these honeyed words were false. I never found that they were, nor probably did anyone else; there were murmurs that behind your back she was not so sweet; but I doubt if she was any more critical of people than anyone else. Eric, hearing her say, 'Look out, the cat will have it in a trice', realised that her way of speaking was grounded in a Victorian child's story book.

I think she wasn't a very intelligent woman but she was serious and probably unconsciously, ambitious to hold a social position like the Rothensteins did. Possibly her visits to their Sunday evenings at home were at that time her only introductions to a more enlightened society than the one in which she had been brought up; this was also true of Barnett

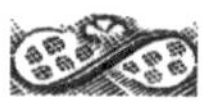

and the last time I saw them together reminded me strongly of Sir William and Lady Rothenstein.

The most attractive of Eric's friends was Betty Rea, she and her husband James were we thought in appearance the personification of the nice sweet couple who illustrated *Punch* jokes. Actually Betty was more intelligent than this and afterwards her life did not at all resemble the probable life of a *Punch* magazine wife. When I first knew her she was at the height of her beauty and charm. She had blue-grey eyes and a pointed face with rather large teeth which gave her a very attractive slightly wolfish look. Because she and James did not make love to each other in spite of their two children, they were both embarking on new adventures in their private lives. As goodness in the accepted Christian manner tends to make people dull, so correspondingly this irresponsibility and bad behaviour of Betty's made her immeasurably attractive and desirable and I shall never forget how lovely she looked at one of Bowk's parties in a white early Victorian dress. She was one of the ladies at the College and they usually held themselves rather aloof from the male students, who were seldom gentle-men by birth. She and Cecilia Dunbar Kilburn did not behave in so superior a manner and Cecilia became editor of the College magazine.

Cecilia had a lot of character, she was very dark with brown eyes and a protruding jaw. She was in the Sculpture School and it seemed a suitable occupation for her, though her drawings were sensitive and resembled Blake drawings, but an unhappy brooding Blake rather than a sublime one. She dressed well in colours that were becoming to her skin; she

was one of the few people who looked well in magenta. She had a flat near Eric in Redcliffe Rd and she was fond of him, whether maternally or otherwise he never discovered.

Both Eric and Edward had been members of the Design School at the College and I learned that there was a gulf between this school and the Painting School which was considered superior; painting, especially oils, being a higher and more aesthetically valuable form of art than commercial design. Eric had an inferiority complex because he was a designer and it took years to get rid of this feeling. It was an attitude I very much resented as I could not see that there was very much reason except tradition behind the scale of values attached to different forms of painting. Why should water-colour which is a far more difficult medium than oil, be less valuable; it is I suppose more perishable but I wonder if that is the only reason? Why should etching have a far higher price than engraving? The only answer I can give is that for some strange reason they have, in passe-partout frames, an irres-istible attraction for stockbrokers and businessmen who don't mind paying high prices for them, collecting them like postage stamps. I always felt strongly about things that weren't fair. I didn't like this prejudice against the designers, nor did I like that attitude towards inferior artists that their brother brushes adopted. In fact there were a lot of snares and pitfalls for an artist. To begin with, the word 'artist' was not used. Paul Nash, who taught Eric, used to say about something in his work that was not original, or some trick that he had employed, 'we want to get away from that sort of thing'.

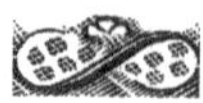

It was fatal to be too successful because your admirers invariably tired of your work and the unfortunate idol was left either dead or if he was lucky later on he might be resurrected if he adopted a new style and successfully changed his work in some way. Eric aimed modestly at being a good second-rate painter and engraver.

The students of this period were exceptionally successful ones, because a considerable number of them were older than is usual, having been soldiers in the 1914–18 war. The most brilliant painting school students were A K Lawrence who won the Rome Prize and became a painter of dull academy pictures of rather pretentious historical subjects and Gilroy, who also won the Rome Prize. Both of them were rather dashing painters with a love of display and Gilroy sensibly admitted this and became a very successful designer of Guinness posters, probably the best known posters in the country: 'Goodness my Guinness'. He also founded the Mustard Club for Colman's.

Another dashing student but in a different way was Basil Taylor, who was tall and dark and more sophisticated than most of the students. He was an irresponsible creature; coming into the room with a handful of paint brushes, he looked at them for a second, then impulsively threw the whole bundle of them into the air and left them lying where they fell and did the same thing another day with a handful of small change. He was gay and charming to women, making love with success to quite a number of them; strangely, they were nearly all called Lucy. His favourite at this time was an Eastbourne girl called Irene, with his north-country accent he

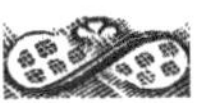

called her 'Reeny'. He had fashionable clothes, danced well and was friendly with a ballet dancer called Billy Chapel. I didn't meet him till years later and I never met Gilroy or Lawrence, so these descriptions are from hearsay.

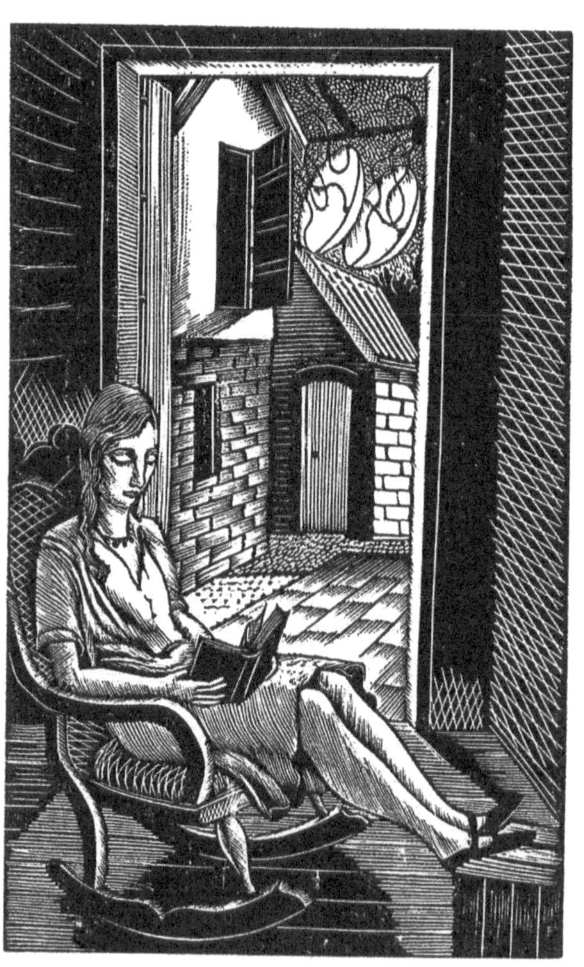

CHAPTER ELEVEN

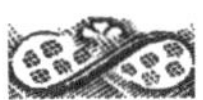

One day Eric was very surprised by Edward asking him if he would mind letting Charlotte Epton have his room when he was away for a weekend at Eastbourne. This was the first that he knew of the friendship between Charlotte and Edward which had begun in Italy where Edward had gone for his travelling scholarship the year after Eric. We were very pleased to think that after all he really had got a girlfriend.

Edward had met Bowker and Epton in Florence. Being strangers together in another country dispelled his shyness and he made friends with them, and he continued to write to Charlotte when she taught at Cheltenham Ladies' College. Now she was assistant to Bernard Leach's pottery in St Ives and learning that we had arranged to go to Cornwall for our honeymoon, she invited us to spend a day or so with her at Leach's Chinese-style home where she lived by herself.

Edward most bravely consented to be our best man and our wedding was arranged for July 5th [1930] at the Scottish church to which I used to go with the aunts in Kensington. Eric did not at all look forward to this intermingling of our families and friends. Though it was supposed to be a small,

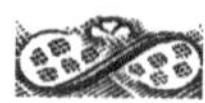

quiet wedding, somehow the number of people that we simply must invite seemed to swell.

On the day Edward put us all in a great state of alarm by arriving very late. He explained that he had intended to take a bus: but had changed his mind at the last moment as it was a fine day and decided to walk. When the moment came for him to produce the ring, it was carefully sealed up in an envelope.

I felt quite sure that I was in love with Eric by now and we neither of us felt apprehensive at having to make so many solemn promises.

The reception was at the aunts' house [13 Argyll Road, Kensington], and as it was a fine day we went out into their little, crazy-paved garden and ate strawberries and Vita Cream; this was a synthetic cream in which Aunt Edith had invested some money and as she was anxious to advertise it, she thought this was a splendid chance. My Uncle John took a cinematograph film of us coming out of the church and of people at the reception, most of the film he only managed to get either people's legs or their top halves and very few people seemed to accomplish any plan of action; like cats, they advanced a few steps and then suddenly turned abruptly and started away in a different direction. Eric was very nervous that his family would do something embarrassing and when my father who was sitting gloomily at the top of the garden with Uncle Harry, remarked to him: 'Hullo, you're looking very dejected', he was furiously angry with him and he was also enraged by the vicar's wife who, when I answered a toast which he should really have done, said: 'I hope you

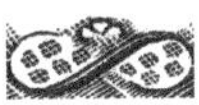

don't always intend your wife to speak up for you'. It was with a pretty disgruntled husband that I finally left the house, my spaniel Charles on a lead in one hand and a tennis racquet in the other. Nothing seemed to go right, we went to Kew on top of a tram, but when we got there we weren't allowed into the gardens because we had Charles with us.

For our honeymoon, we went to the Lizard in Cornwall. We didn't really want to go away very much but in the same way that we had obliged my family by doing the conventional thing and marrying in a church, we meekly went on honeymoon. The journey didn't start very well, our seats were booked in a carriage with a funeral party of three people in black, one of whom, a neurotic-looking woman, shrank away in terror from Charles and said that she didn't like dogs. We calmed her, reassuring her that he wasn't an ordinary dog and his respectful gaze soon reassured her and before the end of the journey, she had timidly patted his solemn head.

We spent a day at Falmouth so that I could meet my sister-in-law Evelyn and her husband Vernon and daughter Gwen and then we went on to the Lizard. We didn't like it very much; Eric thought the colour of the vivid green grass and the intense blue sea wasn't the beautiful combination of colours which it was reputed to be and we ate far too much cream and had to go for long walks to digest it. After a week we were glad to go to St Ives to see Charlotte Epton. She was a very lively and energetic person with short dark hair, dark eyes and a small mouth and a long face. She welcomed us very warmly and laughed long and loudly at our troubles. She was dressed when we first met her in a coat and skirt, felt hat and a fur

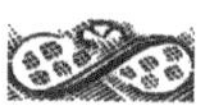

tippet round her neck, things that Eric particularly disliked. I thought how much my mother would have approved of Charlotte in these clothes which were I believe ones that Mrs Epton had bought for her daughter. She was living in a Chinese kind of house that Mr Leach the potter for whom she worked had built outside St Ives. She worked very hard, getting up very early at six o'clock in the morning to dip hundreds of tiles in glaze.

The next day we made some pottery and dipped a number of tiles in glaze. Mr Leach was an awkward-looking man; he made pots and dishes like the old English ones with a pattern like the trail of a rat running across them. He wasn't I suppose a very original craftsman but he was a very able potter and having lived in China, which country had visibly affected him, he knew a great deal and had taught Staite Murray who was considered the best potter at that time and Michael Cardew and Charles Vyse, a friend of Aunt Edith's.

I found a real leech at the bottom of a dried-up pond in the garden and as I had never seen one before, I brought it in and we put it in a bowl of water where it swam round quite contentedly. Later on when we were having supper, it came out and we found it crawling in a sinister manner towards us.

Charlotte asked our advice about Edward who was writing her most affectionate letters and who apparently wanted to marry her in theory; but when he met her would stay on the other side of the room and look very apprehensive. It was a difficult problem and we didn't quite know what to say. Personally I felt that Edward should be overjoyed that anyone

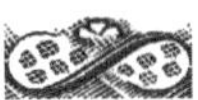

as nice as Charlotte should even contemplate him as a husband but I couldn't say that.

Our first home in London together was a flat in Stratford Road on the borders of Kensington and Earls Court. The landlady Miss Parker lived with a cousin in the basement, she was a most dismal creature with the sallow complexion of one who has seldom seen daylight and her eyes, as though unaccustomed to light, goggled weakly through strong-lensed spectacles. She spoke with an accent which we later decided was peculiar to Earls Court, it was slow and terribly sad, the words falling unwillingly from a mouth already filled with something else.

We had only been there a day or two when Eric was called upon by an insurance agent, who let loose a flood of persuasion upon him. Eric confessed that he couldn't understand this kind of subject. The man eventually left, after half-convincing him of the advisability of being insured. The next day six pages of explanation from the man arrived. Eric attempted to read them but the phrase 'loan against the bonus' was too much and feeling slightly guilty, he wrote a firm refusal.

At none of my six schools had I learned anything that was at all useful in a house. I had as a Girl Guide taken Cookery, Domestic Science and Child Nurse badges but I had failed to pass any of them, although I did get a lot of other less useful subjects. Mummy had a theory that the cook would leave if we went into the kitchen so that I knew nothing about cooking and when I first lived in Hornton Street I didn't even know how to make tea. Eric was quite good at doing a few

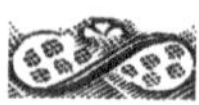

simple things like boiling potatoes and making custard and omelettes, and having grasped the rudiments I found it wasn't really very difficult.

We had a daily char called Mrs Ainger, but she wouldn't do the cooking because she wasn't strong enough; she had recently had a stroke and three of her fingers remained paralysed. She was a wonderful old lady and the whole time she was with us, she only was the cause of one saucer being broken; she had put it on the window sill and the cat had knocked it off. She was a Yorkshire woman with a flat, rather owl-like face. She was extremely small; she had been a six months baby and had worked in a factory in the north when she was a child for 9d a week. She had spent most of her life in London; her husband who was now retired had been a Kensington road man and had started work every morning at five o'clock. Her previous place had been with a hat shop woman called Madame Clare and she still did for her on some afternoons, but Madame Clare wasn't doing too well herself and Mrs Ainger used to find her sometimes the worse for drink. She herself liked a half pint every evening which she would drink with her husband at the pub across the way from their basement home in Child Street. We found that she couldn't resist the temptation of finishing off any bottles that Eric left about. As it was her only weakness and she never took very much, Eric enjoyed leaving her small quantities and nothing was said. She was also deaf in one ear because a waiter had banged a paper bag behind her one day when she was washing up in a hotel in Cromwell Road. In this same place, she had accidentally shut a cat in the oven but she smelled his

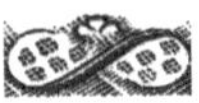

singeing fur in the nick of time. She walked with a queer rocking motion, her feet very much turned up at the toes and often Eric, coming down in the morning, would fail to see her, his normal line of vision being inches above her head and colliding with her he would sweep her half across the room before he could stop.

As Eric's father had always cooked the breakfast at home, Eric cheerfully cooked the breakfast for me. He loved bacon and thought I couldn't fry as well as he could which was quite true. I hate frying things because the fat flies out and burns me. I never cooked breakfast but I managed the other meals. He liked to choose pale pink back bacon in the shop. I didn't know the names of the different pieces of meat or what it ought to look like and I found shopping very difficult because the shopkeepers were always in a hurry and had no wish to explain the differences. We used to play 'rummy' after lunch and the one who lost had to clear the meal away.

The Rothensteins used to have open house every Sunday evening and I went with Eric to one of these parties very soon after we were married. As well as Professor William, I had met his brother Albert Rutherston at the private view of *The Haggadah*, which Albert had illustrated, and his daughter Betty Rothenstein. She was a dark and small-featured girl and made me feel very uncomfortable when we were first introduced by looking me up and down in a strange way. Albert Rutherston was like his brother in appearance but was far more genial and less dignified. We didn't think much of the illustrations, they were too mannered and now he obviously never took the trouble to really look at an object like a tree or

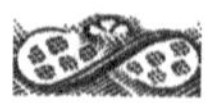

a gate and draw it with care and love as he probably did when he was younger and less successful.

This first party was a special one for Eric because he was to meet Max Beerbohm. He loved Max Beerbohm's drawings and books, and Geoffrey Fry had given us a set of his works for a wedding present. He came in late wearing a ginger-coloured tweed suit, which made him look rather conspicuous among the other smooth and darkly clothed men. Eric was introduced but his conversation with him was rather spoiled by Lady Cunard, whom Eric complained afterwards to me would whicker at him so that Max Beerbohm's pearls were constantly being lost.

Rothenstein had that morning taken him to see the wall decoration at Morley College and he was very pleased with them. When he heard that Eric was wax polishing them, he offered to come along and help. Already he affected to be a very old and very decrepit man, so that this offer was in no way serious. James Stephens the poet was also introduced and he made an arrangement to meet Eric at Morley College one afternoon, so that he could be shown the decoration. Eric dutifully went along but no James Stephens arrived. Eric had half expected that he wouldn't and ruefully said: 'Never trust an Irish poet'.

These Rothenstein evenings were rather an ordeal from my point of view. I didn't mind if I was left alone so that I could watch people but Mrs Rothenstein was always conscientiously introducing one to new people just when you had broken the ice with your latest neighbour. I'm happiest really with one or two people, and don't like talking parties. They were embarrassing

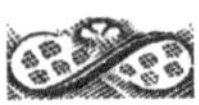

too for Eric because Rothenstein was so pleased with Morley College that it had gone to his head and he was constantly referring to it and introducing Eric who felt that people must be sick of the subject and somehow think him pleased or responsible for this shower of praise. There were at these parties some of the silliest women that I have ever come across.

Cecilia [Dunbar Kilburn] asked us to supper at her flat in Redcliffe Road and this turned out to be one of the most extraordinary evenings that we ever spent. She had staying with her a pretty girlfriend of her younger sisters and this girl returned unexpectedly after we had eaten our supper and were looking through a book of the collected works of Dr Heinrich Hoffmann, the author of *Struwwelpeter*. Presently the telephone rang and the girl, Lucy, asked if Mr Baird might come and join us: she had I think intended to spend the evening with him but their previous arrangement had fallen through. We looked forward to meeting Baird who at that time was busily perfecting his television transmission for the BBC. We were warned that he was a little strange and that he didn't approve of intoxicating drinks. I can't now remember his face, there was nothing remarkable about it, he was a small very ordinary Scotsman who seemed to be defending himself against imaginary criticism; he was more truculent towards Eric than to the rest of us. When it was about eleven o'clock, he asked if we would all accompany him back to his house on Box Hill where he would show us his television set. While he was telephoning directions to the Daimler hire people, from whom he hired a car every evening, Lucy hastily

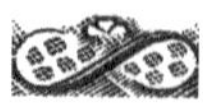

whispered to us that this was not an unusual request as he was frightened of going home alone.

Driving into Surrey, the conversation turned to murders and Eric said that the overwhelming interest and space taken up by them in the newspapers disgusted him; this seemed so obvious a distaste to us that we were surprised when Mr Baird warmly defended the public interest in crime and continued with a talk on the various methods that a murderer might employ in getting rid of a body. It was quite dark by now and the car climbed up the final hill which was shrouded on either side by overhanging trees. The last time that I had driven up this hill was with my cousin Bobby on his Norton motor bike when I was fourteen, it looked so different now that I didn't remember that I had ever been there before. When we got out of the car, blinded by its headlights we could at first see nothing of our surroundings, till slowly we became aware of a great iron gate and Mr Baird fumbling for a bell. A storm lantern came swaying towards us from behind the gate, dimly lighting up the figure of a man dressed in a blue naval coat with large brass buttons like the coats worn by pirates. Apprehensively we walked through and the gate was shut and carefully locked behind us. Led by Baird, we stumbled over the garden and were ushered at last into a typical Surrey house interior with pitch pine woodwork in the hall. Baird rushed to a wooden cabinet at one end of the room and twisted and turned its knobs, but nothing happened. The pirate Roberts informed his master that the electric light had failed but he would try to put it right before twelve o'clock, at which hour television closed down. We were given sherry in the drawing

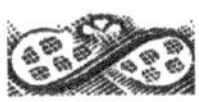

room, part of our minds still speculating as to whether this secrecy and padlocking of his house was really necessary to Mr Baird. If he left his home unguarded, would Russian agents or villainous Germans creep in to steal his latest discoveries?

Mr Baird seemed determined to make our flesh creep as much as he could but whether this was natural or he was trying to pull our legs, we couldn't be sure. The others grew silent but I continued rather desperately to make conversation with him; somehow my aunts kept cropping up in my attempts and I knew that Eric would notice this and probably blame me afterwards. I really was interested in television and would like to have known more about it; I enquired if these discoveries and experiments were alarming to him. I was standing beside him as I asked and we were all disconcerted by his reply, a terrified affirmative and, looking closely at him, I realised that he really genuinely was extremely frightened.

At last the electricity was mended but it was just too late, the BBC was singing *God Save the King*; the words transformed into light and visibility were a stream of spots and dashes like an illuminated piano roll. Before we went, he made a final offer of entertaining, asking if I would like to see the grave of Peter Labelliere, who was buried upside down on Box Hill.

Outside, the chauffeur had naturally grown restless and he seemed very relieved to see us and feeling in a giggling mood after so much intensity and nervous apprehension, we started off. We were however still not out of the wood; the chauffeur confessed that we were lost. He turned down a narrow lane hoping to get back to the main road, but we stopped quite helpless with laughter when the car lights illuminated a sign

post with 'To the Cemetery' glaring in black letters on its shining white arm.

A day or two later, I mentioned this strange visit to Bowker. 'Oh, Baird,' she condescendingly said, 'I know him, he used to live in the flat above us and bring me down his manuscripts to have their spelling mistakes corrected.' It was a relief to find that in her eyes, he was quite a normal human being to be pitied rather than feared.

Eric had painted an interior of Edward in his back room in Redcliffe Rd with the cartoons for Morley College stacked like organ pipes in the corner behind him. Edward had seen how well the arrangement of the room looked and asked him to paint it. Mrs Ainger was very pleased with the fireplace and said she always felt like laying a fire in it which we thought high praise. There were several projects for more mural decorations and Sir Philip Sassoon, a friend of Geoffrey Fry's, toyed with the idea of having Eric to do one of his rooms; but he finally gave it to Rex Whistler, and Geoffrey Fry asked Eric to do a screen for his flat in Portman Square. Visiting the Frys was rather an ordeal because we weren't used to butlers and footmen and though I had stayed with my wealthier relations, I didn't like this way of living. I had a liver attack at a rich cousin's house through swallowing my salmon too quickly, feeling that the footmen were anxious to remove my plate. Eric was apt to knock things over on the Frys' polished table and when absorbed in some topic of conversation, would fail to perform those minor social duties such as lighting his neighbour's cigarette or opening the door for his hostess.

Alathea Fry was very sweet and earnest but was constantly being ill. They had one very healthy-looking daughter called Jennifer with large eyes and a tiny nose. Fry was a bad husband and father because he fussed over his wife and daughter, treating them like children and then was exasperated when they behaved like children. Evelyn Waugh had married Lady Fry's sister Evelyn Gardner and he had evidently been deeply impressed with the family, and reading his early books, I am always reminded of them.

Eric painted very smoothly in oil paint at this time. He did Fry's screen on Essex Board as he preferred painting on board or wood to canvas and when the panels were finished, he sprayed them with wax diluted with turps. Something went wrong somewhere because they came out all over with tiny cracks like an old master, but that was some time later. The scene was a garden formally arranged behind a tennis court, on which people were playing tennis. The garden was founded on the Frys' country house at Oare where Eric made drawings of their hard court. I don't think it was altogether a success; a sophisticated young man visiting the Frys said: 'It's very underground, isn't it'.

When the panels were finished and he was taking them with the help of the porter up in a lift to the Frys' flat, the porter looked at the painting and said that the landscape was alright but he didn't think much of the figures. It was true that Eric wasn't very interested in people as subjects to draw and found it difficult to adapt them suitably into the shapes he wanted them. He was attracted by new faces if they reminded him of pictures or even of other people that he had liked.

I suppose we all are. We used sometimes to divide people into various classes, Bliss had started this at the College and would also find animals or epitaph phrases to fit friends.

Eric and Edward taught twice a week at the College and the money for this paid the rent. Eric did a big drawing (which he later tinted) out of our back window, adding fireworks and figures strolling and climbing about in the gardens. Edward was painting in oil paint, beach scenes stippled in a Seurat-like manner. Now that I was married and had a spare room, we wanted to rescue Margaret from Eastbourne. For a long time I had been urging her to come to London, but always she demurred, saying: 'Well I can't, I'm going to tea with Betty Eden on Friday', or with some such short-sighted reason. A young man of Billy's called Bo Waterfield finally, with Billy's help, persuaded her to make the necessary arrangements and at last she left home and set about learning facial massage and manicuring at a place where they trained people in beauty culture. She lodged with us till she found a room of her own, and directly her training was finished, she got a job at Pontings. Being more of a lady than most of the girls, the old men who look after shops like Pontings readily employed her and afterwards she went to a shop in Oxford Street where they had lice and from there to Harrods.

While she was staying, the Coxons invited us to their boat race party and she came with us. I saw here for the second time Basil Taylor, whose extravagant behaviour at the College I had so often heard about; he was the only man there that Margaret particularly noticed. Later in the evening, Eric went back as Basil had invited everyone to his rooms, but I was unwell so

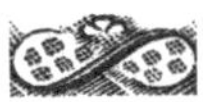

stayed at home with Margaret. When Eric arrived, Basil was so drunk that all the people went back again to the Coxons.

Charlotte Epton also came to stay and became truly engaged to Edward, though he was still being difficult and had made one attempt to get out of it altogether.

We saw quite a lot of the Frys and they invited us several times to stay the weekend with them at Oare [House, Marlborough]. Their having so much money made being friends with them rather more complicated than our usual friendships with people who had similar work or incomes. It wasn't that we didn't believe that they genuinely liked us, but it was the attitude towards this friendship that other people adopted that was annoying.

The more sophisticated might explain it by noticing that Geoffrey Fry invariably had a group of attractive-looking young men whom he entertained in London or at Oare, and that although he obviously wasn't a practising homosexual, his natural instincts were really of this kind. Or, more truthfully, that the Frys liked collecting rum people, it being the only chance he and Alathea had of contact with the outside world. Although money and social position had become a wall over which they never climbed, a selection of extraordinary occupants of the outer world could be invited inside. Geoffrey confessed to us that he had not seen the Piccadilly Underground wall decoration because he never used the Underground Railway. Other more stupid people thought that we would welcome this friendship as a splendid chance for making money which was one of the most annoying reasons, or the equally silly one that we enjoyed social climbing.

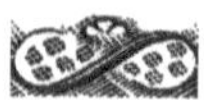

The truth was that their money was slowly destroying both Geoffrey and Alathea and why anyone should imagine that their position was enviable, it was hard to understand.

Staying at Oare was a nuisance in some ways because beforehand I had to try to get all the paint and London dirt off my hands and Eric had to clean himself too and look at the things in his pockets as the valet at Oare used to lay the contents of them in lines on the dressing table. We either went by train or by road in Geoffrey's Rolls-Royce; he had taken great trouble, so that its index number was GF.

Oare House had been a pretty Georgian farmhouse with a lime avenue leading up to the iron gates of the courtyard. The architect Clough Williams-Ellis had enlarged the side of the house with two wings and it had a white balustrade running round the top and a flat roof. Geoffrey told us how one day, Gilbert Spencer had come to lunch and he had asked his opinions of the additions. Spencer had replied that there was too much wood in the windows and later on had remarked what a nice mossy lawn he had. This was a beautifully kept lawn that sloped gradually down to a swimming pool and beyond were fields and a further pond with a plantation of trees on one side and some natural fir trees on the other. The Downs were to the right of this view which Geoffrey preserved with determination. In the centre of the lawn was a squatting lead negro holding up a sun dial and on the left, a walled-in flower and vegetable garden and the red tennis court behind.

A young man whom we met several times was supposed to be one of Mr Baldwin's favourites; his name was Geoffrey Lloyd. I found him a very annoying person because he loved

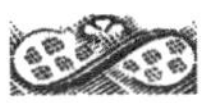

talking to show off what a clever young man he was. He would put us on one side of his arguments and himself on the other, presuming we held views which we probably didn't at all and then, taking the obviously more reasonable side, would oh so cleverly demolish our presumed defence: 'You as an artist will think this' – Oh, will we? I asked Geoffrey Lloyd if he was related to *Lloyd News* which embarrassed Eric but tickled Fry. I think he was a kind young man at heart and he may be better now he is older and taken to testing gas-filled chambers like Professor Haldane.

People were necessary to Geoffrey Fry if only in their capacity as audience, because he too loved talking. Without enough stamina to become an architect or a politician, talking had almost become his career. It was true that he was Mr Baldwin's private secretary, but that was not personally creative work. He loved style and his Cambridge associations and his brief friendship with Rupert Brooke had in their various ways affected him. He loved the works of Max Beerbohm but by the time we knew him, he had almost ceased to read and was already declining into that sad older people's world of exasperation and illness. With his Quaker family behind him, he had high principles and was an excellent landlord and squire to the local people; but he was living in the nineteenth century and paying so that he shouldn't have to be bothered by the ugly reality. He was devoted to Mr Baldwin and greatly admired him. He hated war and was most terribly upset by the Italian attack on the Fuzzy-wuzzies as he called the Abyssinians.

Because we weren't interested in politics and because of Geoffrey's loyalty to his chief, as he called Mr Baldwin, they

were never discussed. Later on when we came to know a little more about the dangerous state of Europe, I tried to judge whether Mr Baldwin had indeed been so much to blame as our left-wing friends maintained. From my limited acquaintance with these left-wing people and judging by the wave of popularity of books about the last war, I think there was a strong pacifist feeling among them. One of the main arguments for Communism was that it was to stop war. I'm sure that Mr Baldwin was wrong in trying to placate the Fascists and Nazis but his reasons for doing so were honestly pacific. I don't believe the Socialists wanted to spend millions on armaments any more than he did, personally I know I didn't. Even if the Labour Party had made an alliance with Russia, events have proved the Nazis wouldn't have changed their plans. But why, if Mr Baldwin knew that there was this danger, didn't he warn everyone? We wondered later when events became even more threatening, whether Fry even knew what was happening; but he told Eric that he too read Mr Cockburn's news-sheet [*The Week*] which at that time was for us one of the sources from which we and our friends had what seemed authentic information. Some time before the scandal of King Edward and Mrs Simpson, he was surprised and alarmed to find that Eric knew about it and had known about it for some months.

It was more difficult for my generation who hadn't been harrowed by details of the Russian Revolution, to understand this quite blindly antagonistic attitude that the older people like Geoffrey and my parents had adopted about Russia. This fear of Communism seemed to swamp their natural judgements and anything, even Nazis and Fascists, seemed preferable.

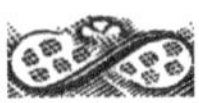

At times I longed to shake Geoffrey as when he made fussy old-ladyish complaints to his butler about draughts and was amusing at the expense of Miss Smith. He was potentially a good and witty person and I felt exasperated that someone as intelligent and sensitive as he was should allow himself to be so silly. There seemed to be quite a number of old retired retainers living about the house, an ancient nurse and Miss Smith who had been Jennifer's governess. She was a snobbish, sweet simple woman and instead of leaving when Jennifer no longer needed her, she had stayed on as a household help to Alathea. Actually there was very little for her to do and she exasperated Geoffrey who felt that she should have left; but with his usual sentimental panderings to his wife's and daughter's wishes she had been kept on. He revenged himself at meal-times by constantly referring to her for her opinion on some subject or other of which she could obviously know nothing and force her blushing: 'Oh, Sir Geoffrey' into conversation in which she was quite out of her depth.

The young man who was at this time his most constant companion was called John Weyman. He was dark and nice-looking, in most respects a typical public schoolboy, correct and sensitive and although he would I suppose writhe at this adjective, 'a sweet boy'. He was very surprised at lunch one day when I revealed to him the rather shocking fact that gravy was made of blood.

A cottage nearby had been let to Lord Francis [probably Sir Eric Phipps] and his wife [Frances] and they came to play tennis with us. He was short and kind and faintly resembled a P G Wodehouse lord and she was very young and utterly

engaging. On the tennis court, her indulgent husband watched over her every stroke and when she got one over would ecstatically cry: 'Isn't she sweet?' She was small and fair and exquisite and at dinner, with round blue eyes, she told us that of course she believed in fairies and even I applauded. The only thing that was worrying was the shadowy future, 'what will she be like when she is older?' and 'isn't it slightly shameful and letting down the rest of your sex to give men so exactly what they want?'

Neighbours who were as different as could be to these were Miss Mona Wilson and G M Young who lived in Oare village. She was I should think about fifty years old, a big woman with a youthful figure and decided features, her face spoilt by her discoloured teeth because she insisted on smoking a pipe. He was, in appearance at any rate, living in an even earlier period than Geoffrey. We placed him as early eighteenth century, small with a round bald head and a wart on his face; Eric said that he looked well with me. He thought I looked like Joseph Highmore's *Pamela* and he was the man in the picture of her who opened the door and perpetually surprised her. G M Young was a critic and writer, and she had written books on Blake and Sir Philip Sidney; he and Miss Wilson read Greek to one another which impressed Geoffrey. She sat on the local bench which seemed surprising to me as she shared a house with Mr Young and however innocent their relationship might be, I knew that a town like Eastbourne would never have tolerated her on its bench because of this. She had known Ricketts and Shannon and had pictures by them in her house. Eric didn't think very highly of the works of Ricketts

and Shannon and seeing him looking at these pictures, I wondered if young men in twenty years' time would adopt this sniffy attitude to pictures by Ravilious and Bawden. Miss Wilson and G. M. Young were great walkers and they knew and loved every inch of their good downland country. There was a pretty lumping hill called Martinsell beside Oare village and to walk up this was a constitutional for Fry's guests. It was very necessary because the food at Oare House was so good that everyone naturally ate too much of it.

Underlying all this surface enjoyment of good talk and excellent food, there was a feeling of sadness because the house and garden were a setting for something which would never take place. Clough Williams-Ellis's architecture with its green shutters and Georgian façades reminded us of *The Beggar's Opera* stage decoration. One felt that it was terrible to Geoffrey that he had no son and yet if he had had a son, one knew that because he would have expected so much from him and loved him so deeply, inevitably they would have quarrelled. Alathea and Jennifer were all very well but they were women and children and Alathea with her lovely generosity and enthusiasms – 'Oh, do let's', was not, however much he might love her, a respectable person. But why probe underneath, let us play golf with Alathea and watch her drive six spanking new golf balls into the swimming pool and later listen to Geoffrey's slow Cambridge voice, drawling slowly and enjoying to the full the flavour of his adjectives and then let us bounce on the large, soft bed so lately occupied by Mr and Mrs Baldwin and in the morning, drink delicious tea: Eric would like a mistress called 'Morning Tea'.

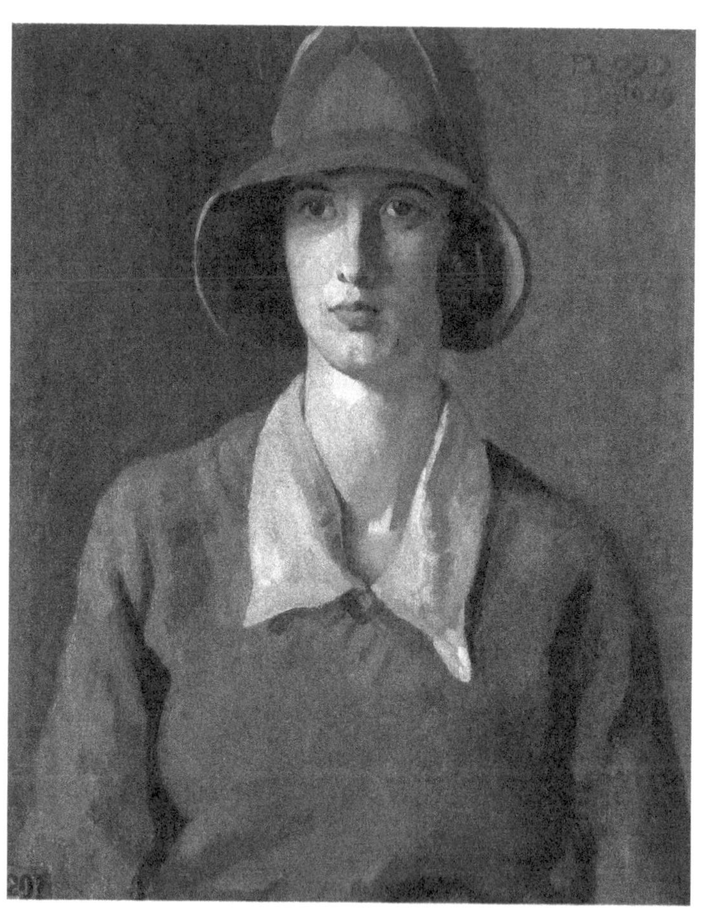

CHAPTER TWELVE

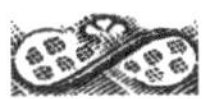

Barnett Freedman had acquired through his wife's Sicilian connections some very fine old Italian puppets. One of them was in shiny armour and they were large in size. He was naturally very pleased and talked of making a painting of them. Eric, who had recently finished his portrait of Edward at work on the picture of Clacton pier, thought that Barnett painting his puppets would be a very good companion piece. I can't remember now whether he wrote to Barnett or asked him personally, but whichever it was, Barnett wrote a letter saying that he didn't want to join Eric's collection of freaks. The other freak he referred to was Bowker whom Eric had also painted and drawn. We were naturally very insulted at this but I don't think Barnett had any idea how insulting his letter was to Eric and came round a few days later to ask if he could borrow £10 which he honestly returned to us later on. Barnett had been very sweet before we were married because he had cautioned Eric that making love to your new wife wasn't necessarily as simple as you might think. Apparently he and Claudia hadn't known what you did on the first night of their honeymoon and Claudia had had to go to the doctor the

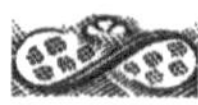

next day to find out. Eric was very touched by this confidence and naturally didn't disclose the fact that we had been already making love for some months, having found out for ourselves how to do so.

Our nearest friends besides Aunt Lilian [Gunter] who only lived a few doors away were the Reas. Betty had just had her second baby; he arrived with one of his eyes blacked which made him look like a pugilist, her other little boy was very sweet but very naughty. They had a very nice house, beautifully decorated, and were as about as charming a family as you could want. The Coxons, when they were visiting us one day, said that there was a flat becoming vacant by the river at Hammersmith. Eric was getting pretty tired of Earls Court and Kensington so we went quickly to look. It was a ground floor flat at the corner of Upper Mall and Weltje Rd, and Eric at once decided to take it. The previous tenants were a couple called Conran. He worked in Scotland Yard and although he was only a clerk and not one of the big five, this gave him a romantic flavour and small boys in the neighbourhood would do anything for him because of this association. They had quarrelled very violently with their landlady who was the wife of an etcher called Robert Austin. Robert Austin was a nice north-country man with a very developed business sense and he also taught at the Royal College of Art. His brother Fred, who was also an artist, lived in the middle flat and an old school friend of Mrs Austin's called Miss Kemp lived at the top of the house. She taught music at Morley College and St Paul's School and played the piano extremely well.

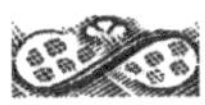

Mrs Austin was small and friendly with a particularly nice voice and at first we liked her and were inclined to side with her rather than the plaintive Mrs Conran, an untidy woman with china-blue eyes who seemed beset with children and household cares. Very quickly our opinion of Mrs Austin began to change and we found that her reputation as the meanest woman and the worst landlady in the district was only too justified. At first this odd behaviour of hers about sixpences was quite amusing but it also stirred in one that feeling of determination that we wouldn't allow ourselves to be so outrageously 'done' by her. A detailed description of all our battles would be too boring for me to tell you, but the interesting thing about the woman was that in every other respect she was particularly intelligent and charming. She had written several quite successful novels and I think had left Oxford with a first class degree, so that it was strange that she should court unpopularity in this way. Her father had been a particularly astute lawyer and I believe he had accused her of extravagance in buying our house which was expensive when she bought it and then moving from it into a prettier house further down the Mall which she really couldn't afford. Obviously this feeling that she had paid too much for our house was at the bottom of her mean behaviour to its tenants; she had behaved just as badly to her brother-in-law and her old school friend, though they were less able to complain and didn't pay nearly as much rent as we did. She was carrying her third baby at the height of her strange behaviour to us and wept on Eric when I was out one day, so maybe it was an eccentricity which she couldn't help. We both loathed quarrelling

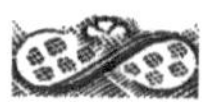

with people and this battle quite spoilt the last year, at any rate for me, of our life in Hammersmith.

In this flat we eliminated most of the marks of my mother's taste which had dominated our flat in Kensington and we left behind in the loft at the old flat the more repellent of our wedding presents. The house had a small front garden and the river ran along under the embankment across the road with Hammersmith Bridge about two hundred yards down to the left and the Bemax factory blocking the view to the right. Moored just opposite the house was an old ship called *The Stork* where orphans and boys from bad homes were trained to be sailors. We had friends and acquaintances all along the waterfront. Beginning with Maxwell Fry's house by the bridge where there were a number of very pretty houses adjoining the boat-houses, where young men in their white short trousers were continually getting in and out of their long, narrow, unsafe-looking boats; then there were twisting passages before you reached our part of the river. There was a very large house beside the passage which seemed empty but was really occupied by an eccentric old lady who walked about dressed in a queer patchwork of clothes like a human caddis-worm, part newspaper, part rag and her grey hair, matted and curled, hung about her ears. She had a big collection of stray dogs and seemed a nice-natured old thing and I never heard anyone speak about or remark on her strangeness. In London these odd people are just accepted without comment. The newspaper shop, run by two queer old women which supplied us with papers, was called The Sabines, yet no one seemed to think this odd. None of our friends told us about Chiswick

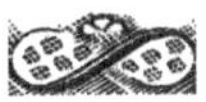

Park either and we had the pleasure of discovering this for ourselves; but before I tell you about this other end of our district, I will continue upstream. At the end of the passage there was a pub called The Doves. The first house on Upper Mall was a nice Georgian one with a magnolia tree in the garden which was occupied by some nuns; it seemed rather a waste to us that nuns should live in this pretty house, especially as Conran said scornfully of them: 'Oh, they are only rich old girls playing at it.'

I don't know who lived in Kelmscott; perhaps Miss May Morris, I think she was still alive then. In another big house with stables lived the writer Naomi Mitchison, but we didn't know her; she looked wildly untidy on the rare occasions on which we saw her. Across the road from our house in Watermist House lived an architect called Randall Wells whose wife did embroidery and who filled the house with decorated objects and needlework pictures. We only came to know her just before we left so we never went inside the house, but Barbara knew her and was very amused when she had proudly told her that she had been married before and that their daughter Rosebud was a love child. There was a very large house before you reached the Bemax factory which was a club for employees of Lyons and we envied them their billiard tables which we could see through the windows, and people liked watching the nippies come in the evenings and at weekends to take their boats on the river.

The next passage was exciting to walk down because after passing a very old shop, it skirted first the water works, through the windows of which you could see two enormous

pumps at work and then it ran by the electricity works, a large new building which jigged and revolved inside with a hundred complicated machines. There were two pubs very close to one another here. First came The Ship, whose sign had been painted by Mrs A P Herbert, and then Mr Herbert's favourite pub The Black Lion. This part of the river bank was called Hammersmith Terrace and it was in the middle of this that the Coxons and the Herberts lived. They were more fortunate than us because their gardens came right down to the river without having the road running along in front as we did. In the last house of the Terrace lived the Bergels; he was in an advertising agency called Crawford's and she had been at the College and was the daughter of the *Punch* artist Lewis Baumer, which was considered rather a shameful thing for her.

There was a barge made into a boat-house moored further along here and the houses again had the road between them and the river. Even further along was our landlady Mrs Austin and then Mr Nigel Playfair's house with its large semi-circle of window which he had had built by Mr Randall Wells. Opposite these houses was a little island called the 'Ey of Ait' which you could visit at low tide. The road ended with a narrow passage which ran along in front of Chiswick Church. Along this was a row of very old cottages like country cottages where once salmon fishers had lived. The road turned right here but there was a footpath round Chiswick Churchyard where one passed the tomb of the painter and accomplished gentleman Philippe de Loutherbourg. Sometimes in hot weather this passage stank of corpses. This walk for us ended in Chiswick Park, a fine house and garden which had originally

been a palace and then a lunatic asylum for well-to-do lunatics, and finally a public park. Unlike the other parks it had wattle fences instead of iron railings and the gardens were peopled with stone statues, many of them squatting animals with breasts and female heads like the Sphinx. There was a very charming lion with a human expression on his face like the early pictures of lions before people had seen them very much. There was a lake and a pretty bridge over it and particularly nice glass houses with elegant columns decorating the corners; these were unfortunately in want of repair and before we left, the pretty columns were removed and the houses rebuilt. Up till the time of the quarrel with Mrs Austin, we used to go often to this park; it had a baobab tree and we saw kingfishers and a jay flying in it besides the usual ducks and swans and herons which one saw so much of on the Thames.

Mrs Ainger moved with us and she came for the morning from Earls Court, quite undaunted for one of her size by this long journey every day. We also acquired a cat from our landlady's brother-in-law. It was a tom cat which Eric named Pybus after the Minister of Transport. He was mostly white but he had a black patch of fur either side of his head like a looped-up curtain over each eye and his tail was black as well, and there were several other large patches on his back. We were all very devoted to Pybus and Mrs Ainger enjoyed going to the Hammersmith market for him and getting huge quantities of oddments of cod for a penny or two. If the fishmonger was in a good humour she brought back enough for supper for her husband and herself as well and she would

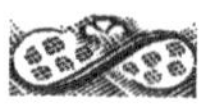

be so pleased with her bargain that after showing it to us, she would toddle upstairs to show it to Fred Austin too. Although she really owned a fur coat, she always dressed shabbily as a matter of principle so that she was never overcharged for anything in her life.

We were very happy and we both worked away at various jobs. Eric was illustrating *Twelfth Night* for the Golden Cockerel Press and I helped him cut away white backgrounds and take prints and I made chair covers and cushions and Mrs Ainger said: 'Well there's one good thing about you, you're always doing something.' Eric used to flatter me a lot, he liked to think that his wife was incomparably better than any other wife and he had a great variety of nicknames for me such as 'Miss Fowlhouse', 'Beast Garwood', 'Chunko', 'Chunkleberry', 'Beast', 'Tushpig', 'Smart Alec', 'Tushbags' or just plain 'Bags'. He encouraged me to go out and about myself and to go and visit museums and libraries to look up books. I didn't much like going by myself because I couldn't really concentrate on the books because of the bored librarians who were so anxious to please. He taught me how to go buying secondhand things in junk shops and we collected books and furniture and cactus plants in little pots. Harry Moore's wife also collected cactus plants and she told us about the awful day when he had dropped on the floor and broken her biggest and best loved cactus, a great round one like a house leek. Eric didn't much like bunches of flowers, he preferred them growing in pots; but later when I could pick my own flowers, he changed his mind.

We were in a very noisy district, because although there were no buses or heavy traffic passing our door, it was always

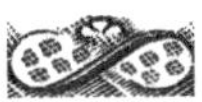

populated with small boys. There was a large blank wall across the road and they used this as a cricket pitch, and they never said anything to each other in a normal-sized voice but they always shouted at the tops of their voices. We didn't mind this as much as Fred Austin, who used sometimes to try and quieten them. My upbringing in Elmwood had blunted my sensibility to noises and Eric and I secretly longed sometimes to go out and join the boys because it sounded such enormous fun. The *Stork* boys were on the whole a depraved-looking collection; they were allowed to meet girls in the evening so long as they didn't leave Upper Mall so that in the evenings there were always giggling knots of boys and girls outside our house. The landlord of The Doves, who used to tell exceptionally dirty stories, told Eric that our porch was called the 'Copulating Porch'. It certainly did seem to harbour lovers and we often surprised them on coming out and there would be a hurried scuffling exodus round the corner. The most strange thing that happened was one morning, when Eric heard a noise of someone in the porch at breakfast time and going out to look, discovered a man masturbating on the mat which spoiled our appetite for breakfast and surprised us very much.

Edward had at first been indignant and scornful about our move to Hammersmith but later on, when he had got used to the idea of our being there, he and Charlotte decided to come too and they moved into the little flat by The Doves above a hand-weaving shop. We didn't see very much of them or the Coxons; somehow when one knows that one can easily see friends if you want to, it prevents one from making plans to

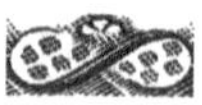

meet them as one has to if they live far away. Barbara [Church] too came to live near after she had married Hugh Gray. She had met him at Oxford where he was secretary or chairman of the French Club; he was quite a lot older than her as he had fought in the last war. In 1918 he had been friendly with Eric Gill and his son-in-law Tegetmeier, as Hugh was at that time a Roman Catholic priest and he had been very upset by the war, and as a result of being shell-shocked, he still suffered from a slight nervous affliction like mild St Vitus' Dance. When his mother was carrying him, she had gone into a church and dedicated her unborn child to the Roman Catholic Church. She and her husband were Irish and both religious, so that when shortly after his birth his mother died, his father had determined that his wife's plans for this child should be carried out. Poor Hugh wasn't at all suited to this celibate life and having an extremely gregarious nature, he was much happier when he broke his vows and married Barbara. He and Barbara both had extraordinarily good memories, though neither of them were particularly creative by nature. They were both very tolerant people and were very much liked wherever they went. Hugh got work with the Gaumont British Film Company and was at first sent to meet American film stars when they arrived in England. Barbara and he used to read plays and do book reviews and then she became Mr [A P] Herbert's secretary.

Hugh became a habitué of The Black Lion but we very rarely went there. We found that if we were too sociably engaged, it prevented our working and as we had to work to earn our living as well as very much enjoying it, there wasn't

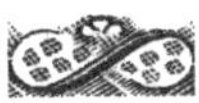

enough time or spare energy for staying up very late at night as well. For this same reason, we stopped taking a daily paper because it took so long to read it, but we did have the *New Statesman* and we had been given a Times Library subscription by Uncle Harry.

Pybus was quite an anxiety to us at this time; he surprised us one day because he wouldn't sit down with his back legs but squatted with his front on the ground and his back sticking up in the air. He wouldn't let us look properly at him and it was quite a long time before I discovered that he had been savagely bitten under his tail. We put this down to rats but it was just as likely another cat because he was always having battles, although he was pretty cowardly with other tom cats. Then he disappeared for a fortnight and Eric and I took to walking along the river bank at low tide examining the rubbish and occasional cat corpses, to see if by any chance it was Pybus. He walked in one morning looking very well and clean and happy and we never discovered where he had been but a little time later, the window of the cat and dog shop at the top of the road was full of little black and white kittens just like him.

Eric did several book jackets for the publishers Duckworth, whose chief editor was a man called Tom Balston. He was a middle-aged man who had become a Major in the last war and he lived in a flat attended by a manservant. Like so many people who live alone, he was a great talker, and although his appearance was male, he had a moustache and was obviously not a homosexual yet there was something about his wink and his slightly malicious stories and the way he talked down his nose, that made one think of him as an eccentric aunt rather

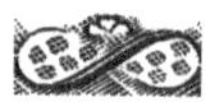

than a kindly uncle. He was a very kind man and helped people without telling his other friends all about it. He had a very large collection of Staffordshire figures which he kept in cupboards and naturally a good collection of books because of his vocation and he also collected contemporary pictures and engravings by [John] Martin, the brother of Mad Martin who had tried to burn St Paul's Cathedral. He knew a great many people, I suppose that he also collected them, and because of his profession had met most of the writers and artists who were in London at that time. We met Ginner at his flat; Eric was a great admirer of the Camden Town Group and was pleased to know this remaining member who still worked placidly and painstakingly in his own satisfactory manner. Being an old man, it was interesting to him to find what a long time it took for the thick paint which he put onto his pictures to dry and Eric looked carefully to see whether Tom's were dry. Sometimes it took years before they were quite hard – he was surprised to find that a picture he had given to an aunt as a young man was still wet. Another person whom Tom introduced us to was Miss Edith Sitwell. She was a good person to meet because she dressed and behaved so like a celebrity that it would be impossible not to remember or be impressed by her almost theatrical display of Edith Sitwell, played by herself. It was a cold evening and we arrived first to meet a nice, friendly, natural married woman and a young man whom Tom was interested in, I can't remember if he was a writer or a painter. Miss Sitwell completely swamped these two so that I can remember neither their faces nor their names. She arrived late, and announced by Tom's

manservant, she swept in in a long white satin dress adorned with a necklace of startling green amber stones so remarkable that they might from a distance have been a collection that she had picked up on the beach somewhere. But more remarkable than any finery was her nose which shone an unexpected rose pink, making it seem like a separate limb from her long face. When she was warmed by her dinner and the fire it grew normal again so that we temporarily forgot it but afterwards, if Eric or I thought again about that evening it was always that first vision of her dressed like a bride that we remembered, with that remarkable nose pathetically making ridiculous the whole effect of her entrance.

She had just returned from Paris where she had been nursing a sick friend; she was I think unused to this kind of work and imagined that we might criticise her for not fulfilling her share of household chores and mending because she made several references to this subject, a quick little remark that women didn't bother to mend their stockings as they should, which is the kind of thing that does annoy a woman who has no idea of the amount of work there really is in looking after a house and family. She talked well and amusingly but always there was this underlying defence of herself and her brothers. She remembered exact verbal insults that people had made against them, quite often I felt convinced that these insults were almost entirely invented because people simply don't take the trouble if they are ordinarily employed to think out ways of subtly discouraging the Sitwells. She had just won the Prix Femina Vie Heureuse for literature and she seemed to me unnecessarily gratified by

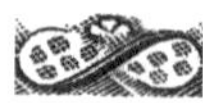

this. I asked her why it was that it mattered to her because surely, by now, her reputation was so established that a prize shouldn't be important. She said that it was always encouraging to have a tangible proof to justify your belief in your own ability. Neither of us expressed ourselves in these words but that is at any rate the sense of our conversation on this matter. At dinner, she told us that she had been to see a show of sculpture by John Skeaping and Barbara Hepworth and how good it was. Eric doubted this and she defended her appreciation by saying that it had given her a feeling and wasn't that surely a proof of its goodness, but Eric, knowing how sniffy Harry Moore was about Skeaping's work, just said: 'No, I'm afraid it isn't'. When we talked about books we felt happier and she recommended us to read Anthony Powell's book *Venusberg*; she thought him more amusing than Evelyn Waugh. Then she told us about her lovely amber necklace and how her father had collected amber and we liked her.

Hubert Wellington, the registrar at the College, was always very kind about offering jobs to Eric and it was he who arranged that Eric should give the comedian Jack Hulbert a course of lessons on art. Jack Hulbert with his enormous chin was a very conscientious man, a solemn person who took photographs abroad and had a large collection of stones and rocks that interested him. He had, before his last film, learned about electricity and he had found that his new knowledge of lighting had enormously improved the film. He felt now that if he could also master the art of stage décor he would be able to better this side of his films as well. Eric found that he was childishly ignorant about colours and seemed amazed to find

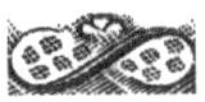

that combinations of colours produced other colours, as though he had never learned that blue and yellow make green. However he was full of enthusiasm and Eric met his daughter and wife Cicely Courtneidge and [brother] Claude Hulbert at tea after they had all been to the circus at Olympia and they were very friendly and familiar, as stage people are supposed to be. Eric didn't think he could be very much help to Jack Hulbert, simply because there aren't short cuts to taste and knowledge about painting and design and Hulbert hadn't got enough spare time to acquire any lasting good from his lessons. Eric would not tell any of our friends about this job.

We naturally went to all the good picture exhibitions there were and to our friends' private views and we wished that we had enough money to collect pictures. David Jones did offer Eric one of his pictures from his last show but he didn't like to take one, though he regretted it later when David Jones had a nervous breakdown and didn't paint any more.

Edward joined a society called the Seven and Five Society and I went one day to see the exhibition at the Leicester Gallery. In an adjoining room, there was a show of Henry Moore's sculpture and I was very interested in this as well. I wondered after examining everything very carefully what he would do next. His love and interest had been in women and the natural resemblance in the shape of stone, of their thighs and breasts; now many of his statues were becoming horrible to me. I could not bear the smooth soapy stone that he was using for some of the smaller figures with their huge ears and idiot's heads. I wished very much Nitchka [his wife] would have lots

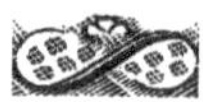

and lots of children for him because having no family might affect his development. It wasn't that I wanted him to use his children as models but he seemed to me to be a man who needed children to make him happy and complete and without them he might become narrow and egocentric.

In the next room I was pleased to find two pictures of Basil Taylor's whom I had heard so much about from Eric. He had been a very dashing and sophisticated student at the Royal College of Art and although I had seen him once or twice, I had never seen any of his work. They were quite good pictures influenced by French paintings; I thought not as smart as one might have expected, but fashionable. I was very attracted to two oil paintings, pictures by John Aldridge, and thought on seeing them that here is someone who loves the same things that I do. They were country pictures, flowers and a water mill and I remembered his name which was an unusual thing for me to do.

A sad thing happened to Raymond Coxon one day. He wanted to send two or three pictures into an exhibition and he arranged for a van to come and collect them. He and Ginesi found that neither of them would be at home at the time the van was expected, so they went next door and asked the maid to give them to the man when he called. This maid was a half-wit and when a rag and bone man knocked on the door, she presented him with Coxon's pictures and that was the end of them, he has never heard of them since. A man who taught at Eastbourne School of Art told Eric a rather similar story, how that he had as a student sent into an exhibition a very painstaking picture that he had worked on with all his heart

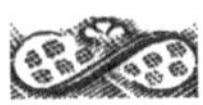

and soul. At the end of the exhibition, the picture was never returned to him and no trace of it could be found. Years later he was visiting an old lady, a stranger to him, and there was his picture hanging in the hall. He explained how he had lost it and she couldn't tell him how she had come by it, it had hung there for years, but she did consent to sell it back to him.

Another person who had strange adventures was Donald Towner. He had been at school with Eric as well as the College and I remembered him very well because he used to live next door to one of my school friends in Eastbourne. He was an aesthetic looking young man with fluffy hair and grey eyes and he was nicknamed the Poet Towner. We went to see him in Hampstead where he lived with his mother and we talked about old times and he showed Eric his old collection of birds' eggs that Eric had given to Towner's cousin, a half-Japanese little boy. He still dressed in an affected manner with a very flat pork pie hat and he told us how one day he had been walking on Hampstead Heath wearing a round deerstalker hat and a large checked overcoat, and a man had come up to him and said: 'Doctor Livingstone, I presume'. Another time he was working on a bridge overlooking the canal and a strong wind blew his canvas off the easel into the water. He told an official about this and they rang up the river police and asked them to collect it for him. By now quite a large crowd had gathered round Towner and when his picture was finally rescued, they were surprised to find that it was a large nude; this had been on the back of the picture he was going to paint, but it was too difficult to explain away.

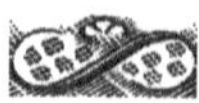

I encouraged Eric to try a painting of London by night. With street illumination and a bright moon, it was light enough at any rate for a drawing. He set off one evening and chose a house nearby in Hammersmith. No one seemed to think it strange that he should be squatting down beside a lamp post, and he worked undisturbed until it was nearly two. Then he noticed the door of the house he was drawing open and a man came out of it and walked up to him: 'I'll trouble you for your card', he said. Eric hadn't got a card and he explained what he was doing. The man then became less aggressive and told him that his house had recently been burgled and that had made him unduly suspicious. Apparently the poor man, a dentist by profession, had been up and about his house all the night peering at Eric from his window and fearing to go to sleep while he still remained outside. It must have wanted considerable courage on his part to finally come out into the open in this way. Eric, feeling rather guilty, came home very cold with a half-drawn picture which he never finished and he never again tried to paint anyone's house by night.

We had of course to give a boat race party and this was great fun. There is certainly something supernaturally exciting about mass enthusiasm. I remember noticing the same phenomenon when I was going through London a year or two ago, when people were waiting to hear the result of the Battle of Narvik; although people spoke to one another, there was a quietened expectation which was pervading the whole town. No one was attending quite wholeheartedly to their business, at the back of their minds this impatience to hear more news

was visibly affecting their behaviour. The *Stork* boys prettily decorated their ship with flags and put rows of chairs on deck and we put boxes and chairs in our little garden for people to stand on. It was an easy party to give because the entertainment was provided for us and with Mrs Ainger to help make a continuous stream of tea or coffee, there was time for us to enjoy the scene as well as our guests. I like strange mixtures of people at parties and we had a rum assortment at ours. The majority of Eric's Royal College of Art friends went as usual to the Coxons and then came afterwards to see us, so that our guests were a combination of aunts and Geoffrey Fry and John Weyman and a young man called Daley-Lewis who Cecilia had introduced us to, whom we only saw on these yearly occasions. He was an excellent social contribution because he was very good at handing round sandwiches with his friend Jock Murray and he was so beautifully dressed for the occasion, even to a pair of field glasses slung round his neck. How gay and lovely it all was and there were people everywhere. There was room for people to stand and every year, a man with a banner about 'Fearing the Lord' pushed his way up and down the waterfront, but I doubt if he did his cause much good because at this time everybody was so excited that they weren't thinking about their souls but whether Cambridge would still be winning again this year.

Eric always particularly looked forward to that charge of small boats and decorated river steamers which, like leashed dogs presses behind the racing boats, keeping their distance only because they must. I believe that most people really enjoy shouting and it is because football matches and races

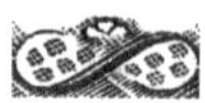

give one licence to shout without appearing to be ridiculous that largely accounts for the popularity of these occasions.

After the race it was no use trying to do anything serious for the remainder of the day; one's stomach to begin with was disorganised by the sandwiches eaten at the wrong time and washed down undigested with cups of tea. One year we collected afterwards at the Coxons and went to a football match at Twickenham where there was more shouting and even greater numbers of people and after this, it was decided that we should go and see some all-in wrestling. In the party there was a young sculptor who was also an all-in wrestler who fought under the name of Black Hawk. He wasn't performing on this evening because he had strained some part of his person. He told us a little about this strange profession, how that if you really were superior to your opponent, you could defeat him in a few minutes. From the audience's point of view this was no fun, so that the management of the theatre insisted that you prolonged the fight so that ultimately you might be defeated by a man whom, had you wrestled with him as hard as you could to begin with, you could have easily overcome. It seemed to be a sport that attracted sculptors because there was another sculptor who wrestled, a handsome young Jew called Rabinovitch, and it was Harry Moore who was particularly keen that we should go.

I don't know if I enjoyed watching this. I suppose I did, it was one of those things like the Eton and Harrow match that are nice to go to once, just to know what it is like. Black Hawk assured us that most of the men were so tough that it really didn't injure them as much as you would suppose.

The last fight was between Rabinovitch and a black fighter called Black Eagle. This man had just invented a new method of attack which was to jump into the air like a gamecock and butt his opponent on the head with his terrifically thick black curly head. Rabinovitch, only having an ordinary average skull, didn't know how to cope with this and the umpire was puzzled because it wasn't strictly speaking against the rules but it was obviously very unpopular with the audience, who screamed and catcalled for all they were worth. The audience at all-in wrestling is not like any other English audience and it made one feel ashamed of it, especially the women who screamed more hysterically and stupidly than the men. Finally when the black man was on the ground and waiting to get up on the eight of his count which is the traditional thing to do as it gives one time to recover one's strength, the umpire as quick as lightning said 'nine ten' and hurried him off the stage in an indignant fury, leaving one to imagine the quarrel that must have ensued.

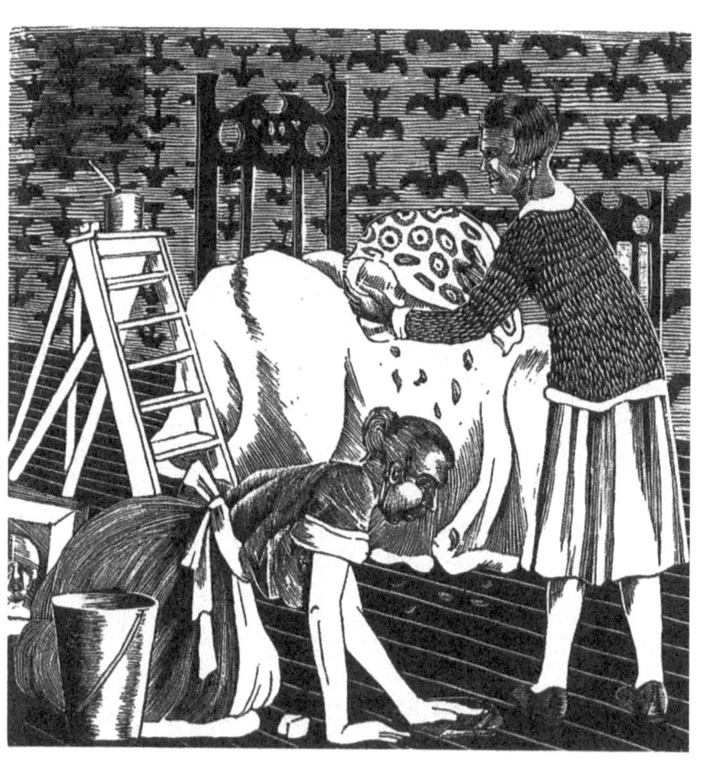

CHAPTER THIRTEEN

By 1931, we had grown very tired of the few walks there were
at Hammersmith and Chiswick, and Eric wanted to paint the
country again and perhaps do some more watercolours. He
was very fond of Cotman's work and he and Edward had been
influenced by his paintings. He had sold quite a number of his
early watercolour paintings when he had exhibited them at
the College sketch club. Anning Bell and Martin Hardie were
among those who had bought them.

One morning, he and Edward took a train to Dunmow in
Essex and from there they hired bicycles and rode round
looking for a cottage or rooms where we could stay. They tried
to take Thaxted Town Hall, a beamed and deserted-looking
building in the middle of the road. Finally they were told to
try Brick House at Great Bardfield which was a prim Georgian
house of red and black brick with a mansard roof and a row of
posts along the front connected by chains. Mrs Kinnear, who
rented it, agreed to let them have half of the house and they
returned to London very excited at their fortune.

The next weekend Eric and I set out on a bus from King's
Cross. It took three and three-quarter hours to get there and

I wondered if any place could really be worth all this boring journey. The bus never stopped long enough to let you get out for tea but it was continually stopping to pick up passengers and waiting while they kissed their friends good-bye. The beginning of the journey through Whitechapel was amusing but the roads on the outskirts of London were bordered by bungalows and villas of a monotonous cosiness. It was this exhausting bus journey that protected the inside of Essex from development and speculative builders. The train service was pretty bad as well, so that very few businessmen could afford the time it would take to get to and from London. The villages were rich in lovely houses and the rents were not exorbitantly high as they were in Sussex. In the same way that before I had met Eric, I had never noticed the difference between good and bad furniture, I had never noticed lovely houses or thought one house more desirable than another except in a purely practical way.

Great Bardfield was a Y-shaped village and one of the most attractive things about it was the shops. The shopkeepers had wonderfully appropriate names and Mr Bone the butcher was the Happy Family Butcher in the flesh and his shop, with its shutter edged with a little wood balustrade, was like a doll's shop. The other butcher Mr Stokes, had a particularly lovely shop with his name written in fine square letters of ochre edged with red on a blue board. The three grocers were called Piper, Dodd and Tanner and the bakers were the Guerneys and the Prances.

Brick House stood in the main village street and was semi-detached on one side to the private house of Mr Tanner the

grocer, whose shop was adjoining his house, and on the other side it was separated by an archway and passage to the police station, a more modern building than most of the others in red brick. The church had a very nice square clock made of wood painted blue and stuck up diagonally on the tower, where it was invisible to the major part of the village.

Mrs Kinnear, who was living in Brick House, was small and thin with large eyes and a pointed face. Her hair was bobbed but it was rather a long bob, and she looked neurotic, smoking continually and jerking the cigarettes out of her mouth when she had done with them. She had two daughters, the prettier one Maisie worked away from home and the other, although quite adult in appearance, still went to school. They both had young men and one of them, Fred, lived in the house because his father who was a police sergeant disapproved of his associating with Maisie. Fred was a great help and did all the unpleasant jobs like emptying the lavatory and he worked in the garden which was a particularly nice one with a paddock behind it containing a lovely big walnut tree. This adjoined a field which sloped down to a willow grove of regularly planted trees and the winding River Pant.

Fred and Mrs Kinnear both owned Alsatians, hers a lovely black and brown dog called Prince and his a bitch puppy. I don't know how Mrs Kinnear came by Prince, she said he was related to a dog belonging to the Prince of Wales. She had been a stewardess before her last job of keeping a butcher's shop in Romford, and possibly one of the passengers gave him to her. As he never had enough exercise he got very difficult to restrain and because of complaints, she dared not

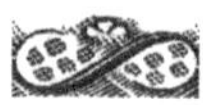

let him out except for occasional walks on which he was kept on a very short chain. He was locked up for hours in an outhouse at the back where he barked continuously while the Kinnears shouted to him 'Shut up Prince' or 'Leave off Prince' a hundred times a day.

As there were two staircases, Mrs Kinnear divided the house vertically. We had the left half and she the right, and we shared the kitchen and scullery where there was a pump. She let one of her bedrooms furnished to us if we wished and gradually we collected furniture for ourselves, though guests sometimes slept on the floor on eiderdowns. I had never known anyone like Mrs Kinnear at all intimately before and it was a strange experience sharing a house with her. She was kind in the way she brought us up tea in the morning and helped with the washing up but the youngest daughter was an awful slut and there was too much work in the house for Mrs Kinnear to be able to cope with it single-handed. They read twopenny magazines and used discarded ones for lavatory paper; we would be continually having our interest aroused by some romantic story with a title like *Lady's Maid to her Sister* but could never get to the end because it would be used before there was time to finish it.

We cooked on an oil stove and a primus provided by Edward's father, and we never used the range though Mrs Kinnear used to boil up lights and other entrails for Prince on the fire while her one hen, quite unmoved by the flames, laid her daily egg in the corner on top of the oven. She would then crow in a deafening manner. Eric would chase her out where she redoubled her cacklings and squawks.

Sharing house with Mrs Kinnear gradually became more difficult. One of the first disasters was the death of Fred who got killed on his motor cycle; he was a nice boy and had been in many ways the backbone of the house. Then the return of Mrs Kinnear's mate upset things. He had been at sea when we first came and the house had many trophies such as a stuffed lobster and bamboo furniture which he had given to Mrs Kinnear; when he arrived, he was so like what we had expected that it gave us quite a shock. He was a terrifically tough-looking man, he went about in a singlet and trousers displaying some remarkable tattooing. He resented our being in the house and we didn't stay very long when he was at home and went back to London till he had gone off to sea again. There was a bath in a little dressing room that led off from Mrs Kinnear's spare room where he slept; there was no method of filling this bath except by carrying up pails of water but it had a drain pipe, so the mate just used it for a lavatory for his night water.

Mrs Kinnear was sensitive about the fact that she wasn't married to this tough and she was deeply hurt when she overheard a conversation between Mr Adams the carter who lived opposite and a passing stranger, who asked who was living in Brick House now. Enquiring further, he asked whether the people were married and Adams said that some of them were and some of them weren't. Mrs Kinnear thought this very offensive of him but it was quite true and I couldn't see that it was very dreadful. Having this sense of guilt, she didn't go outside the house very much and was only friendly with the chinless wife of the builder Mr Crossman, who owned the

house. This woman charmed Eric and Edward one evening when she complained about something to them, saying: 'It wasn't cricket'.

One of the few people that Edward knew in the neighbourhood was A J Symons, who had a bigger brick house in the next village of Finchingfield. Edward felt flattered that Symons should come and see him; he was coy and schoolboyish with him and would comb his hair and insist that we cleaned up the house as well as possible if he was expected. Edward had moved down his big ping-pong table from Redcliffe Road. Symons was very keen on ping-pong and had a barn especially made into a ping-pong room for it at Finchingfield. I didn't like Symons very much and he ignored me. He was a tall dark man, handsome in a kind of continental co-respondent way but too dark to be wholly English. He wore horn-rimmed glasses which exaggerated his large dark eyes in a rather frightening way. He talked intelligently and ignored questions or remarks that he considered stupid. He knew a great many people in Essex, but one guessed that he had insisted on knowing them rather than that they had sought to know him.

Things were a little easier when Charlotte Epton came to stay. She and Edward were now engaged but he behaved very oddly to her, and his love making took the form of rather ghastly schoolboy pranks and tickles and we could hear Charlotte, who was noisy enough in ordinary times, giving the most piercing yells and screams of: 'Stop it E'. At other times he became very respectable and called her 'my dear' in his mother's voice.

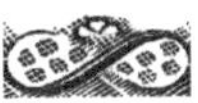

Edward's mother and father came over nearly every weekend to see us. His mother had a weak heart and often thought that she was going to die. Edward got so used to being summoned to her dying bed that he now took it for granted that she would recover and didn't take her condition very seriously. He wasn't very pleased to see them and often I got left to entertain his mother, to whom he was pretty disrespectful. He was a little more frightened of his father but although he pretended to have this scorn for them, he still retained a great many of their characteristic dislikes and beliefs. If Charlotte did something of which he didn't approve, in his mother's flat Essex voice, he would complain: 'It isn't nice.' He talked with an Essex accent and called bulls 'bolls' and fields 'foilds'. He refused to alter his pronunciation and maintained that his was right. Eric talked like an educated man and Edward rather envied his easier social manners, so would dig at him on the subject if he could. He didn't approve of the emancipation of women and thought they should be content to look after the house. When Charlotte was praised for her pottery and offered good posts for teaching, instead of being proud and pleased for her, he just felt jealous and he hated her doing any painting especially in the roadway where everyone could see her.

Once the Bawdens brought some cousins of Edward's, a typical hearty suburban man and his wife; at tea he tackled Edward on modern art, saying that he couldn't see anything in it. Edward shut him up, to our secret satisfaction, with: 'Well there must be something wrong with you'.

Eric and I were exploring one morning when we came upon a sunflower of great size, growing in the middle of a field

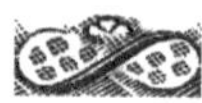

of clover. We hesitated to pick it fearing that it might be the apple of some farmer's eye; its absence too, would be so very noticeable and reluctantly we left it. Edward, on hearing about this remarkable flower, admonished us for having even considered picking it and after tea he set off on his bicycle to have a look and perhaps make a drawing. I remember feeling slightly shocked when he returned rather shamefacedly in the evening and produced the gigantic flower, cut off shortly from its thick stem. Edward is a shy man and easily frightened by people in authority, so it must have required considerable courage on his part to have picked the flower and brought it home tied to his bicycle where all the village could see and speculate as to how he had obtained it. Gratefully we made drawings.

Charlie Mahoney, with Geoffrey Rhoades, stayed for a long time and helped Edward with the garden. During the winter the four men had cleared the yard which was feet deep in years of rubbish. They unearthed all kinds of relics from the trade of past owners; it had been a girls' school and a saddler's and coffin maker's and there were pieces of coffin and piles of old harness which they buried in a huge pit which they had dug in the garden. Geoffrey Rhoades made a painting of the others working in the snow, Eric wearing a black and white striped football jersey. The hedge dividing Brick House garden from the policeman's garden was being gradually choked by a large white-flowered convolvulus. Edward refused to pull up this bindweed as the policeman wanted, and Mahoney and he both did good drawings of it.

In the spring, Mahoney supervised the digging and planting of the garden, insisting on two spits deep, and Edward

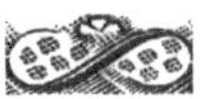

with his usual thoroughness bought lavishly the best of everything interesting or unusual in the seed catalogue so that when we came back from Morecambe [the following season] the garden was already quite changed. It was a fine summer and all the flowers and shrubs were larger than usual. The prize flower was a monstrous double sunflower. We especially loved sunflowers and now we had them growing very successfully in our tiny garden in Hammersmith.

The next year Edward planted numerous sunflowers. There was a row along the wall by the lavatory and halfway up the garden, the cream of the collection, a monstrous double sunflower grew to huge maturity. So large and so splendid was it that looking up to its vast centre I felt that I should never be satisfied with any future sunflower I might grow, this was the limit.

Such a large crop needs strong sticks to support it and what with the number of earwigs they contained and the unfriendly height they grew to, we felt that perhaps we had rather overdone it. Charlie Mahoney made drawings from the top of a ladder, one rather resented his continual presence outside the lavatory.

One night Eric and I were awakened by a crashing and thumping onto the gravel below our window. 'Cats or rats.' Cursing and complaining of the wind that rattled infernally at our window, we turned over and slept again. In the morning we found that the noise had been made by the fall of the row of sunflowers outside.

Living like this with Eric and Edward was very hard work and I didn't have much time to enjoy the country and I got

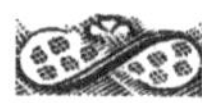

annoyed with Edward if he was unreasonable which he was almost continually, being fussy about his vegetarian food and childishly silly about housework, doing nothing unless Eric did exactly the same amount. When I complained about him to Bowker and the Bransons who came to stay, they said that everyone knew that he was queer but they just accepted the fact and let him be. This was all very well if you didn't have any intimate dealings with the devil, but I thought poor Charlotte was going to have an awful life with him if they married. I determined to do my best with him as I enormously admired his work. I only came to blows with him once when he threw a small fire guard at me and hurt my nose, so I attacked him feeling like murder, but it did no good.

One weekend he asked the Hortons and Geoffrey Rhoades and Joan Jenner to stay without telling me, so that I had made no preparation for them and they had to sleep on the floor.

Percy Horton was a small dark man with blue eyes, he was descended from the Tichborne claimant and he looked far more nobly born than the present Sir Anthony Tichborne, whose photograph I found in a newspaper. He had been a very brilliant student at the Brighton School of Art, he drew most beautifully, but the war in 1914 came when he was about eighteen and inspired by a friend, he decided to be a conscientious objector. I hadn't realised what being a conscientious objector in the last war had meant and Percy told us all about it. His wife Lydia, a large woman with a great sense of responsibility, rescued him from prison in Scotland where he had been so badly treated that it was thought that he wouldn't recover. His case was mentioned in Parliament before he

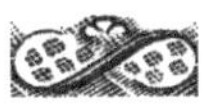

was finally released and he subsequently married Lydia and became a student and then a teacher at the Royal College of Art. He told stories very well and was a brilliant mimic. Possibly because of his experiences in prison and his early marriage to Lydia who was older than him, he had in some respects remained sixteen years old and he seemed much younger than his fourteen-year-old daughter who was very grown up for her age.

Geoffrey Rhoades had been a naval wireless operator in the war. I found it at first very difficult to believe this because he was such a slow and vague-looking creature that it seemed impossible that he should have been able to understand that lightning stream of dots and dashes; but under his shaggy eyebrows his blue eyes were far more alive and twinkling and his brain was far more active than his slow, shambling body suggested. Joan Jenner was in the Ministry of Agriculture with Mrs Horton, they were both very intelligent and could do *Torquemada* and *The Listener* crossword puzzles, for which they won book prizes. Joan had a round, flat head the shape of a stuffed rag doll and her eyes were round and blue and she had a long neck and sloping bottleneck shoulders. She had a school-mistressy voice but she was gay and happy at this time and sang songs in German about the house.

On the morning before they arrived, I came down to breakfast and found the floor covered with water and Mrs Kinnear having hysterics and shaking all over. The oil stove had flared up and become entirely covered in flames. Eric dashed to the pump, feeling that action was essential and he and Edward threw water at it till the flames died down and

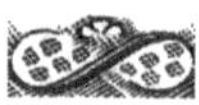

they were able to carry it out into the yard. Later in the day I found Eric laughing because he had just realised that there was a butt full of water outside the door and he need not have pumped. Mrs Kinnear was very upset over this. Her mate was expected in a day or so and she wanted the house to look its best and this had happened and all these friends of ours had come to stay. I went to bed rather early, leaving the others playing ping-pong downstairs. I heard Mrs Kinnear fidgeting about on the landing; the others were making quite a lot of noise but it was barely ten o'clock. I hugged myself warm and comfortable in bed and waited for the storm. She very suddenly decided on action and a wonderful stream of invective poured down on them, there was a dead silence and the staff of the Royal College of Art and servants of the Ministry of Agriculture slunk guiltily to bed.

Charlotte came to stay while the Hortons and the others were still there and Eric encouraged us all to bathe in the river. As we hadn't any bathing suits, and conventions and London were forgotten, we went in nakedly and Percy and Eric and Edward threw soft warm river mud at each other while Lydia who hadn't bathed, stood clothed and indulgent on the bank taking photographs. One of these of Edward putting on his shirt with Eric standing behind him among the trees, looked like the figure in the background of Piero della Francesca's picture *The Baptism of Christ* in the River Jordan. I didn't feel that I was beautiful enough to enjoy bathing with nothing on and I felt much happier the next morning, when I went down by myself to the willow grove to look for Charlotte's engagement ring which she had lost. Willow trees

are lovely if they are let alone, I don't know why they are always pollarded in Oxfordshire, it is certainly a mistake. These ones were planted in regular rows and their light grey green foliage reflected the colours of the sky, so that if the light was red they glowed like opals or if it was dark and stormy blue, they shone like silver against it. The cows had forestalled me and the mud on the river bank was imprinted with the marks of their cloven hoofs so I had to give up the search, idly wondering if anyone would ever find the ring and what sort of speculations about it they would make if they did. It was a cameo ring with a similar setting to mine which Eric had bought at Chapman's, a shop which exchanged jewellery. Mine had a tiny miniature painted inside of a man in a wig of the period of William and Mary. I hadn't realised when Eric had bought it how lucky we had been that it fitted my finger.

The grocer's daughters had a proper wooden boat which floated alright but was rather large for the narrow river and they couldn't go very far in it because of the trees which bent low over the water at several places. There was one near our favourite bathing place which stretched right across the river and Eric used to enjoy daring to climb over by this way. One night, these girls borrowed our canoe and sawed through this tree, much to the annoyance of Mr Ives the farmer who complained to the police. After this we didn't bathe again with nothing on; the river was getting too popular for us to feel happy and private. I loved paddling down to the water mill and relished the lovely peace and stillness and the pleasure of proceeding along without making any noise or movement except the lazy gently splashing of the paddle – even that was

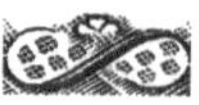

unnecessary if the water was running the same way as I wished to go. In the autumn, I had found some large elephant hawk moth caterpillars on the willow herb and I loved them almost as dearly as I would have when I was small and had collected them with John, but now instead of keeping them for a collection I made drawings and in the spring when they hatched, Edward put them on the brougham in the sun and they flew away. Edward at this time started an aquarium, but he didn't have much luck as it started leaking.

Charlotte's friend Gwyneth Lloyd Thomas, who had attained the august position of a Girton don, came often to stay. She was a dear with lovely grey-blue eyes and black hair and a trusting kind of face. She was about thirty and unmarried and we wished there was someone who would fall in love with her and marry her because one felt she was wishing it too. She started learning how to paint in oils and became very enthusiastic but she insisted on company to support her when she went sketching, in case of possible evils like cows or an audience of small boys.

Charlotte and I both hoped she might marry Thomas Hennell, who was another person we were particularly fond of, but he was unhappily in love with someone else. We had come to know him quite accidentally in the autumn when he had been bicycling through Essex and enquiring after a room in Bardfield, had been recommended Mrs Kinnear at Brick House. I remember seeing from the window this tall figure with a large ornamental top of straw from a haystack tied to his bicycle. To our surprise, he had actually heard of Edward and Eric because he had seen the first show of drawings they

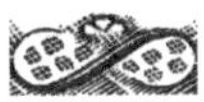

had had on leaving college at the St George's Gallery. Hennell seemed to me to be very learned and I didn't understand quite a lot of what he said. He had a deep voice and a head, which with his large brown eyes and dark curly hair growing on top of his high forehead, reminded me of the portraits which still remained of early Romans or the young men of Pompeii. He was a strange man because it was unusual to meet someone so apparently good and in one sense simple, yet who possessed so much knowledge. When he first came to Bardfield he was writing a book called *Change in the Farm*. He illustrated it himself with careful drawings and he made one of these at Bardfield of the old dovecote which stood in a field by the church. It was a square building with black boarding at its base and lathe and plaster above. Inside there still remained the potence, a ladder which swung round from the centre to assist in the collection of birds from the great number of holes in the plaster interior where they had once roosted, now its only occupant was an owl which lived in the very top of the house. The building was in a very dilapidated condition and we felt anxious for Tom when he drew the place from inside, thinking it might fall on him. The pigeon house belonged to Guy's Hospital but they refused to repair it. Guy's Hospital owned quite a lot of property round about the neighbour-hood, including the white house by the church where Miss Catherine Buck lived. She was a tall, thin-faced woman who had a very big tumour and she walked in, if it hadn't been for her age, what one would presume was a pregnant condition with two or three Cairn dogs darting in and out from underneath her voluminous skirts. She was wholly wrapped up in

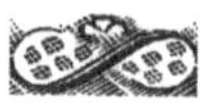

the past and was writing an Icelandic saga for children. This was supposed to have educational value and some publisher had rashly promised to publish all of it. The first volume was successful but she had then, we gathered, been writing for years and we heard that the publisher was nearly broke under the strain of printing her works. This was one of Edward's malicious stories and probably not true. He and Eric got very bored with Miss Buck when she came to tea and talked about Roman roads. She used, with a friend when she was younger, to walk along Roman roads, tracing them across England and she said that she had once seen a ghostly reconstruction of a Roman villa, and that she occasionally saw ghosts in her own house by the church. At one tea party Edward stealthily showed Eric his handkerchief under the table which he had tied in an unusual quantity of knots, while Charlotte above still encouraged Miss Buck to talk about Roman remains because she was interested herself.

A house which Tom Hennell and all of us liked particularly was about a mile away from Great Bardfield and was called Great Lodge. Miss Buck told us that it had once been a monastery or convent and she had seen there the ghost of a nun. There had later been a big house with an enormous hall and servants' quarters, a lovely red-brick building with small slit windows like those in a castle and with a charming clock-tower on top. The big house had come into the possession of a Mr Guy, a rich man who founded Guy's Hospital and he had eventually lost his money and pulled down the big house. Brick House where we lived, was supposed to have been built with bricks from this house. Now all that remained was the

huge brick hall which was used at one end as a farm barn, stacked with grain and calves and a big black and white bull of whom Eric did a painting and gradually the barn became more and more domestic till the other end developed into a house with a pretty white front and charming hall with a circular staircase and then a banister leading to the upper landing and floor which connected with the barn.

Apart from his getting up particularly early in the morning to dig in the garden, Thomas Hennell seemed to us to be in quite a normal state of health and we were very surprised and disturbed a few months later to hear that he had had a nervous breakdown and was in the Maudsley Hospital. He had written once or twice to Edward and had said in one of his letters that he saw visions, but Edward hadn't thought anything very much about it till we heard about his breakdown. After this there was no news, Tom Hennell just disappeared as though he had died and it was very sad. Charlotte found out that he had been in love with a schools' inspectress called Marion Richardson whom she had met once or twice. She was a very enthusiastic art teacher and had trained children to do very good drawings. She was wrapped up in her work, at which she was very successful, and had refused Tom Hennell, or perhaps he being so shy and diffident a person, she may have been unaware of his state; he would not have been a very convincing lover I feel.

Barnett and Claudia Freedman came shortly after I had discovered that there were bugs in the house. I had found one under Bowk's shoe when I was doing her room and another one appeared mysteriously on the dress of my Eastbourne

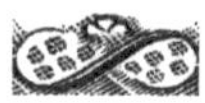

friend Valetta who was particularly clean and refined, when she was eating her breakfast. Claudia and Barnett slept in Mrs Kinnear's spare room and when we were making the bed, Claudia and I found a dead one under the pillow. She didn't tell Barnett who anyway had a horror of the country, its solitude making him feel quite ill after a time. He had already spent a sleepless night because he imagined that the sheets weren't aired, he can't have known Charlotte and me very well or he would never have worried about this; they were thick real linen ones which do feel particularly cold at first.

He and Claudia hired bicycles and set off with Eric and Edward, though Claudia had hardly ridden before and had to be helped on and off. At every farm they came to, she asked anxiously if there were any nasty big dogs. Barnett fell off his bicycle and lay helplessly on his back, 'You look just like a beetle', said Edward and he and Eric laughed and laughed, and Claudia in great distress, cried: 'Oh poor Barnett, help him'. We had pigeons for supper and they both picked the carcasses clean with what seemed to us extraordinary skill. Afterwards Barnett told us about a holiday he had spent with Geoffrey Rhoades and Charlie Mahoney and what a terrible fellow Charlie was. The chief thing that was wrong with him was that he was always right.

The first painting that Eric did at Bardfield was an oil painting of Bowker at the pump in the scullery with Prince lying beside her. He wasn't very pleased with it and after another unsuccessful attempt at an airman coming down by parachute in a farm yard, he gave up oil painting. Edward was

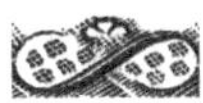

also painting in oil but he was doing beach scenes and not Bardfield; they were carefully speckled pictures with a texture like Seurat's painting. He was finishing off a painting done in small spots of figures on Clacton beach.

In the late summer the weather was bad and the rain started leaking in through our bedroom ceiling: lying in bed I could see it ooze along under the plaster in the corner and finally drip onto a ledge that skirted the wall on that side, making it impossible for me to put a pail to catch the drips. I didn't get much sleep that first night, so Eric asked Mr Crossman if he could mend the roof. He said that he'd come when it stopped raining.

It didn't stop raining all that day or the next night and worried by the ever-filling jug and the continual plop of the drip, I couldn't go to sleep at all; it didn't seem to worry Eric and he slept as soundly as usual. I felt pretty tired the next day so I took some aspirin and tried to have a rest in the afternoon but it wasn't any good, I couldn't go to sleep. We couldn't move into another bedroom because the house was full: so I didn't get any sleep on the third night and it was still wet.

If you don't sleep for a long time, you have a strange disembodied feeling and you go about telling other people about your sad case and how you heard every hour strike through the night in case they don't believe you. I didn't get any sleep for ten nights and towards the end of this time, I started cursing the landlord. I knew he couldn't have foreseen that it was going to rain for ten days, but at least he was something tangible to blame.

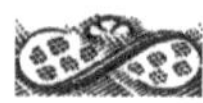

My cousin Rosemary was going to be married and we had been invited to her wedding at her mother's Tudor manor in Kent. We didn't really want to go very much, the thought of dressing up in picture hats and morning coats seemed very ridiculous and remote from Brick House and the preoccupation with work of one sort and another that used up all our energies. My not sleeping at any rate gave us an excuse for not attending the wedding, but we decided to go back to London.

On the way back the bus filled up with children from Dagenham, who had been for a country holiday. They had a man and a schoolteacher with them, he was a fattish sexless looking man and I didn't like the look of him. Almost immediately they were seated, the children started singing a song they had evidently been rehearsing for the return journey, maybe the stout man had made up the words: 'I don't want to go home, I don't want to go home, although I love my mummy and daddy etc – I don't want to go home'. They kept this song up for half an hour and then some of them started on another song while the remainder still bawled the other. The noise was appalling. Suddenly, to everyone's surprise, Eric got to his feet and ordered them to stop; they did for a second, open mouthed with astonishment. The male teacher was furiously indignant with us, the bus conductor looked sheepish and said nothing, and two stout women who were only going to market and hadn't got to endure it as long as we had muttered: 'Shame, let the children enjoy themselves'. I was filled with pride that Eric should have done anything so brave and unlike his usual tolerant acceptance of things. I expect it was that same spirit that prompted his father to stand up in chapel.

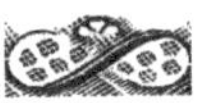

Back in London with the change of air and a dry bedroom I slept again, but when we went back next time to Bardfield, the landlord had grown a nasty carbuncle on his head and I wondered about it.

Sister Margaret now had a flat of her own and she invited me to come to her first cocktail party. She particularly wanted me to come because Bob Church had returned to England on leave and had recently become engaged to [his sister] Barbara's friend Brab and he had promised to go with Barbara to her party. Like Eric when I parted with him, Bob had grown a moustache; it was nice to see him again and we talked about stamp collecting. He did mention his engagement to Brab and said, 'You told me to marry her'. I felt rather perturbed at the responsibility for so serious a step being put on my shoulders but there was nothing I could do about it now. I knew Brab was in love with him although she had been living with another young man while Bob was in Africa, but I imagine that it was only because she had been so unhappy about Bob. He had made love to her before when he was still in love with me and it had been pretty miserable for her, knowing that he really was in love with me.

He said that he didn't want to come and see us at Hammersmith but a few days later, he did come one evening with Barbara and Brab when he was a little drunk and we all went to the cinema together and coming back in Brab's car it felt very strange to be sitting on Eric's knee packed tight together with Barbara and Hugh [Grey] and Bob and Brab. Driving in cars often seems strange to me because ordinary

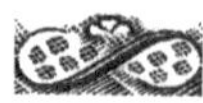

social life is suspended while one sits in unusual proximity to people and because it is usual to sit on other people's knees, it is accepted by people who would be very flabbergasted if you sat on their knees on any other occasion. I suppose ballroom dancing is also strange if you look at it from the point of view of someone who has never seen people dancing before.

Margaret did once meet a Scotsman on a boat going out to India who refused to dance because he considered it improper. One also feels in the power of whoever is driving the car and Eric and I were both infuriated by Hugh Bergel, the young man who was in Crawford's Advertising Agency, because he once gave us a lift home after a party in his Austin Seven; he drove as fast as the car would go and sitting behind in this tiny box which dodged and swerved in and out of the traffic in so dangerous a manner, we both felt angry because it was so unnecessary. There was no hurry and there was this wretched young man risking our valuable necks in this foolhardy manner. When Eric heard that he had been killed when he crashed the bomber that he was flying a little time ago, I wondered if the crew had been suffering from the same bottled fury against him that we had felt so many years before. I don't suppose they had because the aerodrome people said he was a good pilot. Perhaps he was just unused to Austin Sevens.

I saw Bob and Brab once or twice again after they were married. I was disappointed to find that she was quite undomesticated; when I had advised Bob to marry her I had imagined from her shape and face that she was homely and a good cook, but this idea was quite wrong. Still, she loved him which was the main thing that mattered, so I hoped they would be all right.

Edward and Charlotte were now married and Mr Bawden senior, as Charlotte usually called her father-in-law, had bought Brick House for them as a wedding present. They couldn't however quite simply go and live in it because the roof needed mending and Mrs Kinnear had not moved away her possessions, though she herself had gone to be housekeeper to a gentleman in the New Forest. After a lot of difficulty Charlotte at last got permission to move these things into the village hall and with the help of Mrs Townsend who did the washing, she set to, to clear out the Kinnears' possessions. This was in a sordid way a wonderful experience for them both and Charlotte was deeply impressed with their finds, such as the sofa crammed up at the back with old dirty stockings and magazines and the mould growing on the Kinnear combinations and above all the mate's stuffed lobster which had gone bad in the china cupboard. She did things thoroughly and afterwards sealed the rooms and fumigated them with sulphur candles, but the stuffed lobster smell persisted for a year or two afterwards.

To mend the roof, Mr Bawden employed Elisha Parker and Mrs Townsend's son Eric, a charming boy like a fair Modigliani portrait with red cheeks and a red blob nose. He made painted wooden soldiers with revolving arms to scare away birds. Elisha Parker had a peculiar daughter, one of the few people I have heard of who advertised for a husband. The story goes that he stayed a week and then left her already pregnant, but I shouldn't think it was a very reliable story.

While there were ladders up to the roof, Eric and Edward both painted pictures from the top. They used to get up very

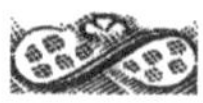

early in the morning and were interested to find how powerful kipper smoke was when it was coming out of the chimney; it drove them in to breakfast. Eric also painted the willow grove many, many times in the early morning, trying in vain to do one that pleased him. He and Edward both painted pictures with the sun shining directly at them.

For a wedding present to the Bawdens, Eric had an ornamental house of trellis work built in the garden; it was painted white and had one of Eric Townsend's revolving soldiers on top. Charlotte finding that their neighbouring farmer Mr Ives had bought, for the value of its wheels, a very lovely brougham with a glass bow-fronted window, borrowed this and it stood for some time under the white trellis house. They both painted pictures of this and Edward did a particularly brilliant one. They worked directly and all on the spot and sometimes one whole painting a day.

Except for his drawings of the steamrollers and the old car, Eric didn't in my opinion, and his own, paint the Essex landscape nearly as well as Edward who knew it intimately and loved it. Eric, whose interest at that time was in Sussex landscape, had for the most part, mainly contented himself with drawing objects in Essex country and was pining for Sussex with its background of Downs. Edward invented a quite personal technique by superimposing bright colours swiftly on top of one another on lettering paper. This paper having a smooth, tough surface did not absorb the paint which, staying very much on the surface, allowed him to scratch lines on it which uncovered the white paper underneath. They had both been experimenting with this scratching in their oil painting

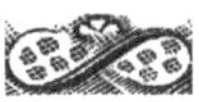

and Eric had used it as a method of pointing his bricks in the painting he did of Bowker in the scullery. Edward had no 'good taste' and occasionally did very bad work, but his love and knowledge of the squat, flat-headed people and the black barns and neat Essex houses with usually a dark line of drain pipe or boarding down the corners, and the thatched and sometimes weather-boarded cottages or the lovely pink plastered ones, produced a stream of 'good ones' or 'stunners', which word we had taken over from the Pre-Raphaelites who used it of their women. If his own work wasn't going well, he would come back and devilishly attack Eric's work or poor Charlie Mahoney or some innocent friend who was possibly deeply wounded and put off by this merciless behaviour till they learned to understand Edward.

There was a big yard near the house filled with derelict farm engines of all kinds and the remains of a very early car. It was a repair yard for steam engines and these were obsolete relics. Some of them were still in working order though the bindweed was climbing over them and there was a hen's nest in one. The door of the shed where they repaired wheels was splashed with a variety of paints and inside were some lovely red wheels. Eric was very thrilled with the yard and set to work drawing the engines and the car, afterwards tinting in watercolour his very careful drawings; Edward drew him at work. He couldn't go on drawing all the summer because he had to go to Morecambe to decorate a tea room and very reluctantly, we left Bardfield just when Edward's father was buying Brick House for Charlotte and Edward as a wedding present.

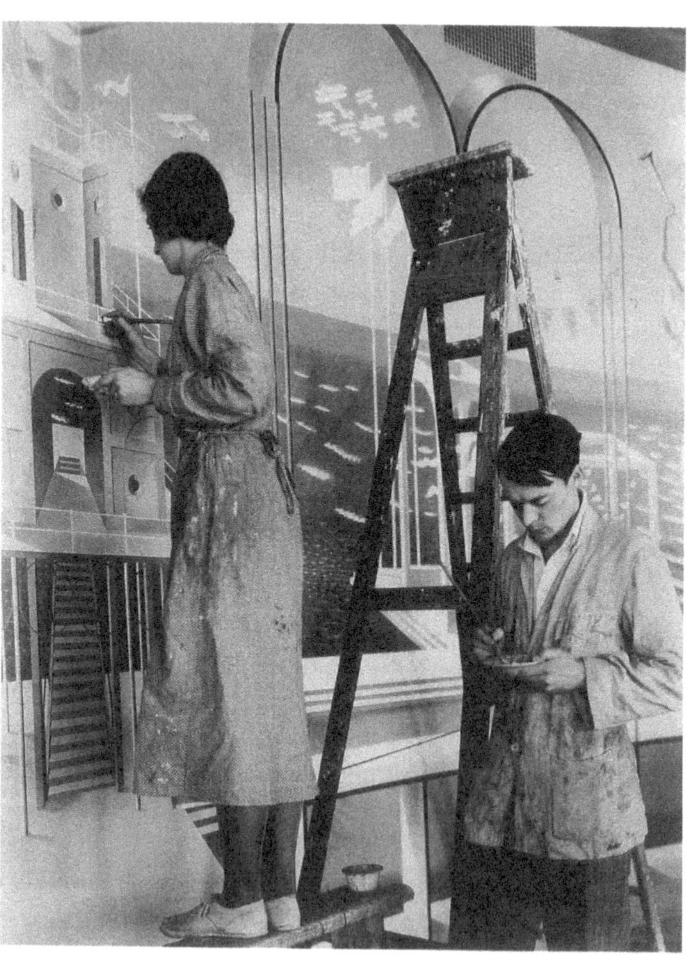

CHAPTER FOURTEEN

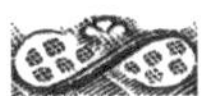

Eric had been commissioned by an architect called Oliver Hill to paint a mural decoration on the walls of the tea room of a hotel which he had designed in Morecambe for the Midland Railway. When Eric's designs for this room had at length been accepted, we set off together to Morecambe which is a seaside place in Lancashire, renowned for shrimp pies and glorious sands and sunsets.

It wasn't looking up to much when we arrived there in April, late on a wet afternoon. We had expected to be put up in the old Midland Hotel on the site of which the new one was to be built, but we found that the old hotel was fast being demolished and there wasn't very much of it left, so with our heavy suitcases we set off to look for rooms.

We trudged past dreary boarding houses with pretentious names like 'Gleneagles' and 'Montrose', their curtained windows draping alternately aspidistras or castor oil plants, till we came to a house which had been recommended to us. It stood opposite a huge ramshackle grey and brown wooden construction, a desolate scenic railway. The door was opened by a dirty-looking man in a collarless shirt and a gust of

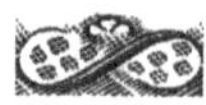

cooking and linoleum smell issued from behind him. He wanted £5 a week so we said no and went on, till we finally settled in rooms with two south of England women who didn't want quite so much money and who were clean, though their house, as did all the houses in Morecambe, reeked of linoleum. This was made in Lancaster which was the nearest big town and the smells of rubbery cooking lino would be blown out to Morecambe when the wind was in the right quarter. The man who had been responsible for this was Lord Ashton; he was now dead but his name was greatly revered by the local people. He had three wives, one of them still living. When the first one had died, he had had erected in Lancaster a mausoleum for her, but there wasn't any grave or relics inside – he couldn't think of anything more original than a miniature replica of the outside of the mausoleum, perhaps he thought you hadn't seen enough of it; it stuck up in the middle of Lancaster from the distance alright, and later his second wife had a smaller one.

The new hotel resembled a big white concrete ship and it stood on the sand in front of the old Midland Hotel. The tea room was circular and was half composed of windows with horizontal strips of glass and the other half, which was divided by a door, was the wall space for the decoration. Eric had designed a similar construction for each side but one was to be daylight and the other side by night. The scene was a seaside, gay with steel and white concrete buildings, a circular tower with a winding staircase and numerous diving boards. In the day the sun shone brightly and flags waved from the seaside architecture and at night there was a splendid

fireworks display in progress, the buildings were whizzing and sparking with set pieces and rockets which exploded in the dark sky were reflected in the sea water. There were painted constructional posts and arches to strengthen the design and the base had to be fairly simple, as it would have wear and tear from chairs scraping against it. The sand was to be stippled with a rubber shaving brush, otherwise it was to be painted in a similar way to the Morley College designs. Most of the people who saw it seemed to think it very strange and because the architecture shown was 'the modern school', therefore the whole thing must be 'rather Epsteen' as one man called it.

We were annoyed when we discovered that we couldn't start work as the wall hadn't yet had the three undercoats of white paint that it should. We should have to wait a whole week in this sad town that was only meant for visitors in the proper seasons; now it lay like a sluttish prostitute who hadn't yet bothered to get out of bed and paint her face.

We started aimlessly walking along the promenade that stretched endlessly into the mist, trying to compete with Blackpool which boasted three miles of promenade. The boredom of these endless slabs of concrete was occasionally interrupted by a big, uncomfortable rustic seat made of twisted pieces of shiny brown wood. We walked down to the sand and followed the line where the waves had piled a high watermark of seaweeds and bits of wood and muck. I picked up one of those green glass balls with a net round it, just like the ones Eric had found at Eastbourne and it cheered us up and made us feel less homesick. We came quite soon to a

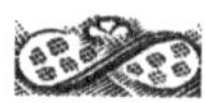

village of stone grey cottages and an old church on the cliff edge. Eric asked at a likely-looking house if they would take us in and to our relief and joy, they said they would.

Decorating the tea room was disheartening work because the plaster was too recently put onto the wall and as well as not being dry, it exuded little heaps of yellowish sand or lime or whatever it is that plaster is made with. When we were drawing out the design, if we used an India-rubber or disturbed it in any way the white paint peeled off, so we decided that it had better be scraped off and repainted. This delayed us for some time and even then it was never satisfactory. Eric fumed at having to waste so much time when he was longing to paint watercolour pictures and be away from this ugly place but nobody seemed to care when we complained that the painting hadn't a hope of lasting, so long as it looked alright on the opening day that was all that mattered. So there was nothing for it but to go on drying the damp wall with our overalls before working on it and hoping for the most improbable best. There was a part of the roof above the tea room that Oliver Hill hadn't decided how to finish and the workmen just left it, so that when it rained the ceiling got wet. Then another workman left a pipe uncovered across the ceiling and he knew that it would eventually make a stain, so every day he would come and gaze up for a minute or two. He looked like Leslie Howard and it made us laugh to see his gloomy face uplifted day by day, till at last the stain began to show. It was brought to the attention of Oliver Hill who happened to be paying one of his very occasional lightning visits. He looked like a benevolent uncle and was dressed in an open-necked shirt

which barely covered his developing stomach. His manners were very bad but we came to the conclusion that an architect had to be pretty tough if he wanted to get anything done. He came into the tea room and glanced at the ceiling and then said: 'Spray it with cork'.

Spraying with cork was a nightmare for the workmen, it blew into their eyes and throats and up their noses and they had to do it several times because they first of all used too fine a cork. The final catastrophe was when the plank on which three of them were standing broke in the middle and tumbled them and the pails of cork all over the place. Most of the painters were Londoners and we felt more at home with them than with the north-country workmen who didn't like the way Eric and I spoke. Occasionally we overheard them doing charades of our 'lah-di-dah' southern accents. Bible Jack, a religious one, was north-country. There were two Italians who made Bian Cola stone and polished tirelessly day after day. They were enthusiastic about Mussolini. I was shy as I was the only woman working there and if I passed a group of workmen, they would boldly compete with one another with noises and whistling to attract my attention but singly or in pairs they were very sweet and obliging. North-country people seemed extraordinarily warm and kind after the more reticent south of England people I was used to. I was very touched one day by a stranger in a bus presenting me with a passion flower, not intending it to indicate any passion, but because we were artists.

Eric Gill with two assistants and his son-in-law Tegetmeier were also decorating the hotel. Gill was carving a figure

in Portland stone in the lounge and doing a ceiling painting of Neptune above the well of the staircase. Tegetmeier painted a map of the neighbourhood on the walls of a sitting room. We all found conditions for working about as difficult as they could be and the noise of hammering iron bars into concrete made it quite impossible to think coherently at times.

Gill and his friends all bravely stayed in the old hotel; there was a bedroom left intact at the top and the laundress had supplied some high iron bedsteads. There wasn't any water left and they had to fetch it in pails. Eric and I enjoyed seeing them one moonlit night emptying their slops from the top of the half-demolished ruin. Mrs Gill joined them later but she stayed in the rooms that we had thought so dirty; going back to them they seemed better and the view of the switchback was very good. The upstairs room was papered with a wallpaper of almond blossoms against a black background.

Eric Gill wore a navy-blue tunic with a belt round the waist, a black beret, golf stockings and bloomers under the tunic. I don't think I saw these but I believe Robert Gibbings told us about them and how at one time Gill had worn pink Oxford trousers, but maybe I've remembered this wrong. He didn't dress like this from personal vanity but because it seemed to him the most suitable costume for the conditions under which he worked. It must have been very trying to be stared at so much everywhere he went, but I suppose people tend to suffer in one way or another if they have the courage of their convictions. He wasn't very at home in upper-class

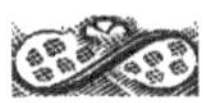

society, we went with him one evening after work to see some people called Reynolds who lived at Carnforth and he felt just as uncomfortable as we did to find them wearing full evening-dress and living in a house that was almost a castle. We all thawed later on in the evening and enjoyed Mrs Reynolds' singing. She also could make a remarkable echo by shouting at the park which sloped gradually up in front of the house.

Geoffrey Fry also told a friend of his, Lord Balniel, that we were at Morecambe and he came over one day and drove us to his father-in-law's house where he was staying. We were surprised to find how much we liked this young man, he reminded me of Bob. We had heard his father the Earl of Balcarres give a speech when he gave away diplomas at the Royal College of Art and we hadn't expected this old Scottish dragon to have such a charming son. His father-in-law was a brother to the Duke of Devonshire. I don't remember what he was himself, if we ever knew; he also lived in a house that looked like a castle, perhaps it was one. We had a happy afternoon watching the family trying to catch trout and looking at one of the first monkey puzzle trees that ever came to England which grew in the garden. There were a lot of the family: Balneil's own wife and children and his mother-in-law and her numerous children. I felt rather sorry for her two daughters, who had everything that the majority of women are supposed to wish for in life given freely to them but in return they were deprived of their freedom and the fun of trying to earn their own living or intimately knowing people outside their own limited society.

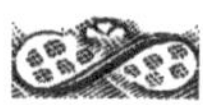

All that was expected of them was that they should make a suitable marriage and produce a suitable family. Perhaps I imagined their troubles, I suppose they could leave home if they liked, but it would obviously be more difficult for them and I remember thinking that this is not an enviable life for women.

Our landlady we knew would be so thrilled and interested in this visit if she knew about it that we dared not tell her and met Lord Balneil a little way down the road, instead of letting him call at the house where she would surely have recognised him. She had a tremendous interest in the big houses and their occupants and invariably knew the number of bedrooms and bathrooms of the ones in the neighbourhood. She was a staunch Conservative and would undertake the most long and complicated journeys to catch a glimpse of Mr Baldwin or the Princess Royal.

At last the hotel was finished. The railway people had insisted that the interior should be a warm colour and Hill had had to have the walls of halls and staircase a pinkish brown; this was combed in the prevailing fashion and looked exactly like Edinburgh rock. There was a big opening lunch, Lord Derby opened it and hurried away. The speeches were amusing in the sense that they almost openly said 'we don't like this hotel ourselves, but we hope to attract Americans with it'. The railway's pattern of perfection for hotels was Gleneagles. Lord Stamp, whom I took an instant dislike to, made a speech and was followed by the Mayor of Morecambe who built dreadful houses and had a slogan: 'Buy a Gardner Built House'. At the beginning of the meal, a grace was said

and in the sudden hush that preceded it, a waiter's clear voice rang out: 'They aren't giving them any shrimps'.

The people of Morecambe were quite determined to see this lunch and while we were eating, they stampeded like a herd of difficult cows and treading all over the newly-sown grass, they pressed their noses to the windows and watched us eat till they were driven away.

Sitting in the lounge afterwards, we came to the conclusion that we had never before seen a room full of more unattractive business toughs. Their suits were black and smart and their faces narrow and alert; money, position, success their only goal. Eric Gill among them looked like a different species of animal and I hope we did too. Outside, Lord Stamp's enormous car seemed explanation of why the railway didn't pay enough dividends to its shareholders. Already the Corporation were silently protesting at the modernity of this whited sepulchre of a hotel and trying to make it more homelike, they were planting crazy pavements and setting up rustic seats.

When we got back to Heysham and told our landlady and her husband all about this great opening day, they told us a nice story about a similar civic luncheon when the guest of honour had been the Princess Royal. She was placed next to the Mayor of some north-country town and presently they were served with very delicious ham. Princess Mary left the fat from this ham at the side of her plate till, unable to bear this waste and forgetting who she was, the Mayor enquired if she was going to eat the fat and if not, could he have it. It was graciously given to him.

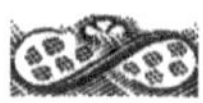

Re-reading a notebook of engagements of this period, 1933, which I kept, it seems almost impossible that people could cram so much work and entertaining and visiting into one year as we did without getting quite worn out. I wasn't unhappy or happy; there wasn't time to be either and I longed for a peaceful holiday away from people and house-work. I did have two blissful days with Bowker when we had Brick House to ourselves. We did as little cooking as we could and ate bread and cheese and painted as much as we liked. I tried to paint in oils and enjoyed myself like anything.

Both Eric and Edward held exhibitions in the autumn of 1933, to take place in a new gallery that had been started in Lichfield Street by Zwemmer's, the book shop in Charing Cross Road. His show of watercolours was fixed for the end of November. The young man in charge of it was Robert Wellington, an old friend of Eric's, because his father Hubert was registrar at the College and had always been very kind and helpful to him. Robert came down to Bardfield several times to look at the pictures; he was not a tactful man and both Eric and Edward were made so miserable by his attitude towards their work before their shows that the whole house was filled with gloom. I don't think he realised how disheart-ening he was and he was quite happy himself, bathing in the river and dancing about on the banks. He made us laugh when someone said they had heard an owl; he said, 'Where? City boy must hear the owl'.

Edward's exhibition of watercolours took place in October; it was very successful and he sold nearly all of them. They both had well designed invitation cards to their private

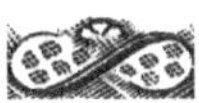

views and the catalogues were also decorated; this was an original idea as the other galleries at that time had very dull, stereotyped cards. Eric also sold nearly all his pictures which was a great relief.

Another friend of Charlotte's was a girl called Diana Low who had been a pupil of hers at Cheltenham. Gwyneth had also been a mistress at Cheltenham and had taught Bob's wife, Barbara Bowers. Charlotte hinted to us that Diana was a naughty girl and how she had been studying with William Nicholson, whose mistress she had become. We had never seen William Nicholson but we were used to hearing that kind of gossip and didn't think ill or well of Diana Low because of it when she arrived. Incidentally it was quite untrue, but because she talked a lot about William Nicholson and played a wooden cup and ball game that he had taught her, we took it for granted that he loved her. She wasn't a beautiful girl, she had to wear glasses because she was very short-sighted but she was very attractive in rather a feline way and she had a lovely figure and fair skin. She was full of energy and dived beautifully, but perhaps her chief charm was her naturalness and she dressed more beautifully than any other woman I have met. Eric fell in love with her at once and it seemed quite natural after what Charlotte had said that she should take him off in her car for a day's painting. I had been used to Eric being in love with other girls at Eastbourne but this was the first since our marriage and I felt rather strange but not unduly disheartened. An unforeseen result was a shower of criticism from Eric. I was no fun and did nothing but housework and I hadn't any initiative and didn't go off and do things by myself. I did try

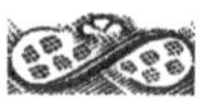

to give a little more time to being with him but the only result was an angry Charlotte who thought I wasn't doing my fair share of housework, so I thought it wasn't much use and any spare time I had I was doing needlework pictures.

Being in love with Diana had changed Eric's way of painting and instead of his dry, careful drawings he did a series of more boldly coloured pictures painted freely with quite wet watercolour. Poor Diana was terribly upset at what had happened and firmly banished him, although it made her perfectly miserable because she too was in love by this time. At first I hadn't minded his loving her but when it stopped him being able to make love to me I began to be hurt; I remember waiting for him late one afternoon when he should have come back but hadn't done so. Actually it was the day that Diana was saying she couldn't see him and that he mustn't make love to her any more, but I didn't know about this. I was standing in the bow window looking at the river and I realised that something had changed in our relationship to one another which would never be restored. I had felt for a few minutes that I hated him and then I knew that the real sadness for me wasn't that he didn't love me but that I had ceased to love him. When he came back he was so upset by what had happened that I didn't hate him any more, but I didn't have again that feeling of being a part of him that for four years had been so precious and I realised that we'd been lucky to have loved each other as long as four years.

We never told other people about this; I had a great aversion to being pitied and also it seemed to me to be

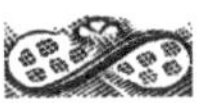

bad-mannered to worry other people with your private miseries; and for another thing, sympathetic friends might be far more worried for you than you were yourself.

Eric's wish to paint in Sussex was due to another new friend we made this year, Peggy Angus, a lively Scottish girl who had also been at the College. She had been to stay at Brick House with Diana at Christmas time, and tried to convert us all to Communism. This was the beginning of our interest in politics and gradually it encroached on our time and interests and although we hated this interference with our work in the years that followed, we were continually aware of the Spanish Civil War and we went about feeling unhappy and ashamed and filled with foreboding. Charlotte became more involved than myself or Eric and Edward who, if they had attended all the meetings and given the subscriptions which the more fanatical left-wing people in the neighbourhood wished, would have been left workless and penniless.

The new people at Place House were also becoming interested, at least John Aldridge was; but I remember stopping with Basil Taylor outside a left-wing poster on the front of Brick House and his asking confidentially, 'What do you think of Communists?' and replying, 'I don't like them, they're so ugly'; and feeling that we agreed, like guilty conspirators, we said no more.

John Aldridge came to Bardfield in 1933 and having an affection for the country, and particularly his own garden and flowers at Place House, he painted them in oil paint directly and richly, with a naturally sympathetic understanding. He

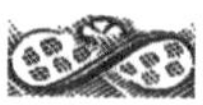

was not at all interested in Bawden and Ravilious's pictures and couldn't tell the difference between them. His own painting was so different in style as well as medium that there was no challenge to Edward in this, but there was in the matter of house and garden. Edward must have naturally admired John's taste in clothes and furniture and they quickly made friends over their gardens.

Eric had seen John Aldridge and Lucie Brown before but we weren't sure who was living with whom. Basil had had two or three mistresses called Lucie and we supposed that she was one of them but he was also reputed to be, as he had said himself, slightly homosexual and we wondered about John. Their friends were mostly homosexuals or people reputed to be so. It is difficult to judge truthfully in these matters because there is no definite proof as people don't usually make love in front of others. These three all looked after each other very carefully and Lucie mothered them both.

We had rather resented John and Lucie's and Basil's arrival in Great Bardfield because apart from the usual feeling of slight annoyance when one painter plants himself in another painter's country, they seemed to gradually be affecting the Bawdens and to a lesser degree, ourselves. In having Place House done up and repainted and beautifully furnished, they unconsciously issued a challenge to the Bawdens. Edward's competitive mind we knew would never be content to let things stand as they were in Brick House, having seen Place House, and Charlotte with her love of thoroughness was naturally affected as well.

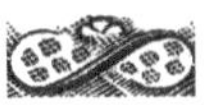

We went to as many auction sales as we could at this time and we all loved going, with the exception of Edward, who was too shy to be happy. I liked John Aldridge very much, he slightly reminded me of my rather sinister cousin Bobby. I felt there was something wrong with him somewhere but I was quite at ease with him and he gave nearly everyone that feeling of easy familiarity and understanding. We all liked Lucie [a divorcée] more than we thought we should. From hearing stories of her more disreputable past we had imagined a much more positive and confident person from the timid and tremendously respectable woman that she really was. I didn't think that she liked me very much; she was intensely interested in people and their appearance and mannerisms and I was conscious of this watchfulness of hers and sometimes I felt that she resented my coming into her house. She had a mysterious illness, a kind of indigestion which attacked her in the morning, making a nasty taste in the mouth and giving her a headache. The doctor thought it was nerves, but that didn't make it any better. She was very devoted to cats. The first cat they had was a huge gelded tabby called Smith which they had found was homeless after an auction sale. He would sometimes fiercely attack your legs but he had a nice habit of putting his paw into a Marmite pot and licking it and he would go on doing this almost indefinitely. The next one was a half Siamese black female cat called Trippet who lived to a great age and they also collected a number of grey cats with short smooth hair that were very charming. Trippet had constant families and John once horrified everyone by cutting off the heads of some of her

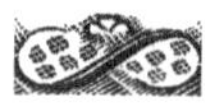

newborn kittens with a garden spade. He defended it as being quicker than drowning which I suppose it is but it seemed rather a queer alternative.

The worrying thing about John was that he slightly reminded me of Betty Rennison. He had a mouth like hers and the same dent in his chin and now I knew that Eric no longer wanted me, there was a danger of my falling in love with him. Symons came one evening to Brick House and we all sat at the table playing paper games and I looked at John's handsome but weak face and Eric's charming, honest head and thought what an ass I should be if I ever thought him preferable to Eric; but Lucie's watchful jealous eyes made us aware of one another and I imagined her discussing me with John as I knew she must, because of this tremendous interest she had in people.

These three now moved into Place House, an Elizabethan house (dating from 1564) on the outskirts of the village. Eric and I once considered taking this house which had stood empty for some time, but Eric didn't like it very much as he didn't like the idea of living in a Tudor house, preferring a more simple plan. This one had an odd little attic bedroom up irregular steps and it seemed to him dark and depressing. I liked the garden which had run wild and was a perfect garden for hide and seek. One never seemed to reach the end of it, it went on indefinitely into swamp and undergrowth. But the house was, apart from anything else, far too large and inconvenient.

John Aldridge bought the house and Mr Crossman put in central heating and a bath and mended and painted it up.

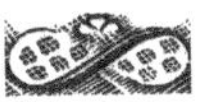

Outside we were rather disturbed to find that the brown beams had turned blue, though the plaster remained the same white as before. John and Lucie and Basil didn't like it very much either and later on, they had the blue painted over and the house colour-washed the usual Essex pink.

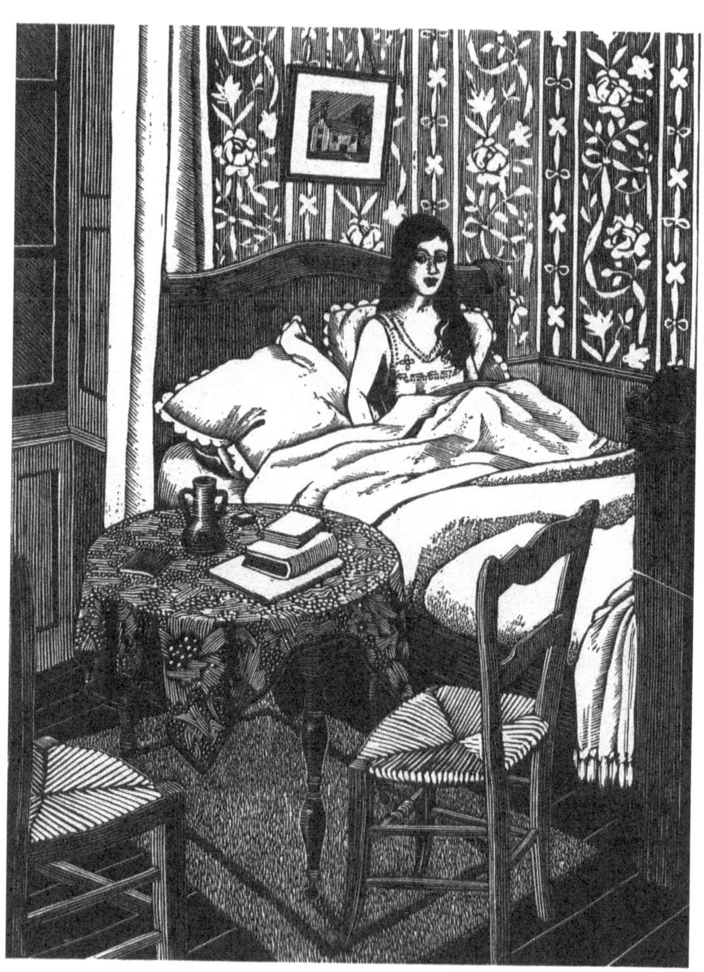

CHAPTER FIFTEEN

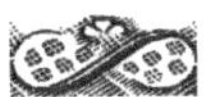

Peggy [Angus] also invited us to stay with her in her cottage at Furlongs near Glynde in Sussex and Eric went there early in February. It was a lovely place and he came back very pleased and full of plans for future watercolour paintings which he would do there.

I was also full of plans because, with Charlotte, I was learning how to marble by a new method of using petrol which Charlotte and Edward had discovered. It had been suggested to Edward that he should try marbling for wall-paper designs but he did not carry out this plan. Charlotte and I used his new method of marbling to produce pattern papers while he [later on, in 1939] collaborated with John Aldridge to make wallpapers from linoleum blocks, which method he preferred.

If anything, that year was even more productive than the last, as my notebook shows, and added to the excitements of work there were discussions on politics and lovely walks on the Downs when we stayed at Furlongs, more lovely walks on the Downs at Oare when we stayed with the Frys in Wiltshire, visits to Eastbourne and Bardfield, and innumerable games like

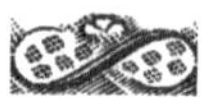

heads bodies and legs or more complicated pencil games when A J Symons came over. We had rather given up dominoes and rummy by now, but Eric and I still loved billiards and had bought ourselves a quarter-sized table for our London flat.

My sister Billy had been married out in India to a soldier whom we always referred to as the King of Poona and now, much to the family's relief, Margaret while doing her manicuring work at Harrods met again on the stairs her old lover, Joe Calverley, who was doing the auditing for that shop. He was still unmarried and in January they announced their engagement, and Margaret thanked heaven that she had had the courage to leave home and work, and to have a life of her own, which had rewarded her in this wonderful manner.

It's very difficult to write about these crowded years and I haven't time now to tell you as I should like; I can only write when I am ill and my preoccupation with my past life is not a good thing when I am up and should be attending to my house and children and yet I feel that if I don't write now, perhaps I will never have another chance with the Germans menacing our peace.

Early in March we had to go back to Morecambe to repair the wall, but the greater part of the summer we spent at Furlongs. Furlongs was a long-shaped flint cottage attached to a farm owned by four brothers called Freeman, who had funny high voices and worked endlessly. Conditions were even more difficult than at Brick House because we were miles away from shops and the cottage was in a lane which became almost impassable for cars in the winter. To fetch water, we had to

wind a well handle in the well-house across the farmyard ninety-five times because the well was ninety-odd feet deep. When the bucket eventually came up, it was leaking very fast so you had to pour it very quickly into the pails before it had all run away again. I was hardly strong enough to deal with the huge well bucket and usually lost half the water.

The great charm of Furlongs was the wonderful feeling of freedom which we had there. Behind the cottage the Downs stretched sharply up but in front there were flat fields and a railway line before the Downs rose again with that lovely hill, Mount Caburn. There were two cement works nearby, one called Greta and the other Garbo, and Eric was delighted with them and the funny little engines which drove the trucks. He was very happy there and did a series of cement works pictures. Then Peggy showed us Firle Park and the house where Lord Gage lived; an ancestor of the present Lord Gage had been responsible for greengages and Eric found some big greenhouses and a nice gardener with a beard. He got permission to draw inside the houses and the gardener told him about his early life when he had gone on an expedition to South America to pick orchids in the tropical jungle.

In a very overgrown lane by one of the cement works, Eric discovered two covered wagons and on enquiring about them, he found that they had been used by the manager when he was first prospecting a site for the works. He cheerfully sold them to Eric for 15/- each. They had been in the lane for some years and a thin coat of cement dust covered them up and at first, we were doubtful if they would stand moving. They had shafts for a horse but Eric hired a car to tug them away and

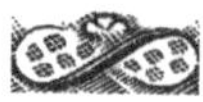

they were safely moved to the lane in which Furlongs stood. We got a man to mend them inside and fit up one for a bedroom and the other for a living room and I nailed new canvas over the top of them and painted them green with red wheels. It was tough work, especially the underneath parts and it took about a fortnight, although occasionally I had some assistance.

Peggy was very hospitable and streams of friends came to stay at Furlongs, sleeping in tents or on the straw mattresses inside which Peggy had made for the beds. I added to the general muddle by having my marbling tank on the copper in the tiny scullery but as I provided wallpaper, Peggy didn't mind. In fact nobody minded anything, we were all so busy and you couldn't say anything rude about anyone else, because the walls were so thin that you would have been over-heard. Peggy didn't paint very well herself but she was full of enthusiasm, she didn't mind how her pictures were done provided the final result pleased her and she would enlist other people's assistance to paint bits which she found diffi-cult. She was unhappily in love with a man called Horace Wilmott, a dark-haired, blue-eyed young schoolmaster who was rather like an effeminate version of Bob. He liked music and Peggy had a gramophone and lots of records. Horace was lazy about getting up in the morning and to get him out of bed, Peggy would half wind up the gramophone and then put on one of his favourite records which presently ran down in the middle, making such an excruciating noise that he was forced to get out of bed to take it off. Peggy taught us a lot of songs and Percy Horton brought his violin and they would

sing rounds. 'Turn Amaryllis to thy swain' and 'Twine gentle evergreen to form a shade around the tomb where Sophocles is laid' being two favourites. I could learn the words of songs, but I couldn't sing. Another friend who couldn't sing was Helen Binyon.

Helen Binyon's father was a poet and she had a twin sister called Margaret or Peg and together they ran a marionette theatre. So besides painting in watercolour, very pale sensitive pictures, Helen at this time was also carving puppets in wood. She had been brought up very carefully and her father was very fond of her and he had written sentimental poems about her when she was a child. He had worked in the British Museum, and was an authority on Chinese painting and having had a surfeit of it in their youth, his three daughters didn't feel very attracted to this subject. Helen was rather big and fair with grave grey eyes and a small nose and mouth. She was nearly thirty and it was surprising, being so very nice and charming, that she was unmarried. She had been engaged once when she was very young and now there was an American in America who wanted to marry her. She was, possibly because of her father, a very romantic girl and she wanted someone a little more exciting than the polite, correct museum young men that she was constantly meeting at home. Peggy enjoyed teasing her about her upper-class upbringing and the fact that she knew two lords and she was constantly saying, 'Now Helen, don't be a lady'.

Helen was very humble about her work and used to ask Eric for his advice and criticism and I wondered if he would fall in love with her or if he was still enough in love with

Diana to make this impossible. Furlongs certainly encouraged people to fall in love. There were obviously no aunts or parents about, none of them could have faced the primitive conditions, and the air and fields and downs all radiated an open, happy feeling of freedom.

Peggy had been to school with Ishbel Macdonald and after Ishbel had been on a visit to Canada with her father who was then Prime Minister, she invited Peggy and Helen to bring us to Downing Street one evening when she was showing a film of their tour in Canada.

Ishbel was a dark, squat-figured girl, I only met her on this one occasion and I noticed how bad she was at being a hostess which was surprising because, as the Prime Minister's daughter, it was after all her main occupation. It wasn't that she didn't try to be a good hostess but that she overdid the part, so that at once, under her too-helpful organisation, one became self-conscious about one's position as guest. Peggy and Jim, who knew her better than I, said that she was a very self-centred person; but I didn't from her appearance guess that she was the egoist they assured me she really was. She looked a homely, kind person, which was the way she thought of herself I expect.

She prided herself on keeping her old friends in spite of her elevated position, so that the room was filled with an odd assortment of people, among them another school friend, red-haired Pauline Gough who, like Amy Johnson, was an air pilot. Snobbishly, I thought these people don't look well in these dignified rooms. The film kept breaking down and halfway through, Ishbel went out to boil milk for her sister's

baby which was in her care for the evening. She showed us the room where cabinet meetings were held on a lovely shiny table and some pictures which they borrowed from the Tate Gallery I think. Eric sneaked away to the lavatory and returned with a piece of prime ministerial lavatory paper; but it was disappointingly ordinary and there was no white velvet seat like the one King George was reputed to own. Later, when we were sitting round the fire in the drawing room, Mr Macdonald came in and shook hands benevolently with me because I happened to be nearest to the door and he handed Eric a copy of *Punch*, the page opened at a picture of himself with a none-too-friendly caption underneath. He was in very good spirits and seemed to have taken no offence from it and although he must at that time have known how unpopular he was getting, he stupidly refused to face the truth. Hearing him speak, I wondered if he had reached the responsible position that he had because he sounded like a Scottish minister in the pulpit, and unconsciously connecting the two, simple people thought that he must be reliable. Geoffrey Fry had told Eric that you really did have to have ability to do well in politics, so I suppose that when he was younger he really had been a helpful man; Peggy said that he was very changed now and wouldn't condescend to argue with her as he had done before he was Prime Minister.

Ishbel's faithful lover was Horace Wilmott's cousin Bert Kelly. He was a short, friendly man rather like Owen Nares in appearance but he wasn't quite a gentleman and had a rather servile nature so that Ishbel scorned him. The more dashing young man that she really wanted to marry wouldn't propose

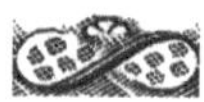

to her and she finally married an uneducated labourer who according to Peggy, looked a little like Bert in appearance. I liked Bert very much and thought she was a silly one not to marry him.

In London when Jim Richards came to see me one afternoon I talked enthusiastically of our new friend Peggy, who was brave enough to camp by herself in a field with a bull and cows in it and how enterprising she was. Suddenly I was aware of Jim's interest and thought, Jim thinks he might marry this girl. I didn't like this thought and I stopped my eulogy of Furlongs. When Eric got home I told him about this feeling I had and he agreed that Jim was not the right sort of person for Furlongs or Peggy. Jim was hopelessly bad at housework and he and Peggy both being unhappy in their love affairs, would almost certainly fall on each other's necks; and viewed dispassionately really they weren't suitable people for each other. However, we couldn't keep Jim out of Furlongs if he wanted to go there and sure enough, he went to stay for a weekend and all that we had foreseen came to pass.

Just before we finally left London, we went to stay with Helen's parents in Berkshire. Her father had worked as an authority on Chinese art in the British Museum but was now retired and I don't think he was writing any more poetry either. He was a short man with Helen's rather sad, slightly drooping eyes like a faithful dog's and a small mouth. Mrs Binyon was a cheerful, busy kind of person who had when she was young been very bossed and organised by her mother, a social snob who had at first not at all approved of her marriage to Laurence Binyon who was a north-country man with

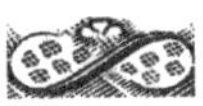

nothing distinguishing about him. When he had become a successful poet, she tried to organise her granddaughters into making good marriages.

We now wanted a house of our own in the country and Charlotte and Edward discovered two empty houses in a village called Castle Hedingham near Bardfield, and they wrote and told us about them, so Eric went off to have a look. One was at the corner of the village street called High House and the other, semi-detached to the grocery business of the landlord Mr Henry Baines, was called Bank House. Charlotte had already interviewed Mr Baines and Edward in his letter described him as a charming and venerable old man with a beard. Eric went with Charlotte and Basil Taylor in the car and when they arrived, old Mr Baines mistook Charlotte for Eric's wife and his opening remark to him was, 'Does your wife sing or play hockey?' Eric looked very surprised and Basil said: 'Do you want her to do so now?' Apparently this remark was because Mr Baines hoped that we should befriend his favourite daughter Marjorie who although married to a farmer at Gestingthorpe, spent three-quarters of her time at home, and these were her favourite pastimes.

Eric decided to take Bank House, a long-shaped red-brick Georgian house, rather than the more elegant Queen Anne High House which stood at the corner of the road, because Bank House had a bathroom and lavatory. High House only had an Elsan which stood quite openly in a passage with no door or screen. Neither house had very nice gardens, they were both small and shaded by high walls but Eric wasn't

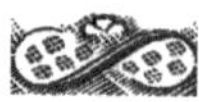

interested in gardening and their rents were very low; Bank House was only £50 a year including rates which was less than half of our London rent. There was gas in the house and we arranged to have electric light put in. The house had been a shop and it had a room with a bow-fronted window that was fitted out very prettily with shelves all round it which had held the stationery and toys, these were very useful for our large collection of books.

Old Mr Baines was very tall and resembled George Bernard Shaw in his appearance but not in any other respect. He had, we soon discovered, a reputation for being extremely mean and very wealthy. After our London landlady we felt capable of dealing with this because he was a silly old man and very simple minded, so that it was easier to see when he was being dishonest. Showing us round the house, he tapped the beams and said with satisfaction: 'Solid oak, solid oak'. He had at one time lived in the house himself and had uncovered and painted a sticky brown varnish over all the beams he could find and he very much objected to our wish that they should be a lighter colour. Eric tried to explain that he didn't think it right to have Tudor beams in a Georgian house; but Mr Baines didn't understand what he was talking about and said that he had lived in the house himself and he knew that the grey-purple wallpaper and brown beams were a perfect combination and if only we would wait till we too lived with them, we should realise that he was right. He wore strange old-fashioned coats made of smooth, very good material that was in spite of its strength very unattractive, and like most of the shopkeepers he wore a straw boater hat in the summer.

Up in the attic of his shop next door, there were two lovely straw hats that had belonged to his horse. When his sons convinced him that he should exchange his horse for a motor van, he had put the horse out to grass, resolved that it should do no more work. He forgot about it and years later, he passed the field and was surprised to find it still alive and standing.

I drove over to Hedingham one afternoon to talk to the painter who was decorating Bank House. It was a boiling hot day and I didn't feel too well by the time I had arrived. Mr Baines and Mr Wiseman the painter, a man with seraphic blue eyes placed very widely apart in his head, talked and talked, saying the same thing in as many different ways as they could think of like a repetitive theme in a symphony, as Essex village men do, and I started feeling sick. At last Mr Baines went away and I was left with Mr Wiseman still talking about paint and wallpaper: 'I suppose you'll have a nice chocolate in the toilet'. 'No', I said, 'excuse me, I'm going to be sick' and I went upstairs and was sick in the lavatory. I came down again and he made no comment but went on with his sentence, telling me in detail just how Mr Baines was trying to get out of his agreement with us that he should pay half of the interior decoration. Mr Baines's plots of this kind were always given away by his workmen. The plumber didn't charge us for plumbing that he considered Mr Baines's responsibility, but knowing that he could never openly convince him of this he would just charge him more on his own private plumbing bills.

I was introduced to the two sons, Harold and Cyril Baines, who now ran his grocery business which was semi-detached to

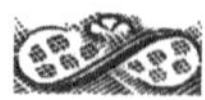

Bank House, so that the rats, of which there were any number, used to run between these houses and the adjoining one on the other side to ours; here lived the two Miss Westrops, middle-aged spinster sisters who worked in the shop and whom Mr Baines still called 'the girls'.

Harold Baines was rather like his father to look at, so all the villagers were agreed that he was just as bad; but Cyril who was quite a nice-looking young man and who disassociated himself from any of his father's house property, was quite popular.

Mrs Baines had been a Miss Gotobed and old Baines, at the christening of one of his grandchildren, told how when he was deciding whether to marry her or not he had been driving along in his trap and the wheels had rumbled 'go to bed, go to bed, go to bed', so he had of course proposed and very prolific they were. She was a soft-voiced stout woman, as mean as her husband, and the favourite daughter Marjorie was also dark and carefully spoken. They told me that I spoke like Princess Marina which I took to be a compliment; I don't think I've ever heard her speak so I can't judge.

Marjorie had recently married Scantlebury Philp who was as remarkable as his name. His father and Edward Bawden's father had both come from the same district in Cornwall and Scantlebury had dark Cornish eyes, or eye; one of them he had accidentally put out when a boy 'assing about' as old Bawden scornfully told us. He was a very big man, as large as a carthorse, and he and his whole family whom I once visited at their remote farm Kirby Hall, reminded one of people out of a Brontë novel. Their mother was as powerful as her sons and

the old-fashioned kitchen was filled with large dark-eyed Philps, amiable and uncomfortable with somebody as strange as myself but potentially violent people because I felt that they were really hostile to everyone except their own kin. Marjorie who was with them, seemed frightened of her mother-in-law. Scantlebury was a very good mechanic and he kept a number of enormous steam engines for farm work and he had a small terrier bitch and a big Labrador dog called Ringer. His main income came from pigs which were all around his farm at Gestingthorpe. He had no pride in the exterior of his house and Marjorie wasn't interested in gardening, so that the outside of the farm was derelict and unkempt-looking, but inside Marjorie had furnished it with loving care and fashionable Drage-like furniture and patterned linoleums.

Marjorie was rather silly when she came visiting with him because instead of accepting him as a good mechanical farmer, she pined for him to be more of a gentleman like her favourite brother who was a house decorator in the suburbs, and she was constantly pricking his considerable vanity with comments on his uncouth behaviour. This naturally made him more ill at ease and resentful towards the gentlemanly patterns that she upheld. She was as her father had said a very nice girl and she made him an excellent wife in every other way; she bottled fruit and cooked very well and had won so many certificates from the Women's Institute for her household skills that she reckoned that she could have papered the lavatory with them.

When we had been in Hedingham for about a year, Marjorie gave birth to a baby girl. On the night the baby was

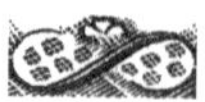

born, she had woken Scantlebury up and said that she thought it was starting, but Scantlebury, resentful at being woken up, had just turned over and gone to sleep again. There was a nurse sleeping in the house and as the baby arrived remarkably quickly, the nurse had to deliver it without the help of the doctor. Scantlebury had a guilty feeling about his behaviour and the next day he went into town and bought her a second wedding ring. Marjorie Ellen was born round about the same time as the Coronation and Scantleberry stood two of his huge engines between the fir trees in their front garden, cleaned them up and decorated them with flags so that they looked very fine.

Eric and I did not like very much going to their house because Marjorie expected us to stay such a long time. If we were asked out to tea, she wanted us to have supper too and then to go home at about nine. Scantlebury didn't like these high teas either and, scorning Marjorie's serviettes and pretty buns, he called for the golden syrup tin and put it straight from the tin onto his hunks of bread. I think it was after the birth of their second child Wilfred when we had been invited over to chase rabbits while the corn was being cut, that Marjorie told me that she was employing a nursemaid and she proudly showed me a little attic room that she had furnished and said: 'Well, she won't do badly if she never fares worse'.

Winnie was a pretty, dark girl, rather shy and she became very fond of Marjorie Ellen, and Marjorie liked having Winnie to train and she liked being in a position of a lady employing servants which she thought so desirable.

I didn't see very much of the Philps for some time and it was Mrs Turner who worked for us and for Marjorie once a week, who first hinted that there was trouble up at Rectory Farm and it was soon all round the village that Scantlebury was carrying on with Winnie the nurse.

I kept meaning to go and see Marjorie, but my own life was pretty complicated by this time and I never seemed to have time and it wasn't till much later when she had decided to leave Scantlebury that Marjorie eventually came and told us about her troubles. Scantlebury had taken to climbing into Winnie's attic window at nights and Marjorie had discovered his unfaithfulness when, in turning out their desk, she had come upon bills for jewellery which he was giving to Winnie; this, really more than his infidelity, hurt Marjorie and she reproached him bitterly for it. She tried at first to go on living as though nothing had happened but Scantlebury with his love-making on his conscience was very difficult to live with. His chapel upbringing must have worried him that he was doing wrong, but Winnie was a romantic girl, a reader of *Peg's Paper* and *Women's Weekly* journals and to him infinitely more desirable than the solid, practical Marjorie.

Marjorie told Winnie that she must go and she eventually got another place, but Scantlebury still continued to make love to her. Both he and Marjorie neglected their work and the farm started deteriorating. It was when the war began and Scantlebury shot Ringer that Marjorie became too frightened to stay, and consulted the village doctor as to Scantlebury's sanity. He was pronounced sane and as he was asking Marjorie to divorce him, she made up her mind to do this and she

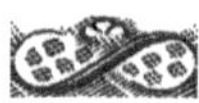

withdrew what money she had invested in it from the farm and came back to Castle Hedingham with her two children who, strangely from such dark parents, were both fair and blue-eyed.

We tried to dissuade her from divorcing him but she put the responsibility for this on Scantlebury's shoulders and to everyone she said: 'It is his wish'. We thought it a bad thing that she should have taken away her money from the farm when it was already doing so badly but he was a hard-headed man himself and if she had not done this, he would probably have hated her more for making him feel even more guilty, or he would have despised her for being weak. She talked very freely about her troubles to her friends and her mother also chatted quite cheerfully on the subject and said that Scantlebury had made Marjorie a beautiful lover. When the divorce was made absolute, Scantlebury quite often visited Augusta House. He was very fond of his little daughter who was a particularly forward and nice little girl and the boy very early in life showed an intelligent interest in machinery. Marjorie would rather proudly tell her neighbours of the numbers of times he visited and the presents of eggs and petrol that he brought for them. Winnie never appeared in the village and having been sacked from her job as housemaid at which she was very incompetent, she went to live at Rectory Farm with Scantlebury, but he didn't marry her.

There were soon three officers billeted in Augusta House who appreciated Marjorie's good cooking and she became happier and more attractive and confident. When we left Hedingham, she and her mother came back to live at Bank

House. The old man had died and they spent quite a lot of money making the paint a nice chocolate again and taking out the few remaining old fireplaces and putting in Devon grates.

The last news I heard of them was from Mrs Turner. Winnie has a daughter; but Scantlebury has never married her. When Mrs Turner went to fetch her meat from Mr Wheeler the butcher, whose shop is almost opposite Bank House, he did a charade of Marjorie coming across when Scantlebury comes into the shop which she does nearly every time he goes there and he imitated her mincing voice saying: 'Oh, do please Scantle come across and help move some furniture' and Scantlebury is always very ready to go with her; but whether what Mr Wheeler and Mrs Turner think is true there is no way of knowing.

I think about poor Winnie, no one will come and see her or her baby. Scantlebury is an exacting man, and she will get no help in the house nor any invitations out to tea, as her own family turned her away from their house when she was seduced, and I wonder what will happen to her.

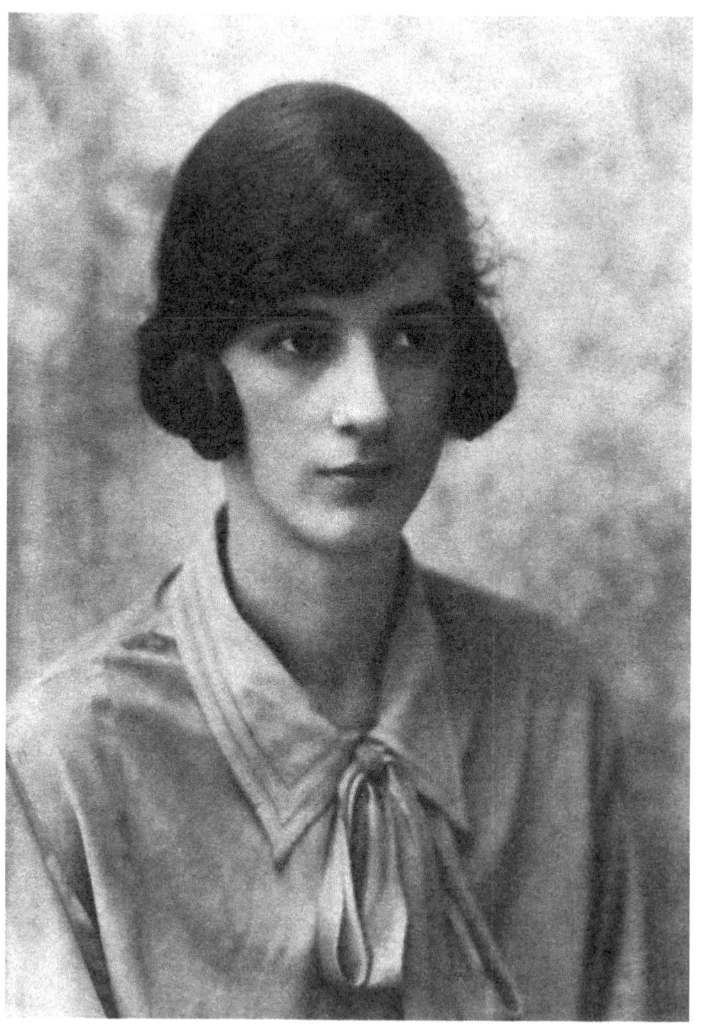

CHAPTER SIXTEEN

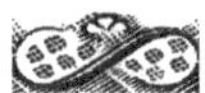

My being sick proved to be the beginning of a baby. I wasn't sick again and I felt better than I had ever done before; it was a wonderful relief not to be unwell every month. Charlotte was also pregnant, but she was unhappily sick every morning right up to the day on which she was delivered. I was staying with her in March when her baby was expected and looking at her in her bath in the outhouse that had once been Prince's kennel, I marvelled at the immense size of her stomach. We knew very little about babies or childbirth and Charlotte collected an incredible number of superstitions about our condition. There is always that warning to expectant women that they mustn't run or jump about. Charlotte's reason for this was that it was supposed to stretch the baby's umbilical cord so that there was more danger of its strangling itself at birth. Another version is that it affects the navel of the baby which protrudes afterwards with umbilical hernia. There may be some truth in this because the navels of my children do stick out and I used to run when carrying them. We took calcium and for the last fortnight, small doses of quinine which the Braintree Dr Edwards had ordered. Edward

Bawden had heard that raspberry tea if taken beforehand made you have a painless labour, so Charlotte drank a little of that too, just to make sure.

Early one morning, Charlotte produced a small show of blood so I went for the village doctor who said that there was no hurry but I had better take her into Braintree where we had both booked beds at the Cottage Hospital. So I drove her in, feeling rather important like bringing the news from Ghent to Aix and went to tell the Bawden parents; Edward was teaching in London and we had decided to say nothing till he got back.

Charlotte was shaved and bathed and given an enema and then put in the labour ward, a small room with babies in bassinets standing round the edge. Unfortunately they had accidentally taken away the inside of the commode which was very necessary to Charlotte. When the pains which were doubling her up got more frequent, she went round the room clutching onto the bassinets. The nurses weren't expecting that she would have her baby as quickly as she did and there was a last minute rush for doctors and nurses who urged her to hold the baby back but she couldn't manage to do this, so tore her cervix in shooting Joanna into the world. Joanna was a very charming baby with black bobbed hair and a nice sun-burnt coloured skin, very like those little Japanese dolls that you used to get in crackers.

Apart from the fact that I felt quite well in health, my pregnancy was a pretty unhappy nine months for me. We moved into Bank House and I busied myself painting white the brown paint in the room with the shelves and pasting marble paper round the brown waist-high skirting in the

other front room, while Eric distempered the wall with white ceilingite. He stayed away for long periods doing a pier decoration at Colwyn Bay and more watercolours at Furlongs for his second show which was arranged for the spring. He wasn't very much interested in Bank House or the local country; he did try to paint in a brickworks on the Halstead Road but gave it up after three or four failures. He complained of the unpleasant colour of the Essex earth and he wanted to escape having to paint continually the vivid green of grass which seemed to be present in any possible local subjects. In Sussex, he was experimenting successfully in painting large expanses of downland and was particularly pleased with one he did of a waterwheel near Furlongs.

He came back to Hedingham late one evening after having been away for about a fortnight and he didn't appear to want to talk about what he had been doing. I didn't ask, thinking it was because he was tired. When we woke up in the morning I asked him again and he suddenly turned on me with such dislike in his voice and said: 'You know very well, I've been making love to Helen'. I had known that he liked Helen Binyon and she him, but somehow I had imagined that she being the kind of person she was, nothing would really happen and I didn't know that Eric had never told her that I was having a baby till recently. I felt terribly wounded at Eric's turning on me like this and supposing that I had known all the time what was happening, and I jumped out of bed and went into the next room to weep and feeling indignant, because the shock had made my baby give such a jump in my inside. Eric was very repentant but still determined to

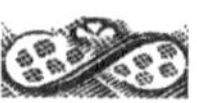

continue making love to Helen. I don't like blaming people for things and I quickly recovered my sense of proportion and when I once knew what was happening, things were easier than they had been when Eric had just been feeling guilty and concealing what he really felt.

All the same it was sad for me, because I couldn't look forward to having my baby when I knew Eric hated the thought of being a father and all the responsibility that it implied. He told me how he and Helen had begun making love after an evening's expedition in the car with Peggy and Jim at Furlongs to see some fireworks. I knew that under the same circumstances I should in all probability have behaved in the same way and I couldn't blame Helen for taking him away from me, because Diana had already done so, but I worried because Helen was such a serious person. Also she was not young but about thirty and I knew what a tremendous change making love made to you both mentally as well as bodily. Eric too was aware of this responsibility but he said that he felt that they couldn't refuse to have this wonderful experience, it would feel like denying life itself. He continued to sleep with me at home from habit or a sense of duty and seeing that there was nothing to be done till the baby arrived, I worked hard in decorating the house and wasn't unduly miserable. I think I must have a cheerful constitution because I don't seem to be put out by misfortunes as much as most people. Possibly this is because I habitually am lucky enough to be completely absorbed in drawing or writing so that I become quite unconscious of people or time when I am working, so there is always that escape from reality.

My sister Billy was also pregnant and she came to stay with me while Eric was away. Her baby was due before mine and she came just after Joanna Bawden had arrived. Billy had had, if anything, even more young men in love with her than sister Margaret. She was more intelligent and sensitive than Margaret but also more helpless. She was potentially quite capable I think, but she allowed Mummy to organise her so long as it didn't interfere with her love affairs which, being of a romantic nature, she enjoyed enormously. She went to stay with my brother John in India and a young man who had divorced his unfaithful wife and felt rather disillusioned with women, asked her to come for an expedition in the jungle with him and his best friend Freddie Newman. This was of course jam for Billy and she emerged from the jungle engaged to Freddie, sending home a number of photographs of herself in a large solar topee, her face very heavily made up in spite of the fact that Freddie had taken away one lot of make up, but she had a second supply so outwitted him.

Before she went to India, her most constant and serious young man had been Bo Waterfield who was large and fair and very good at golf, a plus-four man. He was the son of the headmaster of a boys' prep school called Temple Grove and he hadn't enough money or prospects to support a wife like Billy, as he and his brother both taught in their father's school. The family all liked Bo, he was very good for the Garwood girls because he was such a frank and outspoken person, who never hesitated to say what he thought. When Mummy and Daddy and Margaret and Billy went to Knokke in Belgium for a summer holiday, they had to change trains at

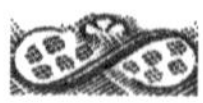

Lewes on their journey out and a bespectacled clergyman got into the carriage with them. It took them quite a long time to discover that it was Bo in disguise, come to see them off. Billy and he used to sing that song 'Trees' while Margaret played the accompaniment. 'Trees' always made Eric restless and sniffy because robins nested in holes in banks and not in trees.

Bo still continued to be friends with Billy after she had married and he came with her to stay in Hedingham. He behaved in a brotherly fashion to her but I think he did mind losing her, because shortly afterwards he went away to South Africa and became a golf pro in Johannesburg. Aunt Edith went to stay with him there and he took her for a motor tour, but it wasn't a success because the car broke down. Then he got diabetes and became religious, bravely writing to the family that he got a lot of comfort from prayer, but they thought he was slightly dotty. Quite recently, we heard that he had got married so I hope he is happy now.

Billy came with me to see Charlotte and the new baby in Braintree hospital and we met John [Aldridge] and Lucie who were also visiting.

Billy was very intrigued with John and Lucie. They were interested in her too and nicknamed her 'Anglo Indian Licemeat'. They enjoyed making nicknames for people and animals and excessively used the adjective 'decent' at this period.

I went too to stay in Eastbourne, where Barbara [Church] was also pregnant and also visiting her parents. My father was very pleased to have so many pregnant women about and importantly, went out with Billy and me and Barbara

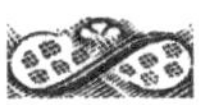

as though he was in some way responsible for us. Billy had her baby in a nursing home in Eastbourne run by a midwife called Beth Smith, whose first customers when she was a young nurse had been my Aunt May and Uncle Robert's twin girls Robin and Wren. She had been fond of my Uncle Robert and was pleased to have his nieces in her Maternity Home. Billy had to have an anaesthetic and when she woke up, she was alone except for a nurse sitting by the window. She thought, 'Oh dear, the baby is dead and how embarrassing for this nurse it is going to be'. She didn't say anything for quite a long time but it was all right after all, because it was being dressed in the next room and was a girl with a head shaped rather like a kettle handle, it grew a better shape later on and she was a pretty little girl with large brown eyes.

Peggy and Jim were now lovers and while he was at Furlongs, Eric arranged with them to sell the caravans to Jim. I felt rather upset about this because I had spent a fortnight doing them up and painting the wheels red and covering the roof of one of them with tarpaulin, and thought that they might have consulted me first. Anyone who has painted underneath a caravan and got paint in their hair would feel a bit possessive about it afterwards. It was the time of the [Silver] Jubilee of Queen Mary and George V [May 1935], when my baby was nearly due to arrive, that Peggy invited herself and Jim to stay. We were also expecting Robert Wellington to come and look at Eric's pictures preparatory to his show and I told Eric not to invite anyone else, but he said he couldn't very well refuse Peggy and Jim when he had stayed so much at Furlongs.

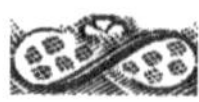

Peggy arrived first and kept Eric up till two o'clock in the morning, making coffee for her, while she feverishly did some mural decoration designs for a hotel in the Channel Islands. When Jim arrived, they wouldn't get up in the morning. The first morning, they didn't get up till nearly twelve and as Mrs Turner went home about that time she couldn't do their room and we didn't know whether to give them breakfast or lunch. The next morning, Eric went up and pulled Peggy out of bed while Jim was in the bathroom. Jim came down to breakfast looking black with fury about this and Peggy was pleased with him for being jealous. Eric and I were both very surprised because we never thought of Peggy with any respect, to us she was like an old Scottish terrier that one turned off the chairs. We both deplored their relationship because they were so fundamentally different to one another and it was unpleasant to witness something occurring which we had so vividly foreseen.

When Robert Wellington came, Eric felt rather like a cat on hot bricks because he didn't like having his pictures looked at by Robert after the way he had been so depressing before his last show, and Peggy and Jim being there made it very awkward as there never seemed an appropriate moment for showing them to him.

My legs hurt if I stood for a long time and I tried to rest when I could, but there wasn't much opportunity. We all walked up to the castle grounds on Jubilee afternoon and later went up to watch the bonfire and fireworks in the field at the top of Sudbury Hill. The villagers tried to sing songs round the bonfire to the accompaniment of the local band but unfortunately,

the only song that everybody knew was Tipperary. Miss Musette Majendie [whose family owned Hedingham Castle] was there organising her scouts and Peggy was being her most Communist and publicly embarrassing self, making sniffy remarks about the village gentry which Eric and I were nervous they would overhear. It was all very well for Peggy, she was only visiting but we were living in the village. She also complained a lot because she loathed bangs and hid her head every time a firework went off. Eric had been feeling indignant with Peggy for some time because he didn't like her lack of respect for him and Helen and he thought that she expected them to do too much housework for her at Furlongs. Her behaviour now made him even more resentful and I was glad to have a common grievance with him because it made us more friendly.

When we came in from the fireworks, I made a silent bargain that if Jim wanted another cup of tea I would write him and Peggy a letter saying what I thought of them. They were blissfully unaware of having annoyed us and Jim innocently accepted his cup of tea, leaving me resolved to write my letter. They went off early next morning with Robert Wellington who hadn't seen Eric's pictures, and I sat down and wrote two letters and showed them to Eric. He refused to let me send the one I had written to Peggy but passed the one I had written to Jim, which I suppose now was a bit unfair because I had been more annoyed by Peggy than Jim.

In this letter I returned the £7 which he had so far paid towards the caravans. I don't remember exactly what I said, I remember writing that he imagined that if he praised the

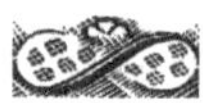

cake, he was entitled to eat all of it and urging him to be more thoughtful and considerate to people when he stayed with them in future.

Jim was terribly upset by this letter and wept about it on Peggy. He did worry that other people might have been thinking the same way about him as indeed they had, but he soon forgot about this and thought it was a personal attack on my part because I was pregnant and because of what had been happening between Eric and Helen.

Peggy had encouraged Helen in her love affair with Eric and Jim, although not actively encouraging, did nothing to discourage it. After my letter he did try to help Peggy a little more, but he was very bad at doing domestic work and she found it was quicker to do it alone than have his assistance. There was something lacking in Jim's brain; he just wouldn't consider or understand other people's feelings, though he was extraordinarily capable of understanding abstract ideas and remembering facts. They both wrote back, Jim saying he had torn up the returned cheque and Peggy sending us 10/- for their expenses which I was glad to have, as we had hardly any money after all the expenses of moving into the house and there was the baby still to be paid for. We knew it would be alright if Eric's show sold as well as his previous one, but there was always the possibility that it might not do so. I went to stay in Bardfield for a day or two with Charlotte and she arranged that John Aldridge should drive me to London where I wanted to buy a cot mattress. I didn't want to be with John when I was pregnant and spent a sleepless night before this drive which was the first time I had been alone with him.

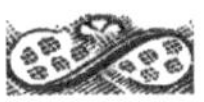

I had a funny felt hat like a shepherdess's hat which I didn't want to wear but it was the only one that went with my dress, which was a rather brilliant blue with white spots on it and trimmed with a narrow red binding. I didn't like John's wearing a knitted cap which he did at first and I was glad when he took it off. In fact I wasn't very happy on this expedition. John was apt to be a bit of an embarrassment to go about with because he was so big and oddly dressed that people noticed him and I feel happier if I am not particularly noticeable. We went to the Caledonian Market because I hoped to find some china door handles. There were one or two with painted patterns but they were 8/- each so I couldn't buy them. John argued with the stall woman who kept saying that they were real antiques and he tried to explain that it was a pity they were because we only wanted good door handles, but she didn't see the point of this argument and just looked cross.

Eric came back for the month when my baby was due but weeks passed and it did not arrive and Eric got more and more impatient and annoyed because he was missing Helen and I was longing for my labour to start and be over and done with because living as we were was miserable and I felt it was sad, because it spoilt my pleasure in having a baby when he was so violently resentful about it. When it was a fortnight overdue, I began to think it never would arrive while he was there and Ruth and Oliver Simon, hearing it was so late, drove over anxiously from Bardfield where they were staying with Charlotte and insisted on taking me to the hospital to see the doctor. Dr Edwards was a big, pink hearty Australian and

he said everything was alright and he expected my labour would start at any moment now and I went back to stay at Bardfield. Eric hadn't made any arrangements for driving me into Braintree from Hedingham because he said that someone would always offer a car in such circumstances. Charlotte arranged that John Aldridge would take me and I felt relieved that I should be with friends because I imagined it might be awkward to be in labour with people you didn't know very well. Eric went to London where Helen was very anxious that he should go with her to some dance.

As we had played racing demon the night before Charlotte had Joanna, Charlotte arranged another session for me and in the early morning I did have a feeling like the gripping pains from the senna that Mummy used to so frequently give us when we were small. As it recurred at regular twenty-minute intervals, I knew it must be labour so I got up at about half-past five and told Charlotte.

I made tea while she went to Place House and came back with both John and Lucie. I felt rather uncomfortable at being the object of so much solicitation because Charlotte had given us such a lively description of her labour that John and especially Lucie were being I felt unnecessarily harrowed on my account. Lucie was particularly sensitive to pain or embarrassment and I chatted bright and cheerfully to them because I really felt bright and cheerful as it was such a relief to really be going to have the baby at last and I longed to know what it would look like. I had borrowed two books from Place House the day before, one called *The Mongol in our Midst* I left behind but I took Evelyn Waugh's *A Handful of Dust* with me.

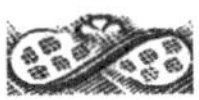

They left me sitting in the armchair of the same bedroom that Charlotte had occupied in the Cottage Hospital. It had a French window looking out onto a garden. I was told to walk about this garden so I walked up and down with my big stomach reading my book, an object of interest to the bored patients of the next ward and a sixteen-year-old boy who was also up and outside. The hospital was being painted and there were quite a few housepainters who propped up their ladders at windows at awkward moments. During the day I was shaved and given three baths and three enemas, but I went on having pains but no waters broke or shows of blood appeared. John and Lucie sent round a bunch of flowers which they later told me they had picked in the garden of an empty house they had gone to look at in Braintree. They enjoyed looking at houses from curiosity, and John I think enjoyed petty thieving of this kind.

At lunchtime the doctor had urged me not to have my baby because he was delivering another baby in the town. He had expected that mine would arrive first, but the other one came at lunchtime weighing 10 lbs and he did a good charade of the distraught husband sitting at the bottom of the stairs saying: 'Strewth, she's dying', till Dr Edwards pushed him outside to go and get a drink. Eric was teaching in London and he didn't arrive till the evening. By this time my pains had got much weaker and had almost stopped and the matron, who was a six-feet tall Swedish woman, allowed him to come and visit me in the labour ward; she had a soft spot for artists as she had been engaged to one in the last war but he had been killed. The bassinets and babies that had been there in Charlotte's time were gone and everything was strangely

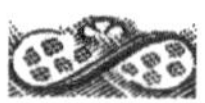

labelled 'Root'. I wondered what this meant and was told that there was a Mrs Root whose baby had been expected before mine so that her belongings were all there in readiness. Eric, who looked very anxious on my account, talked to me for a little time and then went off to spend the night in a hotel in Braintree; I was feeling very tired by now and had finished my book. By about ten o'clock, having encouraged me to push the baby's head down as far as I was able, Dr Edwards decided that he would deliver it with forceps as it evidently wasn't going to come naturally and he sent for an anaesthetist. The sister and he were very amusing together and they now had a lively argument as to whether I was going to have twins or not. He had a proper stethoscope and she had a small one that had a tiny horn like a miniature gramophone at one end and they kept listening to my tummy and she said that she could hear two hearts beating and he said she couldn't. Then we talked about lunacy, because he happened to mention the hospital Claybury Hall from which Tom Hennell had written and he said that Hennell would be recovering if he was there.

The anaesthetist was a carefully dressed homosexual looking man and he asked me the proper questions as to whether I had false teeth, while Dr Edwards urged him to hurry up. When I came round, the matron said in my ear: 'It's a fine boy, just like his father'.

John Ravilious weighed 8 lbs 11 oz; he had been slightly *occipito posterior*, or at least that is what it sounded like and that was why he hadn't arrived normally. Personally I thought he was a fortnight overdue because he never seemed as infantile as most babies. He always looked like a boy as he had large

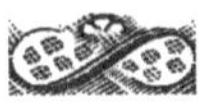

feet and hands, like the claws of some large fowl. He was fair with large eyes and long, turned-up eyelashes and when he was first brought in to see me, he was very pink and crying indignantly and his blue eyes shone with indignation like my mother's when she is angry.

I had three stitches so that lying down and sitting up was very painful but otherwise, everything was alright till the third and fourth days afterwards when my milk arrived, so much of it that my breasts swelled up and became quite hard and white and Dr Edwards, coming into the room stopped and pointed at them with a shocked: 'Look at those breasts'. I had massage and poultices and a dose of salts and gradually they got better but there was too much milk for the baby and it didn't do well and lost weight nearly all the time I was in the hospital. I had very large milk glands and afterwards, when I had other babies, all the nurses and midwives said that in all their twenty or thirty years' nursing experience, they had never met anyone who swelled up quite solid with milk as the way I did. I have had other babies since and I know that I got off fairly lightly that first time because I didn't have the final kind of pain which actually produces the baby. It is very exciting to look down between your thighs and see what you have given birth to and how indignant they are. My second immediately piddled onto my leg just to assure me he was another boy; he looked very brown and handsome so I forgave him for not being a girl.

Outside the sun shone all day, making the garden which I could see in front of me through my French windows look so bright and glaring that I had to ask the nurse to pull down the

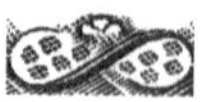

blind over it as my eyes got so sore. Eric used to bicycle over from Hedingham to visit me, complaining bitterly of the heatwave. There were no buses whose times fitted in with visiting hours and he nearly always arrived at the wrong time. I didn't have many other visitors; John and Lucie came once and towards the end of the fortnight, Charlotte and Gwyneth brought Joanna to see me, and my mother came all the way from Eastbourne looking very exhausted by the heat. The baby was by now covered with spots; he had been left by a probation nurse with too many blankets on while there was an operation which had removed all the more sensible nurses and so he developed this heat rash and I felt sorry for visitors, who couldn't really be enthusiastic about such a white-faced, spotty child. I longed to be home and looking after him myself and I felt very miserable and spent quite a lot of time crying when I was alone. The nurses and doctor thought I was particularly carefree and when I was leaving, Dr Edwards asked if Mrs Bawden and I were always such cheerful people.

I liked all the nurses except the night-nurse, not because she wasn't a nice girl but because, being deaf and nervy, she was no good as a nurse and getting behindhand in her work she put out of gear all the rest of the nurses. She was very funny one day when she came to me complaining about the incompetence of one of the other nurses, saying, 'And there she was giving bread and butter with her tea to the fractured skull'. Mrs Root started her baby a few days after mine and she made a terrific noise. She shouted abuse at the nurses and I heard her ordering them to let her go home. The night nurse was very upset by this and kept repeating, 'She's no courage',

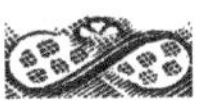

and wondering how she was going to get through the night's work with this hysterical woman as well as everything else. The next morning they brought Jean Root in for me to look at; the nurses didn't like her, but she was I thought quite a nice little baby.

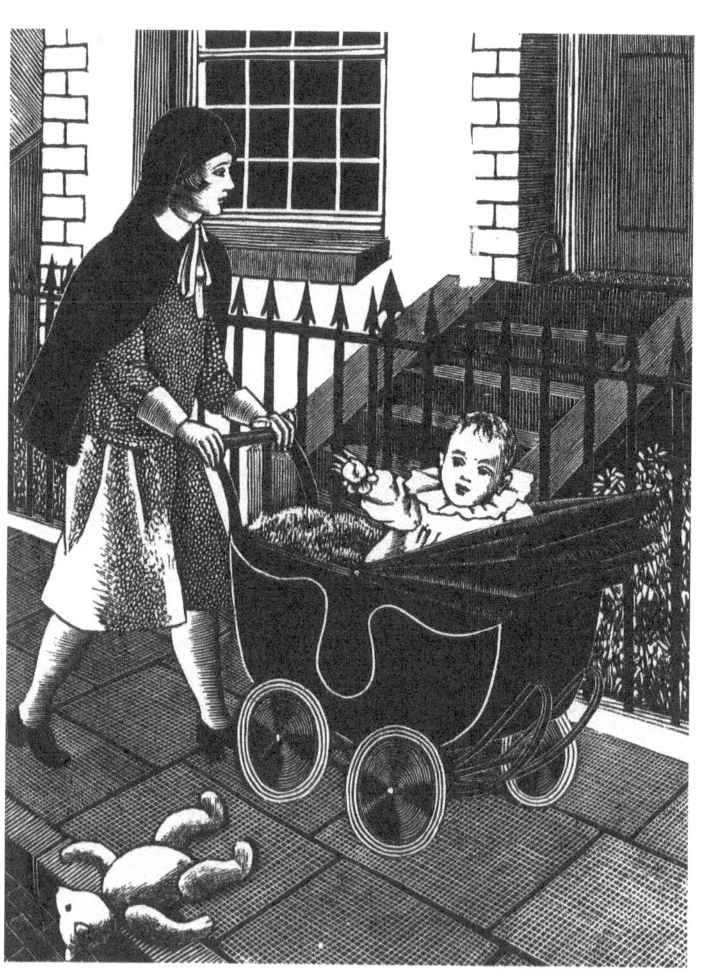

CHAPTER SEVENTEEN

Lucie hoped to arrange a marriage between her she-cat Trippet and the Brick House cat Terrakin. Trippet's only distinction was that she was reputed to be half Siamese. She looked very much like any other black cat and her taste in lovers wasn't good. The tom who was usually the father of her kittens was a black and white cat Lucie called Willis; he was a wild farm cat and Lucie had once surprised a tea party she was giving by suddenly saying in an anguished voice, 'Oh look John, he's mounted', because she had been watching Trippet and Willis out of the window. She didn't like Trippet very much but feared to get rid of her because she felt superstitious about her black coat being lucky. Terrakin was very young but his coat was prettily marked with grey and black stripes. Charlotte and I took him over to Place House one evening. The next morning the grocer congratulated me on having had a baby and I couldn't think how he knew that I was even expecting till I remembered that I had been carrying Terrakin wrapped up in a shawl. Shut into the dining room, the two cats didn't take much notice of each other; we stood watching indulgently, hoping that at least they would play. Basil Taylor, who was in

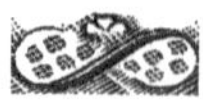

the room too, suddenly growled something about not being able to bear these cats any more and left us all feeling rather self-conscious. I followed him presently to the other room and he explained that it wasn't that he didn't like cats, but it was watching them like that. This wasn't exactly said but I was left with the impression that that was what he meant.

I was shy of Basil who had been such a figure at the Royal College of Art, his bravado and his mistresses and his magnificent appearance had appealed very much to the unsophisticated Eric. I knew that I could never have fallen in love with him myself. My fastidious, Eastbourne, lady-like self labelled him a gypsy's warning of a young man, not for me anyone so resembling the dissipated King Charles. I was beginning to lose my fear of him and to find that he was a kind-hearted person. We talked for a little time before the others came in and he said that he wanted to come and see our house now that we had properly moved in.

The next time that I saw him was when Eric and I were having dinner at Place House, and he came in after we had eaten, looking dreadful. He had been drinking practically neat spirits and Lucie was terribly worried about his inability to work and his getting into debt with people in the village, which made John very annoyed with him too. He had now stopped living at Place House and was staying at a village quite near with two sisters. The elder of these sisters was a cripple called Fairy and he helped to carry her about and with the arrangement of their house, into which they had just moved. This evening, he did not sit with us long before going out and I don't think he said anything much.

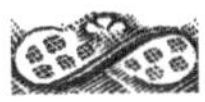

It was now nearly Christmas time and Eric was away from home when one evening I was sitting over our dining room fire at Hedingham. It was bitterly cold and I managed to keep the front of my legs warm, but my back remained chilled as the draught blew under the door and in from the rat runs around the skirting, where it was inadequately patched by old Baines with brown paper. I tried to settle down to reading a book by Bertrand Russell called *Possible Worlds* but after a chapter or two, I was so intensely depressed and miserable that I shut the book and moved to the table and tried to play Patience. Still the feeling of utter unhappiness filled me and I found myself picturing the inside of a gas stove, vaguely wondering why it was an unfamiliar gas stove. I thought, perhaps I am going to start feeling unwell again and that is why I am feeling so miserable. Then I heard a car slowing down outside and I thought, how awful, Basil is going to come and see the house as he said he would. The car didn't stop and I got up, wondering why I should be so foolish as to imagine Basil would come so late at night and, to reassure myself, I walked into the front room and pulled the curtains round the bow window and went upstairs to feed the baby and everything was normal again.

Eric came back the next day and I said nothing about my misery the night before. He brought with him various Christmas presents, among them a dozen prettily coloured balloons on which we painted Christmas greetings to our friends which would enlarge when the balloons were blown up.

The next morning, Charlotte rang up warning us not to send presents to Place House because an awful thing had

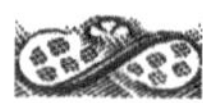

happened: Basil had committed suicide. We felt very low on hearing this because Basil had been such an amusing person and we both wept.

We went to see Charlotte a few days later and she told us that Lucie had been frightened that this might happen because Basil had tried to kill himself before by this same method, with the exhaust from a car; on this other occasion he hadn't succeeded because he said he couldn't stand the smell. Lucie thought that one of the reasons he had killed himself this time was because he was going home for Christmas; he was an only child and she thought that he couldn't stand being such a disappointment to his parents; she had gone with him the Christmas before. I wondered if the feeling of misery I had had was really connected with his death. I didn't want it to be, and standing by Charlotte's primus doing some frying for lunch, I casually asked when it had happened, but it seemed that I had got to face the fact that it had been connected, because it was that same evening at about the time that he had gone into Place House garden after quarrelling with John and Lucie and cut a piece off John's hose pipe to fix into the exhaust of the car. I suppose he may have remembered that we have a gas stove in our house.

I told Eric, wondering and half hoping that he would just dismiss the story as morbid imaginings; but he didn't, because Cecilia had had just such an experience about a young man who had hanged himself at College and she had been moved to write a letter inquiring after him because she had felt so anxious.

It seemed a breach of confidence with Basil to spread around this thing that had happened between our private selves. Eventually I told John Aldridge and, learning that Basil too was unhappily in love with him, the affair seemed a little more explicable.

All that remained of Hedingham Castle was the tall keep which was built of enormous blocks of stone. It had originally had four turrets on top, but two had almost disappeared and there were only the remains of the others. The castle stood on high ground and the village was clustered to one side of it, so that the gardens in the village were not as large as they should have been because in sheltering so closely together round the base of the keep, there was no room for them though the grounds surrounding the castle were very extensive and lovely. Before the last war, the keep had been in habitable condition and was one of the best preserved castles in England but during the war troops were billeted there who accidentally set it alight. Instead of going at once for help, they tried to put the fire out alone so that when the villagers were finally collected and formed into a chain to pass buckets of water from the lake, it was too late and the whole place burned like an enormous chimney. The government later restored the interior with stout wooden floors and it was used for occasional dances and boy scout meetings.

The people who now owned the castle were called Majendie. Mrs Majendie lived in a big house which stood about a hundred yards away from the keep. It wasn't a particularly fine house, just quite a nice Georgian one. When we first came

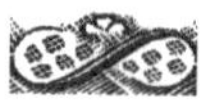

to the village, she lived there alone with her children's governess Miss Bryan and the castle servants, a lady's maid and various others like Bryner the butler. Her husband had been very popular in the village when he had lived there as he was very generous with his money and they had gay parties and plenty of guests for weekends. Jim Andrews, who lived in the cottage opposite Bank House, told Eric how he used to drive a brake to the station to meet the castle guests and what fun it had all been and how nice Mr Majendie was. Old Jimmy Turner who brought us vegetables used to be groom and he too told us about the good old days at the castle. But Mr Majendie was unfortunately too extravagant and, having spent all his own and nearly all his wife's money, he left her and went to live with someone else. He was now very old and decrepit and lived at Torquay. They had had three children: two boys and a girl. Both of the sons were abroad and neither of them had married well; that is to say they hadn't married wives as well born as themselves. The daughter Natalie Jacqueline Frances Musette Loveday Majendie was the most successful and the most extraordinary member of the family. She had from a very early age wished that she had been a boy and as a small girl, she loved boys' games and make-believing that she was a cowboy or a boy scout, and she wore a belt with a knife stuck in it.

When she grew up, she had a man's voice but she was a girl in spite of this, with nice eyes and dark hair and a determined jaw and she danced beautifully. Young men did fall in love with her and want to marry her, but she refused them. She much preferred men to other women and judging from the fact that she had a nervous breakdown, she can't have been at

all a happy person. She was always interested in scouts and she ran a pack which held their meetings in the keep.

It was when unemployment was at its height that she made up her mind to do something active to help and started her camps for training youths in useful employments, such as domestic work or electricity and plumbing. The first camp at Hedingham was very successful and when we came to the village, she had five camps running in different parts of the country and she was awarded the CBE for her achievement. She very rarely visited the village and it wasn't till the war had started that she returned home and we came to know more about her.

Jack Gold also had a boy scout troop and he told us how, when he brought his scouts over to Hedingham one day, she had fixed up an apparatus for swinging across the lake on ropes. Saying that she didn't believe in trusting her boys onto anything that she hadn't first tested herself, she swung off in monkey travel position over the lake. Her heavy weight caused the rope to sag too greatly, so that her behind submerged in the middle passage of her journey; but a guide smiles and sings under all difficulties and she made no comments or appearance at having even noticed this accident when she rejoined Jack and the scouts.

I think that we first met Jack Gold at Bardfield when he called at Brick House, but it wasn't till he arrived unexpectedly one afternoon to fetch pictures for a show that he was organising that I really remember him.

He dressed very immaculately and obviously enjoyed choosing his clothes; usually he wore gloves and a cap or a felt

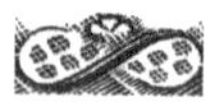

hat turned down all round. Although he was quite tall, he seemed to be a small man because of his neatness and his shyness. It was difficult to tell how old he was because, like my Uncle Harry whom he resembled in some ways, he had gone bald when he was young. When we came to know him better, he would sometimes walk unannounced into our house and call 'Tirzah' in a voice so like my uncle's that it was quite startling to me and I wondered if one day I should do something indiscreet like changing my skirt in front of him and, like Uncle Harry, he would never appear again.

At this first tea party he took such an intelligent interest in John that I asked him if he had any children of his own, to which he replied: 'I am not married'. With children about, his shyness and self-consciousness vanished and I found him a wonderful person to have at children's parties; without them he seemed a cold, aloof man with something of Edward Bawden's distaste for the human race. He had an alarming habit of not answering questions, which was disconcerting because it made you feel that you had asked something indiscreet or silly. As though he refused to admit that he was shy or awkward, he would say rather challenging things which drew attention to him and he enjoyed paying compliments to women, as though these small tributes would make up for the larger insult to them he had made in not getting married. Why Jack Gold had never married was of course a matter of some interest to women and we all had our various theories. He wasn't particularly handsome, but he was a personable young man with round grey eyes, a turned-up nose and cleft chin and his upper lip was also deeply ridged. Although he

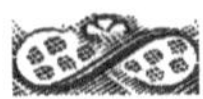

appeared to be indifferent to women, he had a sensual mouth and he didn't in spite of his elegance show any signs of being a homosexual.

He very rarely talked about himself, so that we didn't know much about his private life. We heard vaguely that his father was a conservative old man with whom he didn't get on very well and that Jack had been trained as an architect but whether he was a practising one or not, we didn't know. He ran a troop of boy scouts and was interested in the education of the local children. He began arranging the series of exhibitions of the work of Essex artists, primarily so that the schoolchildren should see them and he gave the children talks on the pictures, and afterwards they all wrote essays on their visit and their opinions of the work of the various artists.

He invited Eric and me to dinner and we set off in the car on a fine evening. We got rather lost as his house was in a part of Shalford with which we were unfamiliar. It was very good country, a valley with the River Pant from Bardfield flowing through it with occasional willow groves and hills on either side. There had been a sunset and we turned the car down the lane and through the ford which ran across the road, winding up a steep hill to his house. At the corner there was such a lovely white weather-boarded mill that we had to stop the car to properly admire it. The sunset made it look a delicate pinkish yellow and the hill rose sharply behind it, the grass was dark green in the evening light and silhouetted the trees which grew about on the steep slope, one of them a light grey dead ash. 'You ought to come and paint this', but Eric never would because he never painted things which we discovered

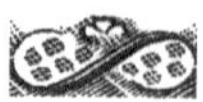

together. Jack's house [Little Codham Hall] stood at the top of the hill with some trees behind it. It was a small, upstanding house colour-washed the same green as a light emerald moth and down the middle of each end it had a red brick chimney running vertically the whole side of the house. It had a nice wide front porch with two steps leading up to it and on either side there stood a plaster cast, one a young man and the other a lady. Jack didn't know exactly what they were; he had bought them at a sale and presumed they were Graeco-Roman casts.

Inside there were more statues in the dining room, but they were busts on pedestals and not full-length nudes like the two outside. The dining room had shiny mahogany furniture and a dark red wallpaper patterned with white wreaths which looked well behind the Roman emperors. The sitting room had yellow and white striped wallpaper with mats and chair covering that imitated tiger skin. The round table had a patterned marble top which with the busts outside gave one the same air of cold aloofness which was characteristic of Jack himself. He had a good collection of books and the *Peerage* stood open on an ornamental lectern in one corner of the room. The walls here were hung with a few pictures by Ruskin Spear and on each side of the fireplace there were two very charming little models of Adam's design for Edinburgh University cut delicately in white paper which he had bought in an auction sale in the Bell yard at Hedingham.

It was a well proportioned house with generous windows and high rooms. Jack described it as a gentleman's house but the coldness of the high ceilings didn't matter very much to him because he told us that he usually spent the winter in

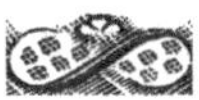

Italy. The plan of the house was simple, like the plan of a doll's house with rooms on either side and a staircase up the centre which curved very prettily to the upstairs, the landing papered with wallpaper imitating yellow and brown marble. His bedroom was remarkable for his bed, which was a very grand one with a small round canopy above it and round wooden legs like wheels.

He was a good host in his eighteenth-century way and we enjoyed the evening very much and like Edward when he was feeling congenial Jack could also become quite warm and friendly. He took us for some very good walks in the country around his house, nice rolling fields almost like Sussex Downs with sheep paths across them and he showed us a small wooded hill with a ditch all round it which had been made by early Britons to protect their cattle from marauding thieves at night.

One evening Mr R A Butler came to speak at Castle Hedingham. He was the Conservative member for the Halstead district and was a friend of Geoffrey Fry's. Eric had called on him and his wife some time before when they lived near Bardfield and he thought that it would be polite to go and listen to him on this occasion. When we reached the school we found that the meeting had already started and, not liking to interrupt, we stopped outside and listened to a man making an opening address. We asked the policeman who was at the door how long Mr Butler had been there. He laughed at this and told us that Mr Butler hadn't come. 'That's our Musette,' he said.

Another story of Charlotte's at this time was about a man who lodged with the Communist Nell Somerset. He worked at the nearby aerodrome and obtained information about conditions of work for the *Daily Worker*. Nell Somerset was just going off on a visit and she went out, leaving a bundle of leaflets of Communist propaganda on the table and several pounds of money which she was going to take with her. The lodger returned unexpectedly and, finding no food in the house, he felt annoyed with her so he took some of the money and the leaflets and went into the pub and got quite drunk. That afternoon in Bardfield Mr Butler, the Conservative member, was holding a private meeting of the executives of the Conservative Party and somehow this man got admitted and he sat down quite contentedly with the rest of the audience. At the end of the meeting, he solemnly distributed his leaflets and Mr Butler sent for the policeman. The policeman walked him home and finding he was an old school friend, they had some more drinks and sat in the police station till they were both drunk.

A few months later a new vicar was appointed to Hedingham to replace Canon Horne who was retiring to Lincolnshire from where he had originally come. The new vicar was a young man called Hepher. He and his wife were both very fair-haired with blue eyes and rosy complexions. Their little boy was called David and he looked a prize baby with his fair curly hair and big apple-red cheeks. We very soon made friends with them. Guy had a very warm-hearted nature and an infectious enthusiasm and Evelyn was the nicest kind of typical English girl with a wonderfully calm nature which she needed to counterbalance her husband's erratic behaviour.

Miss Bryan, the castle governess, together with two or three other spinsters in the village, had loved Canon Horne and they had all assiduously attended the early communion service so that she and Mrs Majendie were sad to see him go, but they at once liked the Hephers. It was at a tea party at the castle that they were first introduced to Musette and also to the Butlers. Mrs Butler was small and dark and rather like Mrs Robert Austin. When she was talking to Evelyn Hepher she asked her if we were Communists like those awful people at Bardfield and Evelyn, who hadn't really considered the matter, said that she thought we were. Mrs Butler replied that it didn't matter as we were so nice anyway. Guy laughed about this later to us. We hadn't really classified ourselves as anything in particular and he said: 'Well, you aren't Conservative anyway'. Because she had been to school with Gwyneth's mother we had met a Miss Rachel Barrett, a talkative Welsh woman with strongly socialist leanings for which she was labelled a Communist and as we were known to be friendly with her, we were ever after this known as Communists among the local gentry. Seeing that it would keep the more stupid ones from meeting us, I thought this on the whole a good thing. Still, it was disquieting to find that even the wife of the Conservative MP could make no distinction between the Labour Party and the Communist Party. Mrs Majendie had called on us one afternoon. She had pale china-blue eyes and a rather goat-like expression. She was interested in painting and liked sketching. Later when they came to the village she called on the Gooddens, a young architect and his wife, and she said that she thought Mr Goodden couldn't be a Communist because he had such good

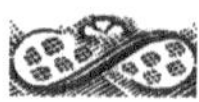

manners. She gave Eric permission to draw in the castle grounds and he tried several times to paint there, but the castle was so romantic looking that he couldn't accomplish anything that he liked and he was also put off by the enthusiastic praise of the boy scouts who gathered round to watch him and he came to the conclusion that anything they liked so excessively couldn't be good.

He also made a start of Mrs Majendie's drawing room under dust sheets. This was a very elegant room with light walls and a black carpet and each chair had a specially shaped-to-fit dust cover over it and Mrs Majendie brought in an ornate gilt easel that she used when she herself was at work, and Eric painted that as well.

He made a good beginning but he got depressed with the way he had painted the view out of the window which had a swan swimming on the lake, because it seemed out of tone with the light interior of the room, and finally to my sorrow, he tore the picture up.

Mrs Majendie told Guy Hepher that she thought that she was disliked by the village people and as she was rather crippled by rheumatism, she never walked anywhere except in the castle grounds. Had we known how seldom she ventured from home, we should have been more honoured by her call, which I never had the courage to return. Dressed in my best clothes, I used to feel uncomfortable on the very rare occasions when I did call, or repay a call as though this social custom was making me appear in quite a false light. In Great Bardfield I had come to identify myself more with the working-class people than the upper middle-class ones and

although having lived in the middle classes, I knew the right way to behave among them, this behaviour was only a make-believe return to the drawing room manners of Elmwood Palace.

When we first came to the village the only people who called on us were the Bishop of Colchester and his family, who came one day when we were out. He was, I believe, a pompous man who had married one of Aunt Gladys' sisters. Aunt Edith forced me to return this call but the Bishop was in his turn out and I only saw Mrs Bishop, who was a high church edition of Aunt Gladys though totally without her charm. I was amused by Aunt Edith urging me before we set out on this expedition to put on more rouge. We were told later that the reason no one except for Mrs Kelk who did drop in after a month or so, called on us was because when Mr Baines had previously let Bank House he had told the sort of people like Lady Rycroft who did call that he had let the house to such a nice family. These people dutifully called on the Ulphses but there was great consternation in their breasts as well as in the bosom of Mr Baines himself when Mr Ulphs revealed himself in his true character which was that of a saddler, and to crown this disgrace, his pretty daughter seduced away from his family the only son of Mr and Mrs Kelk the auctioneers, whose father never forgave him for this and he left home in disgrace. Mr Baines who had especially stipulated in his lease that the house was not to be used for trade as he was afraid of any rivalry in the village, was extremely annoyed by this deceit of Mr Ulphs. They didn't pay their rent and Mr Baines refused to repair the house for them so they pretty soon left Hedingham

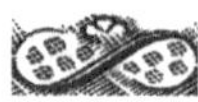

and went to live in Braintree. When therefore we arrived and again Mr Baines said that he had let the house to such nice people, this was received with scepticism and it was not until Mrs Kelk had had me to tea to meet Miss Bryan the castle governess that I was passed as having the right kind of accent for people to call on. Being pregnant and very busy decorating the house, I missed all this and it didn't enter my head that people weren't calling on me. I was fairly contented and it surprised me very much when some years later, a woman called Mrs Rawlins who was acting as midwife for me, when she recalled our first settling into Bank House said: 'I did feel so sorry for you.' I certainly wasn't feeling sorry for myself.

Guy discovered that there were death-watch beetles in the roof of his church. It was estimated that to mend this side roof would cost well over a thousand pounds and Guy set about collecting this with his usual indefatigable enthusiasm. Various rich people in the neighbourhood promised to contribute and the Pilgrim Trust sent £100 and he collected promises for money in the future from the people in the village. The doctor's wife collected about £40 but was very incensed with him because he never wrote to thank her for it. Guy's excuse for this was that the money was for the church and not for him personally: he was very bad at answering letters and often put them into his pocket unopened and forgotten.

When Eric was playing shove half-penny in The Bell one evening, Guy came in with an alive death-watch beetle in a bottle. He wanted to put a collecting box in the church, alongside a display of how the beetle did its destructive work,

showing it in its various pupa stages among sample pieces of oak wood. He couldn't think how to kill the beetle without harming it, but a bright idea seized him and he ordered some gin and filled the bottle right up to the top with it. Eric brought it over for me to mount and I thought I would put it in a box with a glass front which we had got in the house, one that had really been intended for a postbox in a gentleman's residence. In a few days, the beetle had swollen enormously so it was a particularly imposing specimen when I had finished it. Guy's brother Paul came round just after 11 on Sunday morning to fetch it and he hurried off with the box and marched up the aisle through the intrigued congregation and settled it in its place. After the service, there was quite a rush to look.

Next, Guy planned a vicarage fête and he asked Eric and me to run a side show. Eric was very pleased at being asked and decided on crockery smashing, he always enjoyed those comic films where people threw things at one another. Knowing how good Mr Thomas of The Bell was at making anything, Eric asked him to help and he came round to look at the garage which Guy had given us as a stall and he and Eric were both bursting with good ideas. While we drove about the nearby towns collecting any old crockery that we could buy cheaply, Guy set to work and with surprising speed he erected a dresser at the back of the garage while Mr Thomas worked on the 'pièce de resistance' which was a table and chair that collapsed when a target was hit. He made it with a spring underneath and the table tipped upwards, so that anything standing on it fell off too, excepting a lamp which was nailed on.

He made a woman's figure which I dressed in some old clothes of mine, a smart hat and white gloves and I made her a face from an old sheet which I painted and she wore a pair of spectacles. When she was seated in the chair and it tipped over backwards her legs went up in the air in fine fashion. The garage already had shelves on each side and we put old lamps and pots about on them and hung cups and jugs on the dresser with a selection of plates balanced along the shelves which I had decorated with a zigzag of red paper. The walls were hung with pictures, the whole scene framed by some fine large white lace curtains that Evelyn's mother had given to her which we hung up on either side in front. Among the junk which we collected were some quite nice Victorian pictures and we kept one for ourselves, a roll of honour of soldiers who had mostly died of diseases in the war against Afghanistan and we also kept a set of six plates decorated with a pattern of knotted rope and gave in place of these some of our wedding present dinner service, of which we had grown very tired.

Since they had sacked Kathleen, the vicarage had employed an orphan girl called Kitty Tansy. She was not as attractive as her name but was a heavy, squalid Dutch doll of a girl with her eyebrows plucked away to a tiny hard line. Evelyn didn't like her very much although she was a good worker, because she made such a noise stumping about in the kitchen. She went into the garden a day or two before the fête and tripped over a guy rope and hurt her leg and for weeks after she never appeared at the vicarage, though she was up and about the village fetching her water from the pump in the street and carrying it back to her room above Mortimer's

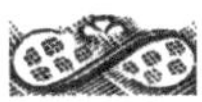

stores. At last Evelyn became so overworked with her continued absence that she employed someone else, but this was not the last of Kitty Tansy because she then sent the Hephers a letter through her insurance demanding £30. She had only been in their employment for about three weeks but the village doctor, who loathed the Hephers, had signed a paper saying that her bad leg was caused by an accident and they had to pay up. Fortunately, their insurance covered this, it was a very long-suffering insurance company. They had already paid for a new bag which David had thrown in the fire, the handbag of his grandmother containing three pounds which he quietly burnt just as she was leaving the house to catch a train; she had never come to stay again. Then he had lit a fire underneath one of the armchairs and only Evelyn's prompt behaviour saved the house from being destroyed because the flames had just reached the curtains; and the insurance company had paid up for this damage too.

After this, Kitty Tansy evidently decided that she had had enough of domestic service and she set up on her own as village prostitute, a fact which Eric found a grateful client had advertised in The Bell outside-lavatory. Eric always read messages in lavatories and we used to speculate about the writers.

It was a lovely day, and early in the morning the stalls were assembled all round the big sloping back lawn with the monkey puzzle tree standing at the top. Mrs Marshall had provided a fortune-teller who sat in a very hot tent on the sunken lawn to the right of the house; it was overshadowed by a large chestnut tree but it did not seem to help. Mrs Marshall insisted that Eric should have his hand read and reluctantly,

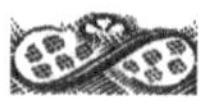

he was shepherded in. He said that she didn't do too badly, she dropped one brick when she said that he was keen on gardening. He had been playing tennis and had blisters on his palm which she mistakenly attributed to spade work. He was amused when she said: 'You've been married twice'. He denied this and she said: 'Oh well, perhaps it was a long engagement'.

At our stall, the prizes for a bull's-eye hit on the target were chocolates or cigarettes. Eric gave permission to children to stand halfway. Early in the afternoon a boy appeared who seemed to have plenty of money and in spite of early failure he persevered until he had won quite a lot of chocolate. Having once given permission for children to stand closer, it was difficult to revoke this when one of them took advantage of it. All day long this boy threw, until Guy had to bring a new supply of chocolates. We discovered that he was the son of Mr and Mrs Ashley Ripper, members of the family who owned Ripper's Wood Yard and he was much older than he looked, being a short stockily-built child. We heard about his prowess at cricket at school and loathed the boy more and more as the day wore on and he quite took away my pleasure in the success of our stall.

Mr Thomas ran a sweepstakes spinning wheel, a hexagon which Eric coloured for him in six numbered segments. He and Mrs Cooke didn't mix very often with the village; they were very tied to The Bell and could only go out in the after-noons. Mrs Cooke who was big, 'a damn fine woman still', always wore splendid furs and opulent hats when she drove out with Mr Thomas.

The fête made enough money so that in a few months, Guy had collected enough in actual and promised money to start on the repairs. These were done by a firm called Rattee and Kett, and Eric called our tortoises after them. I had bought the tortoises from Woolworth's to save them from death in the same spirit that we [later] offered our home to German refugees.

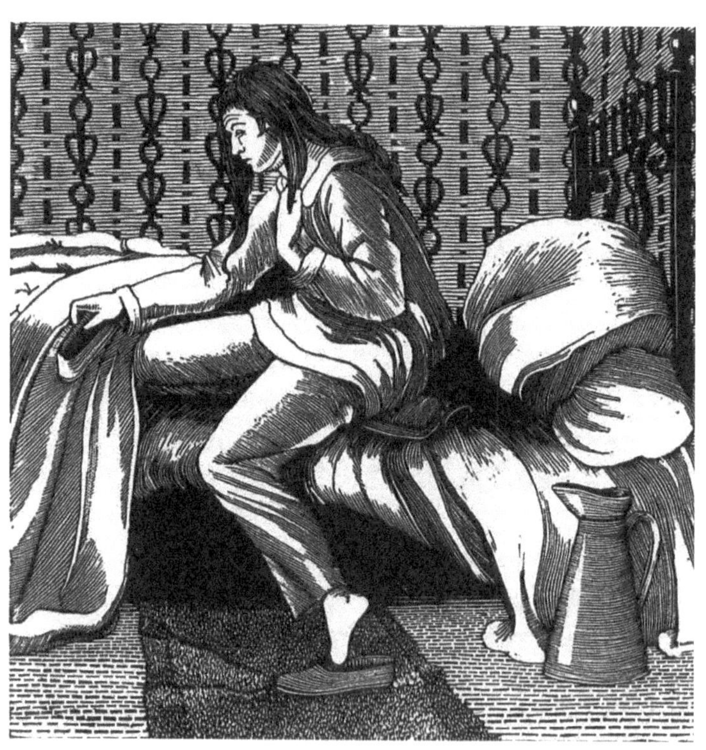

CHAPTER EIGHTEEN

When we first heard that Gwyneth [Lloyd Thomas] had a lover, we were very pleased. It was unfortunate that he was already married but she was doing work that she enjoyed and it was amusing to think of a Girton don having a lover. We felt the same peculiar satisfaction that we would feel on hearing that a nun had escaped from a convent. Our feelings did rather change when confronted with the lover in the flesh. He was something like Jack Gold in appearance, but a coarse, sensual Jack Gold with a warm intimate manner. We all thought it was a thousand pities that as she liked men who looked like this it wasn't Jack Gold who was obviously so much nicer and who had no wife, but the harm was done and she was tremendously happy.

Joe went at first to stay with Gwyneth at Place House. They slept in the big spare bedroom which had a little window opening onto a passage which led to the bathroom. On the second evening, John and Lucie both went into the bathroom and started talking about their impressions. They had nick-named Gwyneth 'Snake' and Lucie said: 'He's not half good enough for Snake', and John said: 'I wish they wouldn't come

here just to do their rogering, it makes them so dull in the day'. After they left, Gwyneth told Charlotte to tell Lucie that she and John had better be more careful what they said in their bathroom because it could be very plainly overheard in their spare bedroom. It was nice of Gwyneth to tell them, but poor John and Lucie had a pretty worrying time trying to recall their remarks and remembering possible insults that their previous guests might have overheard.

Edward and Charlotte not only had Gwyneth and lover to stay but his wife as well. His wife was a lady doctor and as Joe had already been unfaithful to her before, she pretended to be indifferent to his behaviour and from self-defence had also slept with someone else. Edward didn't like this lot of embarrassing visitors and forbade Charlotte to have them again.

The first time we saw Gwyneth and Joe together was when they came to dinner on their way to London, where they were going to see a play. It was impossible not to be pleased to see Gwyneth in a new hat, glowing with happiness and we invited them to stay for a weekend in April.

When they arrived, we told them that Eric was also having a love affair and they discussed the difficulties of making illicit love and Gwyneth talked about writing a handbook on the subject with helpful hints for the innocent. As both of them would have lost their jobs if they were discovered, she and Joe were compelled to be extremely cautious.

It is I find much easier to make friends with men who are in love with someone else because you can speak quite intimately without feeling that your intimacy will be mistaken for anything but friendliness. Not knowing anything about Joe,

I presumed that he really was in love with Gwyneth and was as nice to him as I should be to any friend of hers. Very quickly, Eric and I were disillusioned about him because he immediately began to try to make love to me. This was terribly embarrassing because he didn't on principle disguise the fact and when I complained that it would upset my relationship with Gwyneth, he said that she agreed with him in his theories of free love. This underground scuffling was very unpleasant and Eric and I felt worried for Gwyneth who naturally as he was her first serious lover, doted on this disreputable man. We realised that only a tough man like Joe would have dared to make love to Gwyneth because obviously someone who had been suppressing all their sexual emotions for such a long time would be a heavy responsibility. Joe was beginning to be alarmed at the seriousness of his actions and asked my advice and I told him that whatever he did he mustn't desert now; he had become responsible for this change in Gwyneth. She continually worried that they might be discovered and imagined all sorts of possible pitfalls into which they might fall and I think this bored Joe. It was true that Eric had behaved in the same way about Helen but he did realise the importance of this responsibility and he didn't want to make love to every strange woman that he happened to feel attracted to.

Saturday April 12th was such an eventful day that it is hard to believe now that so many fateful things could happen all on one day. It started very early in the morning when Eric woke and decided, because he had had a letter from Peggy the day before saying that Helen had cried for a week, that he would

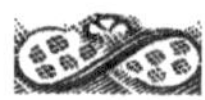

leave me and go and live with her. She was staying with Percy [Horton] at Bures so that it would be quite easy for him to go and see her.

I had recently told him that I was in love with John Aldridge and he got up early and went downstairs to talk to Gwyneth who was also up and I could hear their voices faintly coming up the stairs. I knew that he was explaining to Gwyneth about my loving John so that his leaving me wouldn't seem so wrong. I lay in bed and thought: 'I ought to be feeling very sad', but somehow I didn't, the world seemed so mad and such improbable things seemed to keep happening that I started giggling to myself. Joe next door probably thought I was crying and he asked me to come and see him. I went and sat on his bed and he held my hand and presently started rubbing his thumb up and down my palm so I snatched it away quickly. I was wearing some old school pyjamas of my sister Betty's and he said that what I needed was some proper night dresses, but how silly people like you are who think that between Eric and me such things are the least important.

I got up and dressed and went walking with Eric up Sudbury Hill. 'You can't go away this morning because it's rude to Gwyneth and Joe who have just come to stay the weekend,' I said. This didn't change his mind and desperately I hazarded: 'You can't because it's Betty's birthday.' This one made him laugh so much that I knew I had won and he agreed to wait till Tuesday when Helen would have gone to stay in Devonshire. Gwyneth said that she had some important letters she must post and she wanted to drive in her car

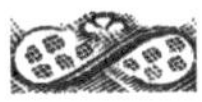

to a town. Quite suddenly, I made up my mind to tell John Aldridge that I loved him and that Eric was going away. I thought that after all he might be able to do something about it and anyway, he was a kind person and Lucie having had at least two lovers herself, might be sympathetic. I was still not absolutely sure if John was her lover or not or if he was just a homosexual young man that she looked after. I told Eric and Gwyneth what I was going to do. They didn't think it was a very good idea, but seeing that I had made up my mind, Eric said that if he was John he would do something and I was worth six Lucies.

Feeling as though I was setting out for a visit to the dentist, I drove off with Gwyneth who made a plan that she would say she wanted to talk to Lucie while I went on to Braintree to post her letters. We were lucky because John was outside his house: we got out and he put his hand on my shoulder while I explained what we wanted and it was quite easy to push him into the car and I drove off with him to Braintree. Having got as far as this, I felt very frightened and, like the pain that disappears when you have reached the doctors, I didn't feel that I loved him at all. However I had to go on now and I made a very bad beginning ending up with the phrase that I felt physically attracted to him, at which he gave a big start of surprise and I felt more and more miserable and cursed my Eastbourne upbringing with Margaret that made me use these dreadful expressions when I was nervous. 'How much did you hope for?' he asked. I hadn't hoped anything but I thought rapidly now and said: 'That you should make love to me once a fortnight.' John said that we had better post the

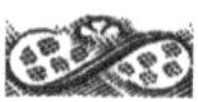

letters first and talk about it on the way home and I agreed that it was probably on occasions like this that one ran over people. I drove without accident to Braintree and back as far as the green lane to Hobby Binns, where he suggested we got out.

It was a very cold and windy day, the hedges were still bare. The green lane starts as quite a wide open road which later on narrows and by the tumbledown cottages on the left it turns gradually and the hedge of overgrown bushes and trees shuts it in on either side, so that there is no direct view of where you are going. John seemed immensely tall as I trotted along beside him: 'I must think', he said and he didn't say any more till we had nearly reached the cottages where he explained that Lucie was a very jealous person and that it was because of Basil's infidelity to her that she had stopped living with him and also that the unfortunate things that had happened to her before had made fidelity particularly important to her.

I knew that it was hopeless but I couldn't stop and I thought even if I am ridiculous, it is all to the good because it would be sad for John if he really did love me after this. It was bitterly cold, we had passed the cottages and stopped by a large clump of bushes with red bare twigs which rustled against one another in the wind and I thought, I have never done anything as brave as this before and I feel that I will regret it all my life. 'Your pictures have all got walls round them.' I opened the attack which gradually developed into a kind of auction sale and I was extolling the virtues of Lot 1 – myself – 'worth six Lucies'. John had been leaning over a gate but naturally stung by this, he turned on me and defended Lucie and his love for her in quite a long coherent speech, but

it just wasn't perfectly convincing and I grinned and said: 'I don't believe a word of what you're saying, you'd be in love with me if I wanted you to'. Poor John, the hateful green lane seemed to force us to speak truthfully; 'I suppose I should'. It was only a very muttered admittance but it made a tremendous amount of difference to me. For all that, I accepted the fact that we couldn't do anything about it and I mustn't because of Lucie really try to make him in love with me and we walked back to the car without saying much more.

I was feeling quite ill and exhausted by the time we reached Place House and John brought me into the drawing room, where Gwyneth expected that I would say something about what had happened. I felt, I shall be sick if I talk about this and in the hall I said desperately to John: 'Don't tell Lucie', and he said: 'All right, I won't'. Coming back in the car with Gwyneth, I told her that it was hopeless and she said that she had felt sure it was but she hadn't stopped me as I'd seemed determined to settle the question this way. Afterwards, as one tends to do with bricks that you have dropped, I didn't think about that day if I could help it.

Eric and I went to tea on Monday with Rachel Barrett, the Communist school friend of Gwyneth's mother and met there her neighbour Mrs Marshall. He was still determined to leave me on Tuesday and we both laughed inside ourselves when Mrs Marshall asked where it was he was going the next day and hearing it was Devonshire, enquired which parts he was going to sketch.

We made love for the last time that night and he said: 'How well you kiss, you ought to have a lover.' I went up to

London with him the next day and in the railway carriage, he taught me the tune of one of Peggy's songs:

See here you false young men,
Do not leave me to lament.
The grass that has often times been trampled under foot,
Give it time it will rise again,
Give it time it will rise up again.

When I got back to Hedingham, I wrote letters to Charlotte and Barbara [Church] saying what we had decided to do and they both came to see me. Barbara was particularly vehement against the whole plan and said that Helen was wrong and in time Eric would be sorry: she likened being in love to mumps which made me laugh.

Eric had arranged to come back and see me in a fortnight but he arrived sooner, because Helen had seemed rather dazed by this sudden change of action and hadn't wanted to tell her mother yet as her sister was just going to have a baby and she thought it would upset them both. She had asked him to wait till the baby was born. This didn't seem a very convincing reason to me and for the first time I felt angry with Helen. After all, it isn't easy to give up your husband and your sense of security when you have a child to look after. She had never shown any consideration for my baby and it was cruel to have Eric back when I had made the effort of parting with him. I cried at supper one evening because I felt forlorn and not at all confident about my future and when Eric asked what the matter was, I said: 'I haven't got anything left'. He

reminded me that there was little John but it wasn't much comfort. He said that he didn't know what Helen would do if she knew that I felt like this and that he couldn't leave me if I really was so unhappy. I felt rather mean because I knew that if John Aldridge had only been free I shouldn't have minded Eric going, so I made an effort to cheer up and Eric advised me to go and stay with Peggy who had invited me to Furlongs for the weekend.

When I arrived at Furlongs I found that Horace [Wilmott] and a couple called Andrew and Jane Boyd were staying with Peggy; Andrew Boyd was a soft silly man, his wife was the daughter of the painter Philip Connard and was herself a singer; she was a fair, dissatisfied girl.

I thought that Barbara was in Eastbourne so I walked over to Firle village to ring her up. The telephone was answered by Colonel Church who said that Barbara had just gone back to London; he was ringing off when he said: 'Hold on, here's Bob just come in'. It was good to hear Bob's voice again and he arranged to come over and see me the next day; Barbara had apparently told him about Eric and me separating from each other.

The next morning was a lovely one and looking at myself in the glass before I set off to walk to Glynde station to meet Bob, I thought, you will never look any prettier than you do now. There is always that compensating factor that if you are having a horrid time, the days that aren't horrid are more enchantingly beautiful in comparison.

The train came in with Bob's head sticking out of the window. He had grown a moustache, his hair was going grey

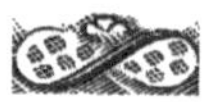

each side and he was fatter, but I knew it would never matter to either of us what we looked like just because we could always remember so much about each other in the past.

Outside the cottage he made me promise that there was no one inside that I loved because he would feel so jealous that he would rather not go in and meet them. I reassured him and having been introduced, we went out for a walk. There was a ridge of bushes and trees dividing two fields and I disappeared among the bushes to pee, but was surprised to find that Bob had followed me and was watching this undig- nified procedure. We walked along inside the cover of the hedge and sat down to talk; he pulled up a blade of grass and twisted and tied it round my finger into a ring. Dear Bob, of all the best things that have ever happened to me, that was surely one.

At lunch, he and Horace, who slightly resembled him, seemed to fill the tiny cottage with their brown bodies and the others liked him very much: Jane Boyd was full of curiosity and when we were clearing away the lunch said: 'What a charming man', but I didn't enlighten her as to where he had come from. The truth was that now he was no longer in love with me, he was twice as attractive. We went into Peggy's room and talked about ourselves of seven years ago. Bob realised why it was that I had refused to marry him then and that if he had only been adult as he was now, I would probably have done so.

After a few days, I went to Eastbourne. Billy and Betty were staying at home and it felt like being back at home before I was married, except that my John was there too with Hilda

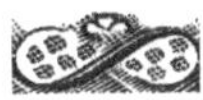

Turner to look after him. Bob and Brab were asked to tea and Billy electrified the family afterwards by saying: 'Did you notice the lecherous way Bob was looking at Tirzah?'

When his wife went to London for a week, Bob took me for a drive and it seemed natural that we should return to Furlongs which was now deserted. I took him for a long walk over the hills to see Muggery Poke, a falling-down farmhouse made of large grey slates in a lonely and deserted valley. It was quite a difficult place to find and it was very hot walking. Bob talked well about Africa and lion hunting and I felt very happy, it was such a refreshing change from politics or art.

Some time later at a party at Helen's flat, I met Andrew Boyd again. More direct than his wife, he asked who Bob was. I wanted to stop him as soon as possible and said that I used to be engaged to him. 'Why on earth didn't you marry him?' he said bluntly. Eric was standing with Helen quite close to us as I replied: 'Because I married Eric instead.' For all that, I didn't think that I had chosen wrongly in marrying Eric, whatever other people might think now; I didn't want to be married to Bob. From this party we went on to a Communist dance, the only one that I ever attended. None of the men that Helen had provided would dance with any of the women she had provided and I found some other people that I knew and when there was a Paul Jones, I joined in. In succession I got two Africans; they had nice voices and spoke intelligently and dancing with them, I was amused thinking how absolutely horrified my father would be if he could only see me. I danced too with Jim Richards and it was the first time I had seen him

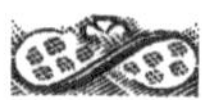

since I had written the rude letter to him. I felt pleased that he asked me: he never had before or since.

I went back to Essex feeling a very different person from the sad one who had left it the month before and all that year; I still loved John Aldridge but I didn't meet him very often and was embarrassed if I did and avoided looking at him. During the winter, he had decorated a little downstairs room with a wall painting, a design of plants and mouths, and looking at these mouths, I began to wonder if perhaps after all he hadn't dismissed my proposal so completely as he appeared to have done.

Helen's sister's baby arrived but she and Eric made no more plans, though they continued to make love and I began to wonder if they hadn't changed their minds.

While I was staying in London in the spring, Aunt Edith took me to John Lewis' to buy a woollen dress, because she had seen one or two that she liked in the sales. Aunt Edith and I didn't really agree at all about clothes but as she was buying it for me, I couldn't be too fastidious. Finally we decided on a green one, which she liked; I only liked the colour and the material but saw that there was a possibility of making it quite nice if I altered it.

It was a long and clinging dress with sleeves that belled out at the cuff and the neck was high, giving it an ecclesiastical air; the kind of dress that an art and craft potter's wife might wear at the opening day of her husband's pottery exhibition.

When I was back in Essex I showed it to Lucie who was deeply interested in clothes and she told me to bring it to her house one evening and she would help alter it. Since I had

been with them to a fitting at a Cambridge tailors, I was beginning to realise the intense interest the inhabitants of Place House took in their clothes. Anyone looking casually at John might suppose that his careless appearance really was careless. His clothes had a slightly nautical look or possibly he might be just going to do some painting, or was it gardening? He didn't look well in ordinary conventional suits which was the reason I suppose for these fancy dresses. Lucie more obviously gave care to her appearance. Her dresses were usually long and though roughly conforming to fashion, they were very personal, which is of course what clothes should be. Basil said that she reminded him of the old lady in the *Babar the Elephant* books, which was true. On this occasion at Cambridge, Lucie and Basil were having overcoats fitted and John some trousers. They specially wanted me to watch because they thought the tailor was so entertaining. I felt sorry for him because every little tiny detail of the garments was discussed and alterations, possible and impossible, suggested. Basil's overcoat was made of a remarkable red brown tweed and lined with checked horse cloth. He looked enormous in it and reflected in the three-sided mirror, he unnaturally filled the room. Now poor Basil was dead and we looked at a book of his dress designs by lamplight in Lucie's exquisite drawing room.

The same care which they lavished on their clothes was also given to the house. There was always, in the drawing room, a large jug of the most beautifully arranged flowers; at arranging flower bunches Lucie had no equal. The armchairs and sofa were upholstered in butcher's apron blue and white

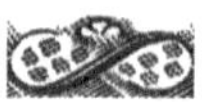

stripes and the carpet was pink. When they had first arrived, the carpet had been red and, with its white walls and white frilled curtains, the room had been very like the one so admired by Charlotte Brontë which is described in *Jane Eyre*. To Eric and me it was a haunted room. When John and Lucie were out of it, unable to bear its close gentility, Eric had felt the necessity to make some protest against it, slap my bottom or do an outlandish clodhopper's caper, a making of long noses at the ghosts. Tonight Eric was away and I felt the room alert and watching us, or were we all watching one another? I thought: 'Lucie, if I take off my dress and try on this new green one, John will one day make love to me.' I felt a pig and took off my dress discreetly behind the big armchair, knowing this false modesty to be useless since John knew that I loved him but there was nothing else I could do.

I am always having these premonitions about the future and I wish I could make up my mind whether they are just ideas in my own head or whether they really are something not in my own control: do I make things happen because I have imagined that they might ?

A month or two later, John and Lucie invited me to come with them to a play at Cambridge. I was alone at Castle Hedingham with little John, so I asked Evelyn Hepher to come and sit in my house to look after him while I was away. She came around after lunch and we sat gossiping by the fire for some time. I was dirty and untidy so when she had gone, I got up to go and change my dress. I wasn't expecting John to come and fetch me till tea time, when to my surprise he suddenly drove up outside the house. Not liking to be found

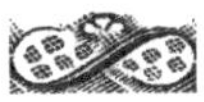

with my nose shining and my hair dishevelled, I opened the front door to him with ill grace and, 'Why have you come so soon?' Like two cats, we walked about the house. I made bright and cheerful conversation and gave him books to look at while I went upstairs and changed into the green dress which now had a ruche of scarlet velvet around the neck. In the car, I felt an excited holiday feeling and John forgot to put back the choke. When we were getting near Bardfield, he told me about an operation on his nose which he had recently had. Going into more horrid details of his operation I felt that it was happening to me and suddenly appalled, I said, 'Oh stop it John'. Glancing at me open-mouthed for a fraction of time, we were vividly aware of one another and he jammed on the brakes of the car too quickly so that we screeched horribly up to the door of Place House.

They had also invited to supper a village woman who had rather an unhappy home life with a publican husband and Nell Somerset the Communist, who suffered from a too sensitive nature. Her face was slightly fanatical but she could be very charming and I admired her very much; she bicycled around the villages in Essex delivering books and *The Daily Worker*. Having been introduced, we left the drawing room; the other three went out first and I was left with John following behind. There was a belt of green around my dress, the tails tied behind and tipped with red, my mother would have called it 'Suivez moi jeune homme'. It seemed quite incredible to me that the superior John should really be holding on to them as we entered the dining room with such innocent faces.

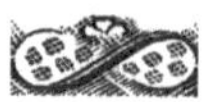

The play was about the Tolpuddle Martyrs and was written by Miles Malleson, the actor. They did it well and I enjoyed it, though I wished that I could have sat next to John. I was between the two guests, and Mrs Somerset became very overwrought and moved to tears by the play. At the back of my mind, there hovered Eric's description of a completely chinless Miles Malleson portraying a stage butler who put his face round a curtain and just looked.

After the play we drove directly back to Castle Hedingham. I was feeling worried that I was so late and would be keeping Evelyn up. I was relieved to find Guy sitting with her too when I got back and leaving the others in the car, John came in and was introduced. I followed him back to the hall and unexpectedly, we kissed one another goodnight behind the front door. Going back to the drawing room I caught sight of myself in the big wall mirror; I was surprised to see myself transfigured, my head surrounded by a shining light. Guy and Evelyn noticed nothing and asked politely if I had enjoyed myself.

When they had gone, I squatted down by the fire and touched my glowing lips, wishing now that I could keep them un-licked and unwashed for evermore. I spent a sleepless night and the next day I went to stay in Eastbourne. Here my feelings of happiness changed to deep gloom. I had told Eric what had happened and he wasn't particularly interested nor did he think anything else would happen, but I worried and worried because I didn't know if John loved me or not and if he did, what ought I to do.

Eric was now in London painting a showcase for the Paris exhibition. It was to display tennis racquets and acquisitions of sport, and I went to help him. Edward was doing one for trunks and leather goods and John Nash for guns and sporting equipment. These were all set up in the Imperial Museum which happened to be empty after the removal of the War pictures to Dulwich. I hadn't met John Nash before and I liked him at once. He was short with a nose rather like Dante's but his head was longer and a nicer shape. He had large grey eyes which, protruding slightly, made him look delicate. I don't know why but he made me think of an unusually dignified piano tuner and it was, I found, true that he did play the piano as well as paint. While we were working, the telephone in the room rang: the clerk, an unprepossessing-looking man who whistled: 'A fine romance with no kisses', wasn't there to answer it so John Nash picked up the receiver to stop the noise. 'Hullo', he said, 'Hullo', a pause, 'Who are you speaking to?' He had a high, inconsequential voice and I think he was quite surprised when he put down the receiver and turned round to find us in fits of laughter. I was glad to laugh again, I had got so gloomy in Eastbourne that I couldn't even smile. I cheered up now and bought some red, white and blue silk and started to make three pairs of French knickers.

Eric was again away when about three weeks later John Aldridge unexpectedly bicycled over to Hedingham. He arrived one afternoon when a shower of rain was just starting and I wasn't feeling very well and the shock of seeing him again so unexpectedly made me feel even worse. I felt quite

panic stricken to see him standing at the door and I half wanted to run away, so I borrowed a bicycle too and said that I must change into some suitable bicycling bloomers. When he followed me upstairs, I felt certain of the reason for which he had come. Bicycling in the rain I rode with him to Sible and round Ruchey Green, worrying because he had already had a long ride, yet I felt that I must go somewhere very quickly. Back home again we drank tea and he sat in my grandfather's big armchair while I squatted down by the fire and said, 'I can't go on like this'. I don't remember exactly what we said after this; John rarely finished his sentences at the best of times and in this nervous state, he was more incoherent than ever. I know we talked about jealousy and he said that he must feel sure that I really liked Lucie and I reassured him about this. I knew that because of her he wanted our love making to be my responsibility and I cheerfully accepted this but wished I didn't feel so sick. Whatever we said now didn't alter the fact that the harm to Lucie was done whether we made love or not, because I knew he wanted to, and I had been right. Actually it never entered my head to stop him at this moment and our second kiss, which was as though I had never been kissed before, left no alternative to us. We stood up and I thought of the Border ballad which Bliss had illustrated: 'A bed, a bed, Clerk Saunders cried', but upstairs I knew that more than anything I really wanted rest like the shepherd in that lovely Somerset lambing song, 'I had rather rest on my true love's breast than any other where' and just to lie down and know that everything was all right.

During that summer John made love to me every two or three weeks. We made love so perfectly together that it was impossible to think of it as wrong or harmful to anyone else. But we both knew that it couldn't go on indefinitely and every time that he came, I was aware that it might be the last and I would look carefully at him while I still could, trying to store in my memory what he looked like and the feel of his thick hair while I rubbed his head with my hand. We didn't say very much and he never said that he loved me or anything endearing to me at all, so that I imagined that he was making love to me because he was sorry for me. I was so much in love with him myself that I felt humble and frightened of him and I didn't think it possible that he could love me back, nor did it seem to matter.

I would like to have had a baby by him but Eric would not allow this and I saw that it wasn't really a good idea; but I longed to give him something back for the happiness he had given me, though goodness knows, Englishmen don't usually accept a present of a baby with gratitude. We arranged that if Lucie discovered our secret we should stop. On the few occasions when I saw her, she didn't seem more unhappy or unwell than usual; in fact she looked rather better, so I didn't worry about her. I had very little time for thinking at all as Eric and I were constantly entertaining and being entertained in the village and little John and marbling left me fully occupied. All that summer I was aware of being absolutely happy and knew myself to be most awfully lucky; after all, how very rarely do the hopelessly in love have what they desire.

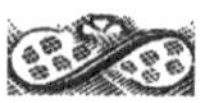

I enjoyed too the feeling that I had a secret and wherever I went, I felt more charitable to other people and good. I realised that it was strange that I should feel good when I was doing something that was generally accepted by society as being bad, and if I thought about the future when I should no longer have John for my lover, I was afraid that I might change, and looking back on my behaviour, think it was wrong. Because I knew that John loved Lucie I accepted her as being part of him and as I didn't have time to see him very often or for very long, I felt that I wasn't altogether taking him away from her. It was difficult for him to come and see me because she did not like being left alone, so that he could never be away at night or give me very much warning before his visits. Eric was sometimes at home when he arrived but he didn't mind because he liked John and pleased to have me happy again, he began to be more interested in me himself. I didn't really like this benevolent attitude of his and would have preferred him not to have been about but as he was doing lithography on large zinc plates which were hanging in our front room, he couldn't very easily go away. Then he quarrelled with Helen and this upset me because it seemed such an anticlimax after all the fuss and trouble that they had made. Unkindly, one morning I said that after all, she was only a north-country girl. Eric, who had never thought of her as that, agreed and I knew that he would never leave me for her again. The truth was that when it came to the point, neither of them really wanted to face the upset and trouble that their parents would create if they openly started living together, and they both felt guilty about me and little John. Gwyneth's love affair we heard from Charlotte was also finished and she and Joe were no longer seeing one another.

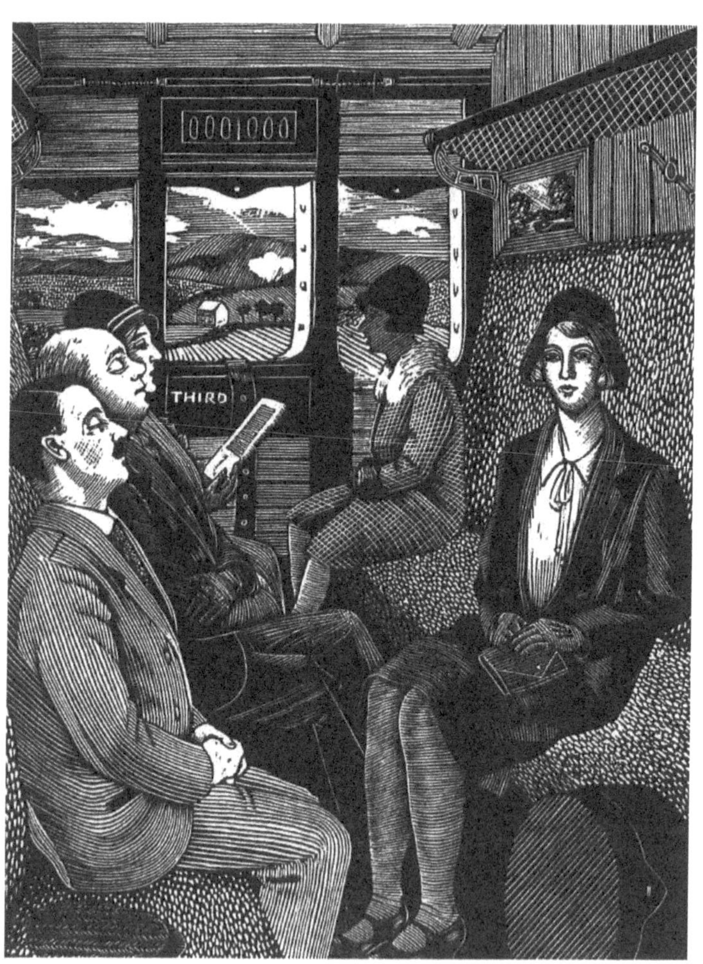

0001000
THIRD

CHAPTER NINETEEN

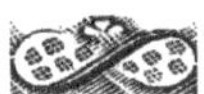

I was invited to a tea party with the Hephers by Miss Care, a delicate woman who had been a nurse until she overworked and strained her heart. She was an enthusiastic woman, an active member of the Women's Institute and she particularly enjoyed doing charades in which she grossly over-acted; the two stars at play acting were the Miss Westrops who lived next door to us, the elder one was extraordinarily good.

Lady Rycroft also came to this tea party and another big widow with a double-barrelled, high-sounding name which I have forgotten, who lived at Yeldham with her daughter. The only topic of conversation was the impending abdication of King Edward VIII. How these women enjoyed it; what keen pleasure that scandal gave to millions all over the world and nowhere was it more thoroughly enjoyed than in Miss Care's cottage that afternoon. At first, there was the competition for who had first known about the existence of Mrs Wallis Simpson and then a collection of stories about her and finally their opinion of his behaviour. The verdict was that no one minded his having a mistress, but it was wanting to marry her that was so wrong. The Hephers and I went early, Guy took a

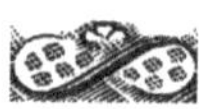

deep breath of nice, fresh air outside the cottage before climbing into the car which I had just bought: a shiny black Morris Eight.

The two hundred shares in Shell Transport that Aunt Edith had given us for a wedding present had this year given all their share holders an extra number of shares as a bonus. I didn't like the way this appeared just at the same time as the Italian attack on Abyssinia and, in case it had some connection with the war, I decided that I would sell them and buy a car instead. The Morris was secondhand and cost £70 and I let Guy and Evelyn use it if they wanted to and they allowed me to garage it at the vicarage.

In May [1937], the coronation of the King and Queen was to take place and we began planning how we should decorate our house. Mr Thomas began first by putting up his big Union Jack on the post of the yard gate by the gents lavatory: but he didn't leave it there because Mr Baines went over to him and suggested that they hung a rope right across the road between their two businesses. He had two big flags, one of them a fine one of the castle arms, and with the Union Jack, they made a good start. We hadn't got any flags, except a faded Royal Ensign with a repellent-looking female torso incorporated in the harp of the Irish quarter. She had flat drooping breasts, wispy Victorian hair, a beak-like nose, savage eyes and wing feathers like hair sprouting from under her armpits. We also had an old Royal arms made of painted lead and we nailed it up over the front door, where it looked as though it had been there for hundreds of years. We couldn't buy flags because there weren't any in the village, so I cut up my

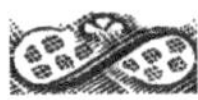

blue spotted maternity dress and a white sheet and made strings of pennons which Eric nailed along the railings and under the roof and porch.

Once someone had had the courage to begin, the rest of the village started and decorations came up like fine flowers. If there had been a competition for the best decorated village, I think Hedingham would have been anyway highly commended even if it hadn't won a prize. The trouble about the Coronation was that it all happened at the same time and you didn't have a chance of seeing all the places before you got a little tired of flags waving everywhere.

Mrs Turner and her neighbour covered the pump in their garden with coloured paper and made a lovely crown on the top of it: but it didn't soften the heart of the old perisher Baines and make him have it mended for them as he ought.

It was such a beautiful village that first evening when the flags appeared and walking round with Eric I felt that the people were specially glad to see him there admiring it so, because they'd all been playing at being decorators themselves and were pleased at being complimented by a real professional. Everyone talked more freely as people always do when there is an occasion, making one wish there were far more.

On the next day the carts and bicycles were decorated too. Hedingham carts were lovely enough without decoration; the milkman and the bakers had stunning yellow ones. Our milkman was called Jethro Stimson, he'd only had one holiday in his life which he had spent at Eastbourne. He was a very typical Essex shape, short and broad with a flat top to his head

and wide-apart eyes. He made his cart so pretty with blue, yellow and white flags that I went and did a picture of it for him at Hostages Farm where he lived.

On Coronation morning, Eric was restless and impatient for things to start happening and he wandered aimlessly about the street wearing a red badge with Committee written on it of which he was very proud. He came in and looked at the autobiography of Benjamin Robert Haydon which had an excellent description of the coronation of George IV: 'The room rises with a sort of feathered silken thunder.' The Gooddens came in to listen with us to the broadcast of the ceremony. Listening to it, I couldn't really imagine at all what it would look like and I wondered if the King had got to say anything and whether he might not break down and stutter at this most important moment. Eric was charmed with the clear sweet voices of the choir singing: 'Vivat, Vivat'.

The village wasn't so much interested in the real Coronation but were intensely preoccupied with their own share of the festivities. The more authoritative and capable men like Harold and Cyril Baines and Beard and the fussy little schoolmaster, could be seen about with their red badges gleaming on their coats, pointing their arms and directing people who pushed barrowloads of chairs or cars full of fat women and crockery. The garage boys put a finishing load of old motor tyres on the huge bonfire that had been built in a field on the top of Sudbury Hill and we wondered if they would smell.

The programme started with a fancy-dress procession to the castle keep and as we and the Gooddens had been asked with Mrs Majendie to judge the children's dresses, I went

round with the procession trying to make up my mind which I liked best. It was surprising how many people there were and what a lot of noise they made, the women's voices clacking and the men's rumbling underneath, interrupted by the ugly shouts of the excited boys. The very tall handsome milkman called Percy Sneezham, who worked for farmer Ruffel with the roving Groucho Marx black eyes, was shamelessly beautiful as a bridegroom, so resplendent that you just didn't notice his bride, and there was a very masculine-looking girl dressed as an apache, clothes which I felt she would probably have preferred to wear every day. At last we got to the keep and the children were lined up for their judging. Neither we nor the Gooddens knew their names and Mrs Majendie didn't appear. It grew colder, the sky was overcast and the fancy dresses looked every minute more unreal and fancy while a few drops of rain started spattering the forlorn children. Anxious mothers put coats round the shoulders of one or two of them, trying not to let this detract from their dresses underneath. After about five minutes Mrs Majendie arrived, I felt so coldly angry that I could hardly wish her a civil good afternoon, and looking at her pale blue eyes and goat-like face I thought, no wonder Mr Majendie won't live with you. I muddled the names of the children and the first prize went to a girl who was wearing a remarkably dull dress.

Meanwhile the school sports were in progress in an area divided off by ropes and marked with flags. There were a lot of races and of course they were dull for everyone except the children, but the grown ups clapped indulgently and with a self-conscious heartiness; with the castle keep towering

up beside them it was lovely to look at. Mr Baines and Mr Thomas tried to send up some small fire balloons but the rain defeated them and they wouldn't ascend and fell below the drawbridge into a deep pit. Arrangements had been made for a first and second tea but the rain made everyone want to be at the first tea. There wasn't room enough for them on the ground floor and Miss Bryan the castle governess refused to unlock the door above, saying that the villagers' boots would spoil the floor. People squashed and jammed themselves on the winding stone stairs, one man slipped and instantly disappeared, horrified we pictured him crashing into a dungeon at the bottom. The last man in was the vicar who had got so gloriously wet that he looked as though he had been under water for some time; his clothes shone with rain and his beaming red face ran with drips from his dishevelled hair. We found a table for the first tea and afterwards I helped dry up about seventy cups and plates with four sodden dishcloths. Miss Bryan having refused the key to the upstairs floor, the washers-up could get no more water and there were many dark mutterings against her.

As the lighting of the bonfire and the fireworks was postponed till a finer night, we were left with no plans for the evening and a feeling of disappointment, so we decided to go over to Bardfield where they were having a fancy-dress dance. We went with the Hephers and Wilma Hessey and a schoolmistress friend of hers.

At the door of the village hall we were given pale blue or pink masks to wear; I don't like people in masks and took mine off as soon as I could. Charlotte wasn't there but we

found John and Lucie looking very fine in Victorian clothes, they didn't at first recognise us in our masks. Of course I hoped I should be able to dance with John, but saw that it would be very difficult because we were burdened with an extra woman and Lucie nearly always danced with him exclusively. I noticed that his face now shone with happiness like mine had done on that first occasion when we had kissed. They had had so many troubles that it was unusual to see him smiling like this: Lucie very rarely looked happy, but she too was gay so that one could more easily imagine what she had looked like as the naughty divorcée whose reputation as a not-too-respectable beauty had surrounded her romantically, in that past of which she was now so reticent and ashamed. I joined in a Paul Jones dance and was rewarded with two or three minutes waltzing with John; the previous uncertainty that I shouldn't be able to dance with him at all made them doubly precious so that I knew that I had never been so happy before. It seemed incredible that this terrific love that I felt shouldn't be obvious to everyone in the room and I wondered if my legs would go through their customary movements of waltzing. Before I had a chance to dance with him again the others wanted to go home, so I left without being able to say goodbye.

It was now about two o'clock in the morning and as we approached Sible Hedingham we saw a distant glow and wondered if after all Sible had lit their bonfire: but the field was in darkness and we turned right towards Castle Hedingham. The nearer we got, the more certain we grew that it was our bonfire that was alight and we raced up the hill

to see. There were two people with a motorbike and two other figures, all expressing the same innocent surprise as ourselves. The fire was burning beautifully, our old cot mattress in its cavernous interior now seethed and bubbled and crackled with the piled-up motor tyres and the lighted sparkling sticks. The trees on Sudbury Hill were lit with strange opalescent light but we were too amazed to properly appreciate the beauties of the scene. All the village glowed red.

Next morning when we woke, we could hear the story spreading round Castle Hedingham like a swarm of bees becoming acquainted with the news that their queen was dead. The schoolmaster called at our house for information; a hay stack had also been fired. His Adam's apple worked up and down rather nervously because privately he thought we were the guilty parties and he said that he was determined to get to the bottom of the matter. He never did and everyone helped to build an even bigger bonfire so that after all, it was eventually a better fire than it would have been.

Eric's interest in harbours and lighthouses was stimulated by a few weeks' stay in Newhaven and he urged Edward to join him. As usual, conditions for working were difficult. At first chiefly because of the fierce wind which blew a violent gale, drowning an old man who was blown off the mole that jutted out on the right of the harbour basin. This storm blew in A P Herbert in a small boat and Eric enjoyed an evening of his stimulating company; but he found that he couldn't stand Edward when he arrived and after suffering one or two of

Edward's most malicious digs, he left him in possession of Newhaven and came home. He also felt a desire to paint mountains, being a great admirer of the watercolour painter Francis Towne. He had attempted to paint them previously when he went to stay in the north of the Lake District but he hadn't been very successful and when he tried again in Wales, the weather was so wet that he could do nothing. However, he determined to have another try now and Guy and I drove with him to Wales where he had booked rooms in a farmhouse at Capel-y-Ffin, a valley above the ruins of Llanthony Abbey.

We passed the home of Lord Faringdon where Eric had recently spent a weekend painting the house. Lord Faringdon was a socialist and he had a camp of Basque refugee children in his garden. Staying in the house was a miscellaneous collection of guests, among them Lord Hastings and the man whose wife had become known as Portia in the newspapers because she defended herself and attacked the companies who built Jerry-built houses. At lunchtime, a carriage drawn by a white horse drove up the drive and in it or rather on it was Mrs John Betjeman, an outspoken girl with an attractive husky voice who asked Eric in the middle of the lunch if his baby was breast-fed. Lord Faringdon sat at the head of his long table underneath the portrait of an ancestor who so closely resembled him that it looked like a picture of him in fancy-dress. Eric found that it was very difficult to make a good drawing of an obviously beautiful house because, if done in a straightforward manner, it would be so dull. Fortunately the grass was being mown and he painted the varying stripes

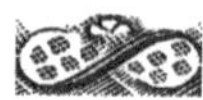

of grass in the foreground and a storm coming up behind in the sky.

When he was leaving he found that he had left his hat behind; the butler hurried off to fetch it and returned with a very odd deer-stalking hat. Eric didn't know if the man was trying to be funny or if he really had believed it to be his hat.

We arrived in Wales by the late afternoon, the weather was damp and the mountains strewn with rocks and patches of brown dead bracken, the sheep on their sides jutted out, precariously attached to their surface by the force of gravity.

The farmhouse though badly lit was very comfortable and the Saunders with their dark, ripely-attractive daughter were very hospitable. We had sponge cake for breakfast and I set off next morning to walk with Guy and Eric to a reservoir on top of the hill above the convent where Gill and his children had lived. I couldn't keep up with them so went back for my car intending to meet them on the road to Ross. When I had driven a little way I lost heart and decided to turn round. The road was so narrow that I couldn't manage this and found myself wedged completely sideways across it with a stone wall on each side of me. I got out and started to take down the wall and build more road behind the car until I was rescued by a one-armed postman who managed to turn the wretched vehicle as easily as anything. I do resent the way cars always behave as though nothing had ever been wrong with them when a man appears on the scene – even a one-armed man.

I drove back the next day with Guy and we were very happy looking at all the lovely Cotswold villages and the fir trees near Tewkesbury.

Six weeks later I set off to fetch Eric back from Wales. I spent a night with John and Christine Nash on the way and while John was fishing, Christine and I had a long gossip about men and husbands in particular.

When I arrived Eric and Mr Saunders both had boils but Eric had done about six good pictures, among them a beauty of the Saunders' double bed, fortunately accomplished in the nick of time because she was planning to have the room redecorated in a few days. He was in the middle of an attempt to paint the chapel, a particularly attractive little one with a pitch pine interior and a small balcony over the harmonium, the whole lighted by a brass hanging oil lamp. The picture wouldn't go right and he reluctantly abandoned it.

The food had been good but monotonous. Eric put the boils down to the fact that they didn't have green vegetables. When a pig was fresh killed, they had lovely fresh pork and everything was fine but after that when it was no longer fresh, they lived on the salted remainder which they hung up in the kitchen and Eric had been continually banging his head on these sides of pig, till he was heartily sick of them. The pigs when alive lived across the way in a muddy field by the river. The lavatory was also in this field and very draughty it was. If the door was accidentally left open, the pigs got in and befouled the whole place and tore up the lavatory paper.

Mr Saunders and his son spent the whole of one day putting up a grindstone that was worked by the force of the river and Eric got up very early in the morning and drew this with some of Mrs Saunders' white geese. He used to enjoy helping her collect their eggs which were laid haphazardly

about in the rushes by the water's edge. He liked the family very much and we took them to Abergavenny to go to a cinema. Joyce loved playing the harmonium but unfortunately she adored listening to Reginald Foort when he played his organ over the wireless.

We did the drive back to Essex all in one day, starting off early with our luggage and a big flat round stone with 17 engraved on it and a parcel of moss which I hoped to grow in our garden at home. Carefully we drove down the narrow winding roads with their high stone walls and hedges on either side, charming little holly trees sticking up from them every now and then. I won't bore you with an account of this journey; there is nothing I detest more than having good scenery pointed out to me and I suspect that most people feel the same.

After this, Eric concentrated on drawing ships and harbours and in May he went to Rye where he lodged in the William the Conqueror and did some of the best paintings that he ever made. The interior of the pub gave trouble because he couldn't decide whether to have a chair in front of the window or not. I think he finally covered it up. He often doctored paintings that went wrong and when he painted two attempts of the railway carriages on the Eastbourne and Hastings train, neither so of which he wholly approved, I cut them up and joined together the best bits and made a satisfactory whole. While he was sketching in Rye, a woman who had a school for watercolour students came up to him and invited him to her studio; he wasn't quite sure whether she was looking for a likely pupil or not but gratefully accepted some sherry. He also went to the pretty house of a

painter called Edward le Bas who booked in advance one of his best Rye harbour paintings. He went on from here to stay at Wittersham with Diana Tuely and her husband. Diana came and slept in his bed, saying that her husband wouldn't mind. Next morning Eric observed that he obviously did mind, so he left for Eastbourne where I was staying. I wrote a calming letter to them and finally the husband became more reasonable about the matter and this relationship with Diana was a good thing because it is always nice to have someone love you and be truthful in criticising your painting.

Entries from the diaries of Christine Nash fill in information not touched upon by Tirzah. Eric had finally given up any idea of leaving Tirzah and living with Helen Binyon. The reason for this sudden dismissal of Helen may well have been the new affair begun with Diana Tuely. Helen, whilst still pining for Eric, rapidly transferred her affections to John Nash, though she and Eric continued to write to each other for the rest of Eric's life. Tirzah's text is interrupted to include Christine's words for the light they shed on the feelings of both women towards Helen (extracts in italics).

Tirzah had left a note of an intended subject for 1937, *Visit to Paris with Christine Nash*, and Christine, writing in her diary on the October 14th prior to going, says:

Alone having tea here on the eve of going to Paris with Tirzah. I never can get away from that feeling of sadness at going, tho really I'm looking forward to it very much. It is the feeling of letting the fires out, and shutting up. J. went earlier in order to have a suit fitted, and is staying the night with Helen, they both go to Furlongs for the weekend.

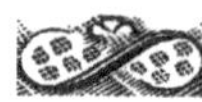

The night Tirzah spent with John and Christine Nash on her way back to Capel-y-Ffin to fetch Eric is also recorded in Christine's diary, March 17th 1938:

Thatched Cottage: Tirzah came on Tuesday for a night, and broke the silence with regard to Helen. It was most interesting to hear what she thinks on the subject, and I couldn't make out if she knows of J's present part in the game.

I think that Tirzah's policy with regard to Eric is not a very wise one, but then she is still young and hasn't been so long at the game as I have.

Further entries in 1938 enlarge on the subject of John, Eric and Helen; and Christine seems to have enjoyed recording events:

April 1st: *Helen was here again last weekend, it was a pity for J & I had a lovely weekend at Wiston the week before, after which he went to Dorothy's & came back here with Helen on the Friday evening, the change in him was particularly noticeable after the easy happy time the week before. He was all nervous & irritable again like last summer & foolishly doting & irritable again, a great pity and she assuming a girlish air. Eric went to spend the night with her on Wednesday. I wonder so much where it will all end. Tirzah told me some interesting things when she was staying here that all fit into the pattern. She said that Peggy (who I always thought a foolish creature) finally decided Eric against Helen by writing a foolish letter to him to say that H. had been crying for a week. I suppose that E, man-like, thought that he simply couldn't marry anyone who cried for a week. Not very clever of Peggy I'm afraid.*

T said the thing that hurt her most was the way that Helen said to

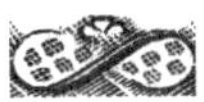

her, 'Eric is so rude to you, it was obvious to me that he didn't love you, so I thought there's no harm in getting him for myself.'

'And I couldn't tell her', said T, 'It's only because of you that he's rude to me, he never was before'. All this is very interesting, and I like to make notes about it as we go along, so that the material is all handy for the complete story when we get it afterwards.

Of course that is the point, one wouldn't mind any amount of girlfriends, if only they didn't make one's husband treat one like something the cat's brought home. I cannot see the necessity. I suppose it's the effect of a guilty conscience. Women have not such troublesome consciences and so they can treat a husband and lover with the same civility and be pleased to see them both.

April 25th: *Easter at the Cottage was one long rush of work and round of gaiety and fixed me even deeper (if that is possible) in my desire for a quiet life. During the first part of the holiday we were a good deal at Castle Hedingham. Eric was on the defensive, cold and snappy. Tirzah says he identifies her with his conscience and me with her, because she is friendly with me. He thinks I'm disapproving of him on a double count, ie, Tirzah and Helen. Why should he flatter himself that I think at all about him! I like to see him when we go to Wiston, but beyond that I can't concern myself with rights and wrongs of his behaviour.*

The thing I do dislike, and disapprove of, is the habit all, or most of, our Suffolk friends have formed of spending the time between tea and dinner at the pub, drinking and playing darts and shove-halfpenny. It seems just an awful waste of time and money; think of how precious time is, and how one never has enough time to do the things one wants to and then to just fritter hours away drinking when one is not thirsty and not talking to any purpose either.

June 25th: *Tonight we are going to see Helen's Puppet Show, and are bringing her back with us for the weekend. The affair seems to prosper, altho J has been very impatient of her preoccupation with the work of producing the Puppet Show. Now no doubt they'll make up for lost time.*

July 8th: *The weekend with Helen was not so good from any point of view, she was terribly over-tired and touchy, thought her Puppets were bad, and that we thought so; her mouth had gone back to that thin, cold line and everything was awkward. She spent most of the time sleeping, and that wasn't too amusing for the old man, and ended up with an attack of weeping over Eric. I came off best that weekend, for I was rung up unexpectedly by T. and invited over to supper alone! This was most delightful in quite the old-fashioned style.*

October 13th: *Eric and Tirzah and John came to see us on Saturday. E restless and wanting something nice to happen. He described Charlotte Bawden's holiday at Skegness with the two children in 'rooms' filled with ornaments. The children smashed them 'pretty freely' said Eric. He is a fickle, impish person, but very charming. H is apparently as much in love with him as ever, which has been a shock for J who imagined that she had 'got over it'. He didn't realise quite how much he'd been made use of. I am glad to think that she is not quite so heartless as to 'get over' an affair like that in a few months, but still more sad to think that our summer's hopes have been destroyed just for her convenience. I had rather it had been on account of some overwhelming passion, which was quite inevitable.*

You cannot get away from that mouth of hers. I would very much like to know from Eric why he sacked her. She says that she despises people like Percy [Horton] who are so cautious that they dare not give

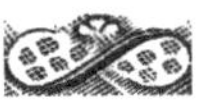

way to their desires for fear of getting hurt, but perhaps the point is that more than one person gets hurt at his game, as in this case, J has. Well, it's a new position for him to be in.

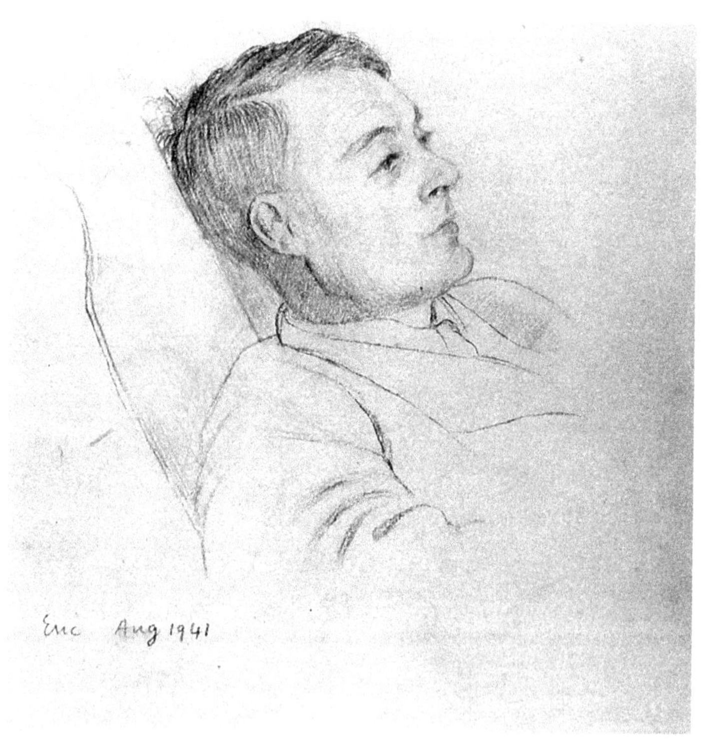

Eric Aug 1941

CHAPTER TWENTY

John [Aldridge] arrived unexpectedly one Sunday afternoon; he looked rather white and ill but he made love to me as usual and afterwards we talked about letter writing and whether we should one day perhaps quarrel with one another. He said that he couldn't write love letters but that he could write the other kind. I wondered what he meant and replied that it would be difficult to quarrel with me because I was very good-natured. He sat up in bed looking unhappy and said: 'I'm not at all good-natured'. I wondered if something had happened at home to upset him, but there wasn't time to think about it any more because someone was knocking on the front door. When I went down to open it, there was sweet Miss Grant with a basket of October raspberries for us and I thought what a wonderful day it was.

I had asked Mollie the German girl to tea; she liked Eric and used to look soppily at him with her sentimental heavy Bavarian face. She had been walking with him and little John in the pram and they all came back for tea. Sitting with John Aldridge opposite and Eric and little John on either side of him, I thought, there will never be three people sitting in a room together that I love more than this.

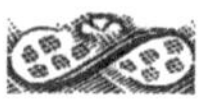

After tea, I took John Aldridge across the road to see the Gooddens who had recently bought one of his pictures and wanted to meet him. Robert came back to the house with us after we had talked to him and Kay for a little while and I left them downstairs, while I went up to bath little John.

I usually sing when I'm running the bath water and I was lustily singing a song called 'The Turtle Dove' when I saw John Aldridge coming up the stairs. I'd just reached the lines: 'The hills shall fly, my little turtle dove, the roaring billows burn, before my heart shall suffer me to fail or I a traitor turn my love or I a traitor turn', and I hastily shut up thinking it wasn't a very suitable song to sing in front of poor John.

He came into the little bathroom where I was fondly washing my other John and he watched for a few minutes and we arranged to go to the cinema with Lucie on Wednesday and then he gravely kissed me goodbye.

I was always so terribly busy that there wasn't much time for considering what John Aldridge might be feeling, although Eric and I did sometimes discuss this. Eric thought that he was in love with me, but I'd got it so firmly fixed into my head that he must not be in love with me and that if I didn't say anything warm or flattering to him he wouldn't be, that I hardly believed Eric. When he had gone, we started talking about him on this Sunday and Eric said: 'I don't know how John manages it, it must be like deceiving your right hand'. I did sit down and think, but deceiving Lucie seemed to be the only possible course now that we were lovers. John was left handed and I think that we both behaved publicly with a social charm which didn't really express at all what we

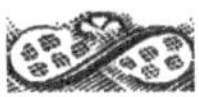

privately thought, as though the expression, 'How do you do?' set going inside us a performance of kindly superficial attention to visitors. John didn't really respect anybody.

The next morning little John woke rather early and I found that he had dirtied himself in his cot. I went downstairs to fetch the letters before cleaning him up. There was one from John Aldridge starting:

Dear Tirzah,

This must stop, not because of what it means to me, but because of the effect it is having on the relationship between me and Lucie. . .

and it ended

Poor Tirzah I told Lucie.

I didn't take the letter in to Eric but went to clean John up without letting myself properly comprehend the awfulness of it till I had washed him. Eric was very nice about it when I showed him and firmly took me for a long country walk. It is somehow impossible to be abysmally unhappy on a lovely day in good country but I felt mighty low.

I wrote back saying how sorry I was to have upset Lucie and he knew that I hadn't wanted to if it could be helped and did this mean that I could not see them any more.

The next day Lucie sent back a parcel of books which she mistakenly thought were ours; they were actually books that I had given to John to return to the Bawdens, to whom they

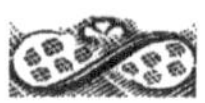

really belonged. She also sent a letter to us both and there was a long letter from John to me, a very unpleasant letter from a man who had obviously been getting it hot and strong from a very indignant Lucie. The gist of both their letters was that they didn't wish to associate with people like Eric and me unless we changed our opinions and developed more moral sense. Lucie's letter was a silly letter, the kind of indignant letter a Woolworth's girl might write to another when fighting over their boyfriend, so I promptly threw it in the fire and replied with nearly as silly a letter myself, saying 'need we discuss something that had been heavenly to me'. Eric wrote to her too:

Dear Lucie,

I refuse to discuss John and Tirzah's affairs. Most people fall in love two or three times in their lives and I think it is best if possible that they go to bed with one another. Do you know that poem of Ogden Nash's: 'When I consider how my life is spent. I very seldom repent.'

Yours sincerely, Eric.

I think there were one or two more letters between the families, ending up with one from John saying that he didn't see why we couldn't all be friends.

I had unfortunately lent my car to Evelyn so that I couldn't go over to see them and try to put things right and as usual we were very busy entertaining. I felt very miserable inside me but all these social engagements and looking after John kept me occupied and Eric discouraged me from trying to see John

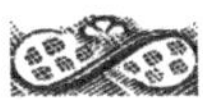

and Lucie. He didn't really want to be friends with them again because he used to get very bored at the long introspective conversation at Place House dinner parties and secretly he had grown rather jealous of John.

It was a particularly hot summer and everything that we did was more impressive because we felt that it would surely be the last time that we should be going to flower shows and dances and parties.

For centuries, there had been a flower show held at August Courtauld's house in Yeldham and whether they wanted it or not, the owners of the house had because of this tradition to have a show. Now it was also a tennis tournament and very unwillingly August, who hated tennis, had his court put in order. He and Mollie did try to behave as the landed gentry should and they gave lavish children's parties and redecorated their house with the help of Mollie's father Mr Montgomery, who had been trained as an architect. He was a nice amiable Sussex man overborne by his large, handsome wife; his taste was mock Tudor but he was so good-natured a person that we just accepted it as something that was too late to alter now and he might have been a great deal worse. There were two daughters, the younger one Pam was married to a handsome Danish artist called Sven Mikkelsen; he wasn't a good artist but they were a sweet couple and both of them were so beautiful to look at that I imagine they would always be liked wherever they went. They had one baby called Leif and Mollie who had married more ambitiously had three children and was just beginning a fourth.

Mollie was a big, gushing girl, I used to feel a bit sorry for her because I don't think August would be an easy person to be married to and the fact that his family had disapproved at first of their marriage made it necessary for her to make it a more than ordinary success. It must have been difficult to keep amused a man who liked Greenland and sailing little boats in dangerous waters and who so young had become a popular hero and I imagine that all this unnatural hostess' gush which overcame Mollie was really a form of inferiority complex. Other people didn't think so, so maybe I am wrong but I do know how much happier August looks now he is at sea again. At one dance at Halstead, he took part in a historical pageant organised by Mrs Marshall and he looked as though he was going to be sick at any moment.

It was very hot at the flower show and Jim Richards who was staying with us came too. We had had Peggy and him to stay at Christmas and our quarrel was never mentioned. It had been rather a miserable Christmas because John had had bronchitis and I was anxiously putting poultices on to his back and keeping him amused by day while he lay in bed. Jim had just met Kay Goodden and being like each other they immediately made friends and I wished he had married someone more like her than Peggy who was so very different. It was fun showing David [Hepher] and John the prize vegetables and the bees in a glass case and three lovely scarecrows made for a scarecrow competition – they were so good that we wished there had been a great many more.

I had lent my car to Guy, and Evelyn, who was expecting him, got rather worried as the afternoon passed and he didn't

arrive. At last he came flushed and obviously pregnant with some great piece of news. It wasn't welcome news but the awful horror that infantile paralysis had started in the village and he had just been taking the mother of the patient into Halstead where it had been discovered that that was what he was suffering from. As he had twice been to the cinema while feeling poorly, the chances that no one else would catch it seemed slight. Guy had offered to have Doreen [the boy's sister] to stay; the mother was in a very hysterical state and he thoughtlessly suggested this plan to be of some help. By now there was another German girl staying at the vicarage, a tall, half-Jewish girl called Nanny aged twelve and of course David. Evelyn meekly agreed to have Doreen while the village gaped at such rash behaviour. In a few days the boy died and Nanny, to comfort Doreen, got into her bed which rather worried Evelyn. Having found out a little more about the disease, Guy realised that he had indeed behaved rashly and he packed Evelyn, Nanny and David off to stay at Angmering with Evelyn's aunt. Most of the cases were at Felstead and a postman died at Sible Hedingham but no one in Castle Hedingham caught it. We wished the lovely summer would end because it was said that the disease spread more rapidly in hot weathers.

There was still another bombshell for the village. The eldest Rycroft girl Alice had married the summer before and we all enjoyed her wedding and the reception at the castle. Eric put on his top hat and borrowed the rest of the outfit from various sources. There was a marquee tent in the garden and even Musette Majendie wore a picture hat. The bridegroom Neil Graham was a friend of one of the brothers at

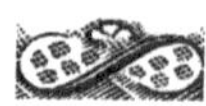

Cambridge and although he wasn't particularly intelligent, it didn't matter because nor was Alice and she was obviously tremendously happy so that everyone was pleased. In the spring she gave birth to twin boys and in the late summer she came with them and her husband to stay at Castle Hedingham with her mother. They took Neil to several tea parties and I imagine he got rather bored with them and, to avoid one at the house of a nearby canon, he decided to drive over to Cambridge and see some of his old friends. They didn't worry over much when bedtime came and he didn't come back, thinking that he had decided to stay the night. The poor village policeman had to go round at six o'clock in the morning to tell Lady Rycroft that he was dead. At first it was rumoured that it was an accident but it wasn't till the inquest that the whole embarrassing and sad story was disclosed. He had been drinking in a pub with his friends and when he got into his car to drive away, he had some minor accident and was accosted by a policeman who doubted his sobriety and this made him very indignant. His friends did try to persuade him to stay the night but he was a rather violent tempered man and he insisted that he was perfectly alright and sober. He was later found dead in his car halfway home, having run into a tree and died of shock. Poor Lady Rycroft had to attend the inquest and then arrange the funeral, an almost exactly similar ceremony to the wedding, which made it doubly poignant. We didn't go and forbade our little Hilda to take John which she was longing to do. It was her mother Mrs Brown who remarked to Mrs Hepher about this funeral, 'Yes I shall go to that, it will be a sad one'. So Neil Graham was

buried beside the old perisher Baines who died on Christmas Day, and Alice stayed on in Castle Hedingham, wheeling in their pram the twins and dressed in black with a hat with a large veil.

John and David Hepher were very devoted to one another and they used to play together every day in the garden of Homeleigh, a house across the road from the big vicarage into which Guy and Evelyn had moved, despairing of ever being out of debt while they lived in the more magnificent vicarage. Evelyn had a lot of trouble with David; he looked the picture of health with his huge rosy red cheeks and golden curls but when he started at eighteen months to walk, it was discovered that he had rickets and he had to have special diet and massage. Evelyn had been very careful about feeding him but she had followed the Truby King book and given him stuff called New Zealand cream instead of cod liver oil after she had weaned him and she hadn't started him soon enough on solid foods and eggs. After the rickets had been cured, a new trouble arose because his neck glands swelled up. We both went to an Indian doctor called Dr Singh and she advised Evelyn to get sun-ray treatment for David at the hospital at Braintree and for a time the gland went down; however it came back later and he started to have a temperature with it as well. By now, having guessed what was wrong, she wrung from Dr Singh the truth which was that it was a tubercular gland. I suppose they hadn't told her because they thought it would be bad for her as she was pregnant. A silly idea doctors have because, as I found from my own experience later, you worry far more if you only guess the truth.

The next disaster was Gwyneth's nervous breakdown. Like Hennell she went to Maudsley Hospital, but she became terribly ill and thoroughly dejected. Jack Gold was having another of his exhibitions of the work of Essex artists in Braintree and John and Edward were going to show the new wallpaper that they had been so long designing together. Seeing how miserable I was, Eric suggested that I showed my marble papers that I had just done to send to Miss Rose as usual; so without considering the possible complications, I went out to the telephone box and rang up Jack Gold to ask him if I could do this. He didn't seem to mind so I set to work sorting them but I couldn't do very much because I got a chill on my liver and a high temperature and had to go to bed. I had been invited to play bridge at the castle with Musette Majendie and I had to send word at the last minute that I could not go; I was sorry to miss this because I was very curious to know more about Musette. Realising that it was probable that I should see John and Lucie if I went to Braintree to put up my papers, I wrote to Edward asking whether it would be better if I did my displaying the evening before because if John and Lucie were going to be there and were likely to be rude to me I should probably burst into tears which would be embarrassing for everyone. Edward rang up and said it would be alright and we could meet amicably on public occasions. Eric was away and Robert Goodden helped choose which papers I should take. I still felt ill but I managed to get up and go into Braintree without having to run to the lavatory which was the thing I was frightened might happen. Jack Gold's neighbour Mrs Tabor was in the hall and I told

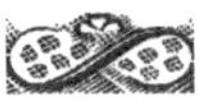

her that I hadn't been well and she showed me where the lavatory was in case I needed it, and relieved to find that John and Edward had already put up their wallpapers in the middle of the room, I started work on my own. They had made a square enclosure which had photographs inside and their wallpapers on the outside, the corners hung with Lucie's inevitable muslin curtains. I didn't approve of this because as it was, the wallpapers tended to have too much of a Victorian flavour for my taste, and the curtains gave them even more of this parlour suggestion.

I was very worried about Gwyneth because I heard that morning from the Rhoades family that she was very seriously ill. Joan and Geoffrey didn't know about her mental state and I longed to know whether she was really worse or whether Charlotte, from whom this news had originated, had told them this without having heard any fresh news of her. When Lucie walked into the room accompanied by Fred, I had almost forgotten our quarrel and thought, Lucie will know. She said: 'Good morning' and when I opened my mouth to ask about Gwyneth, she swept past with her head in the air with Fred following behind. When John came in later, I felt too abashed to try any more conversational openings and as the morning wore on I felt a rising indignation with Lucie who seemed to be acting an enjoyable part. She had her head tied up in a scarf which was fashionable then and I thought it a particularly detestable fashion, but I suppose I was naturally prejudiced. I told Jack Gold about my mysterious illness and my temperature of 104 and John who was standing close to us listened to this, but we didn't say anything to one another and

I didn't ever again go anywhere where there was a possibility of meeting them.

All the village was invited to a Guy Fawkes party at the vicarage. Guy had built a huge bonfire in the yard and Eric and I and Mr Thomas of The Bell made a particularly stunning Guy in a huge black hat; burning him was so realistic that it became suddenly horrible and awe-inspiring. The village children were given sparklers and dancing round in a circle with them all alight and flashing looked enchantingly beautiful.

The end of November was bitterly cold and it wasn't until early in December that at Charlotte's invitation I went over to Bardfield to play Badminton. It had become a new strange Bardfield now, no longer an enchanted village where I might if I was lucky see John, but all the same I enjoyed playing Badminton, with the two white Miss Brunwens and the pink chubby Dr Garland.

It wasn't till after tea that Charlotte broke the news gently to me that John and Lucie had told her and Edward about what had happened and had shown them the letters that had gone between the two families.

Showing our letters to other people seemed to upset me more than the abuse they contained. My indignation was rather like that of Mrs Barnes at Furlongs who, when Peggy had written out a list of the things she had stolen, had come in wild with anguish, saying: 'I never took the sheets'.

Charlotte said that Lucie brooded continually about the affair and instead of being glad that John had tried to make amends for his past unfaithfulness, she tortured herself trying to

analyse why it was that he had found it necessary to make love to me at all. She now hated me and nothing would alter this.

A few days after John had made his confession, she had got up very early in the morning and gone out. By lunchtime she had not returned and poor John with Basil's all-too-recent suicide still haunting him had distractedly searched for her, thinking that she too might be dead. When he did eventually find her, she said that she had lost her way in some fields.

I thought this was a mean trick to have played upon John, however from her point of view it had worked beautifully and I now understood the letter which John had written to me saying:

After what has happened, I don't ever want to see you again. You know we cannot be friends and you can't wish to renew an acquaintanceship in which I should have nothing to say to you.

I was quite cheerful in front of Charlotte and in a way, relieved that she at last knew all about my troubles. I decided at least to attempt a reconciliation with Lucie because I felt that she was making herself unnecessarily unhappy. I had never doubted that John loved her and I hadn't accepted him as a lover to try to make him love me but to cure myself by the only method which does really cure, though incidentally it takes a year or two and is more enjoyable than anything else in the world.

I boldly walked up to Place House and knocked on the door, but there was no one at home, so I went back to Hedingham and wrote a letter trying to explain that John

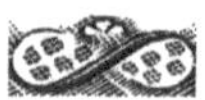

hadn't been in love with me. He and I had believed this, which was the important thing.

The next morning was still bitterly cold but the snow had started thawing, so that it would bind into snowballs. I took John to the vicarage and, with the Hephers' nursemaid Kathleen and Mollie the German girl, built a snowman and a snow woman on the large sloping lawn while David stood crying because his hands were cold.

I felt terribly unsettled and a little desperate so I drove over to see Charlotte again in the afternoon, going slowly along the freezing road to Bardfield. When I arrived, Fred [their gardener] was passing Brick House and he stopped by my car and said: 'John and Lucie had a nasty smash yesterday.' I must have looked alarmed because he added quickly: 'It's alright, they weren't hurt badly'.

A car in front of them had had to brake suddenly and the slippery road made it impossible for John to stop in time and he had run into the back of the car. Lucie bumped her head badly and John had cut his face. I wondered if they had specially gone to Bardfield to avoid me and thought I felt like banging their heads together and the Lord has done it for me.

Eric's next coastal batch of drawings was done [in October] at Dungeness, where he stayed in a small cottage by the light-houses. The few people on this shingle bank rarely saw anyone strange except for birdwatchers in spring.

Eric came back before the snow people had melted; David and John had later added a charming little snow child and we

put a sun shade in its hand. The man was an Essex man with a flat cap on his head; he started leaning over and gradually as the thaw set in, he collapsed over sideways and then the figure of the woman who was of stocky peasant stock became more pronounced and the coal in their eyes made dirty wet tears down their faces, till they were finally left as isolated lumps on the green vicarage lawn.

No one likes being blamed and I was terribly miserable about John and Lucie. The more apologetically I wrote to them, the crueller they became and John's most recent letter ended: 'I hope you will one day find something better than such a one-sided thing could have been.'

I was so much in love with him that the effect of these letters was quite awful and I found that those extravagant phrases like 'A knife in your heart' were really true, only it was in my stomach and if I thought about him suddenly I was unable to stop myself shuddering.

All this misery that I felt was going on behind what appeared to everyone else to be an exceptionally happy marriage between Eric and me. I really was frightfully unhappy and wished I was dead, though I knew I wasn't the kind of person who committed suicide any more than Lucie was and I had my John to look after; but I just felt that I had no spirit or heart to try to be good any more which was what I had been trying in a muddled way to be.

In Braintree one day, I saw a man driving a car whom for a moment I mistook for John. Realising that if it was, he might look at me as though he hated me, my misery was so sudden and utter that it seemed like a curtain of sorrow that had

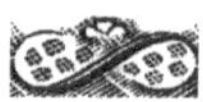

overwhelmed me and I felt it as an isolated phenomenon. I doubted if Lucie realised how utterly miserable she had succeeded in making me, I naturally felt very guilty at having upset her and I suppose it was difficult for her to believe that I really was trying to make what amends I could now. I suppose she may have thought that I was still trying to take John away from her and that, in loving John, I had wished to separate him from her. She was an intensely jealous woman by nature and being so much older than him, she naturally feared that some younger woman might steal him away.

I had at once accepted the fact that he couldn't be my lover any more. It had been my suggestion that we stopped if Lucie knew, but I had never bargained for this flood of hate or for the fact that I could never be friends with John again. Edward had come back to Bardfield; mischievously he seemed to enjoy the whole affair and had a happy time teasing John and Lucie. When John had firmly asserted that he hadn't fallen in love with me, Edward replied: 'Oh, so it was the spring was it?' Lucie put it down to some kind of malignant witchcraft on my part and neither she nor John seemed really to believe that he was in any way responsible for what had happened. John did say in one letter that he was ashamed of his conduct but he didn't seem to think it mattered how much I was upset, as though Lucie's feelings were the only ones that mattered in the world.

Having to write these letters did at least make me decide what I really had believed to be important. I had been so pleased with the discovery that I could still be fond of Helen although she and Eric were in love with one another and that I could love Eric and Bob and John all at once and for

different reasons even though they loved other people as well, because my loving them was the important thing and not my possessing them. I didn't believe in that hateful term 'Free Love' because obviously you must have some sense of responsibility towards those people you love. Oh how I detest blame.

I wanted, as one does when anything is on your mind, to talk about John and Lucie, till Eric became heartily sick of the subject and forbade me to mention their names any more. I still haven't the faintest idea what John's feelings towards me were. I suppose that he must have felt that attraction which haphazardly unites two people whether they wish it or not and which just as capriciously vanishes when they have become used to one another. I imagined that I recognised in him many defects and qualities that were my own, but he was such an impressionable, sympathetic person that many people must have thought this same thing about him. I don't know if he found parting from me painful; he certainly looked very ill but he obediently took down letters at Lucie's dictation to send to me; I felt sure that he hadn't composed the letters which I received because the expressions in them were unmistakably hers. This didn't apply to the earlier ones; the long one was very influenced by Laura Riding who had recently been staying with them.

I think that John must have thought that I was trying to have him back as my lover because his last letter was if anything worse than the ones that went before. In fact, it was very unbalanced and contained this sentence: 'People like you are a dark menace to ordered lives'. I showed it to Eric when we were in bed one morning and he said; 'Poor John, it's funny

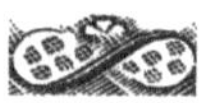

that he should think of you like this, I suppose you really are a menace to him, while to me you're just "the good, old beast".' Eric was more ashamed of his past behaviour than I and said that the truth was that we had both made fools of ourselves and that my love for John was just a physical one. I denied this and said: 'Well I'd much rather be the kind of person that makes a fool of myself and thank goodness you are too'. But after that I didn't want to make love to anyone else because I still felt that I had no heart and I couldn't bear the thought of ever being so upset again.

Finding that they had also told Guy and Evelyn that the families had quarrelled, again without telling me that they had done so, I wrote a little note to Guy and Evelyn when I was having supper with them one evening and went out to hide my blushes in the kitchen while they read it. They had no idea that the quarrel had this origin and were very surprised. They didn't mind as I had feared they might and before long Guy was guffawing with laughter about it. Neither of them would believe that John hadn't been in love with me and as Eric thought that he was too I suppose he must have been, but at this point it wasn't any consolation to me. I was touched by Evelyn telling me a few days later that she had spent a sleepless night worrying over my problems.

At the end of the week Charlotte had invited Sam and Elizabeth Williams, college students of Eric and Edward, to do a puppet show at Bardfield to be followed by a dance in aid of the Labour Party funds. I had intended taking my John to the puppets but Lucie sent word by Charlotte that if I set foot in the hall neither she nor John would go. As John was assisting

as an electrician in the puppet show, it would put Sam and Elizabeth in an awkward position if I had indeed gone; as it was the lights failed in the middle of the performance.

Place House and Brick House both employed a gardener called Fred Mizen, a tall man, attractive because he looked like a pirate as he had a patch over one eye. He had won Edward's heart by covering the garden at Brick House with paper windmills to scare away the birds and he was good at amusing Joanna when she sat up the garden in her pram. Basil had first made his acquaintance in the pub as he was a hearty drinker and at Charlotte's dance he got very drunk and started a fierce argument with the communist Mr Thompson, a kindly but boring man with a beard, dressed like Gill in a one-piece smock tied at the waist with a rope and underneath, bare legs and sandals. Charlotte hustled them into the supper room at the side of the hall where they started fighting which she tried to stop, until John Aldridge arrived to assist her and they pushed them both outside. Charlotte was feeling very tired and she went home and fainted and so missed the rest of the dance. We didn't of course go to the party but were told about it afterwards.

Mollie and August Courtauld gave a very good dance to which we went with the Hephers and Hesseys. They had a very lovely house at Yeldham and this dance was about as good as a dance could be; the overshadowing war made it very impressive because we all felt that we shouldn't ever be going to another at which there was limitless champagne and party food. For the first time in my life, I managed to drink a whole

glass of champagne while talking about insurance and marriage to a young man called Gratton Doyle who was engaged or about to be engaged to Anne Hessey. Anne didn't like the dance as she had a heavy cold and headache and she went home rather early. General Hessey was a very charming person and just what a General should be. They hadn't lived many years in the village before he got cancer and it was very miserable for the family as he lived on for about a year knowing there wasn't any hope for him and when he died, it was a loss for the village because he had behaved very well to the villagers and given permission for a bypass road that was being planned to run through his grounds instead of right through the village. It was Robert Goodden who thought of this idea and everyone was very surprised when the county council adopted his suggestion. Anne didn't announce her engagement till six months after her father's death and he died just as the war was beginning.

We were as usual terribly busy sending Christmas cards and presents. The Christmas cards of our more sophisticated friends were every year getting more and more elaborate and as pioneers of this industry among the Bowker circle, we felt that we had to keep ours up to standard. We had started this phase in Hammersmith when we had sent birds made of folded paper which flapped their wings when you pulled their tails. Geoffrey Fry had taught me to make them and he told us how he had once made money for some charity by having a stall and charging people sixpence to be shown how to fold them. When we sent them for Christmas cards we made them of paper from an old geometry book and Eric painted red on

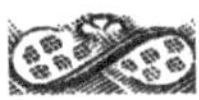

their wing tips and they had paper-clip eyes and guinea fowl features for a crest. Bowker herself made some very ingenious cards and Peggy one year sent the x-ray photograph of Victoria, her first baby, inside her womb.

Guy bought nine large Christmas trees which he put in the church; one in the middle of each of the three arches which flanked the centre aisle and the biggest one in the chancel. Eric helped him to decorate the trees with those lovely fragile glass balls from Woolworth's and with coloured electric lights, till he got such a bad electric shock that he came home and helped unpack a large hamper of goodies which Aunt Rose had sent from Fortnum & Mason. We had never had a hamper before and felt like Porkie boy.

On Christmas Day it was very cold and misty and we went for lunch to the Hephers. We told them about the Christmas in Hedingham when Eric and I had decided we wouldn't give ourselves indigestion like everyone else and, having eaten an omelette, Eric went out and did a good snow picture of the pretty house at the corner of the road. All day the village was quite deserted till late in the afternoon when a few respectably dressed couples with glazed eyes came out of their houses with their children. They walked along quite silently because of the snow but Eric was pleased with the pretty pattern of lines on the snowy road made by the pram wheels and he put them in and came home and had a good Christmas supper.

Guy had been given two turkeys by parishioners, so he gave one of them to us and forgot to thank the woman who had presented it. When we came to the pudding, Evelyn hadn't got any brandy so she poured some methylated spirits

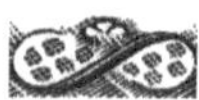

onto it and lit it, but it wasn't a good idea because she put on far too much and the pudding caught fire and it was quite difficult to put out. It tasted pretty strongly of methylated spirits and Guy teased and groaned at her while we ate and she defended herself, saying that her mother had done the same.

I went with Eric to hear them sing carols in the church on the evening of Boxing Day, and it was lovely to see all the Christmas trees lit up and to hear 'The Holly and the Ivy' and that Czech lullaby with its repeated 'lullays'. On the day after that, we all went to follow a meet at Halstead.

It was a perfect day and the huntsmen with their peculiar pink faces looked so like the people in hunting pictures that we stared at them appreciatively and marvelled at their rightness. John and Mollie the German girl were very amusing with their naïve comments on the etiquette of hunting. Eric always enjoyed being quite ignorant of these traditional terms and purposely called hounds, dogs and pink, red if he thought he was in company that minded about such things.

We were lucky enough to see the fox running down a hill with all the hounds and horses cantering down behind him till he took cover in the woods by Cut Throat Lane and found his way back to Dines Hall where he had started, leaving all the pursuing cars quite hopelessly jammed down the narrow lane.

The fox didn't look like the foxes in pictures; it was much browner in colour and the people following looked miserably anxious that they would do something wrong and be sworn at by the Master of Foxhounds.

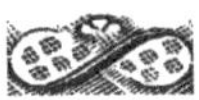

We went with the Gooddens in the middle of the night to hear and see the New Year rung in at the church; Guy too had learned to pull the bells and it was fun watching them all sweating away.

Percy Horton sent us a belated New Year card, a nice picture of a whale with a verse from a poem by Dryden on the back which seemed to express just what I felt about that year:

All, all of a piece without,
Thy chase had a beast in view,
Thy wars brought nothing about,
Thy lovers were all untrue;
'tis well that an old age is out
and time to begin anew.

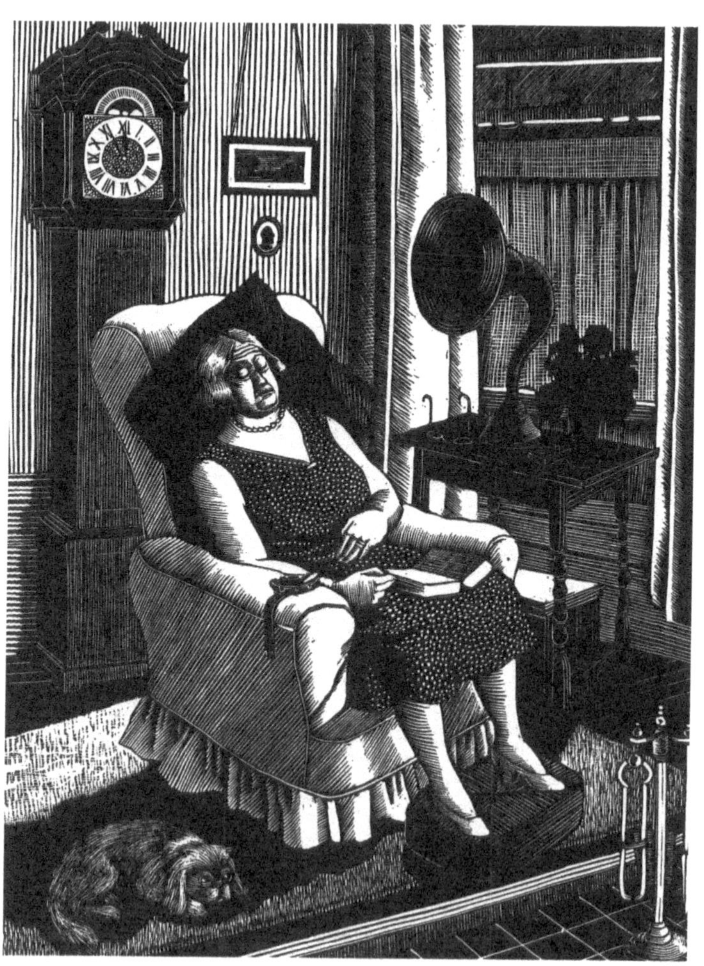

CHAPTER TWENTY-ONE

John [Aldridge] and I had both hated aeroplanes, their sudden droning over our heads on lovely summer days reminded one of the murders and horrors in Germany and the war in Spain, the significance of which seemed to be escaping the British people, and as the months went by we grew more and more ashamed that we were so powerless to do anything. Eric and I attended a few lectures on the war and contributed what we could afford but we had little time for these activities and Charlotte's harried life, now that she was secretary of the Labour Party in Bardfield, was a warning to us of what happened to you if you did really actively take part in politics. It wasn't the views of these people that we were against, but the amount of time that the fanatical ones like Miss Barrett and Mr Thomson in Bardfield wasted in talking. Rachel Barrett invariably recited almost the entire contents of the *New Statesman* at one whenever she came to see us and these people, by being so boring, did far more harm to their cause than they realised. I suppose people with strong political feelings do tend to be people who aren't social successes anyway and they blame society instead of themselves for their lack of popularity. These

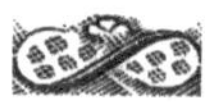

violent people I know resented the apparent inertia about politics that Eric and I seemed to feel but I felt confident that quietly and slowly, we did far more good to their cause by our apparent tolerance of people whose politics were quite opposite, than their indignant attacks. I remember the first occasion when Peggy handed my brother John, home on leave from India, a *Daily Worker*, and how he had dropped it as though he had been stung; but now since his marriage to a wife with left-wing views, he deplored the way the British government were behaving over the Spanish war and had obviously started examining the views of the Conservative Party which most young officers naturally supported at that time. Kay Goodden too had at first joined the Conservative Party when she came to the village, but she had very soon left it and was now more Socialist than we were. It was she who first asked us to take a refugee. If you gave your name to a certain society, a refugee was allowed to come to England if you promised to look after him to begin with. Ours never turned up, but their refugee did arrive and he was a nice young man called Herbert, with glasses and bad asthma. The Germans had released him from an internment camp because they felt confident he was dying, but he had lived, although his heart was affected and he went very blue if he walked too quickly uphill.

We heard later that our refugee, who was also a sufferer from asthma, had been arrested by some SS men. They drove him off in a taxi but he jumped out and was shot dead in the street in Prague.

One day Herbert had a wire from a Jewish friend of his who, although he hated them, was in the employment of the

Nazis as a customs official. He used to help smuggle refugees across the border and had helped Herbert in the past. He wired that he was going to arrive at Harwich that evening and could Herbert find a home for him? As our refugee had not turned up, we of course said that we would have him instead. He had been a wealthy young man who had previously worked as a physical training expert.

I made a nice supper with meringues and cream before setting off in the car for Harwich with Herbert and Eric.

When we arrived at Harwich, we were told that the boat would be an hour late. It was getting cold as it was about seven o'clock and we wandered about the chilly docks and had some tea in a refreshment room. It was almost dark when the boat finally came chugging in and Herbert peered eagerly at the faces packed tight one behind the other on the decks. We waited by the gangway as the people came filing down and none of them took any notice of us. It had never entered my head that he might not come and I didn't grasp the significance of this till we saw another woman, who had also waited in vain, collapse onto a box weeping hysterically. Poor Herbert didn't say much and we tried to cheer him by saying that perhaps he would come on the next boat but he seemed to know that it was hopeless. The meringues were quite tasteless when we got home and we never heard what had happened to the young man.

We were sent the name of another Jewish German refugee, Wolfgang Meunzer, and we agreed to have him for a fortnight. He was already in a hostel in London, having escaped from Prague after the Germans had marched into Czechoslovakia.

He was a small, fair man with thick brown hair that swept backward in a straight line across his forehead and he wore odd square horn-rimmed glasses. He spoke English tolerably well. I am always ashamed at my badness at foreign languages and here was Wolfgang who had learned English in a few weeks.

He was very grateful to us for having him and repeatedly told us how wonderful it was for him to sleep in security in a comfortable bed and, after hearing his account of the last three years of his life, we could well appreciate this.

He had I think originally been employed in a chain store in Berlin; he was now only twenty-five so that he must have been very young when Hitler began rising into power. I don't know how it was that he first came to be arrested or why; he led us to understand that it was for political reasons and that he was given away to the Gestapo by a fellow worker in the store: he felt more bitterly against this man than any other German. He told us how prisoners were beaten every morning to try to force them to give away the names of their friends and how very hard it was for many of them not to weakly succumb and that quite a number of them did but whether he was among them we never discovered; I don't think somehow that he was. He was put for six months with eight other men in so tiny a cell that they could only lie down all together when they lay on their sides. When he was released he left Germany and went to Prague where he lived with a hundred or so other refugees in a disused factory outside the town. Here he became dispenser and medical go-between for people who became sick and the Prague doctors who were very good

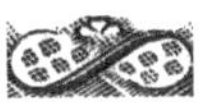

about treating them. After Munich, he said that he saw old men standing weeping on the pavements and added: 'When the old people they cry like this it is not good.' Now his factory filled up with hundreds of refugees and sitting at meals they could hardly wedge their hands onto the tables to eat, so closely were they packed together.

Just before the Germans marched in, one train was allowed to leave for Poland and instead of packing it tight with young men like Wolfgang who would certainly be shot if they were caught, a lady in the British Legion, keeping to the right British traditions, filled it with women and children first. The young men remembered her name and hated her exceedingly for this as they felt certain that the Germans wouldn't bother to molest these women and children. The refugees could now only creep into Prague at night and only their very faithful friends dared receive them into their houses. Wolfgang's work became much harder because the increased numbers made living very unhealthy and they slept on the few beds packed tightly side by side and suffered bitterly from the cold. He went to the British Consul on behalf of a woman who was going to have a baby and it was agreed that she should have a bed paid for her in a Roman Catholic hospital for a fortnight from the date when she was expecting her child. She moved into the hospital but unfortunately her labour didn't start until the time when she was supposed to go back, so the hospital just turned her and her new baby out a few days after its birth and I think Wolfgang said that she slept in a church.

The best way to escape was to cross the border into Poland on a dark night and these escapes were carefully planned.

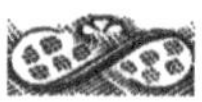

Many people failed and a party of three, among them a very nice woman doctor, were shot while Wolfgang was waiting to make his attempt. He was fortunate and he arrived without money and in rags and dirty in London, where this society who had corresponded with us gave him money to buy a suit and found him a home till they arranged for employment for him either in England or in the colonies. Wolfgang wanted to do riveting and welding as he had a friend who was doing that.

Eric was away quite a lot of Wolfgang's visit and I was three or four months gone with child which may have caused me to see Wolfgang with a particularly jaundiced eye. He was obviously a good and well-meaning young man, but this feeling that it was unfair to criticise him only made it more difficult not to. At first there were only minor troubles like his continual ragging of little John who became quite frightened of all the tickling and pawing that Wolfgang attacked him with. I hate being tickled myself and at last Eric, unable to bear watching poor John squirming and screaming, told Wolfgang to leave him alone. He was at once obedient to any of our wishes but the trouble was to foresee where the next nuisance was going to spring from. He liked his bacon raw in the mornings and continually greeted my best cooking efforts with: 'Is this an English dish?' This quite natural desire of his to understand typically English customs and behaviour was very trying to us, who prided ourselves on our unconventionality. We felt that it should have been obvious to him that if we had been typically English, we should never have had him in our house at all. He didn't go out very much but sat reading in our front room.

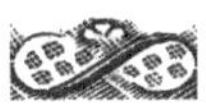

The main difficulty with Wolfgang was the way he would preach Communism to me until very late at night. He spoke volubly and advanced towards one as he became more enthusiastic, gesticulating and breathing all over you. He also convinced me that war was quite inevitable and I hated him for this, because he became in some way the personification of it. His violence against the Nazis was as repellent to me as their violence against the Communists and his attachment to Communism was not for idealistic reasons, but because he hoped that it would benefit him personally. One of his favourite expressions was: 'That would be very good for me'. He read with German thoroughness and concluded that if he had read and learned something, it was now his personal property and that his views on music or architecture or art were sound and naturally right because he had read about them thoroughly. He thought that all art should be propaganda and because he had no experience of aesthetic standards, he refused to believe they existed or were of any importance if they did. Eric found this materialism more of a bore than I did and he would painstakingly try to explain his own views on these tenets but if you have no experience of what the other person is trying to explain, it is quite useless to argue. Most of the people in the village didn't like the look of poor Wolfgang and only Miss Barrett invited him to her house and because he emitted a stream of textbook conversation on such subjects as dialectical materialism, she thought him very intelligent, which, compared to the standard of intelligence of young men in English chain stores, he obviously was. She lent him some books and it was in returning these that he committed his final atrocity.

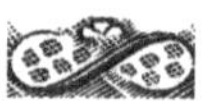

The Hephers when they first arrived in the village had brought with them from Reigate a nursemaid called Kathleen. She was a cheeky, vulgar girl with a long face and bold eyes, a good worker but intolerably noisy. We were thankful when they stopped employing her because she used to frequently come to tea with us with their little boy David and the house would rock with peals of hideous laughter. She stole the Pilgrim boy and became engaged to him; having no parents in the village she was admitted to his home. If a girl was brought into a young man's home in the village, that was a sign of his serious intentions and Jack Pilgrim and Kathleen were very much in evidence with their walking out and frequent quarrelling. When she left the Hephers, she was taken over by Miss Barrett and they got on rather well together.

One morning a note was left at our door from Miss Barrett, saying would we mind if our refugee didn't call any more at her house as he had made advances to Kathleen and frightened her very much. Eric was terribly upset about this and insisted that I take him to Miss Barrett's at once to apologise. Rather fortunately, she was out when we arrived and we saw Kathleen who explained how Wolfgang had come in to wait for Miss Barrett and then tried to kiss her, seemingly unable to believe that she might not want to kiss him and she had had quite a scuffle before being able to get rid of him. She was nice about it and I liked her much better after this. We both gave Wolfgang a lecture and he turned white and miserable about the whole thing. He couldn't understand or believe the typical English girl's attitude to love. If he did, he thought it quite mad and he vowed that never again would

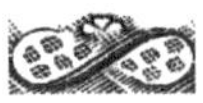

he attempt to make advances to one. I can hear him saying pathetically: 'But these girl, she is not even preety'. Poor Wolfgang, he seemed to be doing all the things that one was warned foreigners did. Jim Richards arrived with John Piper to stay a few days before he was due to leave and we hardly took any more notice of the miserable man because we were so busy. He left for Reading, saying that if ever there was anything he could do in the future to help us he would try and oh, how glad to see him go we were. It is always sad when things that are universally said about people prove to be only too true. He really was a kind man but terribly unfortunate and we never heard what happened to him next. I imagine he may now be in Canada with a wife and at least four children.

I had a letter from Oliver Simon saying that he wanted to see me on business so I dutifully went to London and arrived very hot, carrying a suitcase at Tottenham Court Road Underground which was the nearest station for Russell Square. I went to the cloakroom and produced my case but to my surprise, the man looked at me with horror in his face and said: 'This cloakroom is closed'. It wasn't till some time later that I realised that it had been blown up the day before by an IRA bomb. I wearily carried the wretched case down Oxford Street where I wanted to buy some shoes and then at 4 o'clock, I arrived at the office of the Curwen Press.

Oliver didn't at once disclose his business but we talked about pictures. He expressed surprise at my still being interested in picture shows; he said that he was very tired of them. Actually, I don't believe I have ever been to a private view

where Oliver hasn't turned up sooner or later and shaken his head as rapidly as a dog shaking a rat and muttered: 'I don't know', so it was small wonder he had grown tired of them, especially as he didn't seem to have a genuine liking of his own for pictures. Eric thought that Oliver was like a weather cock and you could judge in a few weeks the general success of a show by Oliver's opinion which would be made up of the collected criticism of his more enlightened acquaintances.

At last he came to the point, which was that he was planning to bring out an edition of *Signature* with an article on marbled papers which he proposed to illustrate. He said that Douglas Cockerel was going to allow him some of his papers and would I do the same thing. The snag to this was that he didn't intend to pay me for them but expected that the honour and glory of being extolled in *Signature* would be enough. He flattered me by saying that I was the best marbler in Europe and I ought to have more recognition. I warmly replied that I didn't wish to be well known and I hated the kind of life led by successful people. After a cup of tea and a biscuit I left, feeling pretty indignant being brought all the way to London for this because he could easily have written to me. I did say I might give him some old papers if I could find enough, because I always felt grateful to him for introducing me to the BBC and Carrington and he had paid me for the last lot of papers that he had used for holding four bound *Signatures*. Charlotte had always told me what a good businessman Douglas Cockerel was and I couldn't understand his consenting to this idea of Oliver's and I wasn't surprised when I heard later that the plan had fallen through, owing to lack of enthusiasm for it from marblers.

We had come to know a friend of the Gooddens, a young painter called Kenneth Rowntree who had been a pupil of Eric's at the Ruskin School of Art in Oxford, and he recommended Eric to go to Le Havre and the northern coast of Brittany which had cliffs not unlike the Sussex ones.

As Robert Wellington had left the Zwemmer Gallery and embarked on a scheme for publishing and distributing contemporary lithographs for schools, Eric decided to have his third exhibition at Tooth's Gallery in Bond Street. His show was concurrent with an exhibition of oil paintings by Sir Timothy Eden, brother to Sir Anthony Eden and both Private Views were on the same day. Eric and I were both pleased with all the pictures this time. Eric very mercilessly rejected any that weren't as good as he had hoped and except for the one of the paddle steamers at Bristol which had too many colours in it, he approved of all of them.

At the Private View I tried to disguise my bulging stomach as well as possible, as it might look as though I thought people ought to buy pictures out of charity, seeing the condition I was in. Actually I felt quite confident that the pictures would sell because it was a better show than the previous two and they had both practically sold out and I was right. We were pleased because John and Christine Nash bought a good one; it is always particularly flattering if another painter buys a picture and also Edward Le Bas had booked one when he had met Eric at Rye. Sir Edward Marsh bought one for the Contemporary Art Society.

Sir Timothy Eden didn't do so well, his pictures were rather dull as was his Private View public, the men in their

neat black suits and the women very much be-furred and high heeled. One of the gallery young men said finally to Eric: 'It's easy to distinguish between your guests and the others, they look more intelligent.'

I can't remember the newspaper criticism, I think *The Times* and the *Observer* were complimentary and as usual the *New Statesman* didn't mention them. So long as Eric felt that the people he admired like Paul Nash and Henry Moore and John Piper approved, it didn't matter what other critics said.

Always our happiness was slightly spoiled, as was every-one's, by the thought of the coming war; the long drawn-out uncertainty making life ever more difficult.

A short time before the show, Eric wanted to take up two pictures to Tooth's. We went to London for the day accompanied by Sven and Pam Mikkelsen who wanted to buy painting materials to take back to Denmark. They came with us to the gallery where there was an excellent show of Impressionist paintings which preceded Eric's. I felt shocked by the lack of interest displayed by Sven. Somehow I had imagined that all painters would naturally wish to look at what were acknowledged to be good paintings, even if they weren't done in a style in which they felt much sympathy.

It was a lovely spring day and the pavements were crowded with well dressed people. We walked along to Piccadilly Circus and turned up Regent Street and I thought how awful it would be if a bomb were suddenly to fall in the middle of them. When we met Sven and Pam again and went back with them in the train, I found that Sven like me had also been seeing in imagination bombs raining down on the people. It was

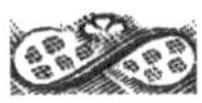

strange that one of the first bombs that did fall should have landed just in this part of Regent Street but fortunately the people were not there. I think everybody's forebodings about the war were not actually more horrifying but quite different from the reality. The newspapers were agitating for deep shelters and only Finsbury Park was sensible enough to build one.

I said how nice it must be for Pam and Sven to be going to Denmark, thinking that Denmark would be in no danger as she had escaped molestation in the last war, but Sven pointed out that Denmark was in a most unfavourable position and could do nothing if she were attacked because of her size. He promised Eric that he would get permission from his father for him to go to Greenland, as Eric was longing to go to Greenland and paint there. Both Sven and August Courtauld spoke highly of it and as far as we know there weren't any good paintings of the country.

When the war started, I was in a nursing home in Eastbourne after having given birth to James. Eric was staying with the family, just having helped Peggy when her baby arrived unexpectedly at Furlongs.

In August I went to Eastbourne with John and Hilda Brown, while Eric went to Furlongs to paint harvest pictures. He wasn't able to do much work because Peggy [who had married Jim Richards in 1936] was there alone with [their young daughter] Victoria, so that there was a lot of housework and fetching of water from the deep well for Victoria's bath. Then suddenly one night, Peggy's new baby started arriving quite unexpectedly. Eric ran down the lane to fetch Mrs Spike who was camping in the field on the right where there is a

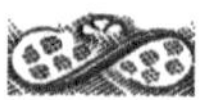

water tap. Unfortunately her husband had gone away in their car for the night, so he had to run on to the village while Mrs Spike went back to Furlongs to help Peggy. He managed to rouse the man in the pub who drove them all in to Lewes where a nursing home ungraciously received the quite unprepared Peggy and a very miserable time she had there. The baby was a boy with a huge bald head like a wooden Dutch doll's and they called him Angus.

After this, Eric, pleased with himself in his role of midwife, came to Eastbourne to see if he could deliver my baby which was really due. I was very uncomfortable and couldn't sit down properly as it felt as though I was sitting on the baby's head and when I looked between my legs there was a bulging membranous sac which was horrifying. I felt like this for a day or two before my waters finally broke all over Mummy's best spare-room eiderdown on which I was resting as it was very hot.

Billy's husband Freddie drove us all down to the nursing home and I remembered how Billy had said that Freddie was the kind of man who gave lifts to pregnant women.

Beth Smith who kept the maternity home was an elderly woman whose first case when she had started out on her own as a maternity nurse had been the twins of Aunt May and Uncle Robert. She retained a surprising affection for my Uncle Robert; it was hard to imagine my dour uncle entertaining an embarrassed nurse for breakfast, but she said that he had been so kind. She had pushed out my odious cousin Bobby in his pram accompanied by a collection of saucepans and kettles from which he refused to be parted; she had found this embarrassing too.

Nothing much happened all the rest of the afternoon. I sat on a towel and dripped slowly but hadn't any pains worth mentioning. The doctor was playing tennis so they waited before giving me an enema until he came in to tea. When he did arrive he looked at me and said he would go away again and come back later, which seems to be the thing that doctors always say to women in labour. I felt by then so angry with him because I was having pains every three minutes that I pushed the baby's head almost out by the time he had reached the bottom of the stairs, so he didn't get away. The final pain which got the head through was accompanied by such a tearing agony that it strangely resembled an orgasm of pleasure, the snapping of an electrical current as though it had fused in your head.

It was disappointing to hear them say: 'It's a boy' and then I looked down between my thighs at the warm wriggling baby and my disappointment vanished on seeing what a handsome boy it was. He had large dark eyes and brown skin and he peed a spray of piss over my leg while the doctor cut through the cord which still attached us, an unexpectedly thick grey cord, as large as chipolata sausages and then they set to work wringing out my stomach to produce the afterbirth, so I just screamed. The doctor thought he had found some strange node on the placenta but decided that it wasn't and my curiosity thoroughly aroused, I asked if I could see it; but he looked quite shocked and refused which made me feel even crosser with him.

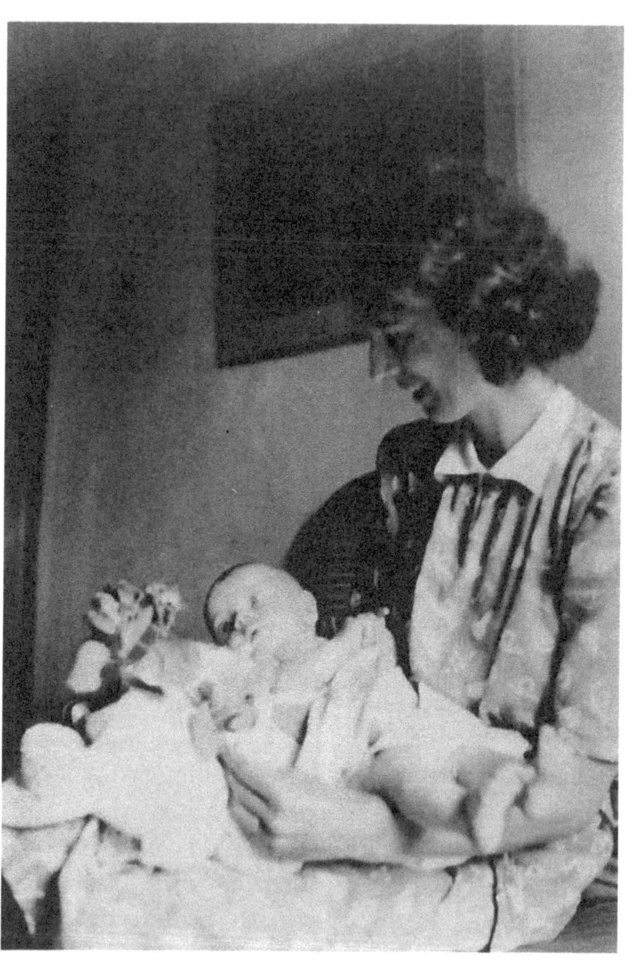

CHAPTER TWENTY-TWO

*Tirzah's second son, James Hugh Ravilious, was born on August
22nd 1939 – a fortnight later, on September 3rd, war was declared.
Tirzah's autobiography starts again on March 13th 1942 with a
description of her mastectomy operation for primary breast cancer.
Tirzah left brief notes indicating what she may have intended to write.
Nearly all the subjects mentioned are covered in letters, and in this
chapter I have used extracts from these to fill in this missing period.
Her list reads:*

War artists
First encounter with baby-faced surgeon commander at
    Chatham, various stories about this man
Inspection by the King congratulating the bugler on his
    bugling
Various arrests
Trip to Norway
Behaviour under action
Sentimental influence of naval men on work
Censoring letters & decoding
Sheerness misery & militant women – my visits & hats

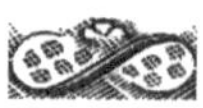

Escape to Southern Command

Charming Admiral Bubbles [Admiral Sir William Milbourne
James, KCB, Commander-inChief, Portsmouth]

August Courtauld's adventures

Submarine work

My visit & day out on the Isle of Wight

Embroidery [for Dunbar Hay]. Possible death of Mother

Lodgings with shell-shocked man from Dunkirk & doctor's
family

Recall to Chatham. Reprimand for his work by Earnley
Earl Drax [Plunkett-Ernle-Erle-Drax] & subsequent
dismissal by Admiral

Subterranean London in the Blitz

Unpleasant Civil Servant & disappearing clothes

Lovely girls

Dover, unpleasant Colonel. Will

Scotland, Dundee, May Island, John Nash's job

RAF dances and pictures in messes

*Following her confinement, Tirzah remained with her parents
while Eric returned home to Bank House. Tirzah, with a new baby
and four-year-old John, was in no position to join in any war effort.
Eric was thirty-six and therefore not included in the first draft of
younger men to be called up but he immediately signed up as a
volunteer with the Observer Corps and took up duties the next day at
the local Observation Post for Castle Hedingham on nearby Sudbury
Hill.*

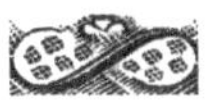

Here is a picture of me saving the country. I work at odd hours of the day and night watching aeroplanes up on the hill, and work with a partner – not in the picture. We wear lifeboat men's outfits against the weather and tin hats for show. It is like a Boy's Own Paper story, what with spies and passwords and all manner of nonsense: all the same, as far as wars go it is a congenial job, and the scene lovely, mushrooms about and blackberries coming along and the most spectacular sunrises.

Meanwhile three small boys and their grandmother, evacuees from Wood Green in London, were billeted at Bank House. You know how good at picking 'treasures' we are, *Eric wrote to Tirzah in Eastbourne on September 3rd*: Mrs Clark is an amazing woman and I don't know what I would do without her. She would be wonderful with babies. The three boys are nice and I am going to keep them all if possible. They sleep in the back room and Mrs Clark in Hilda's bed. . . .

How dangerous Hedingham is nobody knows. The search lights aren't near, not nearer than three or four miles and none actually in the village: also Eastbourne is a town and more of a temptation to the German bomb you would say.

Tirzah returned home with the children and Hilda Brown in mid-October. On the 29th, Eric wrote to her parents saying how busy she had been since her return:

It is very cold in these parts and a downpour of rain most nights and the full moon very spectacular when it does shine. There has never been such a year for berries and fruit and the crab apple by the Post is weighed down with fruit. We would send you them by rail if you have the sugar and I'd enjoy picking the tree on some quiet shift there. We stripped the

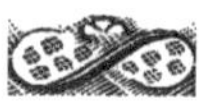

vicarage quince last week just in time I think and Tirzah has made pounds of jam; in fact, the shelves are looking like Fortnum's with so many preserves and bottled fruits, but no mushrooms this year for some reason.

On Christmas Eve 1939 Eric was delighted when a letter came from the Admiralty stating that both he and John Nash were to be offered part-time commissions as Official War Artists with the status of Honorary Captains in the Royal Marines, Eric to make pictorial records working under the Admiralty's Nore Command and John Nash to cover the Western Approaches. Tirzah excitedly wrote to Gwyneth Lloyd Thomas on December 31st:

We are very pleased because Eric has been appointed a war artist for the Navy with John Nash as companion. He is longing to start with his usual punctuality and promises me parrots, monkeys and all those things.

He has also just painted six stunners in the last month which is encouraging because working conditions haven't been too good.

I've been doing baby and housework as we only have our best Hilda three times a week and little Hilda [Brown, only fourteen years old] though a baby charmer, is slow otherwise. However with this new job we can go back to both Hildas and I shall have time to think again.

The baby is called James and has brown eyes and is a pink-cheeked one this time but he also is getting eczema I'm afraid, it is a nuisance. John's has quite gone a long time ago which is cheering. I can hear Eric's cough in the road, he is coming across from The Bell so I must make some supper and leave this roasting fire. . . . Talking of perishing, 'the old perisher'

Baines died in his sleep on Christmas Day. He was a lucky old man. I don't think he ever realised how much the village disliked him.

In January 1940, the weather turned bitterly cold, the pipes froze and the family had to move in with the Hephers; I like exceptional weather, *Eric wrote to Diana Tuely:* but it is making country life rather difficult – and we now live in the Vicarage as Bank House is quite impossible, and all pumps and water frozen. The Vicarage still has running water but for how long no one can say. *And to Helen Binyon:* It is marvellous weather I know, but I can't work in this interval, and anyway there is so much to be done and pipes burst and the snow piles up every day. Now the fish have all died in the castle lake (you can count hundreds of them in the ice) and my ink bottle froze last week so that the pen bounced off the top.

The severest frost since 1894 was recorded in February, 1940. Eric's first commission began in February at Chatham. His introduction included training dealing with the probability of imminent invasion and the assumption that the Germans would use poison gas in their initial attack:

My dear Tush it is borne upon me that gas is going to be used. I do think this is likely and I'd feel better if you took all precautions you can. Have soap and water about where you can get at it. Also it is probably going to be mustard or lewisite so look them up in the book. They are the worst of course. We live so near the coast that a spray might easily reach Essex. Do at least have these things, soap and water (warm if poss) rubber boots and gloves, gas ointment (two kinds), bag for James, anti-dim for your masks.

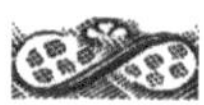

From Chatham Eric moved on to Sheerness and Whitstable and after a brief leave at the end of March to see Tirzah and the children, he set off in April to draw the trawler fleet at Grimsby. In May he was at sea aboard the destroyer HMS Highlander, *part of the flotilla which had sailed through snow storms up the Norwegian fjords to attack the German-held port of Narvik, then sailing further north to protect the merchant shipping lanes. He wrote to Diana Tuely:*

It has been a wonderful trip with excitements here and there from planes and submarines, but the grand thing was going up into the Arctic Circle with a brilliant sun shining all night, Arctic terns flying by the ship – I simply loved it and in fact haven't enjoyed anything so much since the war. The sun is much hotter there than you think and I work without a coat quite comfortably. At sea people wear all sorts of clothes. . . and the whole time we have to wear a rubber life-belt, even in bed, and keep it partly blown up, so that everyone presents a chest like a guardsman. . . Now having at last got into harbour out of the fog we are to sail first thing in the morning. There will be some excitements this time I think. . . . It is strange not seeing land, or women or darkness for so long. It is like some unearthly existence.

By mid June, after a trip of 7,500 miles, Eric returned home to a much-needed month's leave. In July he was posted to Portsmouth, followed by work aboard HMS Dolphin, *a submarine base at nearby Gosport. In August he came home to the news that Tirzah was expecting their third child. His first commission ended with a posting to Newhaven and an assignment to record the pre-invasion coastal defences, from where he wrote to Tirzah:*

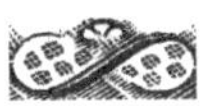

September 19th, 1940. I have at last arrived here after an exciting but rather fruitless two days in London (and what nights!) and a day in Eastbourne. This was a bad dream. It was like the ruins of Pompeii, and both our families gone, the town all but empty. 60,000 people have left. I stayed at Elmwood Palace, all dust sheeted and moth balled. Ethel [cook and housekeeper] was there and the gardener's family living in the cellar and I think they were glad to see me. Grove Rd is a bit of a mess, and the Art School entrance bombed. I put my foot up into Penn's empty window – there was no glass left – to do up my shoelace. Your maternity home is bombed – I think, and a tree outside down. All the windows of that nice white hotel the Burlington are broken and the pier sawn in half. Mrs Church was the only resident I met, holding the fort in some wonderful uniform. Barbara [Church] is happily in California. I left Eastbourne after an early breakfast with a haunted feeling and could have run from the spot.

The autumn of 1940 was a particularly difficult time for Tirzah, one disaster following another. Eric was away when she discovered a lump in her right breast which the doctor recommended should be removed, then John had to go into hospital to have his tonsils out. In October she was upset to learn that Christine Nash, who was yearning for another baby, had had a miscarriage. John and Christine's first child, their five-year-old son William, had been fatally injured after accidentally falling out of the car while Christine was driving. John, in his grief, was unable to forgive her, so the miscarriage was doubly miserable for Christine. Then Tirzah herself threatened to miscarry. Though far from the usual target of bombing raids, a doodlebug

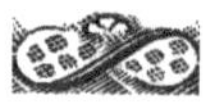

On Tuesday we walked to a nearby farm to see a bomb crater in a ploughed field. Frank Ruffel, the farmer, who much resembles Groucho Marx, he has the same rolling black eyes, was standing about saying: 'I don't know who is going to fill it up'. I think he deserves it as he always listens into Haw-haw and is very pessimistic about the war. Kay Goodden worked for him [as a Land Girl] before she went away to become a WAAF He is a widower with four grown-up children and is a great talker. I left John and Hilda in a Spanish Chestnut grove and took James home, when I was told that Eric had just rung, wishing to be fetched from the station. He had a lot of luggage and had lost yet another cap by putting his head out of the window. He said he had to because the train was so crowded that he could not turn round.

I think his war artist job is probably coming to an end. The committee want him to continue but the Treasury don't want to pay for it. Eric isn't very sorry because he has really done enough work of that kind.

I'm sitting in a slow train wandering about through Suffolk on its way to Cambridge. . . . Tirzah gets as much butter as she wants and handed me out about 1/4 lb for my weekend. I plastered it on the bread, and still have a large lump to take home. I stayed the first night with the Raviliouses, Eric was

restless and had nothing to do with himself. He's finished one phase of the RNVR work and doesn't know if he'll be able to get an extension of the job. Tirzah is much occupied with babies, James is very sweet indeed, a little Puck, he is much more attractive than John was, altho John at his age was better looking, and sturdier, poor James has the same inadequate clothing, cotton suits in this cold weather, and hardly any blankets on his cot.

The operation to remove the lump from Tirzah's breast, which was not considered cause for any great alarm, took place at the end of October; Eric wrote to Helen on the 29th:

Here I still am, leading a quiet country life with Tirzah away in a nursing home for a week in Colchester. I think it is nothing serious. So the day goes rather slowly and I chop up oak logs and walk and read . . . Our future is still uncertain. . . . I've suggested a trip to Iceland later to draw the Royal Marines in hibernas, with duffel coats and perhaps those splendid plum skies. There are the most beautiful women with fair hair in Iceland so they say: it is pitch dark all day and the snow falls and the wind blows and you stay in bed for twenty-four hours.

The offer of a second commission came on November 8th 1940, but Eric asked the Admiralty for six months' leave before commencing as he wanted to translate the submarine drawings done at Gosport into a series of lithographs, the idea being that the War Artists' Advisory Committee might use them in a book for boys to promote life in the Navy: The lithography began on Christmas Eve and goes on all day with occasional visits to Ipswich to see the printer there, and is very good fun. I like lithography. But

now without small Hilda and with no water it is a bit difficult, *Eric wrote to Tirzah's mother Ella on December 31st.* These two things come together as a yearly visitation with flooding the Bank as a finale, and no plumber seems able to stop this, I don't know why. Tirzah and the children are well in spite of all this and John now at school again which he quite likes but is not, according to the report, very good at his lessons. He 'takes an interest' in Scripture, History, Geography and something else but 'is not always willing to work', which made us laugh. His singing has bottom marks. What are called Charity marks. He was very pleased with the two Meccano sets and wants us to get him a battery to light up these cranes and things if there is such a thing in the village.

All the family sleep downstairs – against the bombing – so it isn't so very cold for them at nights. Upstairs is like the Arctic.

Tirzah thinks your offer to come here later on a good one if it is practicable, but the journey from one remote country place to another will be no easy job especially if this weather continues into March. In Essex it might easily. Aunt Edith's hotel is very comfortable so she says. It isn't The Bell. Tirzah has made arrangements with the District Nurse (and doctor) and with a midwife. We like the look of them both. The latter is a sort of Mrs Noah and I should think a queen among midwives. With luck I shall be here at the time as the new six months doesn't start yet, and the lithographs will take some time to do. Aunt Edith may also be holding the fort then. She likes C H as it is fairly quiet. Tirzah will write to you about all this.

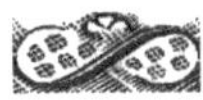

I must go – there was more I meant to say, but water and blackouts and the rest put it out of my mind . . . . James walks very well now.

To avoid the blitz, Tirzah's aunts had decided to leave London, Aunt Edith coming to stay in Castle Hedingham where she could be useful to Tirzah, while Aunt Lucy removed herself to Scotland where she became ill and demanded to be rescued – an impossibility for the family to achieve with wartime travel restrictions. Uncle Harry was bombed out of his flat in Wimbledon and lost his false teeth in the rubble.

Eric's mother, Emma, died in the Princess Alice Hospital, Eastbourne on February 23rd 1941 and Eric, leaving a very pregnant Tirzah behind, departed to arrange the funeral. He was back just in time for the birth of their baby daughter Anne, born on April 1st, and wrote to Diana Tuely the same day:

It's a girl. Isn't that nice? She was born in the small hours before the doctor could administer the anaesthetic (which is lucky really) and they are both well. The daughter weighs seven pounds and has a round head like a nut. What scenes there were in the night; I am jolly glad it was not by day with troops parading just outside the window and fish men and butchers calling. We got to bed about four. I feel a bit tired this morning, but have a new suit on and it is a cold wild boisterous first of April, a nice day to be born.

And in a letter to Helen Binyon a few days later:

Tirzah is in bed recovering and doing this very quickly and the baby well and taking an interest in things. It is nice to have a daughter for a change.

My mother died – did I tell you? and I went to Eastbourne for the funeral. What an awful business funerals are and all

the attendant things, florists and undertakers and wills. It was really a sort of nightmare and I felt very low indeed after it. I was fond of my mother, who was a sheet anchor in our temperamental family. She died without knowing it simply of old age. Her hair was still black.

On April 30th, only a month after the birth of their daughter, the family moved to Ironbridge Farm, an Elizabethan house hidden at the end of a long lane beyond Shalford. This they rented from John Strachey who was an MP and a writer on socialist economics (and after the war, from 1946, Minister for Food). He leased the property with an agreement that half the yearly rent be paid in cash and half with Eric's watercolours to the same value. He suggested that May Holmes, who lived in a cottage down the lane, might help with the children. She was the youngest and only girl in a family of seven brothers and was delighted at this opportunity to look after a baby.

The seriousness of the hit-and-run raids in 1940 had necessitated the Garwoods leaving Eastbourne. They took shelter with Ella's elderly spinster cousins, Edie, Myra and Ethel Scott at Draycott House, Kemsey in Worcestershire. The house was ruled over by the eldest sister Edie.

It is now exactly four months since we fled from Eastbourne, *the Colonel wrote to Tirzah,* and there seems very little hope of our returning there. This is a very safe and comfortable refuge, but it has some decided disadvantages. The atmosphere of perpetual religiosity so far from introducing a spirit of piety has the reverse effect on me. I am temperamentally unfitted for the part of a character in the Pilgrim's Progress. Edie has invented a new form of torture, at family prayers

everybody is issued with a prayer book and has to recite the verses of a children's hymn. It's always a children's hymn and I began to suspect it a case of recession to her early childhood.

To add to this, because of wartime austerity, perhaps coupled with resentment at a man's presence in the house, Edie served him with minutely small rations, so that by January 1941, he was suffering from severe starvation. As early as October 1940 he had written to his brother Harry: Yesterday Edie carved a complete rabbit, which looked like the corpse of an Egyptian cat. She gave Ethel one front paw as her portion, and she dare not ask for more, *and in another letter:* We had salmon tonight and Edie served it with a teaspoon.

There was, however, one redeeming feature at Kempsey. In the disused library Colonel Garwood found a collection of family histories collected by the three sisters' father, Charles Scott, including the diaries of a distant ancestor, Major Thomas Scott RA, who had served in the Peninsula War (1808–14). For the rest of his stay in Worcestershire Tirzah's father was engrossed in the diaries of Tom Scott, which he copied and edited, typing out three-quarters of a million words.

Eric began his second commission in the summer of 1941. The bombardment of Britain had started and he had been asked by the Admiralty to record the cross-Channel shelling of the south coast. The plight of Tirzah's parents was relieved by a visit to Castle Hedingham to help out with the children while Eric was posted to Dover:

I'm glad to hear that your father is going bathing with Ariel [Crittall] and the children, *he wrote to Tirzah on July*

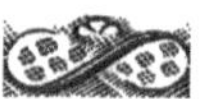

27th, and it sounds cheerful and almost like Elmwood again, gardening and excursions with the children.

Is the beam alright now? Why do houses do this to us; no one else's beams break and plumbing burst out of season.

My father writes that already he is back with [my brother] Frank, and talks of going either to [my sister] Evelyn or Eastbourne again. He still misses my mother very much and is awfully unsettled. Poor old man, there is never any room for him in the West Country and no one much he knows in Eastbourne.

Your drawing is fairly true to life except for the shells. One fell in the town the other night and killed somebody. They make a deafening noise on both sides of the Channel, but by the time I am out of bed and in some clothes the salvo is generally over. They let loose about eight to a dozen as a rule about once a week, sometimes twice.

And Tirzah replied on the August 17th about her life at Ironbridge: There is a great quiet in the house broken only by cries and quacks of different birds. You'll like these birds, they come into the passage much to Mummy's indignation. I can hear them there now. Bats will get into Mummy's room at nights. What is it about Mummy that attracts these minor troubles, it's very strange isn't it. She has gone to church and Daddy has taken both boys for a walk, that is why it is so peaceful.

I have just cut our first vegetable marrow, a fine juicy pale green one. The Goodchild tea party on Friday was again a success, the parents like them and old man Goodchild out-talks Daddy with long tales about livestock in the early nineteen hundreds and the house and garden so beautifully

decayed is looking very good at the moment. Their bottom walled-in field is full of the other sister's rabbits and hares. An old crop of swedes had come up over large parts of the grassland and looks very foreign, it has such large leaves and there are such a lot of rabbits and hares. I imagine parts of Australia must look the same.

John and James had a Fisk birthday party yesterday. James was as usual the life and soul or so they say. I didn't go but Diana and David looked after him. John was happy but unsociable, so they allowed him to collect apples by himself outside so he was alright in his own way.

I've done some more drawings of Anne to make up for the one I sent Thomas Hennell.

It's a good place this and I'm glad we came. James is having a birthday party on Friday so you must come home by then.

When you go to Eastbourne, Mummy would be glad if you'd look up the gardener at Elmwood, only if you have time though. The parents think they may go back there in the winter if it looks as though there won't be an invasion. Daddy was very nervous when they were there, Mummy of course doesn't mind bombs like some do.

I wonder what you were doing while they were shelling Dover. I hope you are still intact. Luckily I only hear about these things a long time after they have occurred.

We are going over to Bardfield tomorrow afternoon to see Charlotte. Fred [Mizen] has been stealing and drinking. He or the evacuees stole all their stores including 40 lbs of jam. I should have been mad with rage. I suppose you have to

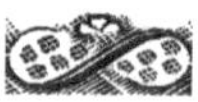

suffer if you leave home. Lucie is in a bad way because she can't cope with Fred yet must have him to pump and do the garden. It's no good living in a haunted house. Fred will make a wonderful new ghost for the future won't he?

By October, Eric was in Scotland, where he stayed with John and Christine Nash, and wrote to Tirzah from Crombie Point Cottage, Dunfermline, on October 20th 1941: I was so pleased to find your letters and the parcel (most welcome to Christine) when I came home today from my ship. . . . I'm glad Ironbridge is warming up for the Essex winter. I hope John's tooth is stopped now and the Baffy [James] well, and Anne growing some hair. How sweet of her to say Golly so young. Now I think of it, charge your Mr Dunn 2/6, which seems a reasonable wartime addition. I hope you will sell him some [marbled papers].

Christine has just gone off to London and possibly Wiston so may perhaps see you. She is a wonderful person in any house, and gets us all up with tea in the morning and a splendid breakfast, then she lights my fire if I work at home and goes off to Dunfermline for beer and cigarettes. What more could you want?

Christine noted in her diary: Eric came last week too, I was shocked by his looks, so thin and sallow and old-looking, but I gather his trouble was just starvation, and he is already filling out and becoming livelier. . . . He is in a mood to be attached to his new home, wife, and children, he really seems to appreciate Tirzah's hardships with two babies under two years, in a way I did not think likely, and tells me anecdotes of

James, I am envious when I think that I might have had a child older than Anne.

While in Scotland Eric had drawn seaplanes at Dundee and, keen to draw more aircraft, he was introduced to Group Captain Lord Willoughby de Broke, the Air Ministry representative on the War Artists' Advisory Committee. This resulted in a commission with the Royal Air Force which started in February 1942, at the RAF station at Clifton, outside York.

Tirzah's minor operation to remove a lump from her breast had seemed at the time to be successful, but now she was told a mastectomy operation was urgently needed. Eric was given a fortnight's leave and summoned home in haste from York. He obtained permission to continue work at the nearby airfield at Debden so that he could be at hand in case of emergency. Then James went down with measles. Tirzah's mother hurried to Ironbridge to help, and to save her from infection, the baby was taken in by May Holmes. She helped again when all three children caught whooping cough. Tirzah's father, left behind in Worcestershire, wrote to his brother, Harry to complain of his wife's absence, on March 11th 1942:

My wife has struck one of the bad patches of her life, and her stay in Essex is now indefinitely prolonged, James Ravilious is in her bedroom with measles, which fortunately does not seem to be a very severe attack. They cannot use the kitchen range for fear of the pipes from the water tank freezing and Ironbridge Farm is a mile from anywhere, situated within quarter of a mile of the River Pant or Blackwater, a very unpleasant winter neighbour.

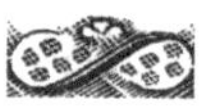

But the most shattering blow of all is that poor Tirzah is in Braintree Hospital and her left breast is to be removed today as a precautionary measure. In vain they comfort me by asserting that the best women all have only one breast, just as the best foxes have no tails. I think it is a horrible disfigurement for a young woman of 33, who has nursed three children, and it is such hard lines on Tirzah who has put up such a gallant fight against adverse conditions for so many months.

Helen Binyon wrote to offer help, Eric replying to her letter; Ironbridge Farm, Friday March 13th 1942: Tirzah has had a successful operation at last, though a pretty drastic one as they had to remove the left breast. Poor Tirzah vaguely was aware this might happen for some time, but thank goodness it is now over. She is pale but quite cheerful and will be alright in about three weeks or so, at least that is what they say: but she had a hard time, with blood transfusions and glucose fed from a tube. I take her in Russian Matisses and Utrillos for the mantelpiece to offset 'Betwixt two Fires' if you know that work, which hangs opposite the bed. Matisse is strong meat for the nurses of course and they think I did it. . . .

Did I say James had measles. He went to Sussex while Tirzah was away the first time and the Hepher children got measles at once from a boy at school. So Tirzah's mother has come here to hold the fort and does so all day long and very well indeed. I'm ashamed I used to dislike her so much at Eastbourne. Now I get on with her perfectly well – in any case we are both too busy to think about anything but

food and fires and measles, doctors and blackouts and ducks
and hens.

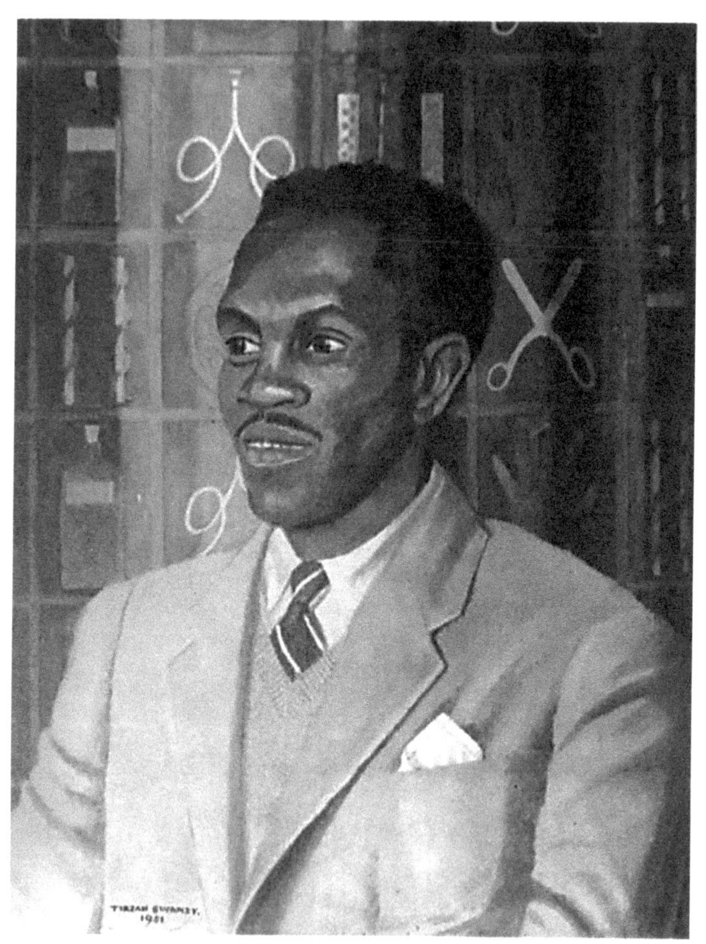

TIRZAH SWANZY.
1951

CHAPTER TWENTY-THREE

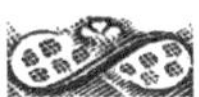

When I woke up after the operation I knew exactly what it felt like to be lost in a desert, because my throat was so hot and dry that it had swollen into a painful burning ache and the first drink of abominable chlorinated Braintree water tasted like life itself.

Sicking up the anaesthetic was of course extremely unpleasant, but the wound was not as painful as I had anticipated and so long as I didn't move my arm, it didn't really hurt much. I was stitched upwards in a long line which curved like the shape of a walking stick into my left arm where they had taken out the muscle which connected my breast to my biceps and it was this part under my arm which was the most painful.

It wasn't till a few days later that I discovered that I had nearly died. Eric came to see me looking very upset and told me how they had rung up on the evening after the operation and been told that I hadn't yet come round. Then later that same evening they were rung up by the matron, who confessed that I had had to have a blood-transfusion and she asked for our telephone number in case they wanted to call for Eric in the night. This of course alarmed him and my

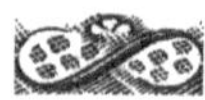

mother and they spent an anxious night before ringing up in the morning to discover that I was alright.

I was surprised to find that my immediate reaction was one of regret that I hadn't died. It was only a momentary regret probably caused by my bodily exhaustion and the realisation that before the operation, I had been perfectly confident of my survival. So that if I had died it would have been without any of that awful feeling of dread which one sometimes gloomily imagines oneself undergoing; and now I should have to face living for a year or two with the fear that the wretched disease might come back.

My right arm was attached to a feed of saline and glucose that ran down from a bottle suspended above me and for a week or so afterwards I felt no desire for sweets which because of the war, I had previously missed very much.

Eric found living at home with my mother and James rather difficult and he was soon his usual grumbling husbandly self. My mother insisted on spring cleaning the house and we both marvelled that she should actually relish the idea of turning out other people's chests of drawers and we wondered if she hoped to find some secret that would reveal to her the mysteries of our private life; she was intensely curious by nature. Eric, like my father, admitted that she was a wonderful woman but as he had to do most of the cooking, it was hard work for him as well. May who was looking after Anne, left them severely alone, saying that Mr Ravilious was as good as a woman in the house.

An unexpectedly good visitor was Jack Gold who came once or twice a week laden with flowers and a picture which he

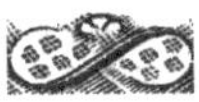

put up for me to look at in bed. Eric brought along reproductions from our collection of pictures from the Moscow Art Gallery so that all the nurses were entertained by this and I got quite tired of trying to explain Matisse or Henri Rousseau to them and the doctor. Of course, the nurses teased me about Jack's attention and when one day I said that I must make up my face because he was coming to see me, I realised thankfully that I was fond of him and that I could love men again.

Not having a very interesting private life, like my mother, Jack was curious about other people's behaviour. I did most of the talking at his visits but he occasionally proffered his odd little confidences, such as: 'I don't like girls' and 'Personally, I like the life of a semi-invalid'. We were talking one day about Sir William Rothenstein whom he had met and I asked if he had found him frightening. 'I am never frightened of anyone', he replied firmly. This seemed a particularly strange remark from Jack who appeared to be so very shy.

He came one afternoon dressed with more than ordinary care and bashfully said that he was going courting. The object of his suit I was surprised to find, was an eccentric old lady of seventy years who wore Russian boots.

Jack never fully told one anything, it was always these little hints which left one guessing as to their true importance. He liked to give the impression that he was a much sought-after bachelor and I naturally wondered who these pursuing women were.

I supposed his dislike of girls was caused by his too great affection for his mother and his baldness had made him look

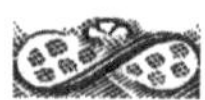

prematurely old. I could imagine that warm-hearted motherly women might wish to look after him. His complete lack of passion was not physically attractive; at dances I noticed he usually danced only with his own family.

He hated any reference to his own ill health and it was a long time before he confessed to suffering occasionally from a duodenal ulcer. His hands, of which he was so careful, were white and tapered at the fingers like a woman's but otherwise they were well proportioned and normal.

He brought in relays all Proust's books for me to read, I had previously read *Swann's Way* but I had never had time to go on. Jack was very devoted to these books and read them before going to bed; he said that he counted as his friends those people who also liked them.

As I read, I became aware that he had identified himself with these decadent Frenchmen. It was Swann who didn't answer questions and Jack's love of paying compliments and his own sensitiveness about his ill health were all symptoms of this identification. The great difference was of course that Proust really did make love while Jack contented himself with sentimental attachments to married women and the collection and propagation of pictures. He was a happy man and seemed only vaguely aware of his eccentricity and, on the whole, proud of it and of his inability to fall in love.

I was also visited for a few minutes by Jack's mother, a small round-eyed person with the same kind expression as her son. She didn't appear to like me very much and I felt the same restraint in speaking to her as I did to my own mother.

Towards the end of my three weeks in bed, I had a visit from Duffy. She was troubled because Lucie, having first rung up John to see if he approved, had told her and Michael Rothenstein all about his love affair with me. At the end of her story, she had appeared a little disconcerted because neither of them said anything. Duffy said that John had hardly come into the story at all and privately, she and Michael had both thought that he didn't seem to have behaved very well which was why they hadn't felt like expressing disapproval of my behaviour, though they felt Lucie had expected them to say something.

Although this had all happened six years ago, Duffy said that Lucie still seemed to think about nothing else. I had been vaguely aware of this brooding hate but it had seemed so fantastic after all this time that I had thought my suspicions imaginary.

We discussed Lucie, and Duffy finally went away very late for her bus but relieved by my attitude which she described as healthy.

When she had gone I suddenly felt so disgusted with Lucie for attacking me in this way, knowing that I had just had an operation, that all my feeling of guilt towards her vanished. From Duffy's brief description of her story, I knew that Lucie did not really know the truth about what had happened and I determined to write down my account of the affair. I felt that if I could read the story I should more clearly be able to judge my own part in it and when it was finished, it would be like a picture that is once painted but afterwards of no more interest to me.

I had started writing small descriptions of our life in Bardfield when I was in Hedingham and [a friend] Shirley Cocks had urged me to go on. I now determined to write an autobiography for my grandchildren. I suppose that an escape from death generally has that effect on people, only most of them don't have the time or inclination to really carry out their desire, and in writing as in drawing, I could completely forget my present circumstances.

I want to write my life while I am still happy. If I read an autobiography, I don't like to think of the author as a poor old doddering person with one foot in the grave. Two months ago, I very nearly died myself. I'm sorry to have to mention such an unpleasant subject but I must be truthful. I had cancer of the breast and had to have my left breast removed. This was not as painful an operation as you might imagine and the convalescence following it I very much enjoyed, and it has made it possible for me to write this account of my life which otherwise I should never have had time to do.

I am so happy sitting here that I find it very difficult to write at all. The smell of May wafting over the orchard wall from the outside lane is so strong and lovely that I feel it should be doing me good in some way! The pony munching the sweet clover has collected round her the flies which might otherwise be irritating me and the cuckoo is cuckooing down in the willow grove. This orchard has a curved wall encircling it with the long white lath and plaster Essex farmhouse inside. Eric is finishing off drawings of aeroplanes at Sawbridgeworth. May the nurse girl has taken the children, James and Anne, away in the pram to post a letter to their elder brother John; now I am

not so happy, poor John! I cannot come and see him for his half-term holiday and that is sad and I hated having to write that I could not come, and see in my imagination his disappointed face when they read the letter for him at school.

I find now that I have started writing my life, that for some years I must have had this intention so that in my brain the sentences have already formed and I have at times that strange feeling that a greater part of it I have already written and mislaid. It is lying in my chest of drawers or scribbled in notebooks, sandwiched between other books on our untidy shelves.

I have just read a short description of his life and fortunes by my great-grandfather [the Rev John Garwood], written for his descendants. In this notebook there is no mention of my grandfather, the only one of his children to have descendants, because my great-grandfather being a clergyman and secretary to the London City Mission, deplored his son's choice of career which was the army, and so quarrelling with him dismissed him altogether from his autobiography.

I hope, dear reader, that you may be one of my descendants, but I have only three children, my grandfather had six and as I write a German aeroplane has circled round above my head taking photographs of the damage that yesterday's raiders have done, reminding me that there is no certainty of our survival.

If you are not one of my descendants then all I ask of you is that you love the country as I do, and when you come into a room, discreetly observe its pictures and its furnishings, and sympathise with painters and craftsmen.

Although I certainly did not begin working with that end in view, I have found the sorting out and setting down of early

fears and hopes has helped me in some way to a better understanding of myself and if you are one of my family, you may recognise yourself strange connections with my mind and habits as I do with my father and he does with his forebears, particularly his great Uncle Tom Scott.

My father asked yesterday why it was that all his daughters had so successfully married, while other mothers with equally pretty daughters often had them left on their hands. I have been thinking since he asked about the answer to this question and have come to the conclusion that it was because we weren't, anyway in the accepted Christian sense of the word, 'good'. Provided you are pretty enough, if you behave in an irresponsible manner you will certainly attract at any rate attention, even if you don't attract a faithful husband.

Personally, I believed strongly in the theory that laughter and humour are divine attributes. It was certainly that capacity for self-conscious humour that had made man so much more remarkable a creature than the other animals. Eric and I, in criticising the church and chapels, were not so much quarrelling with Christ as with the way that certain parts of his teachings were unduly stressed and others, more embarrassing to society, were ignored or explained away in such a manner that Christ himself would never have intended. If we believed that people should be free to love whom they liked, it wasn't because we were ceasing to be good ourselves but because we realised the truth of the fact that you cannot stop people loving other people. In some cases, we should certainly have tried to discourage a love that was, we felt, probably going to lead to disaster and in some cases, we might

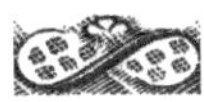

encourage it if we felt that the result would be better for the person, even if it meant their breaking conventional laws. Of course, it is a splendid idea that two people should swear eternal fidelity towards one another and keeping the pledge live together happily and affectionately with the government encouragement for three or four children.

Like everyone else, I don't know if when we die there is an afterlife or not, and as I can't know I don't think about it much as it seems to me to be a waste of time. Knowing the tremendous odds against this particular me being born, I always feel extremely grateful to something which I call God for having allowed me to win the race with other spermatozoa which resulted in my birth. Having entered the world in such a lucky fashion, I think everyone ought to appreciate it as much as they can and admit and enjoy this extremely marvellous place and not whinge about life in the next world. Personally I have tried as best I can to examine all the different sensations and experiences and ways of living and, above all, the flowers and insects and animals that I can. I know fools are supposed to learn by experience but I prefer to be that kind of fool.

Before I had my children, I tried as best I could to express my appreciation by pictures or marbling, though marbling gave me pleasure because I felt that no one else can do this; now I haven't time to do anything except look after the children, I can only scribble this.

The above writing is signed, 'Ironbridge Farm, Shalford, May 1942'. This inclusion of a date may have indicated that Tirzah originally intended to finish her autobiography here.

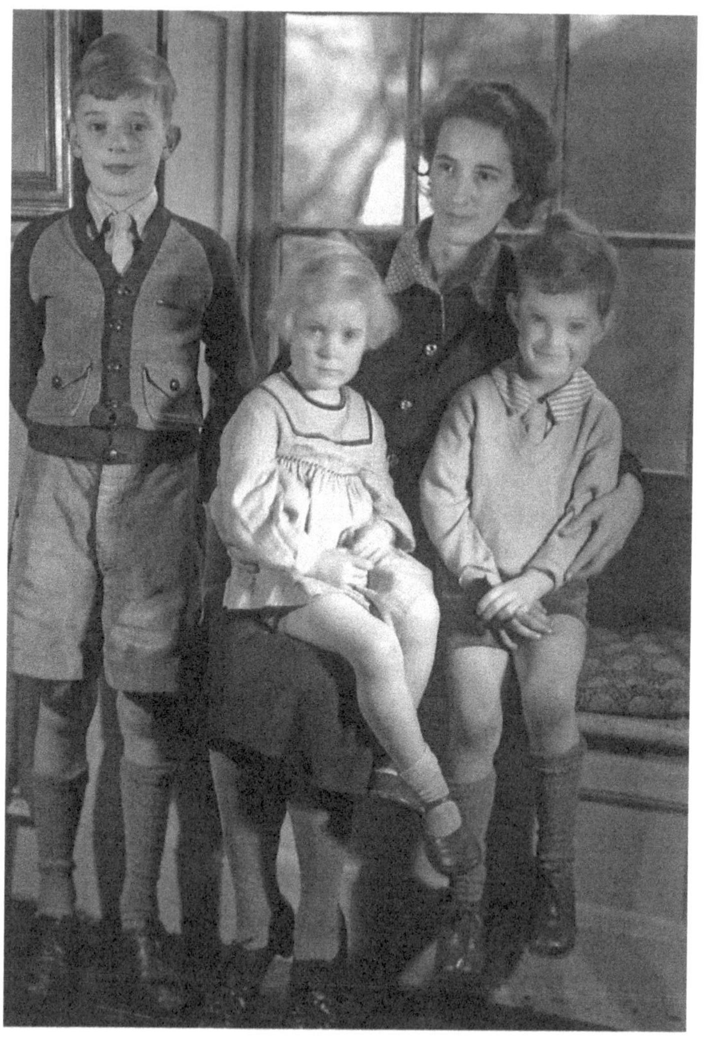

CHAPTER TWENTY-FOUR

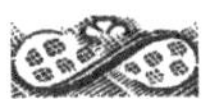

Within three months of her mastectomy, Tirzah became pregnant with a fourth child. Her doctors considered that her health might not stand up to another pregnancy and she underwent a therapeutic abortion in August 1942.

I'm writing this during a visiting afternoon at the hospital. If I look up I get pitying looks from the other women because I haven't got a visitor, I don't like that, I hate being pitied. It was funny at two o'clock when the ward opened and a line of self-conscious husbands filed in, there were a few mothers and sisters, but they didn't come in till a bit later.

There are thirty-six beds in this ward and about half the women in them have had their wombs removed; the doctor's room is decorated with a case of wombs in spirits. Poor fat Mrs Smith's family have just arrived, she only had her operation on Friday and is feeling pretty awful. She said she never felt so awful in her life. We all felt particularly sorry for Mrs Smith because she had to wait a week before they oper-ated on her as the doctor thought she might have diabetes, it seemed worse too for her because of her being so fat. I shan't

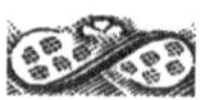

ever forget her rigid perpendicular back view when the two medical students lifted her back into bed after her operation, a nasty little sanitary towel fastened to her noble buttocks: really she isn't at all noble but a nice-natured motherly body, who laughs with all her stomach so that you can't help laughing too, but she did look noble on Friday. We were all staring at her too because we wondered if the medical students would be able to get her back into bed again without dropping her.

We have been laughing a lot in here in the evenings. On my left is a pub-keeper's wife from Stepney, a thin woman who breaks into bawdy songs when she's encouraged. She never gets to the end of a song without some nurse shutting her up, so we never learn the final fate of Maggie's drawers:

> They were tattered, they were torn
> Many years they had been worn
> Those old red flannel drawers that Maggie wore.
> They were baggy at the knees
> And the seat was full of fleas
> Those old red flannel drawers that Maggie wore.

She has a feud with the staff nurse who rebuked her for wanting the bedpan out of season and to revenge herself she complained to the doctor. The staff nurse is rather a tactless kind of Cheltenham girl who issues orders as though she was captain of the hockey team and she's unpopular with this end of the ward. When she is safely off duty, the wonderful Mrs Dormer in the bed opposite mine takes her off and makes us shout with laughter.

Mr Dormer is visiting Mrs Dormer at the moment, they have only been married six weeks and I've found out by roundabout means that she is in here because having been a virgin for sixty years, the poor old woman has too small a vagina and had to have an operation. In a way it seems to me to be a very romantic marriage because she is an ugly old woman and it's nice to think that Mr Dormer finds her attractive. He was a gentleman's gentleman and she was a children's nurse. He is very small and she is only a tick below six feet, they are both over sixty years old. She confided to me that as she was suffering from some form of anaemia, the doctor had told her that half of her brain didn't work and she can't remember very clearly things that happen on the previous day. She remembers her childhood very well and recited right through for us *The Arab's Farewell to his Steed* that she had learnt at school. She said that in her youth she had too much pituitary and she was always on the go, she could swim three miles and sing and play the violin. At the age of fifteen she nearly lost her life through a neighbour giving her half a cup of Epsom Salts when she complained of having a pain when she was menstruating. She has now quite a lot of symptoms of mental defectiveness and she loves showing off and making faces and dancing about with very few clothes on. She waltzed round the other evening opening her dressing gown and displaying a short shift which fortunately came to her thighs. I told her it looked like the *Cutty Sark* but she didn't know what I meant. It isn't much good telling you the funny things that she said because without her grimaces and her Irish 'sure', they wouldn't sound a bit funny.

All the patients are intensely preoccupied with their own operations and the three nearest to me are deaf, probably only a temporary deafness caused by the anaesthetic, but it makes conversation very difficult and a lot of it is wholly at cross-purposes. Mrs Pout across the way in the next bed to Mrs Dormer isn't deaf but she has had so many operations and so much pain from an accidental injury to her bladder during one of them, that her face has now assumed a natural expression of suffering. Mrs Laurie on the other side of Mrs Dormer has more reason to assume an expression of suffering, but she looks wonderfully young and cheerful considering she has been in bed for months with one thing and another and has had to lose her womb at the age of thirty-four. She has six children and a husband in the medical corps in Egypt, who seldom finds time to write to her. She talks an irritating cockney baby talk, very difficult to understand but she is an obviously sweet-natured person and the only outlet for her feelings is the slaughter of wasps; she kills dozens every day. I've promised to draw her tonight so that she can send the picture out to a boyfriend soldier.

Normally the beds have a dark grey blanket on them but on Mondays and Fridays, which are operation days, the next victim for the theatre has a red blanket put on their bed. We get pretty depressed on operation days because usually we've had time to make friends with the new patient and it makes you feel low seeing them doped and lying flat, wheeled so silently away by white-coated students. After the operations, Mr Brews the surgeon comes into the ward with about a dozen young medical students and gives them a lecture on one or two

of the patients. He is a short, fattish man with a pugilist's nose and very arched brows; with his white clothes and round cap, he looks like the head chef delivering orders for the day to the waiters. The first time he came in I did a drawing of him. I only saw him for a few minutes because the students surrounded him and I couldn't see him any more. A few days later when he was going round with the students again, he stopped in front of my bed and gave a talk on therapeutic abortion. I hadn't realised that my operation had been illegal and that he was liable to prosecution for it. He explained that although there was no law, a jury would never convict provided that several doctors maintained that pregnancy and childbirth would in this case subject the mother to more than ordinary risk of life. I felt so hot that I couldn't do any drawing that time.

The most extraordinary case in our ward is a young girl of twenty-two called Barbara. The poor girl has grown a beard. She had been in the ward now for thirteen weeks for observation, walking about in a long blue corduroy dressing gown with her hair hanging to her shoulders, she looks rather like sentimental pictures of Christ. She is a nice friendly girl with quite a pretty face which makes her affliction seem much worse.

The visitors are going now and soon they will be closing the ward by putting a screen up in front of the door; it was funny to see the vicar who was visiting yesterday go out of one side of the screen while a nurse with a superior expression on her face came in at the other with a big pile of stacked-up bedpans in her arms.

We all long to go home. Sometimes I get so miserable that I nearly weep and quite a number of the others frequently cry,

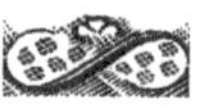

especially when the doctor dashes their hopes of escape and says they must stay longer. The ward doctor is generally liked – 'Ever such a nice young man', they say. He hasn't been there long and is recently married. It's a dog's life for him in many ways; he only had four days' holiday for his wedding and now he seldom gets home before half past eleven at night. I found it difficult at first to get used to the etiquette of the place and to learn what the nurses considered decent and indecent. The whole place struck me as being hideous and repellent, it is composed of ten army huts connected by a corridor open at the sides but roofed over. I offended the sister because she found me nursing a fruit bowl and asked why I had it. I said it was in case I was sick. I'd had three medicines one after the other and was frightened I was going to waste them all, I knew that one of them called Ergot was expensive and the nurse had taken away the dish called a receiver which I had called for. It seemed to me a hideous fruit bowl, it would have been a pleasure to have been sick in it, but the sister obviously thought it was lovely.

The nurses tend to treat the patients with great contempt, and it's difficult to get used to realising that to them you are just a nuisance who has to be swabbed every time you use a bedpan and it's an awful fag for them if you want it an extra number of times. I suffered agonies in the mornings trying not to ask for it, till the woman in the next bed who was up smuggled one in for me. She used to keep one hidden under her knees all day; she spilled it when her husband was visiting.

At last I'm allowed to get up. It seems difficult to imagine that there is still a world where the conversation isn't entirely about Mrs Burke's tumour which weighed twelve pounds,

and, 'Are you a total hysterotomic?', 'Mrs Steele, will you stop looking at your chart, it is put there for the use of the doctors and nurses only'. Mrs Dormer with a knitting needle stuck into her back hair saying: 'I'm joining the army, the naffies, the waffies, the rafies or the wrens. Hell Hitler, that's what I say, my niece says he's the devil incarnate – some people have their second childhood early' and she taps herself. The new patients are just arriving and Mr Brews has just gone away to lunch leaving a bottled uterus on the table: 'For God's sake take it away before the new patients see it' – one of them is a charming NAAFI corporal and I learn to my dismay after-wards that she may be suffering from endometriosis. I shan't ever know if she was and I won't harrow you with a description of what it is in case she hasn't got it after all.

I've just rung up Eric to tell him he may fetch me: 'Have you been bored?' he said.

I was allowed to leave the hospital about a week before Eric was due to go to Iceland and he arrived on a lovely morning to fetch me away. I was still losing a little blood when I got home and started looking after the house and children again. There was cleaning to be done as well as the usual work in the house and garden and I tried to be careful of myself and not do too much but in spite of my caution after a day or two I began getting a pain on my right side which gradually got worse until I became almost unable to stand. We both felt exasperated with my inside as we wanted to make love before Eric went away.

The morning before he was due to leave, he got up early to make the breakfast and standing in front of the mirror

putting on his tie, he said: 'Shall I not go to Iceland?' I knew that he desperately wanted to go and so I said: 'No, I shall be alright'. He seemed relieved at my answer and enthusiastically repeated all the familiar reasons for this expedition to what had almost become to him the promised land, but I knew that he did feel a little guilty at leaving me so prostrate.

When he had gone downstairs I wondered why I had urged him to go and realised that it was because I accepted the fact that his work was more important to him than me and I appreciated this attitude. But I felt so ill I wondered if I should be alive by after Christmas, when he had promised to come back.

Downstairs, he suddenly thought of trying to get Evelyn Hepher to come and look after me and I rang her up at East Preston. It was balm to hear her cool, clear voice saying: 'Of course I'll come, Tirzah', and I thought what a blessing friends and telephones could sometimes be.

There is a strain about prolonged partings that makes them very difficult and it hadn't been a nice week after our first joy at being together again on the day I had come out of the hospital. We remembered how John and Ariel [Crittall] had quarrelled just before he went away and that cheered us up a little. I struggled down to breakfast on the last morning and Eric felt wretched and kissed me goodbye with his face all wet and said: 'I love you, Tirzah', and I said, 'I do you', but at that moment I didn't feel as though I did, but I knew I should when he had gone and I was more calm and less frightened. I watched him walking down the lane and stopping by the Holmes's cottage to say goodbye to James and I knew that he might never come back but there was nothing I could do but

just watch him and remember what he looked like and, with an effort, I lifted Anne up to wave a final goodbye.

Evelyn arrived in the afternoon and I was able to go to bed but I still kept on having the pain, so she rang up Dr Edwards who thought I might have caught a chill. The next morning Aunt Edith rang up to say that Eric had spent the night with them. She thought that we would have heard on the wireless how the plane in which the Duke of Kent was flying to Iceland had crashed and become alarmed, thinking that Eric might have been in the same plane. He didn't leave Scotland for a day or two and when he rang up, Evelyn was able to reassure him about my health.

On the next morning, when I got out of bed a great quantity of clotted blood came pouring out of my inside and, thoroughly alarmed, I hastily lay down again while Evelyn rang up the local doctor. Dr Lasbrey having examined the mess, shyly told Evelyn that he thought it was the natural thing; but he gave me an injection and some Ergot to decrease the violence of the natural thing and after a week or so I was able to get up.

Evelyn went to Castle Hedingham to fetch John home again. He had been staying with Hilda and Billy Turner who had offered to have him when I went to the hospital and he had been there ever since. He was a nice little boy and Eric was fond of him now that school had so changed him and he had bicycled over to say goodbye to him and the Turners before he went away. Billy Turner had always been particularly fond of John and had taught him about electricity and how to make cement.

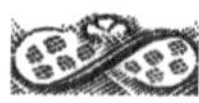

At seven o'clock on the morning after he had got home, there was a funny, thudding noise and a startled flutter of birds and John came running into my bedroom saying: 'The barn's fallen down, the barn's fallen down', and half an hour later there was a second bump and the rest of the roof collapsed. It was a lovely day and there was no reason why it should have chosen that day to fall down.

The next evening I felt extraordinarily sad and when Evelyn was sitting on the window seat after supper, I told her how depressed I felt and she tried to cheer me up but I still felt low and I woke up the next morning with a headache. Jack Gold came round to see us and I told him how sad I'd been feeling and he said: 'Oh why'? I supposed it was the war and he said that he had had such a good life before the war that he felt resigned about the possibility of being killed now and I wondered if he had after all made love to somebody, because to me that was the only thing that was so satisfactory that it resigned you to being dead afterwards.

After lunch I went up to rest on my bed and Evelyn followed me upstairs presently and said: 'Poor Tirzah, there's still more bad luck, Eric is missing now', and she handed me a telegram from the Admiralty. I said: 'I'm not going to believe it', and I got up and she went for a walk with me to the iron bridge. It was a lovely day and when we got back to the house, I said: 'My headache is gone at any rate', and she laughed and said: 'Good for you, Tirzah.'

The next morning there was a letter from Lord Willoughby de Broke who had been responsible for introducing Eric to the Air Force people in Iceland, saying how he regretted this

unfortunate accident; he was quite definite and wrote of Eric in the past tense, so I knew it must really be hopeless. It was an admirable letter of its kind and I felt grateful to him for promptly telling me the truth.

It wasn't till three weeks later that I heard any details of what had happened. Apparently Eric had just arrived at an Icelandic aerodrome on the west coast. A plane was missing from that day's patrol so three planes were sent out at dawn on the following morning, to try to find this lost one. Someone offered to take Eric and so without asking his commanding officer, he accepted and went off in a sea air rescue craft to patrol 300 miles of coast and sea. His plane never returned, nor did they find the other lost one, though with the help of American soldiers they searched very thoroughly for three days afterwards.

The village people at once knew about this calamity because the telegram girl had delivered the telegram to the Holmes family and Evelyn and I felt particularly enraged with the grocer, who rang up to know if it was true. Ariel [Crittall] came on her new pony and I went for one or two rides with her and it was much the best way of taking exercise because I didn't have to stop and talk to people if I met them. Evelyn with her recent loss of baby John was the best person I could possibly have had staying and Christine Nash who came for the day, was also a comfort and we talked about sympathy letters and how after a time, one came to accept their sentiments and began to criticise them as letters. All the same, I dreaded the morning's post and having to weep over my breakfast. Most of the women who wrote were hopeful that

Eric might be safe but the men preferred the acceptance of the worst, which was I thought the best plan because one could always be cheered in an instant by good news but living on uncertain hope was worse than anything.

One morning when I opened the front door, there was a turtle dove with a broken wing on the path and I followed it into the field to throw down some corn, but it was frightened by the children and the Marshalls' cat Esau who had come out to see what I was doing, and it fluttered away into the undergrowth.

While we were in the field, Jack Gold drove up in his car. I hadn't seen him since I had heard about Eric, but he had rung up Evelyn to ask if the news was true and on hearing that it was, he had sent me his love. He brought with him a basket of peaches and John took one and bit a piece out and then threw it away, saying that he didn't like it. Seeing Jack look so white and miserable for us and unconsciously connecting him with the love that he had sent, I quite suddenly felt extraordinarily fond of him and this discovery that I loved Jack was the only stable thing left in the chaos that Eric's death had made in my unsettled mind.

I felt too that the village people were now already pairing me off with Jack, not intending this as an insult to Eric, but in a kindly practical way. James picked a flower and asked what it was. When May replied, 'Marigold' and he said: 'Oh, Jack Gold', she couldn't resist adding, 'That's right, you tell him', and when I was trying to ring him up one day and there was no answer, Emily at the exchange with her sad, weary voice said: 'There's no answer, he isn't there, I'd get him for you if I could'.

After Evelyn had gone, taking John with her on his way to boarding school, Mrs Turner came to stay with me, bringing her new baby Judith. The weather continued to be perfect till one evening after supper time, a sudden thunderstorm blew up. Very quickly it grew dark and the sky was sharply divided into heavy storm and light, until the thunder clouds overwhelmed the calmer evening sky and all the while, underneath the sudden claps and rumbles of thunder the air seemed filled with the drone of aeroplanes.

James upstairs called out for me and I went and lay on the bed beside him while the thunder banged and the planes hummed continuously like a dentist's drill. He wanted me to stop the noise, but I explained that no man could stop the thunder and he reflected on this and accepted it adding, 'Not even an elephant'.

At first Hilda and I hadn't taken much notice of the aeroplanes, presuming that it was a number of them passing over on some raid, but after a while their insistence began to worry us and we went and stood on the front door step to discover whether they were visible. It was too dark to see them and we realised by the noise that they were flying low and apparently going round and round in circles and that in reality, there were only two aeroplanes and the storm must have affected them in some way so that they were now lost.

The sky seemed filled with their fright and we stood watching the storm, unable to do anything to help. Everyone in the village was aware of this feeling of fright, as though the electricity in the storm was transmitting the terror of the airmen down to the earth below.

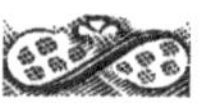

We heard later that a neighbour had rung up the aerodrome to see if they were aware of what was happening; but it was too late by then to do anything and one of the planes crashed at Wethersfield and the other at Gosfield and all the men were killed.

Billy Turner came on his lorry to fetch Hilda and the baby away, and he brought me ten gallons of oil. He was sad because he had expected to see John again, not realising that he had gone back to school.

My next visitor was Barbara, whom I had met at the Brentwood Hospital. She now looked quite normal. I found her rather a depressing guest because she talked sadly and incessantly down her nose and she seemed typical of thousands of English girls and behind her I could hear them all saying the same things and doing the same things and going to the same films and talking all the time about their boyfriends and their girlfriends.

When Barbara had gone and I was left alone, I felt horribly upset and muddled and I had spasms of dreadful sorrow because Eric wasn't there to share some joke or some odd occurrence that would have particularly appealed to him and worst of all, to appreciate the children. I found myself walking about the house crying and had to pull myself together and stop because it would have been so awful for anyone passing to hear. I had told John that he was missing and John, unable to express himself on such an occasion, thought for a second or two and said: 'It's a pity really, isn't it'. I did not dare to tell James because I knew he would be so very upset and if I left it till later, I knew he would have forgotten Eric and so wouldn't mind.

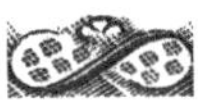

One afternoon, I went to Bardfield to see Duffy [Rothenstein]. Thinking of Duffy, I could see just a large pair of anxious eyes and it was nice to know that she would be waiting at the top of the difficult stairs. Hard to connect them now with the same stairs up which I had once watched John's legs and bottom in his dark green trousers when he had first shown me the chapel flat. But now John and I were quite different, separate people and I couldn't imagine my present self being interested in his trousers.

Duffy and I got down to fundamentals pretty quickly and I was soon explaining that although ultimately I knew it would affect me more deeply, I didn't at the moment feel so utterly miserable about losing Eric as I had John; the difference being that I knew Eric loved me and I didn't have to have those awful letters afterwards and of course, more important than this, there were our children. I thought Duffy seemed a little shocked, so I defended myself and told her about Eric not really wanting to live till he was old; this I suppose was rather false comfort because he can't have wanted to die in Iceland in the very least.

We talked about the Graves family with whom she had been staying and I stood up and looked at a photograph of John Aldridge with two children and a large snow cat, very similar to the snow dog that I had once made on the vicarage lawn. John looked just like a young man, slightly resembling my unpleasant cousin Bobby, and there was no pain or pleasure in looking at him. I looked out of the window onto the Place garden and said to Duffy: 'I am not in the least in love with John now', and sadly knew that it was true.

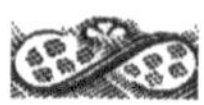

Duffy told me a lot about John and Lucie and how weak and influenced by people John was; how Robert Graves doted on him and had collected so many of his pictures. John's clothes too had been an imitation of Robert Graves and he and Laura Riding had influenced them both. It had been a mutual admiration society indeed and I now understood more clearly why John had refused to even examine other authors or the works of other painters who were not accepted by the Riding-Graves clique.

From Laura Riding, we started talking about Lucie and why it was that she had not been jealous of Laura. As they had quite recently been told about our love affair, I think Duffy and Michael didn't really understand how long ago it had all happened and I shocked Duffy again by saying that even if Lucie was dead I knew that John would never marry me now and how, sometimes in the past, Lucie had seemed to me like a spider devouring him; but as before there had been one leg hanging out of her mouth, now even that was gone and she had completely eaten him. 'How cruel you are, Tirzah', but she laughed and admitted that there was some truth in the simile.

Duffy told me about John's troubles in the army and what bad luck he had about not getting his commission and how this worried Lucie. 'You don't know how demoralised he is now Tirzah, sometimes when Lucie rings up he'll tell her he hasn't spoken to anyone for a week and Lucie instead of helping him, makes it worse all the time.'

I felt glad that Lucie had at any rate stopped brooding about me and Duffy went on telling me about how she had

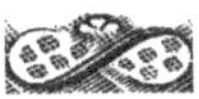

introduced them to her sister-in-law Rachel and he and Lucie had been to a picnic with them and the children and watching John playing with the children, Duffy had seen Lucie with that anguished expression on her face that I knew so well: 'Sometimes Michael and I wonder if she isn't nearly fifty and John is still a young man and he got on so well with Rachel and obviously he loved playing with the children'. Actually Lucie was more than fifty, John was thirty-seven.

Poor John and poor Lucie. I wondered if in Lucie's place I should have been a better wife; I should certainly have been a happier one. Eric had once said of Lucie: 'She displayed John very well'. The children with which I should have liked to populate the garden would have probably spoilt it from a gardener's point of view; as they would have ruined the precious beauty of the interior of the house.

While I was thinking about this, Duffy was still talking about Lucie and with her breathy, carefully-enunciated speech was now revealing more intimate confessions of Lucie's, how she worried because she felt that she had not satisfied John in the physical part of their relationship. I had often wondered myself whether he had been able to make love to Lucie as perfectly as he had to me and now I know that I knew the truth, but so many awful things had happened inbetween that it was barely interesting and I wondered if I was in part responsible for the haunted, sinister atmosphere in his recent pictures. Going home, I felt thankful that John and Lucie no longer preyed upon my mind and it seemed pathetic that John and I, who were both more intelligent than Lucie, should have been so overridden by her condemnation.

I continued to write my autobiography in the evenings but I wondered if it was a waste of time and whether I ought not to start working again at designing, because it was doubtful if I should be given enough money to look after the children and it was an occupation of which Eric disapproved: my writing of him in the past tense had made him feel that he was already dead, and he was afraid that my indiscretions might lead to trouble or horrify our children, for whom I was ostensibly writing: 'Remember this is gunpowder,' he said.

At night I sometimes dreamed that Eric had come back and was telling me not to be ridiculous, of course he wasn't dead; and reluctantly I would have to prove to him that his reappearance was not a possible phenomenon and, after some argument, he had finally to admit in an embarrassed way that he couldn't really be alive. I did feel that he wasn't dead while I could so vividly remember him and because in living with him so long and being influenced by him, I was in part just like him, so he would always be there. I had become so used to him that his hand was my hand or a family hand and it had no power to give me any feeling of pleasure or repugnance like the hands of a stranger. Having this united feeling, I had never felt unfaithful to him if I loved other people because so long as he knew and approved of them, there was no necessity. The good thing about our marriage was that we had at any rate been truthful towards one another, even though we owned to hating each other which we had at times.

Jack was very kind and took me for a day to Colchester and I went to a cinema while he lectured to the troops and I was

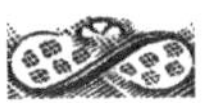

happy because I was with him, but I felt that he was puzzled by my cheerfulness.

Quite a number of people had invited me to stay with them and it was difficult to know which offer to accept; finally James was sent to Eastbourne to stay with Mummy and I went with Anne to stay with the aunts, intending to go on from there to Gloucestershire. Jack took us in his car to Chelmsford with the pram and some hens for Evelyn in a hamper tied on at the back.

The aunts were in a bad way, Aunt Lucy was very tottery and walked slowly along on too high-heeled shoes so that if one hurried her, she looked as though her frail legs would cross and she would fall down in an undignified heap in Kensington High Street. She was very absent-minded too and frequently went out without being sure where she was going and, having laboriously put her onto a bus that was heading for Hyde Park Corner, she would say with a little laugh: 'No, it is Earls Court where the work party is held, dear', as though you had made the mistake. If I went out, she insisted on coming too and the strain of looking after both her and Anne was pretty considerable.

Various foreigners had fastened round Aunt Lucy like blowflies on a dying animal and they frequently called to get money from her. She hated them, but weak-mindedly, as though under the spell of their wordy flattery, handed out money. The worst offender was an Italian woman who had belonged to the Lyceum Club until the war had stopped any money coming to her from Italy. One wouldn't have minded Aunt Lucy helping her if she had been willing to do anything

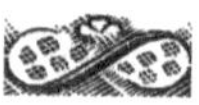

in return but she would do nothing, excusing herself by saying that she was not strong. Aunt Edith had never properly recovered from the Blitz and she was thin and suffering from glands. Her self-control was so weakened that she now openly scolded and derided poor old Aunt Lucy and was irritated out of all reason by small things like Aunt Lucy's capricious behaviour with cheques and money and her rattling of Christmas parcel paper when the wireless was playing.

The cooking was done by a Czech cook, a powerful looking woman with an Egyptian face and the stocky figure of a peasant. She had been married twice, her first husband had left her after six months, while her second marriage to a petty officer called Mason had been even shorter as he died, leaving her the fortunate possessor of a British passport. She claimed to have been a lady in Czechoslovakia and so refused to do any washing up or cleaning in the kitchen. She charged my aunts so exorbitant a wage that she could afford to live in a flat of her own and employ a maid out of her own money to do her dirty work, to the indignation of Lucy, the aunts' faithful parlour-maid. She could cook well if she chose and made the most delicious apple strudel but otherwise, the food was almost entirely out of tins and she spent long hours every day going round to her friends and the shops, wrangling and bargaining to collect extra food, and she entertained her friends at my aunts' expense in the basement kitchen.

Aunt Edith refused to sack her because she feared they would be unable to get anyone else to replace her and if you are incapable of lifting a finger to help yourself, anything is better than nothing. Lucy the maid poured out all her troubles to

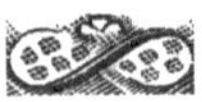

me; one of the worst offences in her eyes was that these foreigners were Communists. It was deplorable that if this was the case, that Mrs Mason should put so much emphasis on her status as a lady. Lucy described how one day she had been scrubbing the front steps and had mentioned to Mrs Mason that this should by rights be her job as she was the cook, and Mrs Mason had said that nothing would ever make her stoop low enough to wash steps, and Lucy had replied that she was no better than a Nazi, and from this they fell to pulling one another's hair, all on my aunts' respectable front door step in Argyll Road and I wondered how the fight had ended. Poor solid, beautiful Lucy, she was like an English cow among a pack of continental wolves, but she did finally triumph because the pack moved off in search of richer gain and she was left alone to look after Aunt Lucy while she could.

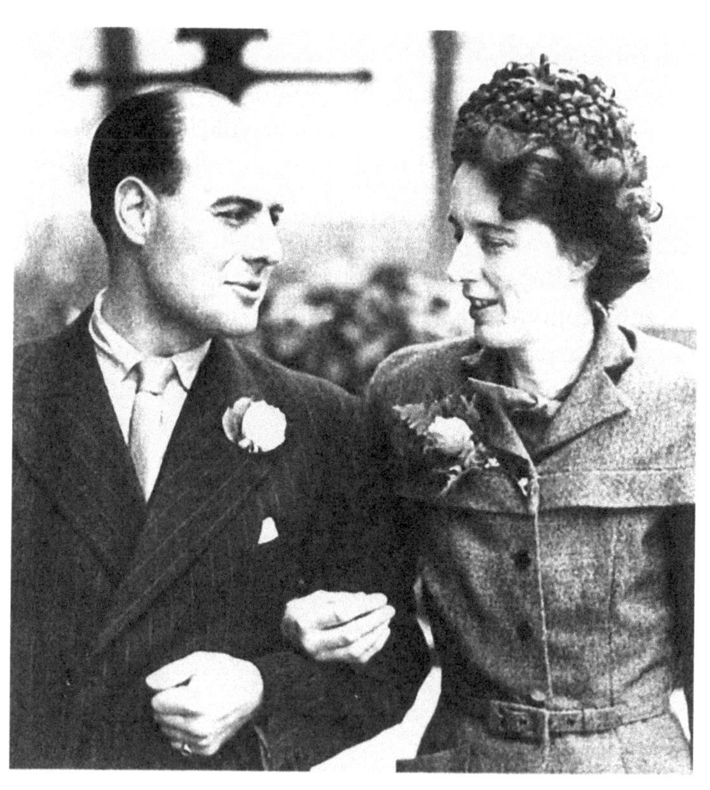

CHAPTER TWENTY-FIVE

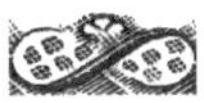

Peggy had been writing to me about her troubles with Jim, who had fallen in love with someone else. When the Blitz had started, she had moved the children to Chichester where she had a teaching job, while Jim stayed on in the flat in Adelaide Road and it became the office of *The Architectural Review* which he was editing, while Hastings had taken over *The Architects' Journal*.

At the beginning of the war, Jim had answered an advertisement in the newspaper for fire-watchers for St Paul's Cathedral and, every Monday night, he joined a strange collection of elderly professors and venerable bearded architects to practise finding their quickest way up all the complicated gutters and ledges of the large roof, where an imaginary fire bomb was supposed to have landed. Their chief anxiety was for the apostles who were rather precariously placed high up round the building and it was probable that a good shaking might bring them all crashing down. They slept in high iron bedsteads in the vaults and, early one morning, a young couple paying a visit to the cathedral walked into the vault and were very surprised to find this queer bedroom of bearded old men.

This job of Jim's caused a lot of amusement to his friends, but as things happened it was this pioneer body of assorted rum birds who saved St Paul's from being quite destroyed on that memorable weekend when the city was showered with incendiary bombs and all the adjoining buildings went up in flames.

During the Blitz Jim slept in the basement of his flat with Bert Kelly, a charming schoolmaster who was a cousin of Horace Wilmott's and the man who had wanted to marry Ishbel MacDonald. Now he was married to a friend of Peggy's called Enid and they had a baby girl about the same age as James, and another quite new one. He helped in the house when he was able and brought us early morning cups of tea. He and Jim had weathered the Blitz together.

Jim's weekend visits to see Peggy and the children gradually became less frequent and when he did come, he was morose and ill-tempered. When Peggy discovered that the reason for this was that he had begun making love to someone else, without consulting Jim she impulsively dashed up to London and took on a teaching job at a tough boys' school which would necessitate her being in London again for half the week. Jim was furious with her for this move and firmly moved out of the flat and took rooms near the Ministry of Information, where he had just started working.

Peggy, very upset by this desertion, rang me up to say how miserable she was and would I come and share her empty flat [in Adelaide Road] so I put off my visit to Gloucestershire and went to stay with her.

After I had been there a week, Aunt Edith rang up to tell me

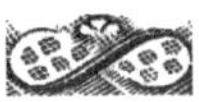

that Aunt Lucy had been run over by a bus. They had both gone separately to a meeting at which the King of Greece was present. This combination of lecture and royalty was obviously irresistible to Aunt Lucy and she had insisted on going in spite of the fact that it would be dark when they came out. After the meeting, Aunt Edith had as usual hurried out in front of everyone else and as she had been unable to see Aunt Lucy in the audience, she presumed that she hadn't come after all.

Having been knocked down by a bus outside Pontings, Aunt Lucy was taken to a nearby hospital with a nasty cut on her head. Fear and worry had made Aunt Edith quite callous and she seemed to have no sympathy for Aunt Lucy, only an exasperated contempt for someone who was letting down their façade of respectability by publicly making an exhibition of herself. My father was equally indignant and exasperated by Aunt Lucy and couldn't understand why she didn't resign herself to the fact that she was an old lady and stop pretending that she was able to go on living the same social lecture-going life to which she was used. She was a bad patient at the hospital and, after she had fallen out of bed one night, she was removed to a nursing home, still protesting that she was perfectly all right.

I found that even the aunts hoped I should marry Jack, and Aunt Edith openly tackled me on this. 'Why don't you marry Jack Gold?' Rather flummoxed by this direct attack, I said: 'Well, he loves his mother'. 'I don't see that that's an insuperable obstacle, lots of people do you know, it's quite natural.' His feelings didn't seem important to them.

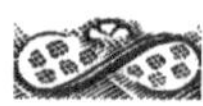

Whereas before Eric's death when it hadn't mattered, I had felt sure that Jack did love me; now that it was important, I doubted whether he did because passively loving someone else's wife is a very different thing from marrying a widow with three children.

Staying with Peggy was very hard work because there was no help in the house and she was out all day teaching. She went to Chichester for weekends to see the children while I entertained Jim, who returned home in her absence. He was in a queer state and obviously needed a rest. Finding that his wife objected to his love affair, the other girl was trying to discourage him and this of course made him feel doubly indignant with Peggy. I tackled him one morning at breakfast, asking what he really intended doing about his family and wrung from him the promise that he would in the future try to reconcile himself to living with her again. He complained what a difficult person she was to live with and I had to admit that she was; still he had married her and there were Victoria and Angus to be considered.

Peggy too looked very run down and in need of a rest but she was not a person who could rest; immediately a new idea seized her she would instantly carry it out. She could never resist asking people to stay, without ever considering whether there was room for them or even whether she would be there herself to entertain them, so that there was always someone new sleeping in the house and the supply of sheets ran out and the beds of the permanent residents got blacker and blacker.

She was continually thinking of ways to organise her friends and, finding that Helen Binyon was unhappy in the

flat which she was sharing with another friend, she arranged that Helen should take the flat above hers in Adelaide Road, and of course she was full of schemes for me and my future. Just as Charlotte had arranged without consulting me that I should go and stay with the Russells in Gloucestershire, so Peggy arranged with Oliver Hill that Evelyn Hepher and I should go and live in his London flat and be his house-keepers. As I didn't want to do either of these things, I had to extract myself from both these arrangements, leaving both Russells and Hill offended by having their plans upset. She also urged me to enter a competition for a children's book and when, in a desperate hurry I had nearly finished it, I took the drawings under my arm with Anne on my other side to go and visit Shirley Cocks who had promised to amuse Anne while I finished the lettering. I clambered onto a bus upon the seat by the door and the book slipped from under my arm, down between the seat and the side panel of the partition and was hopelessly gone. Fortunately, it was the wrong bus and it was quite near its terminus. The driver and conductor were very nice about it and the inspector gave them permission to take it to a garage that night and get the seat unscrewed and they promised to give me the book on the next morning.

When I called for it, they were quite mystified why I should have been so anxious to remove a school exercise book. I gave the conductor some ducks' eggs for his trouble as I was afraid he might be insulted if I offered him money.

I was supposed to go every three months to see a doctor to make sure that I was alright and I dutifully went to the aunts' doctor in Kensington. I had noticed that my urine was odd,

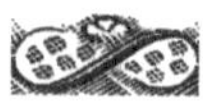

especially before I was unwell and since my abortion I found it sometimes very difficult to control it at all, so I gave him some to test. He found, as I had thought, that it had quite a lot of sugar in it and he told me to wait until I was unwell and then he would take another test after that. When he had examined my chest, I asked him if I could consider myself alright now and he frightened me by asking if my arm hurt. It hurt like anything as I had been carrying Anne about as it was impossible to take the pushchair on buses, and he measured it to see if it had got bigger than the other arm. They seemed to be about the same but I didn't feel at all reassured by him and felt terrified that I might be getting cancer again.

Christine Nash came unexpectedly for a night and we both bought some silk material and made petticoats, hers green and mine magenta pink, and I felt happier with some calming sewing to do. Her lodger John Langston rang up when she was out and I asked him to come to tea when she was expected back. Eric had often talked of John Langston who was Christine's diabetic lover and a believer in free love, but neither of us had met him.

He wasn't, when he arrived, at all what I had imagined as he was a thin dark young man while I had pictured him as much older and fair. He had an unhealthy colour, but was a handsome young man with large greenish damp eyes and a confident manner, so that we were soon easily discussing the sugar in my water over our tea and he told us all the symptoms of true diabetes.

When Christine had gone, he rang me up and asked me out to dinner and as Bert Kelly's wife and children had now

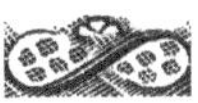

arrived to stay in the flat as well, I was able to leave Anne and John who had come back from school with them and I accepted his invitation.

We walked down Adelaide Road, past the gaps in the rows of dilapidated houses with their plaster falling off and here and there a bombed one with ivy running along the front steps and in at the empty windows, as though it had taken possession of the house. He enquired after my water and I informed him that it was found not to have sugar in it any more which was a relief, because I didn't want diabetes as well as everything else.

We had an early dinner in a newly opened club. It was nicely decorated with light walls and striped material like deckchair stuff which gave it a holiday feeling, but the walls of the bar were ruined by some bad decorations like indifferent fashion drawings where it only needed an elegant abstract, something designed by Cassandre or Edward Bawden.

John left me in the bar while he went away to inject some insulin into himself and then we went into the dining room where the women were either in uniform or coats and skirts, looking very proper in surroundings which one associated with such a different fashion. It was a good dinner and John told me about his lecturing; his chief interest was in politics of a left nature.

We wondered what we should do after dinner, because it was too late to go to a movie and the only other occupation left was one which he said he didn't indulge in. He had a little scar at the top of his nose and I wondered how he had got it. I suggested we went for a walk, so he paid the bill and the

manager presented us both with some cardboard matches printed with a picture of a bride and bridegroom on each matchbox and outside, he ordered a taxi.

Inside the taxi, he immediately started to make love to me and I sat bolt upright feeling like the picture in Frans Masereel's *La Ville* of the woman with the fat Frenchman making love to her, while she sits with a blank bored expression on her face. All the same it is very difficult to know what to do when someone gives you a good dinner and then makes love to you and I suddenly remembered this old problem when I had lived in Hornton Street and I said to John: 'This feels like twelve years ago'. Seeing that I wasn't going to bed with him, we got out of the taxi and went into Green Park, which I remembered so vividly because I had often walked there with Eric listening to the distant rumble of traffic between Hyde Park and Piccadilly, but now it no longer sounded the same.

We walked along in the moonlight and I explained that I couldn't make love if I didn't know him, and I told him how Eric had found the same thing because he had, in the spirit that one ought to try everything once, gone home with a prostitute in Le Havre and when she got into bed, found that he had no desire to make love to her at all but was deeply moved by the beauty of her room and a lovely striped sofa which he longed to paint, but he hadn't the courage to ask if he might do so when he was unable to make love to her. She was quite amiable about it and hadn't, like the girl who Bob had refused in the same way at Tours, thrown things at him the whole time he was dressing.

We sat on the only unoccupied seat by the water and I found that he didn't know about my losing my breast and he asked about it and I said I had run into a door and got cancer, but the doctor had said it would be alright. I added ruefully that it shook me and he said: 'It would have me'. It didn't seem to deter him from wanting to make love to me, for which I liked him and I told him how unhappy I'd been when I had had a lover before and that if I accepted him there mustn't be any blaming afterwards, and he said that he was still friends with nearly all the women he had made love to. He appeared to have been the original young worldly, as he had started his career by seducing his house mistress at school and he told me about this and his subsequent affairs. I didn't much fancy the idea of being one of a collection, but it was fun make-believing that I might and the searchlight was lighting up the tree in front of it so that it shone like a magic Christmas tree, and it was warming on a cold night to have someone wanting to make love to you, even if they did call you 'dear one'.

I walked up Park Lane holding his hand till we reached Grosvenor House and I had to go the other side and have the other hand held because it had got so cold. We went into the Cumberland Hotel where he was staying and I waited for him downstairs, watching some foreigners behaving in an odd and suspicious way until we got a taxi and went back to Adelaide Road. I asked him if he had read that book by a taxi driver and told him how taxi drivers knew if people were making love in their taxis because they sat together and weighted down one corner. He asked if there was any reason why he couldn't come back and share my bed and I said it was full of children, glad

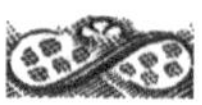

of so concrete an excuse. He was going to Scotland the next day, so that I was safe. I said that I would possibly stay for a day or two in London with him and in Peggy's kitchen I had a good look at him to see what he was like, before pushing him out of the door feeling rather a pig to have got him into such a state when I didn't intend doing anything about it.

This evening with John Langston made me feel much more cheerful and the next day I went with my children John and Anne to stay for Christmas with Evelyn at East Preston. I found that I didn't miss Eric indoors but when I was outside, I would suddenly become miserable about him and weep as I walked along the road, too tired with trailing Anne round to be able to control myself and it was a wonderful relief to leave London to go and stay with restful Evelyn. I told her all about my adventures, and John wrote love letters and rang me up and sent me a Shetland shawl in a parcel with string tied up into forty knots which alarmed me and I didn't like accepting presents from him, and I made up my mind not to go to London.

I felt he was really Christine's young man and I wrote to her for advice, drawing a little picture of myself and three children at the crossroads with a signpost with three arms, one saying lovers, the other marriage, the third career. She wrote back saying I ought to aim at having all three and there was nothing like having a lover for setting a girl up. All the same, I wrote to John saying I could only be his friend and I knew that I had never really intended accepting him because I wasn't in love with him.

I wished I knew whether Jack really would want to marry me and I felt very much in the same state as I had before I told

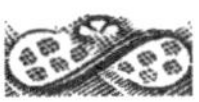

John Aldridge that I loved him, a state so well described in the Elizabethan song by Jones that Eric had taught me, 'What if I sue for love of thee' and I wrote Jack Gold a silly letter about letting him read the rest of my autobiography.

Evelyn thought that Jack would probably wait at least a year after Eric's death before saying anything if he did want to marry me, and she was worried that I might mind too much if he didn't. I knew that I would have to face the prospect of this, but I had had far worse things happen to me before and survived.

John and David were so pleased to be together again that it was a pleasure to watch and they said that they liked one another even better now than they had done before. I had given John a Gamages conjuring outfit for Christmas and they gave a wonderfully bad performance through the hatch, explaining how each trick worked before attempting to perform it. Guy had got David a bicycle which he wasn't allowed to ride as yet so we had to have it indoors, till Susan fell over it and knocked the handlebars through the pane in the French window that had just been mended on the previous day. Guy came for his last leave before going abroad and he rang up every night till he sailed.

One morning at Evelyn's I noticed that a small white lump had appeared near the base of the scar on my chest. It was a long scar beginning at my upper arm where the breast muscle had joined the arm muscle and curving round above my armpit ended up beside the region of my heart. Looking something like Gandhi down one side hadn't mattered when Eric was alive because being so used to me he barely noticed

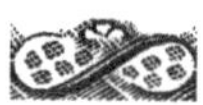

what I was like at all, but I worried about it more now his reassuring 'It doesn't matter at all', was gone. When in Eastbourne my father had diarrhoea, he summoned the doctor and seeing that there was a doctor in the house, I thought I had better enquire about the spot. Dr McQueen, who looked like a golfer, thought it was possibly caused by a stitch and said he would look at it again in a fortnight.

The next time he came it was much the same, so he thought it probably wasn't anything and I might leave it alone, but on hearing that I was going back to Essex he advised me to show it to the surgeon who had done the original operation. This wasn't very reassuring and I began to worry that it might be cancer again. No one ever said I had cancer but I just presumed I had; it didn't seem to be a word that doctors ever mentioned, but I suppose that their having removed my entire breast because of a lump the size of an acorn had meant that it was.

When I went back to Essex, I showed it to Dr Edward who peered at it through a magnifying glass but after a month he decided he'd better remove it just in case, so back I went to the Cottage Hospital to the same old room with *Between Two Fires* still hanging over the mantelpiece. He kept me waiting for two hours because a soldier had had an accident to his arm which he had to put right and when he came, he immediately started talking about [Jack's sister] Diana Gold and we got in a muddle because I thought he was talking about Diana Rowntree. I remembered Jack sitting in the chair and my thinking how nice, I can love people again and then I remembered Duffy's visit with her anxiety about Lucie having told

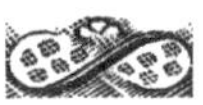

them about John and me and how afterwards I had felt so disgusted at Lucie doing such a thing knowing I was having this operation and also at the falseness of her story, that I had felt no more guilt at having upset her. Yet now I was back in the same old position, only it was Jack instead of John and I couldn't tell Jack after the mess I had made with telling John. Actually there wasn't any better way of describing it than in the song Towner had taught Eric, who had sung it to me:

What if I sue for love of thee
Shall I find
Beauty kind
To desert that still shall dwell in me.

For if I live and love forlorn
Then alas never was any wretch
To more misfortune born
Though thy looks have charmed mine eyes

I can forbear to love
But if ever sweet desire
Sets my willing heart on fire
That can I never remove.

I longed to tell Jack Gold but I knew it would just be embarrassing and there wasn't anything I could do but just go away from Shalford until I felt more normal.

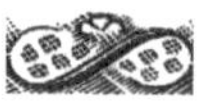

The next day I took part of my autobiography round to Jack and left it at his house to read with a letter saying that I was miserable. I met him unexpectedly as I was leaving the house and felt that idiotic grin of pleasure on my face that I had at first been unable to control when Bob had loved me so many years ago at Eastbourne.

It was a nice month with Evelyn, the only eventful occasion was a visit to London with John because I wanted to take him to the Great Ormond Street Children's Hospital to have an X-ray photo as there had been a slight suspicion that he might have TB.

We stayed on Evelyn's advice at a comfortable hotel. After we had visited the hospital, which was over much quicker than I had expected as the doctor thought that as John was cured of his asthma there was no necessity to X-ray him, I took him along to the National Gallery. He enjoyed identifying the name Eric Ravilious on his father's works which were unhappily hung under some shockingly bad, long-shaped pictures by Stanley Spencer. I suddenly found myself standing next to Sir Kenneth Clark who was taking round a superior-looking woman, and he asked quietly so that she shouldn't overhear whether I had got the £81-7s-9d which he had sent. As he had sent it to Peggy and Jim's address, I hadn't. Next I took John to the collection of French pictures which I really wanted to see. I thought he would find them very boring but he surprised me by being very interested though critical of the untidy painting of the Impressionists and Van Gogh. He stopped however in front of a large Renoir nude and said

enthusiastically, 'I like that, it's so lovely and smooth', and he went to peer more closely at her inviting bottom, and the people nearby nudged one another and said, 'Did you hear that little boy?'

After we had had lunch at the hotel, I rang up Peggy because I wanted to go and fetch my hat which I had left behind; I was wearing a funny black velvet cap of Evelyn's. She told me that Edward was back and if I hurried, I would find him having lunch at the Garrick. I grabbed John and we dashed into a taxi and when we got there I could see Edward's head through the glass window. Inside Bowker was there too, sitting beside Charlotte. Edward looked well, his face was a healthier colour, his hair had receded even further and the springy wires were a speckled black and white. I told him that it had been rumoured that he had gone completely bald and when Bowker made some comment, he replied with his old malicious spirit: 'Well, I don't mind so long as I don't develop your waistline Bowk'. I hadn't seen Bowker for some time and she really was prodigious in size, bigger than I had ever remembered her.

Edward was wearing Canadian battle dress and he told us a little about his experiences of being torpedoed and his five days in an open boat with a daily allowance of half a ship's biscuit, 2 oz of water and 2 oz of chocolate. The men who were used to drinking plentifully went mad, but Edward only suffered from having to sit in one position for all that long time and he had scraped all the skin off his hands scrambling down into the lifeboat. I could imagine Edward sitting pale and aloof, bolt upright in the boat, only speaking when

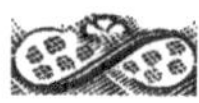

spoken to. Losing fifty drawings and all his collection of junk and hats was very tragic. However he was socially much improved and his voice had lost its ugly Essex accent.

When I reached Peggy's she was out, so I sat down to tea with Victoria and Angus and the nurse. Angus's eye hadn't got any better, he had a funny soft little voice and manner like a dormouse which was disconcerting because when he was a baby he had looked as though he was going to be a terrifically tough child. Peggy came charging in presently and upstairs she embraced me and told me that Jim had returned to her bed and wept on her and said that she had won; so I went back to Preston very cheered, feeling that my exhausting stay with her had done some good.

I enjoyed staying with Evelyn and didn't look forward to staying in Eastbourne, but poor James had been without us for two months and I knew he was looking forward to our coming. They had had one very nasty raid just before Christmas when Focke-Wulfs had dropped three or four bombs close to one another at the top of Terminus Road. They had landed all among the Christmas shoppers in a post office and blown the proprietress of Scholl's Correcto shop right across the road into Bobby's Arcade, and the ARP wardens had thought that her naked body was one of the wax models. When Mummy told me this story and pointed out the fatal spot, I remembered Barbara's story of their mother's insistence that she should go and look at the lion in Whipsnade who had eaten the man.

Because of this raid, all the occupants of Elmwood were in a very nervous condition and the gardener's wife never

failed to hear a cuckoo warning. However late at night it was, up we would all have to get and down to the cellar we would go, as though the cellar was some charmed place where a bomb couldn't land. A cuckoo warning was made by the siren, sounding very much quicker than its usual wail and it was intended to warn people that there were enemy planes overhead. The maddening thing would go just before meals and the gas in the kitchen would be turned off and our dinner left to get cold. The gardener's little grandson Dennis was a clever boy who made remarkable model aeroplanes, horridly like the real things, and he wanted to be an aeroplane mechanic when he grew up. He had once been machine gunned on his way to school and never tired of telling us about it.

My father had five wireless news bulletins a day and insisted that the children kept quiet while he listened to them all over again. This was very trying.

Michael Rothenstein, thinking they might be a good thing to draw, wanted to know more about the barricades on Eastbourne front which Eric had described to him and which he thought might be good material to add to the series of drawings of barricades which he had already made, so I went one afternoon to have a look at them.

I walked down the hill past the roofless St Anne's Church where the sunbeams, straying inside, shone through the stained glass windows so that I could see them the other way round to when I sat inside the church listening to old Reverend Jay's sing-songing voice not so very long ago. Hartfield Gardens was deserted, the majority of the houses

unoccupied. Occasionally a small front garden would be thickly spread with tiny pieces of broken glass and dirty bits of material that had been used to block up glassless windows that had blown down and flapped untidily onto the square gardens. They were freed now from their railings but there was no one to take advantage of their lack of protection. The basement of Wagga Wagga was overgrown with 'snow in summer' but the corner house where I had once on my way to the Art School been intrigued by seeing the mistress of the house, conducting morning prayers for her maids, was occupied.

It was Sunday so the shops were closed, but there were quite a number of people in the streets, not elderly people but Canadian soldiers and Air Force boys and girls wearing sailor hats. They looked, if one came to think about it, far more appropriate than the over-dressed and over-painted tummy huggers who had sauntered round Cave's Oriental Café when I had lived there and I felt as though I was the ghost of a Garwood girl still haunting Terminus Road.

I walked down through Memorial Square where the bronze angel who had superseded the much prettier tree was still standing on her block of stone. A modern flat had been built at the bottom of Devonshire Place and a few of the most outrageously opulent-looking houses had been pulled down, houses which with their white façades laced all over with plaster patterns had looked like Nottingham curtains and which my mother had particularly disliked. I suppose she thought they were vulgar but to my generation Victorian vulgarity of this kind was merely amusing.

At the end of the road, the Duke of Devonshire's statue, still undamaged, was supported by a row of bathing machines, their wheels removed and their bodies tipped up and filled with shingle. The white Imperial Hotel that had been patronised by the boat race crew looked superficially unaltered but when I passed close by, it was empty and most of the windows were bare of glass, and black curtains flapped untidily out of some of them. The corner of the Cavendish Hotel on the other side of the road where the bomb had landed, that I had seen falling from the aeroplane in April, still looked the same as when I had seen it with Vern as though a section of the hotel had been taken away to show what type of interior decorating the management favoured. The heap of blocks of cement and rubble that had landed on poor Mrs Matthews as she cycled past had been removed.

I crossed over the deserted promenade and stood looking down at the squat blue domed bandstand which was like a huge piece of barbola work, a powder bowl on some modernist dressing table, and the hungry gulls flapped and mewed around my head. As I walked along towards the Wish Tower, each road was barricaded in a similar way, with bathing machines full of shingle and the Wish Tower Hill looked like some fantastic pantomime set with its drapery of imitation grass and it was protected from the shore by the most lavish display of barbed wire that I have ever seen, the newly added grey wire in front making a pretty speckled pattern against the rusty red jungle behind. There were a few cold soldiers here who were looking after the guns, and the hotel across the road was occupied.

I felt fond of this new Eastbourne, as though it had been reformed by a baptism of fire, and I noticed that there were quite a number of pretty houses and shops still there and I walked back to Memorial Square appreciating these deserted buildings that still remained. Some of them looked infinitely pathetic, like the Fudge Shop which had plastered its windows with a fantastic display of criss-cross strapping; but it wasn't the blast that had forced its owners to abandon it but the lack of fudge and custom.

I wished I had time to explore the other end of town, the mutilated pier and Splash point but the children would be waking up from their rest and, as it was, I had had to miss visiting old Dad Ravilious to undertake this small journey 'down town'.

After dinner on the next evening, the Infirmary rang up my father to say that Mr Ravilious was sinking and in their opinion, he wouldn't last very much longer. Groaning inwardly, my father ordered a car to take us to St Mary's and slumped back into his easy chair to wait till it arrived. The idea of a deathbed scene was very alarming and my father, being particularly frightened of dying himself, hated these constant reminders of our mortality. He was every now and then forced, in his position as chairman of the Old Contemptibles, to attend their funerals, and their dwindling numbers were very depressing to him.

When I had seen him on Wednesday, Dad had looked very much the same as he had in the spring; his complaints against the nurses were not quite so frantic, but he still muttered that they had no respect for the sick and dying and that he had

seen dreadful things. It was very difficult to feel sympathetic with such a confirmed egotist as Dad and I expect they were heartily tired of his moans and groans. The visitors of the other patients hinted to Miss Alce and me, as though we as his visitors were responsible for the old man's behaviour, that he was a great nuisance. Actually he wasn't in any great pain. He complained that his knee was stiff but then so was mine, and a stiff knee is only a thing which hurts when you move it. He also said that he had horrible dreams and wished he could be taken. He was quite clear in the head and had asked if I had heard anything further about Eric. When I said: 'No', he said. 'Well, it's a good thing really, he is better where he is', as though the more of his family to greet him on the farther shore there was, the better it would be and typical of his evangelical views. Miss Alce thought that he knew that he was not going to live much longer because he tried to give us all his pathetic belongings to take away and his collection of letters from Evelyn and Frank.

Daddy and I groped our way through the backwoods to Mr Mailey's car and drove off, unhappily, on our unpleasant mission. Inside the hospital, nobody was about much and the wards had dim lights but the night sister soon took charge of us and conducted us to a different ward, explaining that Mr Ravilious had become very restless and fallen out of bed in the old one.

I don't know whether they had drugged Dad but he was propped up in the end bed breathing strenuously, his mouth slightly open and his face pink and thin because he was no longer wearing his false teeth. In the next bed a man tried

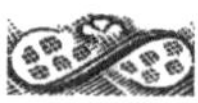

frantically to attract my father's attention; it was one of his Old Contemptibles, a man who had been a great talker but who in having some minor operation for tonsils or adenoids had suddenly become tongue-tied and paralysed. This combination of Dad and the Old Contemptible was too embarrassing for my father and he stood aloof and talked to the sister, saying things like: 'Well we can obviously do no good and how long do you think he'll last?' I tried to rouse Dad but it was no good and feeling that I must make some gesture, I planted a hearty kiss on his warm cheek. He gave a startled grunt, as though the kiss had interrupted his last dream and I hoped it had changed it to something less horrible than the ones he had complained about on Wednesday.

Poor old Dad, he was one of the few remaining links with that Victorian world of boater hats and penny farthing bicycles. A man who had loved picnics is no good in a hospital and my father said as we walked away: 'Well, I've not been to any deathbed at which I felt less regret than this one'.

As though to atone for his past rudeness to Eric, Daddy had been very good about visiting the old man and he and Louise Alce and Maggie Gosden had all gone regularly to see him. Dad had been flattered at my father coming to see him and as my father was a friend of the matron's, he looked on him as a possible source of escape from the hospital. He only counted visits from the family as being important and Eric had been amused when he had complained about his lack of visitors, and on Eric reminding him of Miss Alce and Miss Gosden, he had replied airily: 'Oh, those girls'. For all their forty-five years they were still girls to him, because of their

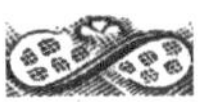

being friends of [his daughter] Evelyn's. His friend, poor old Mr Roader, had been bedridden himself all the winter so he had been unable to come. Only a year ago he and Mr Roader had been for long walks together on the Downs but being two years younger, Dad always treated him with scant respect and continually made personal remarks about his friend's appearance, which being deaf, Mr Roader seldom understood.

Vernon Ledger and Frank both came to Eastbourne for the funeral, Vernon as matter-of-fact and solidly Yorkshire as ever, and Frank still remarkably handsome and young looking in spite of his being nearly fifty. He no longer looked dishonest as he had done when I first met him, but he was still morbidly sentimental; Vern and I sat heavily upon him when he started saying what a tragedy Dad's death was.

Eric had been impressed by his mother's funeral but there was nothing impressive about Dad's, except the remarkable amount of chunks of clay that the sextons had had to dig up to make room for the coffin. It was a very informal chapel funeral and the preacher gave us a little talk on Mr Ravilious, whom he had visited occasionally in hospital; he did it very well.

I had never been to a funeral before and my father assured me that it wasn't at all an ordinary funeral, as it completely lacked the usual air of misery and regret. Occasionally the widows and relatives of Old Contemptibles threw themselves into the open grave and had to be dragged out very muddy down the front, because Old Contemptible funerals were always on wet days.

The last few days of any stay at home were always ones to be dreaded, because of the fuss and noise that my mother made

about packing and plans for the journey. There were two alternatives open to me, either I let her alone to do all the packing, in which case she would exhaust herself and turn on me for being lazy, or else I could pack quietly and quickly before she had discovered that I had done so and then she could unpack and do most of it again, putting things in the particular order that she had in mind. In either case, she exhausted herself and was rude to me. Although it was never admitted, she must have loved packing. She thought up all kinds of probable and impossible difficulties and problems and so complicated things that I always left the house in a bottled fury at her intolerable interference. Of course, it would be lovely to have any number of trunks and one's clothes carefully folded in tissue paper, but my method of packing a few suitcases and a hold-all as full as possible, didn't really do any irreparable harm. I could always iron our dresses when I got home if they really needed it.

On Sunday just after lunch, I looked up and saw an aeroplane flying parallel with the tops of the houses in the town below and then we heard the noise of another plane thundering over our roof and crump, crump, crump, crump. All four bombs had fallen by the time we had reached the door and the cuckoo alarm started sounding.

The next day we drove down the hill to the station, going slowly past the Technical Institute and Art School where the bomb had landed. It had killed two girls in the adjoining fire station but the fire engine was safe because it happened to be out in the road and not in its house. The outside of the Institute still stood but the inside, where there had been a

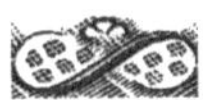

public library and museum below the school, was all blown to little tiny pieces. Miraculously one of the two studio windows at the top of the Art School was still unbroken.

This destroying of the Art School gave me a feeling of finality; the Eastbourne that I had known was, so far as I was concerned, gone for ever and Eric and his parents with it.

We waited anxiously in the shattered station till the train arrived and James climbed in and solemnly gave his reins to a strange woman in the corner to hold while Anne perched on my knee in her smart new bonnet. Underneath the bonnet her head was an exact replica of old Dad's and her eyes were the same innocent blue, while James with his round felt hat pulled well down over his tensely excited face was a small Mum. We were off back to Essex to discover which of the arms of my signpost we were going to follow.

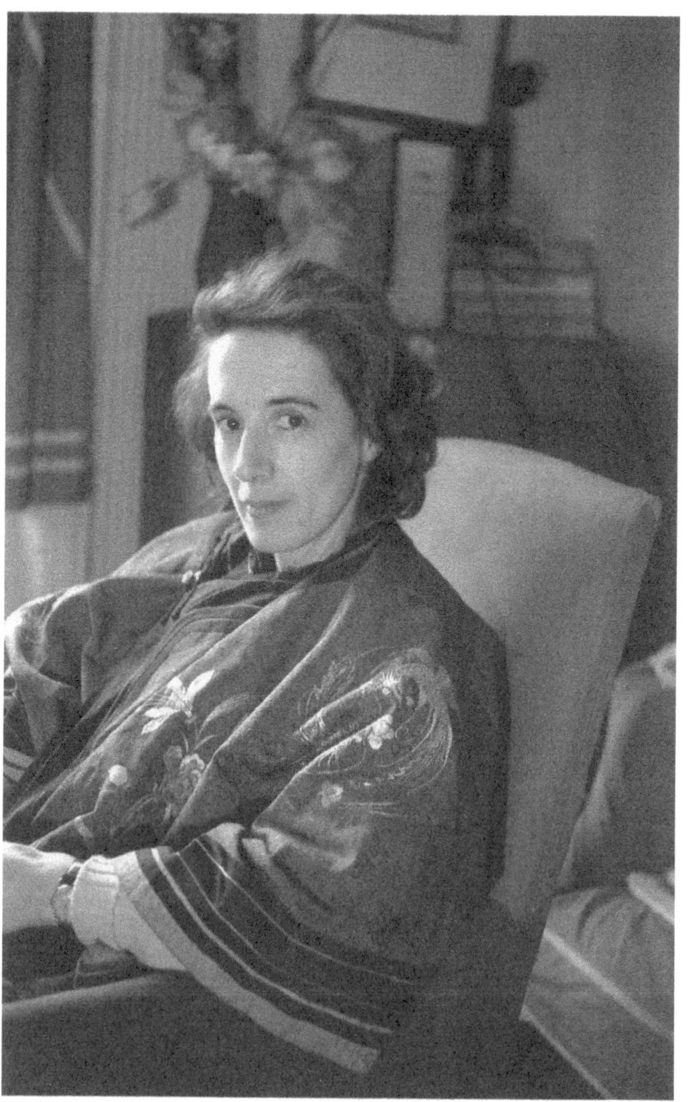

CHAPTER TWENTY-SIX

My mother finished writing her autobiography at a crossroads in her life in February 1943. Following her visit to Eastbourne she arranged to meet Peggy Angus in London and together they took the children to Ironbridge. Peggy's marriage to Jim not having survived the war years, she too was alone, and the plan was that while Peggy taught in London during the week, Tirzah would look after Victoria and Angus, Peggy joining them at weekends. When the wartime ban on travel to the coast was lifted in 1944, Peggy, taking the children with her, moved to Furlongs. Sometimes we joined her there and my brother James's first-ever memory was of Furlongs: of standing in a deep-rutted lane watching thousands and thousands of gliders passing overhead on their way to the Normandy invasion in the early summer of 1944. My brother John recalls how incredibly poor we were at this time, for a statutory six months had to pass before anyone 'missing' in the war could officially be 'presumed dead'. It was not until September 1943, a whole year after Eric's death, that Tirzah had finally been classed as the widow of an officer and given a war widow's pension.

On March 24th 1944, Tirzah moved from Ironbridge to nearby Wethersfield, renting half of Boydells Farm which lay a little way outside the village. Dick Crampton, the cowman, and his wife Betty

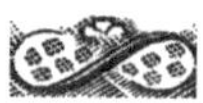

lived in the adjoining half, with the yard and cowsheds at the back. Mrs Crampton was remarkable in that she ate bluebottles, treating the flies like prawns, discarding the head and legs. John vividly remembers this too. Gas lighting was in the house, but no geyser, so water still had to be boiled in a copper. We kept hens and a few ducks which paddled in a Victorian foot bath.

In January 1945 Tirzah become engaged to Henry Swanzy. He worked for the BBC at Bush House where, from 1946 to 1954, he produced and edited a literary radio programme Caribbean Voices which sponsored young West Indian writers. Novelists Derek Walcott and V S Naipaul (later both Nobel Prize winners) were among those whose work was first broadcast during his years as Editor. Henry had been sharing a flat in Hampstead with the publisher George Weidenfeld and when looking for a new room had become one of Peggy's lodgers. Henry said that apart from the obvious reasons of attraction, he had first been drawn towards Tirzah because, like his own mother, she had been left widowed with three small children to support. The wedding took place on March 12th 1946 at a London registry office, followed by lunch at the Café Royal, and a short honeymoon at the Hotel Grosvenor on the sea front at Swanage. Tirzah once again packed up all the furniture and her belongings and moved to London, where she and Henry rented 169 Adelaide Road.

Adelaide Road ran between Chalk Farm and Swiss Cottage near to Primrose Hill and to the Zoo, the lions and tigers of which we could hear roaring in the still of the night. Another noise was the subdued and distant rattle of trains rumbling underneath the house in one of the great mainline terminal shunting tunnels. The house was in a poor state of repair owing to the semi-detached half next door having

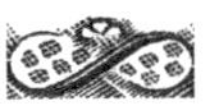

been bombed in the war, completely demolishing it. Number 169 was precariously supported by two enormous flying buttresses made up of giant timbers which in theory counterbalanced the entire four storeys. This was not entirely successful and occasionally large pieces of plaster crashed down from the cornices. All the houses were owned by Eton College and let out on repairing leases. The previous occupant had been the artist Ivon Hitchens, but he wanted to move to the country so he was delighted when Peggy suggested to him that Tirzah and Henry might take on the house, especially so as he had been worried about all the cracks from the bomb damage. (Incidentally, at about this time Tirzah bought an Ivon Hitchens painting, but after the show he said he could not bear to part with it, so she had felt obliged to give it back. The name of the picture is not recorded though Tirzah referred to it as 'one of his best'.)

Ivon Hitchens had been absent from the house for some time and may not have known that it was suffering, as were very many in London, from the post-war plague of fleas. Henry taught us how to catch them on bars of wet soap, but eventually they became too much to bear and we had to move out while the house was fumigated. Helen Binyon was now renting rooms with Peggy Angus and she and Tirzah were soon good friends. Helen and the Gilbert Spencers with their daughters were planning a holiday to the Isle of Canna, in the Inner Hebrides, and invited Tirzah and the boys to join them while the fleas were dealt with. Alas, I was considered too young and was sent instead to stay with my grandmother who was alone in Eastbourne, my grandfather having died in 1944. The following letter to my mother arrived from Henry who had stayed alone in London.

29.8.47.

Darling,

I write in a seething fury. The floors are all bare in all the house. The garden looks like an Eastern market with carpets and hangings everywhere. There is a dense smell of powdered naphthalene, and the fleas still cling and bite, and bite and cling. This morning I picked two out of my hair. I have lost twelve hours sleep during the last three nights. And the pest squad will not come. All they do is give this advice for dealing with the plague, and it will not work. I cannot tell you how irritated and degraded I feel. The only thing is, I feel glad that you and the children are not here. I hope I shall get the thing settled before you return. I think the house will really have to be sealed for several days. Kitty has not yet gone to the vets.

Apart from all this (but what is apart from fleas), I grind away at work, and go to the endless colonial functions. I have also been to Gabbitas and Thring, the school agents, or Scholastic agents, as they like to call themselves. I will tell you what I found out when I see you again.

I feel bad at forgetting James' birthday, but really, I have quite a lot of things on my mind! – you can't imagine what it is like to have a plague like this, where there are clouds, everywhere you go. Pascal said something about fleas driving out the thought and love of God! I do not think I will send him (James) anything as yet, I might send money, but I don't think that would be good for him – he would only hoard it on your barren island. However I enclose a brief letter.

Your loving and distraught husband.

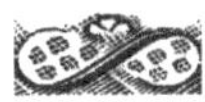

The fumigation must have worked because the fleas were all gone when we returned to London.

In nearby Kings College Road there was a millinery and haberdashery shop run by two elderly sisters and I shall never forget my mother's excitement when, being invited into the back of the shop, she found shelves packed high with rolls of Victorian and early Edwardian dress material, tiny print patterns on cotton and chintz. The sisters had stopped selling lengths of material after the the First World War when they had taken over the shop from their father. Henry mentions this shop in a revealingly perceptive description of Tirzah written some time shortly after her death in 1951.

What the insensitive saw, besides the face and the legs and the feet, were the clothes. These were always idiosyncratic, but depended, to some extent, on the occasion. They were partly determined by her memories of her mother, who was very conventional, with firm ideas about magenta: and by her experience as the wife of a very poor and struggling artist, who was so modest that he 'queered the market' by his low prices. Thus her dresses were nearly all dowdy, like village women's, with brogue shoes, crêpe de Chine, curious cloche hats and inappropriate eye-veils, but they were often composed of rare and curious materials, with colours of pistachio or maroon. Her belts were remarkable, one in particular made of gymnastic welting in red, white and blue. In design, her single idea seemed to be square lines around a square throat, very often black on red. When I first knew her, I noted that her clothes were all five years old. Her best dress, she told me, she had used for lying-in. Needless to say, she was not one

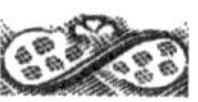

for fancy pants, as she would call them. But for certain types of taste, those voguish structures, elaborate but impersonal, have not got a tenth of the charm of Tirzah standing in red knitted jumper and blue bloomers, with the crude stockings as ever rucked at her ankles. (On such an occasion, I compared her to Saint Joan, whom, to cover her pleasure, she called a swanky old dotard).

It would be absolutely wrong to dismiss Tirzah as a conventional frump or freak, only made beautiful in the eyes of the beholder. As a village woman, she was brilliant at suggesting and designing fancy-dress clothes for other people. She could run up, in a night or two, the most perfect Grimaldi harlequin suit and pantaloons for her son James. Out of the brilliantly coloured bits of cloth that littered all the drawers of the house, she would compose a perfect lace ruff, indigo blue breast with a great sun burst in the middle, striped pink and white trousers ending in another twirl of lace, and red stockings. Nor was she backward in designing for herself at public appearances which I believe she regarded as occasions for fancy dress. I remember the pleasure given her by the discovery of a milliners shop run by two old ladies, who had been round the corner since H. G. Wells was a haberdasher's assistant. Out of their late Victorian and Edwardian remnants, she ran up the most delectable lilac dress, with bustle and swathe hanging in front, along the oval line of hip. Above this, she put on a little straw hat, with fruit fillet and dark red velvet band, and a three-quarter length coat of corduroy of the same wine-red colour. The effect was so astonishing in its infinitely aristocratic and fine-drawn appeal, that (and not in my

opinion alone) she made all the other women at the Royal Garden Party look worn and heavy. But she was so nervous of her finery, which was new in 1948, that she took a cab, and started like a fawn under the 'hostile' eyes of the people in the streets. On another occasion, she made another new look dress, of scalloped pistachio, with which she managed to out-shadow the crowds watching the jumping at the Olympic Games. More often, it was a single beautiful feature that she wore, invariably offset by another that was not quite so successful. Thus, she could have a very pretty Cossack hat in soft grey, its lower antennae twining in the most enchanting fashion with the tendrils of her hair, and yet below there would be a stained coat, twisted stockings, and heavy green suede shoes, with a dollop or two of candle-grease darkening the toe.

And he again records the dress for the Buckingham Palace garden party in his diary – Royal Garden Party, Thursday. July 22nd 1948. I wish I had a photograph of her, the most elegant there, in the tip-tilted straw with plum band, the little grey home-made dress with the bustle, the half-length velvet coat in cherry.

Tirzah nearly always made her own clothes, and ours too. I had the prettiest dresses made up from the Victorian printed cottons. The only new clothes I can remember I wore on an occasion when James and I, dressed in smart stiff tailored outfits, modelled at the Tower of London for a fashion magazine, The Ambassador. This introduction was probably through the auspices of the graphic designer and typographer Robert Harling. An admirer of Ravilious, he came to know

Tirzah well after the war. These are his words, written some fifty years later, of his remembrance of Tirzah:

From the moment I first glimpsed Tirzah Ravilious at her husband's 1939 exhibition of watercolours in Arthur Tooth's Gallery, she seemed to me to have stepped straight out of one of those brilliant, brittle yet poignant novels by Michael Arlen, now so curiously and inexplicably neglected.

For starters, she looked the part: a slim, extraordinarily pretty heartbreaker, somehow touched by sadness. A gleam of fateful gaiety seemed always to attend her enchantingly fey persona. And when, some five years later, I came to know her well, I had no call to change this view. Rather the reverse. This impression of carefree sadness was enhanced by her vivacious chitter-chat, well-laced with zany throwaway lines, wholly captivating to listeners, especially more susceptible males. And, despite her seeming (and actual) fragility, she was always game to the last.

John was now at Cotters Bow, a boarding school in the Cotswolds. Richard and Joanna Bawden and Jane Tuely were also pupils. During the war it had been the habit of the headmistress to read out at morning break in the school playground the names of fathers who had lost their lives: this was how John had first learnt of Eric's death. Joanna Bawden remembered that one small boy had both his parents' names called on the same day, the father killed at the front and his mother in an air raid. When Cotters Bow closed at the end of the war, John joined Peggy's son, Angus, at the country half of St Mary's Town and Country School near Rugby. John was happy but Angus was

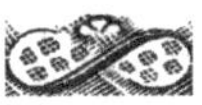

bullied by the older boys and John had watched horrified when Angus had been thrown through a trapdoor into the beer cellar below. He landed on his head and Peggy used to maintain that this was the cause of the epilepsy from which he died in his early twenties. John had been a slow reader but he was brilliant at things that interested him, especially electronics and had made a radio in a matchbox at a very early age. Tirzah may have now considered Summerhill, the A S Neill school in Suffolk, as she recommends this to Peggy for Angus. This was a very progressive school where the children made all the rules and worked as and when they pleased and at their own pace. This philosophy was much in tune with Tirzah's own ideas on bringing up children. In the end, she chose for John Long Dene, a progressive boarding school at Chiddingstone Castle in Kent.

James at this time was infatuated with a radio character, Dick Barton, Special Agent, an interest which seemed to occupy his entire day. He had been sent to Cotters Bow when he was six and was now at Dane Court, a prep school formerly named Whatcombe House, near Blandford, Dorset. Many of the boys moved on to Bryanston School in Dorset, where Charlotte planned to send Richard and Tirzah hoped to send James (though in the event he did not go there). This boarding school education was made possible by Tirzah's uncle John Garwood who died in 1948 leaving a bequest to cover the cost of not just Tirzah's children, but of all the Garwood grandchildren. At this stage I remained at home and attended Primrose Hill, the local primary school.

A tragedy in 1947 was the death of Tirzah's brother. Having chosen to follow in his father's footsteps as a Royal Engineer, John had survived the war and had been commended for his bravery in the retreat from Dunkirk, from which he returned wearing his major's

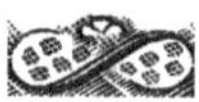

crowns. He then served in the Far East and had risen to the rank of Lieutenant Colonel, being awarded the DSO in 1946 for his part in the Burma Campaign. After the war he continued his career in the army. In 1947, now married to a young doctor, Dorothea Leslie Smith, and with two children, he was posted to Nigeria. Leaving their baby daughter, Prue, behind in England with Dorothea's parents, they took their eight-year-old son David with them. On August 3rd, while paddling in the sea near Lagos, David got into difficulty caught by a strong current. The child, both parents and a passer-by who had also gone to his rescue, all drowned.

Tirzah had made her first oil paintings in 1944. Now settled in London, she had time again to pursue her artistic career. I loved to come home from school to the smell of oil paint and turpentine. Reluctantly my mother would stop work and clean her brushes. In winter we would have tea and crumpets round the fire. Later Henry arrived home, usually bearing a gift for my mother, flowers or a pineapple; then habitually he would sing Schubert's Lieder, accompanying himself on the piano, and woe betide the child who interrupted him with a call for supper before the end of a song. As well as painting, Tirzah also became increasingly engrossed in making houses set in box frames which were a mixture of 3D, collage and print. She had started making these in Essex where she had been inspired by the simplicity of the pretty houses in the villages nearby. She exhibited her paintings and collages at the annual Pictures for Schools *exhibitions run by Nan Youngman. The aim of the exhibitions being to improve, by example, the aesthetic awareness of children.*

I loved this new exciting life in London, though I was always timid out on my own as the streets were full of men out of work, many

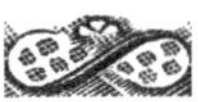

still in army uniform. Having a father figure too was a new experience and I adored Henry. He loved people and parties and was always organising exciting outings – boat trips down the Thames, or climbing up inside the dome of St Paul's. He was very partial too to long walks, especially if there was a view to be had, and would wax lyrical at the city spread before him as he gazed out over London from the top of Hampstead Heath or Primrose Hill while we children, behind his back, tittered at him. Sometimes we went to the coast, once travelling on the beautiful train, the Brighton Belle. On the beach, Henry would organise French cricket and then sunbathe with his handkerchief knotted at the four corners over his balding head and we would join Tirzah making sandcastles. These sandcastles, or more often large sand churches decorated with shells collected from the rock pools under Beachy Head, and with pebbles, were marvels of artistry and the wonder of the beach until the tide turned.

Tirzah kept up with all her old friends; we saw Peggy Angus in London and at Furlongs in Sussex; we had holidays with the Hephers who now lived in Malpas, Cheshire, and with the Tuelys in Kent and the Rowntrees in Essex; they were regular callers in London too as they now had a town house on the Thames near Putney Bridge. Tirzah's great friend Duffy Rothenstein and her husband Michael, were also constant visitors, as was Christine Nash.

New friends were the photographer Edwin Smith and his adorable wife-to-be Olive Cook. Olive thought it was probably Tom Hennell (who had once been in love with her) who had first intro-duced them to Tirzah. Edwin was a photographer only by necessity; he had had an architectural training and took truly superb archi-tectural photographs, but he always wanted to be a painter. Olive had been in charge of publicity for the National Gallery during the war

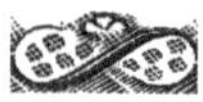

while the galleries were empty, the permanent collection having been moved out of London and hidden for safety down a slate mine at Penryn quarry in North Wales. Olive, as Supervisor of Publications, was appointed to write about the pictures in order to keep the main collection in the public's mind. There had been lunchtime concerts in the gallery and the young Joyce Grenfell served lunches in the canteen.

Another new family of whom we saw a great deal were the Uhlmans, who lived in Hampstead. Fred Uhlman, writer and self-taught painter, had been born in Stuttgart where he had been a barrister. He came to England in the late 1930s and married Diana, daughter of Sir Henry Page Croft. They were greatly involved in assisting refugees to Britain and their home in Downshire Hill had been a meeting place for refugee intellectuals and the headquarters for help to the left wing in Spain. For the duration of the war, Fred Uhlman had been held as as an enemy alien and interned on the Isle of Man.

In the spring of 1948, Tirzah's cancer returned and she nearly died. She records coming back from treatment at the Royal Free Hospital on March 4th with £70 worth of drugs, and she must have felt very weak for she writes in her diary, 'Henry walked me to the window and back.' Her illness necessitated a housekeeper and a large moon-faced lady named Mrs Precious, a former bus conductress from Cardiff, was hired to cook and housekeep; she lived in and looked after us, though in term-time my brothers were away. Eventually it was decided that I too should go to boarding school. I was sent to Shingle Ridge on the sea front esplanade (Crag Path) at Aldeburgh. This was a tiny school of only nine pupils run by Miss Thompson, the retired headmistress of Cotters Bow. The Rowntrees' son Adam also became a pupil there.

*Tirzah's cancer was well advanced by the time she wrote the
following undated letter to Duffy Rothenstein in 1949 from the Royal
Free Hospital in Hampstead:*

My dear Duffy,

Thank you and Michael very much for your sympathies
and all the news from Bardfield.

I am supposed to be going out tomorrow but don't really
see how I can as I am in an awful state of emaciation as I have
no appetite.

Having accepted the fact that one is inevitably dying I find
myself, except when feeling badly ill, quite normally cheerful.
One can't after all go on moaning for an indefinite period.

After radium treatment one feels perfectly frightful. I'm
supposed to be having the final of this today, but fear I've got
a new sore place on my left ribs now. I am wondering where
the male hormones that are injected into me come from and if
I live a bit longer, do you suppose I shall become unusually
domineering?

It is a badly run ward and the men who wheel one about on
a trolley are terribly careless about bumping me about. They
have one idea in their heads and that is the hope that they will
get a pretty nurse to accompany me and their faces fall when
they get an ugly one. I'm often left about for odd half hours on
a board hard trolley among the outpatients who look at me like
James Fitton char ladies and murmur when they see me go in
for radium treatment; 'I wonder if she knows what she's got?'
and I found it amusing in a macabre way when the girl medical
students were being lectured round the ward yesterday and

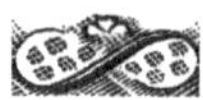

were hastily shepherded away from my bed to a discreet distance by the sister and the lecturing doctor remarked in a
jocular fashion; 'Yes, she looks peculiarly orthopaedic'.

One of the night nurses last week was a strange sadistic girl
from Little Easton, this week there is Lisette from Italy, a
friend of Olive Cook's which is nice.

I'm not at all looking forward to one of the painful deaths
I have unfortunately been witnessing in the Middlesex,
especially as I can't take morphine.

There seems to be a crop of mercy killers at the moment.
They've all my custom but I suppose if they're going to be
blamed one should commit suicide – perhaps Edward could
think up something ingenious for me or should I write to
Agatha Christie?

Poor Duffy, I'm probably upsetting your morning milk.
I'm so glad about your children, how satisfying they are. I've
been much luckier than most people apart from wishing that
I could have had more time for getting on with painting, one
can't have everything and I shall always feel guilty about
Henry not having his own children.

Can you share this letter with Charlotte? I shan't probably
feel like writing any more today. I suppose I ought not to
embarrass John Aldridge by wanting to see him so give him
my love and thanks for the happiness he once gave me.

Long live Great Bardfield and love to you all,
Tirzah

Just back from treatment. I suppose I shouldn't write these
death-bed letters and then linger on for years.

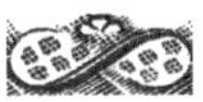

Tirzah's 1950 diary vents her frustration with the doctors who because a few seem ignorant, imagine all their patients imbecile. *Her diary also reveals that after trying unsuccessfully to write to her, John Aldridge, bringing John Langston with him, did visit Adelaide Road. Henry's sister, Helen, who was nursing Tirzah at the time, was very firm that he should only call for half an hour, but eventually he stayed to supper and met Henry.* He looks smaller, *Tirzah wrote,* and as John Langston cruelly said 'digested by Lucie', we talked distortedly about painting. Anne brought us all some party biscuits with our initials and finally presented John with a heart saying 'You can eat your own heart'.

A few days later she commented, Henry. . . . Also jealous of the fun we seemed to be having in my past life and feeling he had no part in it and that I still love John A although I deny this, and point out that most of the time I was terribly over-worked and latterly, after Eric's death, unutterably miserable. He is the most intelligent of my lovers, John Langston the best looking, John Aldridge the best lover and Eric the most charming and good.

In the early summer of 1950, secondary cancer of the spine was diagnosed. A new helper, a Scottish lady, Mrs Severs, was hired to housekeep in London but Tirzah would now need full-time care. Christine Nash suggested a nursing home run by her friend Susannah Sharp, daughter of Cecil Sharp, the collector of English folk music. This was Copford Place, a fine Georgian house set in its own grounds with a farm attached, at Copford near Marks Tey in Essex, which Susannah ran with a partner, Dorothy Curtice. Henry could commute to London and children were welcome during their holidays. Tirzah

still went back to London for treatment and the last photographs of her taken by Edwin Smith in March 1950 were at Adelaide Road.

Naturally the children's future became an anxiety. Many friends offered to adopt one or other of us, but here good fortune was on our side and we stayed together. Kay Goodden who had parted from Robert at the end of the war had met Henry's younger brother, John Swanzy, who fell madly in love with her and they married on August 9th 1946. Kay, who was unable to have children, longed for a family, and she and John became our legal guardians. During the summer of 1950, Tirzah took us herself to Hopkins, their lovely mellow stone farmhouse at the foot of the Cotswolds at Long Marston in Warwickshire; we did see our mother every school holiday after this but mainly we stayed at Hopkins whilst Tirzah remained at Copford. Letters from Kay concerning our welfare show that after Tirzah's death, she made sure that we continued to spend time with Henry in London and that we stayed regularly with our granny in Eastbourne, who also took a great interest in our welfare until her own death on August 6th 1952, aged eighty. She was the last of the three Corry sisters, Aunt Lucy having died in 1944 and Aunt Edith in 1947.

During the last year of Tirzah's life, sometimes in bed and often in pain, relieved by deep ray therapy and testosterone, Tirzah completed no fewer than twenty small oil paintings. Olive remembered how she amazed her friends by her determination, courage and unquenchable gaiety in what she declared 'the happiest year of her life'.

Tirzah died suddenly and without pain on Easter Monday, March 27th 1951, a fortnight short of her forty-third birthday. She is buried in the county churchyard at Copford. I and my brothers did not

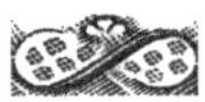

attend her funeral but the church must have looked beautiful for I watched Christine Nash pick every single hellebore from the legions in John's garden. John and James were told of Tirzah's death by their headmasters. Henry records that they sang 'Now the Day is Over', but for Tirzah the 'birds and beasts and flowers' will never be 'asleep'. In a typically thoughtful gesture he also recorded Eric's name on Tirzah's gravestone:

IN

LOVING MEMORY OF

TIRZAH SWANZY

(EILEEN LUCY GARWOOD)

1908–1951

AND OF

ERIC RAVILIOUS

LOST IN THE ATLANTIC

1903–1942: ARTISTS

BLESSED ARE THE EYES WHICH

SEE THE THINGS THAT YE SEE.

ACKNOWLEDGEMENTS

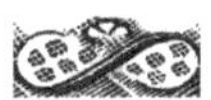

My grateful thanks are due to the following people for their help and encouragement. To my late stepfather Henry Swanzy, and to his second wife, the late Henriette Swanzy, and their son Martin, for their gift of Henry's reminiscences written about my mother. Also to the late John and Kay Swanzy. To my late brother James Ravilious for re-photographing the family photographs in the diaries of my grandfather Colonel F S Garwood, and to my sister-in-law, Robin Ravilious; to my brother John Ravilious for his early memories of our parents. To my late aunts, Margaret Calverley, Billy Newman and Betty Darwell-Smith, who identified places and people in Tirzah's writing, and to my Garwood cousins, Brooke Calverley, Jenny Bates, Rosemary Poole, Prue Smith and Marylou Warren.

My thanks to Duffy Rothenstein (Ayers) and to my mother's late friends for their helpful information and reminiscences. These include Peggy Angus, Edward Bawden, Helen Binyon and her twin sister Peg Higgens, Meg Campbell, Olive Cook, Raymond and Ginesi Coxon, Ariel Crittall, Diana Croft, Ralph Currey, Peggy Garge, Jack Gold, Robert Goodden, Barbara Gray (née Church), Robert Harling, Evelyn Hepher,

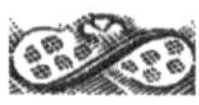

May Langford (née Holmes), Joan Lumley, Enid Marx, Diana Rowntree, Clissold Tuely and Wilma Hessey.

My thanks to Sarah Baker, Edgar Bartlett, Richard and Joanna Bawden, Prudence and Rosalind Bliss, Dominic Brookes, Nick Chaloner, Tamsin Currey, Tim Davis, Sasha Devas, Sarah Dixon, Andrew Friend, Victoria Gibson, Peter Goodchild, Beryl Graves, Richard Perceval Graves, Peyton Hall, Susanna Harrison, David Hepher, Andrew Higgens, Jane Howell, Jill Howell, the late Ian Tregarthen Jenkin, Ash Kahn, Juliet Kindersley, David and Kate Lavender, Andrew Lawson, Michael MacLeod, Maggie Le Mare, Peter Le Mare, Stephen Massil, Peter Morgan, Mike and Jeannie O'Connor, Henrietta Phipps, Alan Powers, Philippa Price, Harriet Proudfoot, Ben Ravilious, Ella Ravilious, Kate Ravilious, Julian Rea, Nicholas Rea, the late Adam Rowntree, James Shand, Peyton Skipwith, Kim and Mike Timms, Carolyn Trant, Miles Tuely, Barry and Saria Viney, Iris and Nigel Weaver, Brian Webb, the late Dr Anne Whiteman, Susan and Guy Woolfenden, and Ruth Yates. My thanks to Christopher Whittick, Senior Archivist, Document Services, at the East Sussex Record Office, Lewes. And thanks to Jeremy Hill, Librarian, and Jonathan Makepeace, at the RIBA Library Photographic Collection, for photographs by Edwin Smith; and to Simon Lawrence for the other photographs.

My children's interest in their grandmother's writing and artistic life has been my greatest incentive to see her work published. My especial thanks to my daughters Sarah and Martha for the marathon task of typing Tirzah's original manuscript. To my son Tom for his interest in the project and

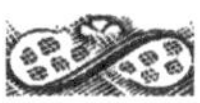

to his partner, Tamsin Meddings, for her help correcting punctuation in the autobiography. My thanks to my husband Louis for his patience with the years of work involved in this project. Lastly my thanks are due to Simon Lawrence for producing the magnificent and profusely illustrated 2012 Fleece Press edition of this book; and now to Persephone Books for bringing the work to a wider audience.

Anne Ullmann, June 2016